Confederate Sympathies

GENDER AND AMERICAN CULTURE

Martha S. Jones and Mary Kelley, editors

Editorial Advisory Board
Cathleen Cahill
Rosalyn LaPier
Jen Manion
Tamika Nunley
Annelise Orleck
Janice A. Radway
Robert Reid-Pharr
Noliwe Rooks
Nick Syrett
Lisa Tetrault
Ji-Yeon Yuh

Series Editors Emerita
Thadious M. Davis
Linda K. Kerber
Annette Kolodny
Nell Irvin Painter

The Gender and American Culture series, guided by feminist perspectives, examines the social construction and influence of gender and sexuality within the full range of American cultures. Books in the series explore the intersection of gender (both female and male) with such markers of difference as race, class, and region. The series presents outstanding scholarship from all areas of American studies—including history, literature, religion, folklore, ethnography, and the visual arts—that investigates in a thoroughly contextualized and lively fashion the ways in which gender works with and against these markers. In so doing, the series seeks to reveal how these complex interactions have shaped American life.

A complete list of books published in Gender and American Culture is available at https://uncpress.org/series/gender-and-american-culture.

Confederate Sympathies

Same-Sex Romance, Disunion, and Reunion in the Civil War Era

ANDREW DONNELLY

The University of North Carolina Press
CHAPEL HILL

Designed by Lindsay Starr
Set in Warnock Pro by codeMantra
Manufactured in the United States of America

Chapter 5 was previously published in different form as
"The Sexuality of Civil War Historiography: How Two Versions of
Homosexuality Make Meaning of the War," *Civil War History* 68, no. 3
(September 2022): 295–321.

Chapter 6 was previously published in different form as "Henry James'
Confederate Sympathies: Ingenuous Young Men from the Past and
Corrupt Postbellum Politics," *ESQ* 69, no. 2 (2023): 155–200.
Copyright 2024 by the Board of Regents of Washington State University.

LIBRARY OF CONGRESS CATALOGING-IN-PUBLICATION DATA
Names: Donnelly, Andrew, 1987– author.
Title: Confederate sympathies : same-sex romance, disunion,
and reunion in the Civil War era / Andrew Donnelly.
Other titles: Gender & American culture.
Description: Chapel Hill : University of North Carolina Press, [2025] |
Series: Gender and American culture | Includes bibliographical references and index.
Identifiers: LCCN 2024051348 | ISBN 9781469685588 (cloth ; alk. paper) |
ISBN 9781469685595 (paperback ; alk. paper) |
ISBN 9781469685601 (epub) | ISBN 9781469687650 (pdf)
Subjects: LCSH: Male homosexuality in literature—Political aspects. |
Men, White, in literature—Political aspects. | Male friendship in literature—
Political aspects. | Male homosexuality—United States—History—19th century. |
American literature—19th century—History and criticism. |
United States—History—Civil War, 1861–1865—Literature and the war. |
BISAC: SOCIAL SCIENCE / Gender Studies | LITERARY CRITICISM / LGBTQ
Classification: LCC PS217.H65 D66 2025 | DDC 810.9/353—dc23/eng/20241104
LC record available at https://lccn.loc.gov/2024051348

For product safety concerns under the European Union's General Product Safety
Regulation (EU GPSR), please contact gpsr@mare-nostrum.co.uk or write to the
University of North Carolina Press and Mare Nostrum Group B.V.,
Mauritskade 21D, 1091 GC Amsterdam, The Netherlands.

CONTENTS

ILLUSTRATIONS

Confederate Sympathies

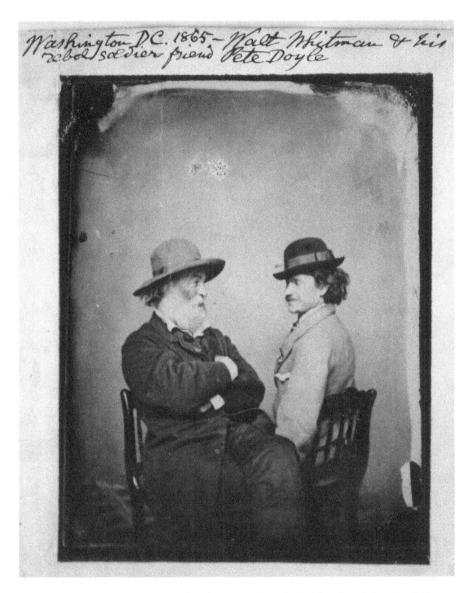

"Washington D.C. 1865—Walt Whitman & his rebel soldier friend Pete Doyle."
Moses P. Rice. Feinberg-Whitman Collection, Library of Congress.

Introduction

I N EARLY 1865, Walt Whitman was the only passenger seated in a horse-drawn streetcar traveling down Pennsylvania Avenue. The car moved through a snowstorm and the forty-five-year-old poet held a blanket around his shoulders to protect himself from the wind entering at the window's edges. He had noticed the conductor, a young man in his early twenties, of average height, with thick curls pouring out from under his uniform cap, arms that hung low beside his coat, a thin moustache—and the conductor appeared to have noticed him. Something drew Whitman's interest to the young man, perhaps the sense that something had drawn the young man's interest to the solitary passenger, or at least Whitman's interest seemed mirrored in the blue eyes and white face that now moved toward his section of the car, toward his seat, and sat closely beside him. "We were familiar at once," the conductor would later say. "I put my hand on his knee—we understood." The young man sat beside him to his destination, but the poet did not get out. He rode the car back along Pennsylvania Avenue with his new, intimate friend.[1]

For the next eight years, Whitman and Peter Doyle remained intimates, with Whitman riding frequently in Doyle's car, taking him to restaurants, on vacation, to the opera, and to dinner with Whitman's mother. Today, the scholarly consensus is that, of Whitman's many possible homosexual affairs, the man referred to by Whitman's acquaintances as his "intimate friend" is Whitman's most likely lover and his longest intimacy.[2] When Whitman's letters to Doyle were published in 1897, a critic wrote dismissively that "they throw all the light that is needed upon the poet's friendships with younger men, and upon that section of 'Leaves of Grass' called 'Calamus' in which he celebrates 'the manly love of comrades.'"[3] Doyle was, in those letters, Whitman's "dearest comrade," and with lines such as "My love for you is indestructible," the letters represent the nearest real-life analogue to the ideals of same-sex love that Whitman defined in his poetry.[4]

When the pair met in 1865, Whitman had just begun a new federal job in the Department of the Interior's Office of Indian Affairs. Two years earlier, he had moved from Brooklyn to Washington, DC, to be closer to the war effort and share in the suffering it produced. His younger brother George had enlisted with the Union and fought at New Bern, Antietam, and Fredericksburg, where an exploded shell sliced open his cheek. The poet went to Washington to find his brother in an army hospital; he spent the next two years tending to wounded soldiers, as the Union war effort became a project of his life as well as his poetry.[5]

Peter Doyle had also been at Antietam, or Sharpsburg, as it was known to Confederate soldiers. Born in Ireland and immigrating with his family to Virginia as a child, Doyle enlisted in April 1861, at age seventeen, in Virginia's secessionist army, which would later that year become the Army of Northern Virginia under Robert E. Lee's command. He was wounded at Antietam and, from a Richmond hospital, petitioned for discharge. He avoided Confederate service for several months before being captured by Union soldiers in Washington and imprisoned in the city's Carroll Prison. He was paroled that spring on the condition that he would not rejoin the Confederate army or aid the rebellion. Despite that oath, and despite avoiding Confederate service, he would remain, in self-conception and to friends, a Confederate soldier. In 1890, he joined the United Confederate Veterans. To the 1898 reviewer who believed Whitman's letters to Doyle confirmed the "Calamus" poems' sexual content, Doyle was "a young Confederate soldier."[6] A now famous photograph shows Whitman and Doyle looking into each other's eyes, with the handwritten caption "Walt Whitman & his rebel soldier friend Pete Doyle."

One axiom of the movement for gay rights has been that "love is love," and I suppose one cannot fault Whitman for having found it across what his Republican contemporaries called the Bloody Chasm. Whitman and Doyle are hardly the only pair, in Civil War or other history, to find love spring from a mighty scourge of hate. Whitman could rationalize it beyond star-crossed love; many postbellum Republicans believed (as he appeared to) that working-class whites, like Doyle, had been duped into the war by wealthy slaveholders, and Doyle was no slaveholder or explicit proponent of the slave system that formed the core of the Confederacy for which he fought.[7] Decades of Whitman's defenders have said that it should not matter whom he loved—yet Whitman's poetry indicates that the poet's attraction, if not to Doyle himself then to the idea of their intimacy, was not in spite of his friend's Rebel past but, at least partly, because of it.

Long before he met Doyle, Whitman celebrated intimacies between men as the solution to political divisions. In doing so, he drew upon imagery and themes common in the post-Revolutionary era, when male romantic friendships bound free men together in service of the new nation.[8] During the 1840s, Whitman, like other Jacksonian Democrats, saw such bonds unifying white men across class and section. By 1860, as the national crisis over slavery intensified, Whitman added the "Calamus" cluster to a new edition of *Leaves of Grass*, predicting, "Affection shall solve every one of the problems of freedom, / Those who love each other shall be invincible." Who are those? "One from Massachusetts shall be comrade to a Missourian." Their cross-sectional "companionship" demonstrates "manly affection, / The departing brother or friend shall salute the remaining brother or friend with a kiss." With Whitman presiding, "I, extatic, O partners! O lands! henceforth with the love of lovers tie you."[9] Whitman's antebellum vision of national union through male intimacy provided a structure for his wartime and postbellum desire. After the war, Whitman redoubled these sentiments and reworked the lines into "Over the Carnage Rose Prophetic a Voice": "Affection shall solve the problems of Freedom, yet."[10] Central to Whitman's idea of the nation was a pairing realized in his own postbellum life, the loving embrace between a Unionist and a Confederate.

Whitman's intimacy with Doyle, to be sure, did not cause his reconciliationist views. Indeed, the "Calamus" poems evidence desire for such cross-sectional love preceding the war. But the intimacies desired in his poetry and those realized in his life went, as Whitman might say, hand in hand. If, as scholars have long demonstrated, same-sex desire was central to his conception of antebellum national union, it also informed his vision of national reunion.[11] His relationship with a man across the war's divisions was hardly representative of a romantic trend in postbellum lives. It was, however, representative of a feeling, one widely evidenced in the nation's literature, that connected homoerotic pleasure with a desire for reconciliation. All his life, Whitman tried to cast himself as spokesman of national feeling. His postbellum reconciliation desires, far more than his antebellum egalitarianism, represented a broad feeling among white Northern men.[12]

The loving, eroticized embrace between white men was not unique to Whitman's imagination but a powerful force within national culture. The homoerotic embrace that he put at the heart of national union and reunion helps explain the sympathies that drove, directed, and inhibited political action nationally. Far from being marginal, the culture of male intimacy deepens answers to the most important questions of the era's history: What held together the antebellum Democratic coalition bridging North and South in support of slavery? What, after the war, happened to the emancipation spirit of the war effort? Why did the nation retreat from the Reconstruction project of federally enforced racial equality and Black political empowerment in favor of a reunion on the terms of white supremacy and states' rights? These very questions suggest answers already within interlocking political forces of race, class, and nation. Homoerotic desire neither supersedes these forces nor adds to them but provides form and content through which they operate socially.

This book argues that the meaning of the Civil War has shaped and been shaped by male same-sex romance and the history of homosexuality. Before the war, homoerotic symbolism enabled the cross-sectional compromises that permitted slavery's expansion, while fictional intimacies between enslaved men and enslavers became a staple of proslavery novels. During the war, homoerotic narratives foregrounded white men as the chief objects of Civil War sympathies. After the war, these narratives would personify the Lost Cause through attractive, dead young Confederate men and allegorize the outcome of the war within a trajectory of male development. Homoerotic narratives were, then, part of a broader culture that cultivated postbellum sympathies for national reconciliation premised on white supremacy and Black exclusion. In short, homoeroticism enlisted sympathies for slavery, the Confederacy, and the Lost Cause.

If homoeroticism helped determine the meaning of the war and its aftermath, it equally shaped Civil War memory and history. By the early twentieth century, Civil War and Reconstruction historians connected the war's outcome to the emergence of racialized sexual perversion and urban homosexuality to develop a sexualized history of the Civil War's social transformation: they associated the antebellum period with sentimentalized romances between men and the postbellum years with the increasing threat of deviant sexuality. The picture that emerged linked antebellum plantation slavery with a longed-for, now impossible homoeroticism and made sexual longing another dimension of the Confederacy's lasting appeal in the United States.

I focus especially on how a group of elite, white, liberal Northerners embraced these views. I do so not because this group had a special preponderance of same-sex desire but because of this group's consequential role in the era's politics, especially in the national retreat from the Reconstruction goals of Black citizenship and racial equality. In his history of Reconstruction, Eric Foner describes a set of Northern white liberals who, after the war, experienced "a remarkable reversal of sympathies," with "Southern whites increasingly portrayed as the victims of injustice" and "blacks deemed unfit to exercise suffrage."[13] Liberals who had been critics of slavery and champions of the Republican war effort would organize the Liberal Republican opposition to President Ulysses S. Grant in 1872 and the "mugwump" defection to Democrat Grover Cleveland in 1884.[14] Their reversal is only one explanation of Reconstruction's demise, though most explanations—whether those of a counterrevolution of property, or Republican adherence to free-market liberalism, or consistent anti-Black prejudice and violence, or the central state's failure to govern the breadth of outpost resistance—return at some point to Northern, white liberals who sympathized with property over workers, laissez-faire over redistributive economics, state autonomy over federal intervention, and white Southerners over Black.[15] Within national culture, the defection of Northern white liberals meant diminished electoral power, less financial support for Reconstruction's educational and infrastructural projects, fewer powerful mouthpieces for Reconstruction policies, and less attention that might stay the hand of white supremacist violence.

Homoerotic reunion between North and South was, to be sure, not the only political orientation fostered by same-sex romance. Intimacies between enslaved men, as recent novelists have imagined, likely enabled both resistance to and resilience under enslavement.[16] We should not be surprised to find interracial male intimacy as a source of abolitionist energies.[17] Certainly, male bonding assisted in the Northern soldier's transformation from Unionist to abolitionist soldier. We do not know the extent to which remembered and continued intimacies fostered the camaraderie, and consequent Republican support, in veteran organizations like the Grand Army of the Republic.[18] Nor do we know the full meaning of Black soldiers' first experience of an emancipation that included freedom from systems of sexual abuse, coercion, and control, within the homosocial camp life of the Union army.[19] Nor should we dismiss the suggestion—as W. E. B. Du Bois appears to make by selecting a stanza of Oscar Wilde's *The Ballad of Reading Gaol* (1898) for the conclusion of his penultimate chapter, "Back to Slavery," in *Black Reconstruction in America* (1935)—that an emerging minoritarian consciousness of homosexual orientation could promote affiliation across class, race, and nation among oppressed people.[20] The political sympathies engendered by same-sex romance and homoerotic desire were likely as varied as the people experiencing that desire.

But same-sex romance operated within a tradition of cultural and literary narratives and developed political meaning within those narratives. Northern white liberals, as the readers, the writers, and the imagined audience of these narratives, were committed to the work of constructing and consuming a national culture. To do so, they looked backward, to the antebellum and founding-era intimacies between men that had transcended partisanship for national union. Even as conceptions of manhood, sexuality, and nation transformed around them, they found in this tradition a way to think about the bonds between white men of the North and South.

The shifting sympathies of Northern white liberals brings to the fore crucial questions about how whiteness operated across the Civil War era. Did a shared racial identity between white Northerners and Southerners produce the affiliations that would doom Reconstruction? Or did the process of and backlash to Reconstruction produce the shared whiteness that would enable regimes of segregation and Jim Crow? Whiteness's appearance as a dominant, and explanatory, historical force depends on the ongoing ways it is strengthened and reinforced.[21] Narratives of same-sex romance, I argue, were a crucial mechanism for constructing and strengthening whiteness. Romances of affiliation between men reflected desire for previous iterations of white-male bonding while also engendering the cross-sectional alliances that would preserve slavery, promote the Lost Cause, and produce a white supremacist reunion. Narratives of same-sex romance, in short, produced these Confederate sympathies.

In some ways, these cross-sectional embraces may look familiar within postbellum culture. Many historians have explored the place of the cross-sectional romance in postbellum reconciliation. Nina Silber, in particular, has emphasized the gendered presentation of these relationships: a Northern man conquering and converting the affection of a once rebellious, now submissive Southern woman. Many prewar narratives, to which these postbellum narratives responded, made political meaning through romances with a reversed gender story: Southern men winning the affections and proslavery sympathies of Northern women, often abolitionists' daughters. Other postbellum romances, of transplanted Northern brides as well as intra-Southern lovers, complicate Silber's gender formula while emphasizing the gendered politics she identifies.²² What difference does it make when the romance is between two men? Male-male romance did not merely complicate the gendered formula but produced different meaning because homosexuality differs from heterosexuality historically and politically.

Political allegories of relationships between a man and woman often draw their power from the perceived unchanging nature of heterosexuality. Even as conceptions of the ideal husband or wife change, love and marriage triumph, especially in the postbellum romance of reunion, over the historical contingencies that would keep a couple apart. Same-sex romance, by contrast, situates itself within history, referential to the changing historical status of same-sex sexuality. To evoke heterosexuality as political allegory is to imagine a transhistorical truth; for homosexuality, political meaning derives from perceived differences between past and present. Homosexuality's political meaning, within a narrative, is historically referential and self-consciously so.

As one prominent example, D. W. Griffith's 1915 film *The Birth of a Nation*, that notorious exemplar of white supremacist cinema, demonstrates how differently male-female and same-sex romances create meaning. Perhaps no other narrative so overtly attempts a gendered North-South balance through the intersectional weddings of sibling pairs, Northern husband and Southern bride, Northern bride and Southern husband.²³ The film's argument for a white North-South reunion victorious over Black empowerment draws strength from heterosexual romance's status as natural, permanent, and hegemonic.²⁴ The film justifies the violence done to Black Americans through the romantic appeal of such stories: it is love, not white supremacist power, that conquers all.

The film also features a third cross-sectional romance, between a male pair, Tod and Wade: "Chums—the younger sons. North and South," an intertitle states. Unlike their brothers and sisters of the marrying type, Tod and Wade die halfway through the film, a "bitter, useless, sacrifice." After Wade has been shot, Tod holds a bayonet over him. Recognizing Wade, he stops short and is shot in the back. He falls, his arm across Wade's bare chest. Tod's hand moves up around Wade's neck as his face leans toward Wade's in what looks like a kiss. They give their last full measure of devotion to each other, dying in this cross-sectional embrace.²⁵ If their siblings' love consecrated the birth of a new, unified nation, Tod and Wade's love was lost in the war.

Their love, unlike their siblings' universal love, is historically contingent, possible only before the war divided and killed them, on a South Carolina slave plantation, where, as an intertitle informs us, "life runs in a quaintly

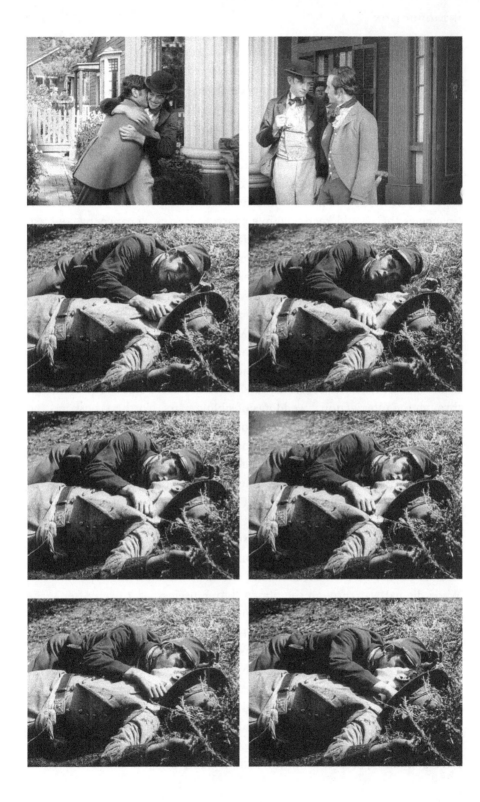

way that is to be no more." In those scenes, their playful touching colors the antebellum world with nostalgia for a youthful homoeroticism. That picture matched a conception developed in the nineteenth century of romantic male intimacy and homoeroticism as confined to immaturity and youth.[26] Because that understanding precluded a homosexually paired adulthood, Tod's and Wade's battlefield deaths, indeed the Civil War itself, enter as a fatalistically preordained event within male development, inevitable but no less tragic. As such, their deaths offer an interpretation of the war: the more intense the intimacies between the two men, the more the war appears as the tragic loss of a past that cannot return. Their deaths make the war both necessary for maturation—the birth of a new nation—and a tragedy of the lost antebellum world, the film's two central themes.[27]

To reinforce the historical dimension of that tragedy, blame for their death falls on the same culprits responsible for, the film asserts, the war itself: Black Americans. Griffith makes much meaning in the silent film through his careful, symbolic staging: the loyal dogs at the feet of the plantation patriarch, the cat among the dogs as the war's upheavals begin. To establish the cause of Tod and Wade's disunion, Griffith stages a Black face—white actress Jennie Lee in blackface—hovering directly between the male pair in their last moment of prewar embrace. Moreover, when the actor who plays the fallen Tod reappears later in blackface as a different character, he is a Black Union spy leering through the Camerons' entryway at their elder daughter, his performance of Black sexuality opposed to the innocent antebellum sexuality of Tod and Wade. Their sepia-toned homoerotic innocence starkly contrasts the later picture of sexuality in the film, the blood-tinged appearance of rapacious Black sexuality in Gus as he chases the youngest Cameron daughter to her death. The chums' intimacy, possible only within slavery's past, becomes impossible in a world of Black emancipation.

The scene's meaning also contrasts another understanding of sexuality developing at the turn of the century. The emergence of a problematized homosexual minority identity, the shift of a whole culture's consciousness, profoundly affected the lives of the actors in this scene. George (André) Beranger, the actor who played Wade, was gay, according to a relative, who wrote in 2012 that the Australian actor had married a widowed neighbor to try to remain viable in leading roles before leaving film for a reclusive life in

Left to right by row: The chums, Tod and Wade, embracing at the Camerons' antebellum plantation; the character of "Mammy" hovering between the pair as they part; the enemy combatants dying in an embrace on the battlefield. Griffith, *Birth of a Nation* (1915).

Australia.[28] Robert Harron, who portrayed Tod, shot himself, either by accident or suicide, and died at age twenty-seven, five years after the film's release. In 1984, film historian Richard Schickel wrote that, "as rumor has long had it," Harron may have been "troubled by homosexual tendencies he could no longer deny."[29] One can only imagine, for Beranger and Harron, the dissonance between the suggestive intimacy they were directed to display and the prohibited intimacies that so disrupted their self-conceptions and careers. That dissonance accentuates the nostalgic meaning of homoeroticism in the scene. The dying kiss between Tod and Wade achieves its nostalgic appeal through the opposition of these two versions of homosexuality: the old, innocent, sentimentalized male-male intimacy and the modern social problem of homosexual identity. This opposition makes the Civil War an event in the development of white manhood, inevitable but no less tragic, and paints the antebellum South as a world of nostalgic, homoerotic intimacies doomed by progress and modernity.

Thus, the presentation of homoeroticism is always historically referential. For the antebellum Whitman, love between men recalled the fraternal attachments of the nation's founding; after the war, it recalled the bonds available before the Civil War's rupture. In *The Birth of a Nation*, it celebrated the innocent intimacies of white men possible within plantation slavery in opposition to the deviant sexualities seen as originating with emancipation. A study of same-sex romance in nineteenth-century US culture, then, requires reference to the period's complex political history, interwoven with two additional strands of cultural history: first, the work and power of cultural production to create, sustain, and develop political sympathies, and second, the history of homosexuality as it transforms and evolves across the century. The next sections provide a brief overview of these two strands, followed by an overview of this book's argument.

Contests of Political and Literary Sympathy in the Civil War Era

When Eric Foner asserts that Reconstruction's demise came, in part, from the "remarkable reversal of sympathies" of Northern white liberals, he treats those sympathies as both a reflection and agent of historical change. Sympathy was not merely an emotion in the nineteenth-century United States; it operated as both an effect and a cause of political action. Its usage represented that expansive political meaning: to be in sympathy with another might mean sharing a feeling or, as often, sharing another's ideas and political views. As a literary sentiment—originating in the moves of some writer, permeating the words of a written page, migrating into the mind, if not the heart, of a reader, and landing upon some object beyond the book—sympathy both evidenced how people felt and accomplished real work in society.[30] To take the era's most prominent example, Harriet Beecher Stowe's 1852 *Uncle Tom's Cabin* reflected the sympathies felt by some white Northerners, but no political history of the Civil War era omits the fact-making, world-shaping power of Stowe's closing admonition that her readers "see to it that *they feel right.*"[31] Feeling was a political action.

Stowe's novel demonstrates as well the power sex and sexuality had to foster literary and political sympathies. Antislavery activists had long marshaled images of sexual abuse, especially of enslaved women, to cultivate Northern sympathies.[32] Stowe's novel, along with Harriet Jacobs's 1861 first-person narrative, followed the success of this framing and united the seduction plot of earlier novels, in which female heroines evaded rapacious male desire, with enslaved women's accounts of abuse to emplot sexual victimization as antislavery argument.[33] The antislavery mobilization around narratives of sexual abuse—in novels, in illustrations, in periodicals, and on the Senate floor in Charles Sumner's denunciations of his South Carolina colleague's "mistress," "the harlot slavery"—were met with proslavery rejoinders recasting abolitionists as the true sexual deviants preying upon sympathetic Southern families.[34] By the time the war began, a war-before-the-war over sex had produced an economy of competing sympathies into which all cultural narratives would be conscripted.

The soldiers of Civil War armies, then, had their sympathies packed with them as they set off to fight. But they also became, for a broader culture, the object of sympathies, a new object emerging almost suddenly, though perhaps unsurprisingly, in 1861. Wartime literature, as historian Alice Fahs writes, resisted mass death with a "sentimental insistence on the importance of sympathy and individual suffering."[35] If the Civil War was, as a body of scholarship has established, a crisis in gender, that crisis engendered both a masculinized sense of duty and a feminized portrait of the suffering young male soldier.[36] A war precipitated, in part, by antislavery activists' image of the victimized Black female body became a war preoccupied with the image of the suffering white male body. Southern sympathies for the Confederate soldier consolidated the symbolism of the national project of a slaveholders' republic onto his body, while, in the North, the replacement of enslaved women by white prisoners as the chief victims of Southern atrocity represented an even more stark, and politically consequential, disruption of sympathies.[37]

The early years of Reconstruction politics also played out within a contest of sympathies. Among the chief arguments for the expansion of civil rights to African Americans, including the right to vote, was the suffering, woundedness, and death that Black soldiers experienced when saving the nation. Demands for federal protections for Southern freed people came through steady dispatches of anti-Black violence in the national press. Meanwhile, Reconstruction's opponents pointed to the suffering of Southern whites, defeated, impoverished, and humiliated, as the reason they should not be further harassed by policies of equal rights or Black suffrage. As had antebellum sympathies, the contests over postbellum sympathies, with life-and-death political consequences, were fought on the pages of newspapers, magazines, memoirs, and books.[38]

Racist beliefs structured the contest over postbellum sympathies, as they had antebellum sympathies. The evident consistency of Northern white prejudice against Black Americans across this period has led some historians to doubt the depth of Foner's "remarkable reversal."[39] Foner does not, however, argue for a measurable increase in liberals' racism but for something different, a shift in the object of their sympathies. Liberals mostly held consistently racist views of Black Americans as social dependents, but by the early 1870s they saw those once in need of emancipationist intervention now as corrupt wards of government intervention. White Southerners, once overpowerful and corrupt as the slave power, were now the victims of government intervention. A reversal of sympathies for the abolitionists turned Liberal Republicans had ushered in this transformation. Its roots were, no doubt, material for those who stood to lose from policies of redistribution. But, for liberals, economic interests became public policy through a discourse of sympathy; sympathy fulfilled liberals' foundational desire to remove public policy from vulgar self-interest and administer governance by sorting groups into undeserving villains and deserving victims.[40]

The period's literary culture both reflected and produced these liberal sympathies. "The political retreat from Reconstruction," historian K. Stephen Prince writes, "could not have occurred without a contemporaneous cultural retreat from Reconstruction."[41] One enabling factor was the near stranglehold that Northern liberal men held on the period's literary production. In the 1870s and 1880s, nearly every Northeast literary magazine had a liberal editor at the helm, many of whom would be prominent mugwumps supporting the Democrat Cleveland in 1884.[42] Despite being a small faction nationally, these mugwump-type men, to an outsize degree, determined what stories got printed in the United States.

One contemporary who rejected this cultural coalescence was Albion Tourgée. A radical, not a mugwump liberal, the jurist and novelist saw literary sympathy as a means of fighting postbellum political battles. "Our literature," Tourgée objected in 1888, "has become not only Southern in type, but distinctly Confederate in sympathy."[43] Tourgée blamed two distinct sets of writers for this cultural landscape. First were those local sketchers of Southern life (such as Constance Fenimore Woolson, George Washington Cable, Joel Chandler Harris, and Thomas Nelson Page) who were disseminated to a national audience through "the great popular monthlies" of the Northeast: the *Atlantic Monthly* and the *Century* (originally called *Scribner's*).[44] Second were the period's prominent realists, William Dean Howells and Henry James, whom Tourgée faulted not so much for sympathizing with white Southerners as for ignoring the political questions of Reconstruction and its aftermath in favor of "trivialities."[45] The field of fiction Howells and James left open to the Southern sympathizers comprised these same Northeast liberal monthly magazines, a cultural world of which James and Howells were far more representative than the Southern writers.

Indeed, James's sympathies are particularly instructive of the cultural shifts to which Tourgée was attuned. For James, as a small boy, *Uncle Tom's Cabin* had been "much less a book than a state of vision, of feeling and of consciousness."[46] "Our sympathies," he would recall of his family during the Civil War, "were all enlisted on behalf of that race that had sat in bondage."[47] When visiting the US South decades later for his travel memoir, *The American Scene* (1907), it would be in the white Southerners' posture of defeat that James would find "food for sympathy."[48] James's reversal of sympathies, from the enslaved to white Southerners, was typical of men of his generation, race, and class and representative of a specific political orientation, mugwumpian liberalism. James meditated on the problem of postbellum political sympathies throughout his writing, most prominently in the 1886 novel *The Bostonians*, which was also initially published in the mugwump monthly the *Century*. For James, as for Whitman, same-sex desire was central to both his thinking about political sympathy and his political sympathy. The prominence of these two writers within this period's cultural history suggests that same-sex desire was not marginal but integrated within these contests of political and literary sympathies. This book will put it at the center.

Whitman and James may be obvious figures with which to begin a study of Civil War–era same-sex romance, but this book will move far beyond them to capture a wider, and stronger, current of thinking across the nineteenth-century United States. In attending to narratives of male same-sex romance, I do not claim to have outed the secret explanation for Civil War–era politics, nor am I attempting to make visible the experience and perspective of a hitherto invisible minority. I take representations of homoeroticism not as a minoritarian discourse produced by and legible to only a tragic fellowship but, instead, as broadly meaningful within a shared social terrain. To do so takes, as Eve Sedgwick suggests, a universalist, rather than minoritarian, view of epistemologies of sexuality, which operate across society and culture.[49] Sedgwick's universalism is not, however, meant to be transhistorical. Much the opposite: it is homosexuality's embeddedness within history that gives it meaning as both an index to and an agent within political history.

The Historicity of Homosexuality

For at least two centuries in the United States, the status of same-sex sexuality has been among the most visible evidence of historical change. Homosexuality, following Michel Foucault's chronology in *The History of Sexuality*'s first volume, was invented during Grant's first presidential term, though it would be one of the few scandals that his administration avoided.[50] The term "homosexuality," developed from German sexual science, did not arrive in the United States until 1888, at which point it began to reshape both medical and legal understanding of sexual desire and its individual self-conception into a pathologized and then eventually organized minority homosexual identity.[51] This development, what Peter Coviello calls "a long moment of singular upheaval and transformation," proves a crucial turning point for any study of same-sex desire across the nineteenth century.[52] But emphasis on this particular rupture, and the discursive inventions of medicine and law that precipitate it, obscures comparison across that century's experience of sexual desire and sexuality's ongoing role in political history.[53]

A broader view of sexuality, one in line with Foucault's approach in his second and third volumes, enables us to see a series of ruptures and continuities in how people problematized sexual desire, thought into existence the problems of desire, and thought to deal with desire.[54] If what we mean in discussing a male *homo*sexuality is how sex between men and same-sex desire was problematized and managed, we can begin to trace that phenomenon's history across the nineteenth century. That view enables us to see, even more clearly, historical change, especially the co-construction of political thought and the experience of same-sex desire. The emergence of homo- and heterosexual identity is a particularly dramatic transformation, but it is one that historians of sexuality now see fractured into smaller, overlapping epistemological shifts: the pre-nineteenth-century shifts toward racialized classification of sex acts during early colonial interaction; the early nineteenth-century shifts toward institutionalizing theories of sexual development within education;

the early twentieth-century shifts from a gender inversion model (men with female interiors) to a gender-based sexual orientation (men who desire men); and the mid-twentieth-century shifts in the position of same-sex-desiring people from objects of surveillance to subjects of resistance efforts for social change.[55] At first blush, recent changes to homosexuality may appear more legal than epistemic, but they were achieved precisely through the assertion of new correspondences between homosexuality and history. These changes, in turn, both set in motion and made visible new ways of thinking about sexuality that are, for many, prime evidence of historical change in their lifetime.[56] Any direct or indirect evocation of same-sex desire, across the history of the United States, situates itself within history; it makes meaning within a historical horizon and by reference to historical change.[57]

To be sure, the same wearing its historical situatedness on the surface is true of many things, such as railroads or computers, that both clock historical moments while symbolizing progress or outdatedness. But the overwhelming depth and visibility of homosexuality's transformations mean that one taking up Fredric Jameson's imperative to strip a narrative to its naked meaning within History finds, with representations of homosexuality, historicity lying there already naked.[58] The presentation of same-sex desire speaks loudly, and quite revealingly, its historical boundedness. If one mode of "queer historicism" would, as Valerie Traub has written, reveal "*how* categories, however mythic, phantasmic, and incoherent, *came to be*," I attempt, in this book, another queer historicist mode, in which the tools of excavating socially constructed sexual categories aim to understand those genealogies as agents and archives of political history.[59] This book uses tools of queer analysis to examine how representations of same-sex romance and desire function as political instruments. In other words, homoeroticism is never the end point of analysis but an entry point toward the horizon of political history.

Homosexuality has intersected, as visibly, with race and class in constructing overlapping, bifurcated, or co-constitutive political identities. Three decades ago, Eric Lott posited that same-sex desire and homoerotic pleasure were constructive of antebellum white working-class subjectivity.[60] A body of scholarship at the intersection of queer studies and critical race studies has asserted the race-making power of same-sex desire. Recent nineteenth-century studies scholars have made clear that interracial homoeroticism—as a desire for, channel through, and effect of power—was a site of race-making within enslavement.[61] If white male desire for nonwhite men has contributed to the construction of race, I find race-making no less evident when the homoeroticism, as in most of the texts I examine, is between men of the same race. Its meaning depends on reference to political history, often through a nostalgic orientation to the past.

One need hardly suggest that the dying chums of *The Birth of a Nation* are homoerotically oriented to a nostalgic past; they are, as importantly, oriented against a distinct political present, one terrified of a Black male sexual threat. Thus, the film draws at once on these two competing understandings of sexuality: the backward-looking memory of past intimacies and the future-looking fearfulness of new sexual perversions. Historians of race and sexuality have shown just how interlinked were the late nineteenth-century projects of racial and sexual science: the same science produced by the same scientists explained racial traits through sexual behavior and sexual identity through racial difference.[62] This science, as I explore later, drew upon Civil War history. If the problems of deviant sexuality were, as sexual scientists posited, the problems of a modernizing, urbanizing society, the antebellum past appeared innocently uncontaminated as premodern, anti-industrial, and agrarian. In this way, nostalgia for a more innocent homoeroticism confederated with white supremacist nostalgia for the happy peace of the antebellum slave order.

To say that postbellum writers, looking backward, saw a more innocent homoeroticism is an old claim, one that Leslie Fiedler put at the very heart of American culture. Beginning with the 1948 essay "Come Back to the Raft Ag'in, Huck Honey," Fiedler argued that the cross-racial male intimates of the US canon represent a longing for a return to an innocent, preracial utopia, before the sins of slavery and racism.[63] More recent retrospectives on Fiedler's thesis have emphasized the implicit homophobia of his phrase "innocent homosexuality." Innocent, literary scholar Christopher Looby has asked, "as opposed to what?" Looby suggests, however, that the oppositions Fiedler established may have been across time: that Mark Twain in *Huckleberry Finn* (1885) "may have been harking back to a prior era in which sexual and gender identities were not so rigidly defined."[64] "Innocent" is, of course, a relative term, and what Fiedler intuited (writing closer to Twain's publication than our own time) was how a nostalgic homoeroticism supported the homophobic regime in which he participated.

Across the nineteenth century, narratives of same-sex romance looked backward. Their political meaning was consistently referential to the past. This book, therefore, begins with male romantic friendship in the late antebellum period. Postbellum same-sex romances, after disunion, referred to a tradition of antebellum romances between white men that were imagined as holding the fracturing nation together. Those antebellum romances were

themselves referential to the male intimacies of the Revolutionary generation, imagined as the ties that bound free white men to one another for the
project of nation-building. To the subsequent generation enduring disunion,
they represented a time before the problems of racial slavery pitted white
men against one another. In these conservative and reactionary associations,
defenders of slavery, promoters of white supremacist reunion, and romancers
of the Lost Cause all found political meaning. Such meaning and associations are, of course, not endemic to same-sex desire, but they demonstrate
homoeroticism's fundamental political pliability. Queer identity and activism
have long been a source of radical politics, but this history challenges the presumption of queerness's radical potential by showing homoeroticism's easy
affinity for conservative ideology. This history points instead to homoeroticism's reactionary potential.[65]

The recent history of homosexuality and queer identity has affirmed
that remarkable political pliability. The expansion of liberalism's promises
of freedom and state protection for LGBTQ citizens has not merely reen-
acted the same exclusions and material inequalities that liberalism has long
failed to redress; if anything, "queer liberalism," as scholar David Eng terms
it, has reoriented the political interests of many toward defending liberties
won rather than combating inequality and racial exclusions.[66] Meanwhile, the
twenty-first century has seen the rise of a phenomenon, which Jasbir Puar
terms "homonationalism," in which the liberal defenses of gay identity are
mobilized against a racial other in service of US imperialism.[67] At the same
time, this century's reactionary right wing has added some tolerance, if not
open-armed embrace, of certain versions of male homosexuality in its ranks.
The at-times quite brazen homoeroticism of this right wing draws again upon
a past—Confederate, medieval, ancient, pagan, who knows—for its antifem-
inist reaction, as if the iconography of male homosexuality serves as the ultimate aesthetic of female exclusion and male supremacy.[68] More important
than any individual gay participation in reactionary politics, as surprising as
this remains, is how homoeroticism constructs these affiliations and political
sympathies more broadly.

This book, therefore, is not one about individual gay Confederates. The
very elasticity of any inquiry into the political meaning of same-sex romance
(What was that meaning for, say, proslavery apologist William Henry Hammond? For Confederate general Patrick Cleburne? Or Secretary of State Judah
Benjamin? What about Confederate soldier Philip Van Buskirk? If Lost Cause
sculptor Moses Ezekiel, then war memoirist Morris Schaff? . . . But war novelist John Esten Cooke? Whitman and James, but William Gilmore Simms?

. . . Or Cornelius Mathews? . . . Or President James Buchanan?) suggests a phenomenon whose boundaries may be coextensive with the imagination of white manhood itself. At the same time, same-sex romance held, for these men and others throughout this book, specific and defined political meaning for imagining the bonds between white Northern and Southern men. This study does not aim to add more individual men to the list of those with same-sex desire and reactionary politics. Instead, it aims to add the experience of same-sex desire to those explanations of why political history in the Civil War era took the direction it did.

The first two chapters of the book treat male intimacy before the Civil War. Chapters 3 and 4 examine images of Civil War soldiers and their legacy after the war. The final two chapters investigate same-sex romance in postbellum memory.

In the antebellum period, homoerotic imagery served to defend racial slavery. The first chapter argues that imagined intimacies between white men kept the antebellum Democratic Party together across differences of class and section. For white working-class Democrats in New York City, homoerotic affiliation enabled party unity; through the 1850s, the imagery of male friendship, including at the top of presidential tickets, symbolized the cross-sectional unity between Northern white Democrats and the slaveholding South. Chapter 2 examines a contemporaneous phenomenon, in proslavery fiction, of romanticized relationships between enslaved men and slaveholders that cultivated sympathy for slavery. By contrasting loving, familial bonds between men to abolitionist threats to the plantation family, these novels analogized a master-slave relationship to marriage threatened by unnatural, antifamily abolitionist deviance.

During the Civil War, the bodies of white male soldiers became the predominant object of sympathy. Attractive young Confederate soldiers, especially those feminized in memory, as explored in chapter 3, symbolized the young life and potential of the Confederate nation. But, with the death of that nation's hopes, the deaths of young Confederate soldiers, such as John Pelham, took hold of a Confederate, and then broader, national imagination in images, histories, and novels. In the erotically charged perspectives of older veterans, and then for reconciliationist culture, the pretty, dead Confederate youth became an eroticized emblem of the Lost Cause. In the North, as well, sympathetic attention turned to the young male soldiers of the Union army. Chapter 4 explores how postbellum prisoner-of-war narratives used the tropes of 1850s sentimental antislavery fiction almost scene for scene and offered, in the place of the enslaved, a new victim of Southern atrocity: the naked, emaciated white Union soldier as prisoner of war. That replacement of victimhood came with an eroticization of the white male body—indeed, through homoerotic depictions of Andersonville prisoners of war in loving pairs. Those homoerotic pairs argued for the model of loving care with which the federal government ought to treat its Union veterans, but the attention on white male suffering served reconciliationist aims in a subsequent wave of narratives of prison experience.

After the Civil War, romantic friendship literature, explored in chapter 5, narrated the nostalgic antebellum intimacy between two young men, often cross-sectional college chums, who break apart with the war. These novels narrated the destruction of intimate male bonds, as if the old dream of white male fraternity lay dead and disenchanted in some small hole-and-corner engagement. As such, they offer an interpretation of the war: the more intense the intimacies between the two young men, the more the war appears as the tragic loss of a past that cannot return. The longing for these intimacies as they are destroyed is not merely homoerotic but a longing for a distinct political past, that of antebellum comity among white men. That interpretation ran parallel, in historical interpretation, to one that followed the period's sexual science that identified a new problem of urban homosexuality increasing with postbellum industrialization. For novelists, sexologists, and Civil War historians, the war-wrought transformation staged an opposition between two versions of homosexuality: the war ushered in the dangerous new sexualities of modernity while recasting the antebellum past's homoerotic intimacies as objects of nostalgic desire.

The final chapter explores the status of the attractive white Southerner, especially the Confederate veteran, in the postbellum Northern imagination. To get at that imagination, I look to Henry James, someone who tried to keep US politics at a distance. That distancing is partly the point: for James, exploring the homoerotic appeal of young, white Southern men was a means of transforming US political issues into the higher, apolitical realm of virtuous culture. It allowed James to accomplish what his mugwump friends sought, to contrast virtuous culture and corrupt politics. James found that opposition in defeated young Southerners, who, through their honest striving and failing to preserve racial slavery in the modern world, became icons of an attractive male attribute, ingenuousness. James's writing and his thinking about US politics provide a case study of Northern liberals' shifting sympathies and the homoerotic desire that enabled, accompanied, and followed it.

What James liked about the South was that it put him in touch with a premodern past, one opposed to a modernity of urban commercialism and corruption. For Northern liberals, that view of a premodern South was a great source of sympathy. Narratives of sexuality helped crystallize the idea of a premodern South for both white Southerners and historians of the Civil War era. While the book's chapters examine how same-sex romance cultivated sympathies toward the Confederate effort to preserve plantation slavery, the conclusion examines how epistemologies of homosexuality have influenced the writing of history. The conclusion posits that as much as narratives of same-sex romance shaped the sympathies of Northern whites toward the white South, they have also had a hand in constructing the idea of the South and our orientation to the past.

Many of the works I examine were widely read, but for few could one demonstrate a measurable impact within the political world. Therefore, in each chapter, to establish a phenomenon broader than any one author, I read across wide sets of literary culture.[69] Some of these, such as the thirty proslavery novels responding in the 1850s to *Uncle Tom's Cabin* (in chapter 2) or the two dozen memoirs and novels about the Confederate prison camp at Andersonville (in chapter 4), may be recognizable as sets to literary scholars, almost microgenres unto themselves. Others, such as memoirs celebrating the brief life and tragic death of a single Confederate soldier, John Pelham (in chapter 3), are wider and yet more cohesive than one might suppose. Alongside closer attention to works canonical in studies of nineteenth-century male sexuality, these texts demonstrate a broad phenomenon of homoerotic political feeling and thinking. This book proceeds with the presumption that same-sex desire is a part of history: not merely that same-sex-desiring people existed in the past but that same-sex desire, as a feeling, narrative, allegory, and structure of thought, has determined political history and its interpretation.

The Conservative, Cross-Sectional Symbol of Intimate Male Friendship in Antebellum Politics

EORGE WASHINGTON, in his 1796 Farewell Address, warned that both sectionalism and political parties threatened "to render alien to each other those, who ought to be bound together by fraternal affection." For Washington and his men, "union and brotherly affection" were one and the same.[1] He had fostered such affections across geographic differences among his Revolutionary War staff: one New York City aide-de-camp, Alexander Hamilton, would write to another, John Laurens, from South Carolina, "I wish, my Dear Laurens, that it might be in my power, by action rather than words, to convince you that I love you."[2] For the Revolutionary-era generation, male friendship was the stuff on which national comity depended, the ties that bound together the fraternity of all men created equal. That fraternity was exclusionary, an imagined equality of propertied white men. It was also backward-looking, drawing on classical models of Greek and Roman friendship as the source of republican civic virtue. Male friendship could be revolutionary in one sense, uniting men to replace monarchical British rule with republican government, while also a conservative counterweight to the revolutionary spirit, what historian Richard Godbeer calls an "emotional anchor" for "social and political stability."[3] As Washington's warning predicted, such stability was threatened by two kinds of factionalism: party and region.

For many, especially post–Civil War commentators looking backward, the rise of party politics—most notably Thomas Jefferson's 1800 ouster of President John Adams or Andrew Jackson's 1828 ouster of John Quincy Adams— meant the end of Washington's union of brotherly affection. As we will see in the final chapter of this book, Quincy Adams's grandson Henry Adams saw Jackson's victory, with which went the spoils of government appointments to members of his Democratic Party, as disrupting the American tradition of virtuous fellowship across party and section. To Adams, Washington's warning had been right: division into political factions had prevented unity across sections. That was, however, a postbellum view. Political parties, through the first decades of constitutional government, proved far more consonant with the US political system than the founding generation predicted. And male friendship proved a unifying force not across parties but within them. Affection would solve the problems of section yet—and not just section but also class—for the Democratic Party following Jackson.

The most remarkable thing about the antebellum Democratic Party, in retrospect, is that it held together as long as it did, until it split in 1860 by section because of slavery. It was remarkable not merely in its pronounced sectional divisions but also in its differences of class. Jackson's party united working-class New York City with the slaveholders of the South. The party's ideological divisions, too, have long been an interpretive crux for historians. Jackson's democratic expansions have often appeared quite radical; the 1850s party of Stephen Douglas and James Buchanan was decidedly conservative. One set of historians sees a party transformed from 1828 to the 1850s: egalitarians defected for antislavery parties, replaced by conservative Whigs during the era's realignments. Another set sees continuity, a party unified across decades through a conservatism predicated on preserving the democratic sovereignty of white manhood.[4]

For a party in flux, the Democrats had considerable continuity in membership and leadership from the 1830s to 1850s. What held the party together across its differences, of section and of class, through Jacksonian radicalism and Buchananian conservativism? One answer is certainly race. "Racial democracy," historian Joshua Lynn writes, "united white men from the slave states and the free states."[5] Political unity depended on symbolism that Dana Nelson has termed an "imagined" "fraternity of white manhood."[6] This imagined racial fraternity, as Peter Coviello insists in *Intimacy in America*, was both abstract and relational, existing within the imagined and real intimacies between men.[7] For the Democratic Party, male friendship was a prominent public symbol that cultivated party unity, across class and across section. Male friendship, the intimate relationships between white men, was the paradigmatic unit and unifying symbol of this fraternity and the national Democratic coalition, increasingly so as the party embraced its most conservative, proslavery platform in the 1850s.

Male friendship, one need not be reminded, is not identical to same-sex romance. Yet exploring the politics of Civil War–era same-sex romance must start here for two reasons. First, male friendship and homoeroticism were not opposed in the period; same-sex romance was integrated within, not outside of, the framework of male friendship. Indeed, part of why romantic friendship worked for men was that it could incorporate expressions of same-sex eroticism, desire, and sex into its framework. Second, narratives of same-sex romance during and after the Civil War drew meaning by looking backward at the antebellum intimacies that had symbolized cross-sectional unity. They could do so because such intimacies held political meaning—the symbolism of male friendship was stabilizing and conservative and within the Democratic Party's appeal to white manhood. That is not to say that Democrats held a monopoly on male intimacies: indeed, some of history's most celebrated romantic friendships were among abolitionists and Republicans.[8] But within the antislavery movement and then the Republican Party, such male intimacies were private, an invisible sustaining source of political activism. For Democrats, they formed a public appeal, a celebrated form and prominent symbol of party unity. In examining the political meaning of these intimacies, this chapter follows Nelson and Coviello in seeing fraternal feeling as constructive of American nationalism. But that feeling was refracted through partisan politics; it was useful not merely in cultivating national identity but especially in keeping the unwieldy Democratic coalition together.

In January 1827,with Quincy Adams preparing for a reelection campaign, New York senator Martin Van Buren wrote a letter to Virginia journalist Thomas Ritchie proposing "the most natural & beneficial" political combination between "the planters of the South and the plain Republicans of the north." Returning to Washington's warning of the dangers of sectionalism, Van Buren offered the opposite remedy, the "all powerful sympathy" of "party attachment," which "in former times furnished a complete antidote for sectional prejudices by producing counteracting feelings."[9] Ritchie's acceptance of the proposal, and endorsement of Andrew Jackson for president in 1828, helped launch Jackson's cross-sectional Democratic Party.

For its first eight years, the presiding symbol of this coalition was the manhood of President Jackson himself.[10] As biographers and historians of the era have written, Jacksonian masculinity became the potent avatar of the fraternity of white manhood by racializing effeminacy as a threat to whiteness and by feminizing nonwhite people as a threat to masculinity.[11] For historian Amy Greenberg, Jackson's "martial manhood" proved an effective mechanism for political organizing by appealing both to the patriarchal dominance of slaveholders and the homosocial world of the Northern white working class. The qualities of this masculinity—militarism, physical dominance, and an unrestrained morality—proved so effective after Jackson that the Whigs' only two presidential victories of the era came when famed generals William Henry Harrison, in 1840, and Zachary Taylor, in 1848, campaigned on their military manhood. Despite Whigs' occasional embrace of martial manhood, it was, Greenberg asserts, the special domain of the Democratic Party. This brand of masculinity, inaugurated by Jackson and running through the party's Young America movement and its expansionism following the US-Mexico War (1846–48), was a through line of party identity, enlisting the urban white North into the proslavery project of US expansion.[12]

At the end of his second term, Jackson's persona, and his party's unified identification with him, propelled his successor, and the coalition's architect, Van Buren, to the presidency. The opposition ran a section-by-section campaign, a different candidate appealing to different regions, in the failed effort to prevent a Van Buren majority and throw the contest to Congress.[13] Four years later, Whigs unified with a new strategy cribbing elements of Jackson's masculine appeal. They ran the celebrated Ohio general Harrison in a cross-sectional coalition with Virginia's John Tyler and succeeded, in part, by attacking Van Buren's masculinity.[14] Democrats divided by section in accounting for Van Buren's loss. For many Southerners, Van Buren's long-standing ties to New York urban politics hurt more than helped, while to Van Buren true believers blame fell on the party's proslavery Southerners who had found the president insufficiently supportive of territorial expansion.[15] Thus, Van Buren's 1840 loss revealed just how potent Jacksonian manhood had been in unifying the party's sectional differences. With Jackson off the ticket, Democrats plainly needed a new mechanism for cross-sectional party unity. They found it in the symbol of cross-sectional male friendship.

Two 1844 political cartoons by a Whig opponent indicate both the failure of Jacksonian masculinity to carry the day and the symbol that effectively replaced it. In the first, a skeletal Jackson pokes James Polk, the Democratic nominee, as the caption states, "in his extremity." The splayed-leg Polk

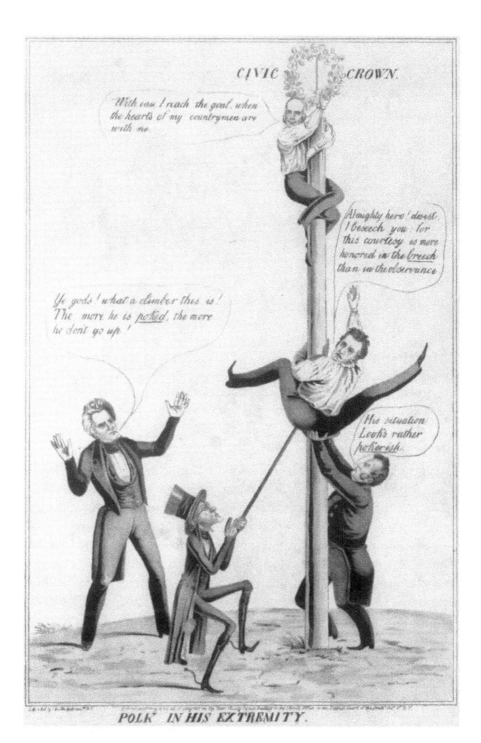

Jacksonian masculinity mocked. "Polk in His Extremity" by H. Bucholzer and
James S. Baillie (1844). American Cartoon Print Filing Series, Library of Congress.

LOCO FOCO TRIUMPHAL HONORS.

The coalition of Democratic manhood: a cross-sectional male pair, carried by white,
working-class, urban men, supportive of slavery and oriented toward expansionism.
"Loco-Foco Triumphal Honors" by H. Bucholzer and James S. Baillie (1844).
American Cartoon Print Filing Series, Library of Congress.

exclaims that "this courtesy is more honored in the *breech*" (not, as Hamlet
says, the breach) "than in the observance." Importantly, the sodomitical sug-
gestions in the cartoon do not feminize Democratic masculinity as much as
satirize its inefficacy. The cheerleader of the scene, South Carolina's John C.
Calhoun, observes, "The more he is poked, the more he don't go up." Nor can
the avid expansionist Thomas Hart Benton hoist the candidate. The cartoon
predicts (wrongly) that the failures of Democratic masculinity, Jackson's as
well as that of the candidate he prods, will yield the victory of Whig Henry
Clay.[16]

The second cartoon, also attacking Polk's candidacy, suggests the political
symbolism that would propel Polk over Clay to the presidency. The cartoon
depicts four cigar-chomping, pipe-smoking workingmen, representatives of
the Locofoco faction of New York City's Democratic Party, carrying the ticket
of Polk and running mate George Dallas, suggestively positioned along a triumphal pole. The friends, Polk, a Southern slaveholder, and Dallas, the former

Philadelphia mayor, follow the Democrat-turned-Whig-turned-Democrat Tyler (who had succeeded to the presidency following Harrison's death) presumably on the defining issue of his presidency, US expansionism through annexing Texas. Two Black musicians trail the procession as a symbol of the ticket's support of slavery. By allusion to the "blushing honors thick upon him," which Cardinal Wolsey looks back on as lost in his "Farewell to Greatness" speech in Shakespeare's *Henry VIII*, the cartoon suggests the demise of even Polk's and Dallas's meek, humble honors. And yet, within the cartoon's farce is the Democrats' winning coalition: a cross-sectional male pair at the top of the ticket supported by both slavery's proponents and the urban white working class.[17]

Male intimacy, as we will see, constituted a crucial component of urban white working-class identity, especially for the faction alluded to in the cartoon. Through the synecdoche of Locofoco, the name given to the late 1830s Democrats organizing the Equal Rights Party in New York City, the pole carriers represent the homosocial world of the Bowery neighborhood. For Whig opponents, Bowery masculinity, and Locofocoism, represented a political and cultural extreme, a working-class rowdyism of hard-drinking, unrestrained sexuality and demands for social leveling. In spite of these attacks, national Democrats would, in subsequent decades, celebrate Bowery Locofocoism as the epicenter of homosocial white masculinity. Within that world, male intimacy was a force for political and cultural cohesion, both in the (often homoerotic) affiliations themselves and in the image of male friendship as a political symbol, one connecting that faction with the larger national Democratic Party.

Thus, ironically, the Polk-Dallas cartoon represents a winning appeal of the antebellum Democratic Party: an intimate male friendship presiding over the party's urban white male constituency—itself a world of real and symbolic intimate male friendships—oriented toward expansionism and supportive of slavery.[18] As a political symbol, male friendship drew upon the conservative and stabilizing aspects of same-sex romantic friendship. Just as romantic friendship could incorporate patent homoeroticism and same-sex sex within its stabilizing framework, so, too, did the symbol of male friendship, for the Democratic Party, incorporate the rowdier and unrestrained sexualities of its constituency. For Democrats, it symbolized the intimacies across region and class within the fraternity of white manhood while also incorporating the party's homosocial, and even homoerotic, masculine appeal. For both reasons, it would prove for the national party to be a symbol of cross-sectional unity, tying the urban, white, working-class North with the slaveholding South in bonds of mutual affection.

Romantic Friendship as a Stabilizing Unit of the Fraternity of White Manhood

Two prominent cultural meanings of romantic friendship made it a potent conservative symbol before the Civil War: first, it was a source of stability in men's lives, a protection against social or sexual upheavals; second, it was a paradigmatic unit of the fraternity of white manhood. Just as the binary of homo- and heterosexual difference worked as a functional, though often unstable and incoherent, system of social organization in the late twentieth century, romantic friendship largely worked as a system of organizing and managing relationships between men for much of the nineteenth. It worked to advance the interests, careers, and fortunes of white male participants; manage same-sex desire and incorporate desire's disruptiveness into a framework protecting participants' social and moral health; and fortress men against social dangers like alcohol, gambling, and sex. Perhaps difficult for us to comprehend, the elements of romantic friendship—loving letters, tender intimacies, bed sharing—were a means of managing the dangers of sex, though not wholly preventative. Instead, romantic friendship provided a structure for male intimacy, homoeroticism, and male sexuality that aspired to contemporary ideals of health (such as avoiding excessive masturbation) and morality (such as an ideal of sexual self-restraint) while having considerable flexibility for falling short of these ideals.[19] The affordances that such friendships provided for breaches of sexual restraint made them a safe training for manhood. The dangers of sodomy and masturbation were made less dangerous by the framework of romantic friendship. Indeed, the pedagogical effectiveness, like all good teaching, depended on a principle not of strict adherence to prohibitions but of navigating, and thereby learning, boundaries.[20] Romantic friendship was the site for navigating these boundaries.

For example, what stands out in the diaries of the Maryland sailor and then Confederate soldier Philip Van Buskirk, one of the century's most notable archives for male sexual behavior, is the young man's fervent desire for a purifying romantic friendship. That wish was why, as a navy sailor in the 1850s, he sought out the impure among his shipmates, lectured them on the dangers of masturbation, and had them sleep tightly beside him, without which they would "certainly sleep with somebody else, and, in that case bad consequences might indeed result." The quartermaster to whom Van Buskirk related this practice responded, "Oh Hell! now do you mean to say that you sleeps alongside o' boys o' night and don't do nothing?" Van Buskirk accused the quartermaster of being "jealous" of his intimacies.[21] Van Buskirk's interests extended beyond his bedmates' welfare: it was not strictly true that he did "nothing" while sleeping beside them. The diaries he kept from 1851 to 1902, the first several of which B. R. Burg consolidated into a history of Van Buskirk's life, document his sex life as it took the form of mutual masturbation, sodomy, and tremendous pining over the other men with whom he sailed and slept. Burg writes that Van Buskirk treated these sex acts with "considerable guilt and humiliation," but clearly a great deal of his erotic interest came from negotiating purity and temptation, whether in his one-handed reading of antimasturbation tracts or in offering his bed to fellow sailors to prevent their having sex with others.[22] Van Buskirk's retrospective self-flagellation derived not from his desire as desire but, instead, from that desire overcoming self-restraint as acts of masturbation or sodomy.

Van Buskirk had an ideal of sexuality for which he strove, and it was not heterosexuality or celibacy. Instead, it was nightly intimacies with bedmates, hand-holding that promised not to use those hands for masturbation, and whispered discussion of sodomy's sins. Now, if restraint alone were what one was into, there would be better choices of companions than those shipmates already tempted by others to sodomy. What Van Buskirk's diaries evidence, beyond frequent sex between men on the 1850s seas, is that the desire for the ideals of a romantic friendship, that negotiating of purity and temptation, that careful construction of the very conditions to be violated, of staying in closest proximity to their violation if not frequently violating them as proof of proximity, was a sexual desire. Romantic friendships and sex between men were not on opposite sides of the ledger; instead, romantic friendships were an ideal by which to manage same-sex desire and cultivate sexual restraint.

What was on the other side of the ledger from romantic friendship was sexual anarchy, often between man and woman, incestuous, or commercial. The period's most transgressive depictions of gender and sexuality contrasted the stability of male romantic friendship with the dangers of sex. In Julia Ward Howe's 1843 manuscript (unpublished until given the title *The Hermaphrodite* in 2004), the college intimacy between protagonist and roommate is celebrated within the stabilizing and edifying pattern of male romantic friendship, until the protagonist's ambiguous gender inspires the roommate to commit sexual violence.[23] In Herman Melville's 1852 novel *Pierre*, sexual anarchy follows only after the breakdown of Pierre and his cousin Glen's stabilizing and romanticized intimacy.[24] And in Theodore Winthrop's posthumous 1861 novel *Cecil Dreeme*, a libertine villain so threatens a young woman that she finds safety only in a male disguise and a romantic friendship with the novel's male protagonist.[25] All three of these novels set the stability of a male romantic friendship against transgressive sexuality and anarchic sexual violence.

Indulging in the intimacies of a male romantic friendship allowed men to cultivate a sexual restraint against the dangerous consequences of desire. For many of the nineteenth century's college "chums," the letters written just after college contain both a homoerotic longing for past intimacies and concern about current sexual behavior.[26] For example, in 1826, a year after they graduated from South Carolina College, future secession convention delegate Thomas Jefferson Withers wrote to his "chum," the future governor James Henry Hammond, asking whether he'd had "the extravagant delight of poking and punching a writhing Bedfellow with your long fleshen pole—the exquisite touches of which I have often had the honor of feeling." Withers's homoerotic remembrance had an added purpose. When he tells Hammond that "your *elongated protuberance* . . . has captured complete mastery over you—and I really believe, that you are charging over the pine barrens of your locality, braying like an ass, at every she-male you can discover," he is using a playful homoeroticism to chide Hammond into more properly restrained sexual behavior. In these words, as well as in his encouragement of "early marriage," the letter exemplifies how romantic friendship, and male homoeroticism, was imagined to cultivate proper sexual restraint.[27]

Withers's worries for his friend would prove well placed. Hammond's later sexual relationships with at least two enslaved women living on his South Carolina plantation were the cause of short-term separations from his wife. In the early 1840s, he sexually molested his four teenage nieces, which caused significant harm to Hammond's career when his brother-in-law Wade Hampton exposed his actions to public scandal. Thus, Hammond's career represents the wide latitude for male sexual behavior that accompanied a social structure in which romantic friendship enabled advancement. His college intimacy with Withers went with a current that propelled his public career; his abuse of enslaved women was confined to a private dispute with his wife. He was free as well to abuse his teenage nieces until that freedom came into conflict with a white man of similar status. For someone like Hammond, the relations between white men appear to be the only positive check on his unrestrained sexual license.[28] Hammond was a public champion of a certain kind of white male freedom. His extensive proslavery writing, which made him among the most notable apologists for slavery, theorized a permanent racial undercaste enabling the freedom of white male enslavers.[29] His sexual behavior accorded with this worldview: the relationship with Withers was part of their mutual advancement; his license to sexually abuse others was limited only by a white man of similar status.

If Hammond's biography indicates where homoeroticism fell in the division between stable and disruptive sexual behavior, his example also demonstrates how romantic friendship functioned within the Jacksonian "fraternity of white manhood." Intimate male friendship, such as that between Hammond and Withers, established a mutual respect for white male self-government, while its elastic affordance for breaches of sexual restraint protected that very capacity for self-government. That capacity, for Dana Nelson, was the unifying concept through which shared race and gender overcame differences of class and region. In one part of her analysis Nelson describes male homoeroticism as a disruptive intimacy that needed to be abstracted away from the body into the symbolic concept of fraternity.[30] But it was precisely the ideal of romantic friendship, with its capacity for accommodating homoeroticism and breaches of sexual restraint, that accomplished this work of abstraction.

If this sounds contradictory, it is a contradiction captured in Van Buskirk's comment that "certainly ninety per cent of the white boys in the Navy of this day . . . are, to an extent that would make you shudder, blasphemers and sodomites."[31] He includes the racial modifier as the reason for one's shudder: not that sodomy is more prevalent among white boys than others but that it is among them, where Van Buskirk's racial expectations presume it ought not be. Whiteness presumes proper sexual restraint while permitting its violation: a 90 percent uptake does not contradict the presumption of surprise. Van Buskirk documents a few incidents of cross-racial sex between men but appears, himself, to have preferred white men and boys.[32] In one diary entry, he expressed outrage that one of his Southern-born male favorites was having sex with an enslaved woman. For Van Buskirk, his friend was defiling himself through this racial contact, guilty not of corrupting the enslaved woman but of being corruptible by her.[33] Van Buskirk's homoerotic longing for his friend imagined their intimacy as a protection from both the dangers of sex and the dangers of racial contact.

Romantic friendship's status as a conservative, stabilizing force, and as a representative unit of white male fraternity, enabled its use as a political symbol. That symbolism proved especially effective in uniting the Democratic Party across its sectional and class differences. As the Democratic Party identified more and more with the expansion and defense of slavery, intimacies between white men were, alongside slavery, part of what the party stood to protect and conserve.

Between Jacksonian Men

Male intimacy achieved two distinct political goals for the Democratic Party. First, it was a cohesive force for Democratic organization, uniting working-class men in shared party affiliation. Second, and partly due to the first, it served as a symbol of that unity. Nowhere are these achievements better demonstrated than in the party's white working-class base in New York City, especially the Bowery neighborhood that produced the Locofoco movement. The symbolism of male intimacy united men within that neighborhood and represented the imaginary bonds that united those men with the wider Democratic Party, especially proslavery white Southerners.

"Locofoco," an unstable term in the period, signified both the Bowery-based political movement of the late 1830s and a broader self-styling of a certain Democratic identity. That self-styling was how those writers associated with the later Young America movement, Whitman, Melville, and Nathaniel Hawthorne, would each brand themselves at different times.[34] The original epithet referred to the self-lighting cigars Equal Rights Party members had used to illuminate their political meeting when more mainstream, Tammany Hall–connected Democrats had turned out the lights. Opponents used the term, then, in the same derisive manner as the suggestive epithet "Butt-Enders," used to describe Bowery men because of their cigar-chomping. For such critics, the caricature of white working-class rowdyism was both political and cultural, connecting the politics of antibank trade unionism with the homosocial culture of hard drinking and the Bowery's notorious unrestrained sexuality.[35] Many of the actual Locofoco leaders tried to distance themselves from such caricature, but a Democratic artist class, especially of the Young America school, embraced both aspects of the Bowery's masculinist culture.[36] For them, Bowery culture meant both a political orientation and a homosocial, white, Democratic identity.

For a Bowery chronicler like Cornelius Mathews, the neighborhood was most notable for its "infinite variety of young men," whom Mathews, a self-described "sketcher of men and things," celebrated in his 1853 *Pen-and-Ink Panorama of New-York City*.[37] In his ambitious 1845 vision, *Big Abel, and the Little Manhattan*, Mathews documented a practice "endemical in East Bowery," namely two men walking with interlocked pinkie fingers, "each in his little finger the finger of the other." These "Pinkeys," as Mathews venerated them, represented the male camaraderie on which, for him, New York City, and America, was built.[38] This pair matches others in Mathews's novel's symbolism: a young white boy and his beloved, dying Black companion; a young male writer and his beloved fiancée; and, foremost among them, Big Abel, an heir to Henry Hudson, and the Little Manhattan, a descendant of New York's earlier Indian chieftains. Though the novel does not quite live up to its almost Joycean ambitions, Mathews explores the urbanscape across a single week through an intimacy of quintessential Leslie Fiedler variety between a white American and his nonwhite companion.[39] Echoing the central theme of male-male intimacies, Mathews, a lifelong bachelor, dedicated this novelistic announcement of a national literature to his "true friend and early school-fellow, one of the six hundred scampering boys of the old Crosby-Street high school," Jedediah Auld, who also married Mathews's sister.[40]

The urban world that Mathews sketched was indeed a homosocial one. Citing Mathews's panoramas of the Bowery, historian Richard Stott narrates the neighborhood as a world of bachelors, one in which the intimacies between men were unselfconsciously displayed.[41] Stott asserts that male kissing, hugging, and hand-holding could be openly celebrated because "such comradeship was explicitly defined in opposition to sexual love."[42] And yet the Bowery district was, at the same time, the epicenter for midcentury panic around sodomy and homosexual seduction. In the early 1840s, sensational sporting men's weeklies such as the *Whip*, the *Flash*, and the *Rake* aimed to expose the Bowery as the locale of "sodomites" ensnaring "youths" with "diabolical enticements."[43] Such sexual notoriety did not at all dim Mathews's celebration of the Bowery as "the greatest street on the continent, the most characteristic, the most American, the most peculiar."[44]

Few American writers have received the contemporaneous or posthumous disparagement that Mathews has. Edgar Allan Poe labeled one of his works "a mere jumble of incongruous nonsense"; Perry Miller called him a "dunderhead"; Ted Widmer's account of Mathews's clique treats him as an annoying, "two-dimensional" writer; and Mathews's own biographer calls him "pompous and vain."[45] His influence, however, was significant. His chants about city men at work anticipate Whitman; his novel *Behemoth* (1839) is a clear precursor to Melville's *Moby-Dick* (1851). Mathews's influence on these two writers in particular is so strong that today he reads like a bizarre Whitman and Melville pastiche. Although Fiedler does not mention him, making an intimate cross-racial male pair the origin of American nationalism was partly Mathews's invention.[46] For most cultural historians, it is not Mathews

but those later two, Whitman and, to a lesser extent, Melville, who most connect New York Democratic politics to male homoeroticism. They are at their
most Mathews-influenced when they do so.

The metonymic role that Whitman's democratic vocabulary plays for historians of Jacksonian democracy indicates that party politics incorporated,
rather than excluded, homoerotic imagery. Sean Wilentz writes about 1840s
New York City in one such Whitman-titled history, *Chants Democratic*:
"This was a world of street gangs, masculine bravado, and noisome enter-
tainments—where Melville's mariners, renegades, and castaways mingled
with the workingmen, where the young Whitman could loiter to watch the
butcher boy-dandy exchange his killing clothes for his 'duds' and launch into
his repartee, his shuffle and breakdown."[47] Much ink (and more) has been
spilled on the democratic ideals of Whitman's and Melville's homoeroticism.
These ideals were not merely democratic in an abstract sense but embedded
within the era's party politics, within the Democracy's language of democracy. In the notorious "Squeeze of the Hand" chapter of *Moby-Dick*, Melville's
paean for the "abounding, affectionate, friendly, loving feeling" of squeezing
sperm is a work task among his "co-laborers" that begins like a work song:
"Squeeze! squeeze! squeeze! all the morning long."[48] Whitman's comradely
love, "by which the nation is held together," was, he would later say, most
evident among a distinct political unit, "the mechanic class."[49] The continued
resonance of Whitman's and Melville's imagery for the spirit of democracy
indicates, to be sure, that such ideals extended beyond one antebellum political party. But to the extent that such language had partisan resonance for
antebellum men, it would have been within the Democratic Party.

I should clarify, at this point, that I do not mean to say that the Democratic
Party was wholly identified with male homoeroticism or that same-sex-desiring people formed an interest group within its coalition the way that they
would by the twenty-first century. Instead, the Democratic Party was the
home for a certain version of male camaraderie, that of the urban white working class, and that camaraderie drew strength from homoerotic imagery. The
Jacksonian coalition succeeded by incorporating homosocial, urban culture
and even homoerotic elements of that culture. Moreover, male friendship
itself would be a unifying force for the party's various elements, especially as
the crisis of slavery's expansion threatened party unity.

Whitman and Melville had both been enthusiastic Jacksonians. They
were, however, just the type of New York Democrats most likely to defect
from a proslavery coalition. As liberal humanists, inspired by the emancipatory spirit of the nineteenth century, especially the 1848 revolutions in

Europe, their cosmopolitan democracy included cross-racial egalitarianism. It was a position, to say the least, potentially at odds with US slavery.[50] But they were also nationalists, believing that the United States had a special messianic role in that global democratic emancipation. Thus, they were also just the kind of Democrats who would associate with the literary-political movement to which Cornelius Mathews, in 1845, gave the name "Young America." The movement originated among Mathews's clique of young bachelor friends in New York, among them future brother-in-law Jerry Auld, the brothers Evert and George Duyckinck, and William A. Jones.[51] When Young America promoters Evert Duyckinck and John O'Sullivan launched a movement literary magazine, the *Democratic Review*, they received funding from that architect of the Democratic coalition, Van Buren, who knew retaining this wing of nationalist Northern Democrats would prove essential to the Democratic coalition. Young America assimilated the nationalistic spirit of Europe's emancipatory movements into a US expansionism that could continue the Democratic Party's support of slavery. Young America did not make men like Whitman and Melville supporters of slavery, but it would help keep them, for a time, within the party of slavery's expansion.[52] Whitman's political advice to a Democratic leader was "Look to the young men—appeal specially to them!" Expansionism did just that: O'Sullivan's 1839 concept, manifest destiny, appealed especially to young white men, the bachelors and the rootless, who stood the most to benefit from new US territories.[53]

That appeal, the promise of nationalism and expansion, was especially effective in keeping urban white Northern men within the Democratic coalition as that party's platform became more supportive of Southern slavery. Such men were the recruitment targets of the 1850s extension of manifest destiny, the campaigns by private armies of US citizens known as filibusters to conquer Central and South American territories. By the 1850s, filibusters were a prominent part of the Democratic coalition, celebrated by promoters like O'Sullivan and highlighted by opponents, just as Locofocoism had been, as representative of the party. The most famous filibuster, Tennessean William Walker, led a private army to invade, in 1853, the Mexican state of Sonora; in 1855 and 1857, Nicaragua; and, in 1860, Honduras, where he was killed. Walker's efforts initially had broad support in the United States, but as the 1850s progressed, his supporters and detractors coalesced on the issue of slavery. Walker's expressed support of slavery in his 1860 autobiography, his relegalization of slavery in Nicaragua, his slaveholding supporters, and his future Confederate soldier comrades all underline his filibustering efforts as part of slavery's expansionist agenda.[54]

Walker's recruitment relied, in part, on a homosocial appeal, with a geographic target, again, in the Bowery neighborhood. In 1856 Walker had a compatriot establish the headquarters of the Nicaraguan Emigration Company within that neighborhood, and Walker himself was greeted by cheering crowds at the Bowery Theatre.[55] Walker's campaign promised to transform the economic circumstances of the Bowery's young men while affirming their privileged racial status and manhood—in short, they could receive the riches due them merely by asserting their white manhood over a racialized and feminized Latin American population.[56] Sex was on offer too: not merely the forcible sex that might accompany a conquering army, but there was also the rumor that elite Nicaraguan women were eager to marry members of the invading army.[57] All of these rewards would be won by means of manly comradeship and the bonds of male friendship. Mississippian John Quitman and Louisianan Chatham Roberdeau Wheat were, as Amy Greenberg writes, "highly visible symbols" of filibustering friendship, but so, too, was Walker in his own writing.[58] Commentators have noted how Walker developed one intense male friendship after another among his comrades. In his autobiography (which Walker wrote in the third person) he remembered his relationship with a fallen subordinate in the language of romantic friendship: "A boy in appearance, with a slight figure, and a face almost feminine in its delicacy and beauty, he had the heart of a lion. . . . To Walker he was invaluable; for they had been together in many a trying hour, and the fellowship of difficulty and danger had established a sort of freemasonry between them."[59] Filibustering's homosocial appeal was equally a focus of the filibusters' critics, who portrayed their endeavors as destructive to the ideals of family, fatherhood, and the home.[60]

If filibustering's sexuality was subject to contemporaneous scrutiny, that of Walker himself has been so for subsequent generations. The idea of Walker's queerness—his treatment by novelists, biographers, and historians as "quite possibly the victim of a sexual disorder," "a sissy," and "a man masquerading as a woman"—has had a long afterlife.[61] As I write in this book's conclusion, historians' interpretation of Walker's queerness has matched assessments of Walker's imperialism as outside of presumed American norms. Walker's popularity, especially within the Democratic Party, should check our sense of his abnormal status in both senses. Walker's promise of male camaraderie, even if homoerotic, should not be seen as the distinct experience of a minority queer army but as operating within the consistent currents of Democratic affiliation.

This analysis of the Democratic Party risks its own sort of expansionism, connecting elements of the antebellum party that historians productively disentangle. The proslavery party of 1850s filibusters was not identical to the suffrage-expanding party of 1830s Locofocos, but neither was it a distinct rupture of the white-male exclusionary politics at the heart of Jackson's appeal. Racial and gender identity—that is, preserving and extending the privileged status of white manhood—ensured both coherence within the party and continuity from the 1830s to 1850s. So too, as a manifestation of racial and gender identity, did white male intimacy. Male friendship was, unsurprisingly then, a central image for Democratic unity. Whitman, again, best represents male intimacy as the unifying stuff of national cohesion, especially as he witnessed sectional divisions over slavery. The inclusion, in his 1860 edition of *Leaves of Grass*, of the "Chants Democratic" and "Calamus" clusters shows Whitman's insistence on male camaraderie as the solution to national disunity. As David Reynolds argues in his Whitman biography, celebrations of male adhesiveness must be seen as a political argument, one rooted in the Democratic politics of the previous two decades.[62]

Whitman's celebration of the camaraderie of the "mechanic class" found a parallel in the political speeches of the Bowery's Mike Walsh, whose "Spartan Band" was an 1840s successor to the Locofocos. The Irish-born Walsh leveraged support among Whitman's mechanic class, what he called the "shirtless democracy," into power at Tammany Hall and then Congress, while also earning Whitman's support and admiration.[63] When Walsh's newspaper, the *Subterranean*, merged with George Evans's *Workingman's Advocate* in 1848, the pair renamed their venture *Young America*. In the *Subterranean* of the 1840s, it was friendship that Walsh most appealed to, calling on the support of true friends while accusing many of false friendship. While Walsh was incarcerated in 1846, supporters formed "Friends of Mike Walsh" organizations, and the *Subterranean* instructed readers on "How to Show a Friendship for Mike Walsh and His Principles."[64] Because his was a politics of personal friendship, Walsh believed such friendship transferrable to his national friends. In the 1840s, he attempted to marshal his urban, working-class support first for the expansionist Virginian President Tyler and then for South Carolina's Calhoun, whom Walsh would support for the Democratic nomination. Announcing a "Calhoun Ball" in 1848, Walsh characterized slavery's foremost defender as "the man for whom I have always battled from boyhood and to whom I will cling as long as a gasp of breath remains in my body."[65] Walsh's endorsement of Calhoun was rendered in the language not of political expediency or strategic alliance but, instead, of a deep and natural friendship between the white working-class North and the slaveholding South.

The idea of male cross-sectional intimacy was a through line of the era's Democratic imagination, for its politicians and for the writers of the Young America movement. It would be one, as well, in the relationship of two of that movement's famed authors. In Melville's seminal 1850 review, "Hawthorne and His Mosses," the New Yorker writes of the New Englander: "He expands and deepens down, the more I contemplate him; and further, and further, shoots his strong New-England roots into the hot soil of my Southern soul."[66] Many have been baffled by Melville's "weirdly sexual language" in describing Hawthorne's influence; more baffling still is why such homoerotic language necessitated Melville's conceit that he was a Virginian visiting New England.[67] But such imagery fits this manifesto of an emerging American literature, written while Mathews and Evert Duyckinck were visiting Melville, for cross-sectional male intimacy was part of the Democratic national imagination. The idea of national literature included cross-sectional homoeroticism, that a Northerner shoots his roots into a Southerner's hot soil or the reverse.

Democrats' Cross-Sectional Friendships

If male intimacy held the Democratic coalition together, the symbol of male friendship proved a potent unifier in the 1840s and 1850s. Every Democratic presidential ticket after Polk and Dallas repeated the cross-sectional pairing: Michigander Lewis Cass with Kentuckian William Butler, New Hampshirite Franklin Pierce with Alabaman William Rufus King, Pennsylvanian James Buchanan with Kentuckian John Breckinridge, and both of the split 1860 tickets, Illinoisan Stephen Douglas with Georgian Herschel Johnson and Kentuckian Breckinridge with Indianan Joseph Lane.[68] Each one of these Democratic aspirants made his own personal friendship with Jackson, however tenuous, part of his presidential résumé. Moreover, the party's North-South alliance, which enabled its protection of slavery, operated through the language of personal friendship. For Northern Democrats, as historian Michael Todd Landis documents, winning national office depended on demonstrating a friendliness to Southern Democrats.[69] A party rule requiring support of two-thirds of the Democratic convention ensured that presidential nominees were broadly acceptable to both a supermajority and a proslavery wing, the Calhoun faction. Van Buren's failure in 1844 to secure that supermajority showed that any presidential aspirant, and especially a Northern one, would have to prove fidelity to the proslavery wing.

Four years later, Michigan senator Lewis Cass, despite being a slave-holder himself, needed to overcome doubts from Southerners that he would permit slavery's expansion as president. His vehicle for doing so was a letter frankly responding to one from Alfred Nicholson, a friend from Tennessee who had been promoting Cass's candidacy since 1844.[70] That letter was, in turn, ushered to widespread publication by Cass's Democratic friends, such as Mississippi's Henry Foote. In the letter, Cass rejected the Wilmot Proviso's proposed exclusion of slavery from territory won in the US-Mexico War and endorsed a policy wherein "the people, who will be affected by this question" (meaning white male voters) would decide slavery's legality in the territory.[71] After Cass's nomination, he responded to further questions about slavery's expansion by pointing to the Nicholson letter: "I had supposed that my senti-ments . . . were fully understood by my Southern friends."[72]

Cass's statements ought to be intelligible to his Southern friends, for this concept of popular sovereignty had itself been the product of the political friendships of antebellum Washington. Friendship among politicians was, as historian Rachel Shelden shows in *Washington Brotherhood*, the lubricant of congressional enactments, sectional compromise, and political comity in antebellum Washington. Congressmen and senators lived there in a very much male world, often together in boardinghouses and messes, where the era's practical politics happened.[73] Senators, in particular, had to be adept glad-handers, for they were a class of politicians elected not through a mass appeal to a popular constituency but by fellow politicians in state legisla-tures. Those politicking skills did not diminish once the senators arrived in Washington but contributed to the homosocial workings of senatorial action. Some senators brought wives and families with them, but for those residing in the city's all-male messes, the experience would be most reminiscent of erstwhile college life. About the importance of such living spaces for Demo-cratic Party politics, historian Thomas Balcerski writes, "The bachelor's mess functioned as an incubator for partisan unity, a proslavery ideology, and, by extension, the entire Jacksonian legislative program on Capitol Hill."[74] Popular sovereignty, as the remedy for the political difficulties of slavery's expansion, developed through the Washington friendships that promoted compromise and fostered respect for sectional self-determination among voting men.

Even with his position on popular sovereignty, Cass's candidacy suffered on both sides of the Jacksonian fraying. On one side, some Southerners had a hunch that Whig Zachary Taylor, a slaveholding Louisianan, would be more supportive of slavery. On the other, the disaffected Van Burenites marshaled the nation's antislavery movements, risking, in the eyes of stalwart Democrats, burning down their own barns. These Barnburners (who included Whitman) pulled enough votes from the Democratic coalition, especially in New England and New York, to ensure Taylor's victory.[75]

Despite Cass's loss, his nomination began the Democratic trend of elevating Northern senators, continued in 1852, 1856, and 1860. As the body in which cross-sectional national compromises were brokered, the Senate was ripe ground for symbolic friendliness. In Senate debate over California's admission to the union, which would shape the Compromise of 1850, Mississippi's Foote returned to classical language to applaud the South's "faithful, tried friends" in the North. Among those "who have always stood nobly by us, and who manifested even Roman firmness, and will so yet," Foote named "such men as George M. Dallas, James Buchanan, Levi Woodbury, and a host of others, good men and true."[76] The first two were Pennsylvanians; Dallas had been Polk's vice president, and Buchanan was the decided favorite among the proslavery South for the Democratic nomination in 1852. The third was the former senator from New Hampshire and Supreme Court justice who had written the 1847 *Jones v. Van Zandt* decision in favor of slaveholders' rights to capture and re-enslave fugitives. After Buchanan's supporters failed to secure his nomination, it went to Franklin Pierce, who had been Levi Woodbury's junior colleague in the Senate. Pierce's friendship with Woodbury, celebrated in campaign biographies, confirmed the proslavery South's key concern about whether he would uphold the compromise's Fugitive Slave Law provisions.

Certainly, friendliness to the proslavery South was a crucial test among Southern slaveholders, but it was meaningful to Northern Democrats as well. If what you wanted on the slavery question was to continue national compromise, as did Northerners remaining with the Democrats after 1850, friendliness was the paramount presidential attribute. But how would a candidate signal to voters his cross-sectional friendliness? By the middle of the nineteenth century, campaign biographies controlled and disseminated a candidate's central narrative. Campaigns collaborated with partisan publishers to aggregate the speeches, platforms, and letters of support into bundled packages, marketed as both news and collectors' items. Biographies advanced a candidate's cause even without the mass of voters reading them. Instead, party organizers and advocates, spread across states, received cues on campaign narratives through these biographies. Therefore, campaign biographies allowed campaigns to manage top-down messaging in a decentralized system.[77] That they were, at their core, biographical meant that issues of platform and policy were channeled through personality. One could know that a candidate would support policies of national compromise on slavery because of that man's friendly temperament and how he cultivated his friendships.

Pierce's campaign biography, written by his novelist friend Hawthorne, confirmed both friendliness and the Fugitive Slave Law. "Our college reminiscences," may not be, Hawthorne wrote, "the material for a biography"; nonetheless, Hawthorne's intimacy with his Bowdoin classmate, and descriptions of Pierce's college chums, provided a picture of a man at ease in male friendship.[78] Pierce's father, Hawthorne explained, had been friends with the father of Levi Woodbury; Pierce lived with the Woodburys and had been friends with Levi.[79] His sympathies were with the author of the *Jones v. Van Zandt* decision, personally and politically.

For the national ticket, Democrats paired New Hampshire's Pierce with the Alabaman King. Because Millard Fillmore had assumed the presidency upon the death of Taylor, King had been elected by the Senate to fill the vacant vice-presidential role of presiding over the Senate. King's election to the vice presidency represented, then, no change at all in his role; nevertheless, his place on the ticket was symbolic of cross-sectional feeling, especially as endorsed by his closest friend in the Senate, Pennsylvania's James Buchanan. In papers around the country in 1852, Buchanan's endorsement of King rang out: "For Col. King I entertain the warmest feelings of friendship."[80]

The friendship between King and Buchanan was politically consequential for both men, but it has also proved a valuable archive for historians of male friendship and male intimacy. The Pennsylvanian and Alabaman were, as Balcerski's 2019 dual biography terms them, "bosom friends." The pair wrote letters as romantic friends for nearly two decades from 1834 to 1853, and spent many years living together in the first decade of that friendship when senators. In recent years, Buchanan and King's intimacy has generated much discussion, some of which erroneously suggests King served a protospousal role for the bachelor president—despite his death three years before Buchanan's election.[81] Balcerski argues against seeing the pair as precursors to a minoritarian homosexual identity. Instead, their intimacy exemplifies a "symbolically powerful partnership between North and South," which "embodied both the political benefit and the moral difficulties of cross-sectional collaboration in the three decades before the Civil War."[82] Their collaboration propelled their individual political careers while their intimacy proved a potent symbol of cross-sectional Democratic unity.

Aside from their well-documented intimacy, much of the evidence used today to point to their relationship as homosexual derives from political attacks on the pair as effeminate. They were both feminized by political opponents, including within their same party, but these attacks were neither uncommon, in the wake of Jackson's winning martial manhood, nor so effective as to prevent the men's respective ascendancies to government's highest positions. The party balked at the idea of nominating them together on a so-called bachelor ticket, and bachelor status was a frequent source of mockery in politics and culture.[83] Buchanan's and King's remarkable political success, however, rebuts the idea of bachelorhood as a dooming political liability. The intimacy between the two was, far from being an electoral weakness, decidedly a point of strength for their national candidacies.

For two decades before his 1856 election, Buchanan was Southern Democrats' favorite Northerner. As such, his endorsements of King helped the Alabama senator among his Southern colleagues. Three years after his death, King could return the gesture in newspapers with posthumous endorsement of Buchanan's willingness to protect the rights of Southern states.[84] By the time Buchanan was the Democratic nominee, the memory of his intimacy with King evidenced his sympathetic orientation to the South. That it was a memory made it no less potent, for it, alongside Buchanan's advanced age, cloaked the conservative appeal in nostalgia. For former Whigs without a party home amid the decade's realignment, Buchanan's conservative symbolism hearkened back to Washingtonian brotherly affection. For Democratic voters, memory of Buchanan's friendship with King abstracted their intimacy into a unifying cross-sectional symbol. The Buchanan campaign narrative, across biographies and letters, depended on his friendliness to the South, and to King in particular. Those Southerners concerned about Buchanan's sympathies need only visit his library at home, one biography stated, where they would find "a likeness of the late Vice-President King, whom he loved (and who did not?)"[85] Love for King, though Democrats thought it universal, had partisan meaning. It demonstrated the Northerner's orientation to his Southern friends, one within the framework of mutual respect celebrated in romantic male friendship.

A mutual respect among equals, as in romantic friendship, implied a distinct policy on the divisive question of slavery's expansion, one of popular sovereignty, which gave authority to determine slavery's legality to a territory's white male electorate. In his letter to Nicholson, Cass had stipulated this policy. So, too, did the next Northern Democratic candidates, Pierce, Buchanan, and, then, one of its chief theorists, Stephen Douglas, in 1860. Popular sovereignty applied the principles of the fraternity of white manhood, combining the power of white men both for self-determination and to determine the status of others. Buchanan espoused the policy of popular sovereignty in his 1856 platform. He also embodied it, as his bachelor status and celebrated intimacy with King symbolized the white male compact, between friends, for mutual self-determination.[86]

Just as romantic friendship was a symbol that incorporated unrestrained sexuality within its framework, Buchanan's manhood also incorporated the unrestrained sexuality of the party's urban, white Democratic base. Indeed, the Democratic Party retained a continued appeal to Bowery homoerotic rowdyism. In 1852, a Democratic rallying song to the tune of "Oh! Susanna" crooned:

> Come brave locos—
> Gallant men and true—
> The Whigs we *Polked* in forty-four
> We'll *Pierce* in fifty-two.[87]

Four years later, a new candidate layered another sodomitical allusion: "We pok'ed 'em in 44 / We pierced 'em in 52 / And we'll BUCK 'EM in 56."[88] Buchanan's appeal entailed the abstract symbolism of cross-sectional male intimacies, nostalgic for a more sectionally amicable past. But the symbol of male friendship was not wholly evacuated of a homoerotic content that had long-standing associations for Democratic camaraderie. Old Buck, the bachelor president, ably embodied both.

The Private Intimacies and Public Sexuality of the Republican Party

The symbolism of male intimacies was not the inevitable product of an all-white-male franchise. Despite what one might expect for a party formed through the affiliation of antislavery Whigs and Free Soil Democrats, the Republican Party that emerged in the 1850s did not cultivate a public symbol of male friendship. Two ideological elements of the party ensured skepticism about the politics of male intimacy: sexual reform made scrutiny on sexual behavior part of the party's animating spirit, and self-made men were the celebrated ideal of political manhood.

Bowery masculinity may have been the antithesis of Republican values. In fact, one origin story of the party narrates that very opposition: the reform politics of temperance and nativism that fueled the initial party developed in response to perceptions of an immigrant culture of alcohol and unrestrained sexuality in places like the Bowery.[89] Reform of sexual behavior cut across the party's "Sisterhood of Reforms": if alcohol led to extramarital sex and prostitution, if immigrant populations brought with them sexual immorality, if slave states were, as antislavery movement claimed, Sodoms, and if slavery created dens of fornication, then the Republican ethos maintained public outrage on sexual behavior.[90]

Republicans cultivated a public politics of sexual restraint. This attitude was not merely directed at licentious Southern slavery but also, importantly, at oneself. Abolitionist William Lloyd Garrison wrote in a *Liberator* article against masturbation that "it is as much the province of purity to hunt out and extirpate lewdness, as it is that of liberty to assail and destroy slavery."[91] On this topic, Garrison was influenced by the period's chief antimasturbation activist Sylvester Graham, with whom he also corresponded about antislavery efforts.[92] Prominent white abolitionists including Theodore Weld, Angelina Grimké, and Sarah Grimké and prominent Black abolitionists including Amy Casey and Sarah Mapps Douglass were also followers of Graham. For Graham's most prominent successor as sexual restraint advocate, Henry Clarke Wright, antislavery and anti-sex polemic were explicitly linked: slavery and self-abuse were mutual metaphors, and one ought to be free from the bondage of one's own lusts.[93]

I do not mean to simplify the two parties into opposing camps of prudish Victorian Republicans and incorrigibly unrestrained Democrats. As I write above, public symbols of male intimacy were, for Democrats, a way of incorporating sexual energies into ideals of sexual restraint. And if the Republicans were prudish Victorians, they were Victorians as Foucault describes, thinking and talking always about sex.[94] Indeed, the classic Foucauldian story of sexuality's birth runs, in the United States, through men aligned with Republican causes.[95] Perhaps no reformer more clearly links these two central stories of nineteenth-century US history—the rise of the Republican Party and the emergence of sexuality as a domain of medicine and the law—than Samuel Gridley Howe. As a doctor, Howe embraced a medicalized approach to social problems: he saw institutions like his own Perkins School for the Blind as part of an approach to social governance, by medical professionals, for public health. As an abolitionist, Howe was one of six who funded John Brown's attack on Harpers Ferry. Because he was both a doctor and an abolitionist, Howe received an appointment in 1863 from Secretary of War Edwin Stanton to the American Freedmen's Inquiry Commission to determine the government's course of action for refugeed African Americans.

At Perkins, Howe concerned himself, as both administrator and theoretician, with masturbation—what a biographer calls his "near obsession."[96] He kept records of his pupils' masturbation, data that informed his conclusions linking masturbation and mental debility.[97] He urged parents and staff to keep "a constant and watchful eye over" children who slept together at boarding schools, "with a view to this insidious and pernicious habit."[98] Like other reformers, Howe believed masturbation was a social "contagion," one not only taught from one person to the next but also encouraged by the "too intimate association of persons of the same sex" sharing rooms or beds, such as in a boarding school.[99] For antimasturbation reformers (as for practitioner Van Buskirk), there was a frequent slippage among solitary masturbation, a performance for others, masturbating within a group, and what might be called mutual masturbation.[100] Homosexual acts were not a special category of offense in Howe's or other institutions, but masturbation, whether performed alone or with a same-sex partner, was.[101] Howe lectured male students that the ideal of sexual self-control demonstrated one's capacity for self-determination. Sexual regulation was, for Howe, a matter of constant surveillance of the self.

For Howe, such sexual self-regulation coexisted with intense male intimacy, a romantic friendship with Massachusetts senator Charles Sumner. Six years into his work at Perkins, at age thirty-six, Howe met the twenty-six-year-old Sumner. The intimacy they would develop was not immediate, but subsequent decades evidence an expression of love as intense as between any antebellum pair, though they did not mention a physical relationship the way some other pairs' writing did.[102] Nor did their intimacy prevent Sumner from, more forcefully than any other antebellum politician, evoking the language of sexual reform for his antislavery politics. In his 1856 "Crime against Kansas" speech, Sumner declared on the Senate floor that the advance of the slave power into Kansas was "the rape of a virgin territory, compelling it to the hateful embrace of Slavery." Referring to the open secret that South Carolina Democrat Andrew Butler was having sex with enslaved women, Sumner, true to the ideology of sexual reform, treated the lustfulness of slavery as a contagion, one that spread and seduced those with whom it came into contact.[103]

Incensed by the accusation, one of Butler's relatives, Congressman Preston Brooks, attacked Sumner at his Senate desk with a cane. For the antislavery press, Sumner became a martyr on account of his victimized, restrained manhood. Sumner's friends, including Howe, rallied to his support. In what would prove a boon for the nascent Republican Party, they organized "indignation meetings" in which participants expressed their outrage against Brooks and sympathy for Sumner. Horace Mann would express that sympathy as impressed from Sumner's body onto his friends: "We are wounded in your wounds & bleed in your bleeding."[104] Sumner's body, wounded and convalescing that summer, became, as would James Buchanan's, a symbol for political sympathies. But friendship with Sumner did not symbolize a cross-sectional coalition or represent the ties that bound men together. Howe and Sumner's friendship, for instance, was politically consequential, as a private source of affiliation rather than as a public symbol. After Sumner's victimization by slavery's defenders, friendship with Sumner was not a public symbol but a private source of sympathy, orienting Sumner's allies to antislavery outrage.[105]

The second explanation for Republicans steering away from the politics of male intimacy rests in the party's ideological adherence to self-made manhood. A self-made man was not necessarily a friendless one, but his success had nothing to do with his friends. Republican ideology was therefore suspicious of political friendship. The very stuff that made Northern Democrats so appealing to the proslavery South was, to Republicans, a danger in that it enticed men to compromise their independent principles. An 1856 campaign biography for the Republican John C. Fremont explained his loss of a California Senate seat in 1851 on a refusal to compromise his principles. "Had Col. Fremont possessed the pliant and truculent virtue of many professional politicians," the biography asserted (most likely using "truculent" to mean something like mercenary), "he might to-day be enjoying the favors of those who so liberally reward, and so gratefully remember their devotees, but he never would have become the standard-bearer of freedom, or have enjoyed the confidence of the friends of liberty."[106] The biography distinguished between two types of friendship: the glad-handing political kind that eases advancement and that which is the product of mutual struggle. The latter kind, which Fremont claimed to share with a fellow California politician during their fight against slavery, Charles Robinson, is "formed in contests and struggles."[107] A onetime political opponent, Robinson, now the territorial governor in Kansas, was a "firm friend," their friendship forged through a struggle requiring mutual conviction.[108]

Democratic attacks on Fremont, targeting especially his wife, Jessie Benton Fremont, and their marriage, are equally telling. Analyzing the campaign literature of 1856, Lauren Haumesser shows how Democrats caricatured Jessie as a frightening figure of female empowerment enabled by Republican policies. Staid tropes of petticoat government and a henpecked husband aimed to emasculate Fremont, but the contrasts Democrats asserted scramble any presumed linkages between male intimacy and emasculation: Democratic partisans painted Fremont as feminine because of his wife, their marriage, and his lack of male friends; Buchanan was properly masculine because of his male friends.[109]

In practical politics, friendship was, of course, no less important for Republican and would-be Republican politicians in the antebellum period. Sumner and fellow Republican William Seward were notoriously friendly across the aisle. Both men, Shelden's study of Washington shows, displayed a public antagonism to Southern Democrats masking their private friendships. The practical politics of friendship also enabled the rise of the first Republican president. Abraham Lincoln, who would be propelled through Republican politics by political friends, had seen the value in joining a caucus of fellow Whigs, the "Young Indians," in the late 1840s. One cross-sectional friendship formed in that caucus, which would prove consequential during the Civil War, was that between Lincoln and future Confederate vice president Alexander Stephens.[110] Lincoln, however, never cited friendship with the Southern Stephens when running for president in 1860.

In contrast to Democratic candidacies of the previous two decades, no friendship featured prominently in the 1860 Republican electoral appeal. Joshua Speed, considered today to be Lincoln's most intimate friend, did not even vote for him. Speed responded to Lincoln's nomination for president, in a letter, as "a warm personal friend, though as you are perhaps aware a political opponent."[111] The campaign kept law partner William Herndon, who was likely Lincoln's closest friend at the time, as hidden from public events as possible, lest his abolitionist views harm Lincoln's candidacy. David Davis, who managed that 1860 campaign, was no close friend of Lincoln and claimed that his candidate had "no Strong Emotional feelings for any person— Mankind or thing."[112] Campaign literature might refer to Lincoln supporters as his "friends" but would use the phrase "special friend" in a derogatory way to characterize Stephen Douglas's relationship with the Illinois Democrat presiding over the proslavery Constitution Convention in Kansas, John Calhoun (whose name recalled the famous South Carolina politician).[113]

Lincoln's election repudiated the symbolism of Jacksonian friendship. Lincoln's Cabinet members were famously rivals, not friends. Appointments would proceed in the same ostensible manner as Lincoln's career, on merit. During the 1860 election, the primary Lincolnian narrative was about an individual's meritocratic capacity to advance himself. Unlike aristocratic politicians, Lincoln had not depended on the help of friends but had earned wages on his own labor, had taught himself the law, and had proved his political skill through his own competence as a speaker. Lincoln's appeal was decidedly not for national friendship, but one targeted for the Northern ideal of the self-made man.[114]

Two things, then, would surprise Democrats who had long believed their party to be the one holding the national compact together. The first was that no man had more cultivated the symbolism of cross-sectional male friendship and sympathies than James Buchanan. Indeed, a personal friendship with an Alabaman had been the most important private and public relationship of the Pennsylvanian's life. But it was during his presidency that such fraternity both within the Democratic Party, and within the nation as a whole, fractured. The second was that his successor, Lincoln, had won through a campaign in which male friendship played no significant public part. His male friendships, however celebrated after his death, were not in the foreground of his candidacy. But Lincoln's political savvy, that which would enable his increasing radical actions across his presidency, was his ability to co-opt the tone of his opponents. Only after his election did Lincoln begin to address those in the border states, especially in his birth state of Kentucky, as friends.[115] Then, more forcefully than any of the Democrats, Lincoln would return, in his inaugural address, to Washington's call for national, fraternal affection: "We are not enemies but friends. We must not be enemies. Though passion may have strained, it must not break our bonds of affection." Lincoln's "mystic chords of memory" played a familiar, recognizable tune, one that hearkened back to the cross-sectional male friendships of the Revolutionary generation.[116] Disunion threatened to break these bonds of affection; reunion would, in subsequent decades, follow Lincoln in looking back fondly on them.

The legend of Lincoln's male friendships developed only after his inauguration. The earliest public attention on a Lincolnian friendship followed the 1861 death of Elmer Ellsworth, who had been Lincoln's legal apprentice. The death of Lincoln's son, nine months after Ellsworth, however, replaced a comradely, though slightly paternal, grief with a fully paternal grief as the public image of the president's wartime suffering. It was not until the outpouring of grief from Lincoln's friends at his own death or even, as I suggest in the conclusion of this book, the culture of reconciliation at the end of the century that Lincoln's public image became associated with male friendship. Lincoln's male intimacies, and their public meaning, emerged, looking backward, only after the Civil War.

CHAPTER 2

The Propaganda of Male Intimacy in the Proslavery Novel

OR LESLIE FIEDLER, in 1948, the homoerotic longing between a white boy and Black man represented a longing to be forgiven for history: "He dreams of his acceptance at the breast he has most utterly offended."[1] It is a dream of escape—Ishmael and Queequeg running off to sea, Huck and Jim running up the river to freedom, Bruce Springsteen and Clarence Clemons kissing while touring for *Born to Run*, Tyler, the Creator running away with River Phoenix in the passenger seat—an escape, Fiedler suggests, for each generation, from history, that is from the history of race and of US racial slavery. History has produced the dream and dooms it: the longing can only be for a mythic before-time, a racial innocence before race. And history dooms it in another way: such a dream of intimacy, we will see, was well integrated within the culture of slavery itself, especially proslavery fiction written in the wake of Harriet Beecher Stowe's *Uncle Tom's Cabin*. The dream there, no doubt among the cluster of references that privileges interracial homoerotic longing in American culture, is not for the male intimacies possible before slavery but for those that slavery enabled, sanctioned, and celebrated.

Proslavery novels, in the 1850s, valorized intimacies between enslaved men and white enslavers as part of proslavery propaganda. Homoerotic relationships between slaveholders and enslaved men are, in this fiction, frequent, celebrated, and sympathetically rendered. Far from abusive and far from portraying an unnatural sexuality, these relationships served, in proslavery novels, to make enslavement appear more natural, more familiar, and more deserving of sympathy. They solved a problem for proslavery propagandists of how to conceptualize young Black men within that most important unit of proslavery ideology, the plantation family. The valorized bonds between enslaving and enslaved men stood in direct contrast to the purportedly antifamily attacks by abolitionists, personified as deviant male predators. By comparing relationships between male slaveholders and enslaved men to marriages, by bringing young Black men this way *into* the plantation family, the novels made slavery look as natural as family life and abolitionist efforts as disruptive as ripping wives away from husbands and destroying families. In short, intimacy between men in these novels served as an argument for slavery.

Depicting intimacy between men was a method of making slavery appear more natural and abolitionism more aberrant. Proslavery writers were attempting not to defend a so-called peculiar institution on its peculiarity but to assert the opposite: using narratives of sexuality to establish boundaries that would normalize and naturalize slave society, while making abolitionist attacks upon that social order antinormative. Contrary to present-day expectations, male-male intimacy did not disrupt a hegemonic order but instead argued for the naturalness of slavery. These novels were not trying to win a national argument over slavery by asserting a Southern exceptionalism; instead, they were trying to paint abolitionism, not slavery, as exceptional to a natural order. The imagined audience were those consumers of a national literary culture, the same audience that Cornelius Mathews, Walt Whitman, and Herman Melville cultivated through their depictions of male intimacy.

Nor should we take the proslavery novels of the 1850s as a particularly Southern genre. Scholars often treat the novels written directly in response to *Uncle Tom's Cabin* as a set of "anti-Tom" novels, but the specific boundaries of "anti-Tom" novels are less than clear. Several white Southern writers wrote explicit defenses of their home region against Stowe's attacks; other established writers across the country saw novelistic opportunities by writing against the current in Stowe's wake; others, decidedly proslavery and in response to *Uncle Tom's Cabin*, have unknown authors. These proslavery novels overlap often in scenes, tropes, and tone, and no proslavery novel written after 1852 can be read as uninfluenced by *Uncle Tom's Cabin*. As such, I treat the set of proslavery novels written between *Uncle Tom's Cabin* and the

Civil War as a sort of microgenre representing consistent formal tropes and ideological content.

This chapter surveys thirty proslavery novels written before the Civil War that respond to Stowe. Twenty-one were published in northeastern states (eleven in Philadelphia, eight in New York, one in Boston, and one in Buffalo), seven in future Confederate states (three in Richmond, two in Nashville, one in Augusta, and one in Mobile), one in Cincinnati, and one in London.[2] Some represented new work by established writers; many appear to have been published by clearinghouses, like Lippincott's in Philadelphia, at the author's expense.[3] What is known of the writers indicates that only a slim majority were Southerners. These novelists were not the South responding to the North but a cross-sectional white coalition attempting to write slavery as exemplary of American family values. Romanticized intimacy between enslaved and enslaving men was not a universal feature of these novels, nor is this trope the dominant element within them. That would be the celebration of the plantation family. These male intimacies are, however, a frequent trope, essential to that defense of a plantation family that incorporates enslaved people as subordinate members. They are essential because they render proslavery argument within the novels' family values.

Often, these novels read like antidotes to Stowe by affirming what a proslavery audience already believes. But to the extent that they attempt persuasion—and I argue that the trope of romanticized male intimacy is a chief persuasion method—they do so for an imagined audience. That imagined audience consisted of both those white Southerners who needed confirmation that their identifiably imperfect system was better than alternatives and, importantly, those Northern whites open to a proslavery appeal. The entire premise of a proslavery response to Stowe rested on the notion that there was a contest for Northern white sympathies. The novels explored here, written by both white Southern and white Northern authors, represent not necessarily success in winning Northern sympathies but a meaningful attempt at doing so. Romanticized bonds between enslaver and enslaved were central to that attempt.

Narratives of Sexual Abuse under Slavery

Before turning to male-male intimacy in proslavery fiction, I want to summarize what we know, and don't know, about male intimacies among enslaved men in the United States. Actual intimacy among men, as a site of abuse, resistance, control, or evasion, resembles its appearance in the proslavery novels of the 1850s about as much as the realities of enslavement resemble the happy, contented slave characters of this fiction. The most notable homoerotic scene in the archive of US slavery is one of abuse near the end of Harriet Jacobs's *Incidents in the Life of a Slave Girl* (1861). The narrator's memory years after her own escape—"When I fled the house of bondage, I left poor Luke still chained to the bedside of this cruel and disgusting wretch"—condenses into a single scene the pattern of violence to which she had been subjected: that slaveholders were "prey" to sexual "vices growing out" of slavery; that slavery intensified these vices as slaveholders' "despotic habits" increase in parallel to their "dissipation" and perceived "helplessness"; and that the law arrived to support slaveholders' power to abuse, as the town constable relieves Luke's enslaver in administering the violence.[4] The implied homosexuality of the scene—the slaveholder in his bed, his head filled with "the strangest freaks of despotism," whipping a half-naked Luke—indicates that same-sex abuse is not different from male abuse of women in kind but only in the degree of the slaveholder's degeneracy.[5] Jacobs may have intended homosexuality itself as an egregious sign of that degeneration, but she paired the scene of homosexual violence with her own victimhood to undermine potential dismissals of her narrative, which came nonetheless from slavery's apologists. Luke's story proved that sexual abuse involved no seduction and was not predicated on female culpability. Nor was the slaveholder, in Luke's case, seeking to produce enslaved children, often treated as a singular motivation for enslavers' sexual abuse. That is to say, one reason Jacobs included a scene of male-male sexual abuse under slavery was to indicate that such abuse operated in ways more similar than different to the sexual abuse of enslaved women.

Jacobs's assessment does not have much corroboration in the available archive of US slavery. Compared either to the sexual abuse of enslaved women by white men in the United States or to the sexual abuse of enslaved men by white men in the contemporaneous slave society of Brazil, limited direct evidence has been identified for the sexual abuse of enslaved men by white men in the antebellum United States.[6] Applying to enslaved men Saidiya Hartman's description of rape as slavery's "normative condition," cultural historians have examined texts and images that evidence rapacious white male attention on Black male bodies as well as invasions of bodily and sexual autonomy structured analogously to rape.[7] Historian Thomas A. Foster has offered a corrective to this archive, assessing the record's homophobic silences and historians' heterosexist presumptions, but his *Rethinking Rufus* (2019), too, documents relatively few incidents comparable to the overwhelming evidence of the sexual abuse of enslaved women.[8] To be sure, homosexual abuse was likely less frequent than heterosexual abuse, but presumably not so less frequent as to explain the paucity of documented evidence. There may be a few other explanations. As the initial stories of slaveholder rape promulgated in Northern discourse make clear, the biological fact that heterosexual sex could produce children and the legal fact that, as more recognizable violations of a marriage contract, liaisons with women produced aggrieved parties made heterosexual abuse more productive of evidence.[9] This was also evidence that antislavery advocates sought out. The unevenness of evidence may be due less to homophobic silence or same-sex taboo than to the incredible success of the antislavery movement to make the sexual abuse of enslaved women an abolitionist issue.

That this took considerable work—work of abolitionists to deliberate over and aggregate common narratives, work of female antislavery societies to influence leadership and marshal compelling testimonials—should not be taken for granted.[10] Given the relative archival silence of enslavers' sexual abuse of enslaved men, it is all the more remarkable that the sexual abuse of enslaved women became central to abolitionism. It did so, in part, because it found shape as a larger compelling political narrative that made use (and even took advantage) of narratives of female victimhood and male libertine villainy.[11] Each were powerful actors in the antislavery discourse: the victimized, subjected woman and the depraved, licentious slaveholder. There was no similar metanarrative for male victims. Contemporary notions of manhood prevented men from being usable examples of sexual victimization. To the extent that there were examples of male seducers of men, their villainy through subterfuge and secrecy did not fit the abolitionist narrative of slavery's villainy with its open claims to expanding power.

Beginning in the twentieth century, a metanarrative of male sexual abuse under slavery developed. Decidedly Freudian, it presumed that not only was sex power but that sexual positions in male-male sex were especially indicative of power: the rape of enslaved men by white men was, then, more than a feature of slavery's abuses and more than an act of domination; it was the symbolic process by which the participant in a homosexual act transformed from a free man into a feminized slave.[12] Such logic, as queer studies scholars have written, makes receptive sex a metonym for enslavement and male homosexuality itself part of Black subjugation.[13] Some men have seen it that way, but there is little evidence that those in the mid-nineteenth-century United States did. This metanarrative was likely not part of the experience of slavery. Instead, sexual violence done to an enslaved man by a male slaveholder appears to have been, as Jacobs theorized it, more a tool of domination than a symbol of domination, and what appears to have stood out most to Luke, in Jacobs's account, was neither emasculation nor a gendered transformation into an enslaved subject but rather the violence.

There was, however, an existing narrative of male-male intimacy in the 1850s into which discourse about slavery could enter. It was the one explored in this book's previous chapter, where male-male intimacy was example, symbol, and source of sympathy. Such a narrative was not usable for those making the public case against slavery; it was, however, useful for those defending slavery. This pattern, then, complicates a transhistorical "queer South," the idea that structures of Southern sexual life, beginning with slavery, have always been exceptional to the normative American narrative. Instead, these instances of queer affiliation operate as not, in that sense, queer; their purpose is to bring the relationships under slavery within the accepted norms of national life.[14] Indeed, what appears most of all not-queer about these narratives is how seamlessly they operated within the ideals of that most important normative nineteenth-century institution, the family.

The Anti-Tom Novel and the Plantation Family

The number of responses to *Uncle Tom's Cabin* published the very year Stowe's novel came out demonstrates that some of the earliest people to recognize the novel's power were proslavery writers. Their responsive novels were recognized as "anti-Tom" novels within that decade, even if, as contemporaneous evidence suggests, they were not widely read.[15] They were even less read and less remarked upon after their publication, until they became a minor site of scholarly attention in the early twenty-first century for what they reveal about cultural history: namely about the cultural dominance of *Uncle Tom's Cabin*, about the proslavery use of Christian ideology, about ideologies of gender and race, and above all, about proslavery thought.[16] On each point of Stowe's argument, anti-Tom novels strove to contradict the picture of slavery in *Uncle Tom's Cabin*: slaves, in their view, were content; Northern wage laborers were oppressed; and Black people needed slavery and it improved them. On one point, however, they agreed with Stowe: that the "worst abuse" was the "outrage upon the family."[17] If Stowe blamed slavery for this outrage, they blamed abolitionism. Where *Uncle Tom's Cabin* demonstrated the system of slavery rending families apart, *Uncle Robin, in His Cabin in Virginia, and Tom without One in Boston* (1853), as one example, showed a slaveholder dismayed in arranging to take his property to a free state, thereby severing the imagined-as-familial bonds between enslavers and enslaved. While the abolitionists were "always croaking" about family separation as "one of the greatest evils of slavery," the slaveholder says, abolition caused "the greatest amount of those same evils."[18]

In the 1850s, "family" could mean different things to the North and South. For Stowe, what was outrageous was intrusion into the private bonds between husbands and wives or parents and children. For proslavery Southern writers, the family was an expanding public network of father and children, husband and wife, master and servants through bonds, sanguine and nonsanguine, and sexual and nonsexual, that all, and as a unit, must be defended.[19] And defended chiefly, in this set of novels, against a singular enemy: the abolitionist.

The plot of nearly every anti-Tom novel contains an external threat to the plantation family from abolitionism, personified as a deviant intruder into the family. Indeed, these novels need abolitionism in order to have a plot at all, for fundamental to their conservative view is the self-sustaining structure of the plantation family.[20] When abolitionism does arrive, it does so as a "wolf" borrowing "the snowy fleece of the sheep," not merely to "seduce" enslaved people away from the plantation but to disrupt marriages and endanger children.[21] In some ways, these seducers resemble the libertine of other eighteenth- and nineteenth-century fiction, as Leonard Tennenhouse characterizes him, "the proponent of sexual practices that threatened the American family."[22] But those threatened here are a distinct subset of American families, ones that held enslaved people. One hardly needs the tools of psychoanalysis to see in these literary figures a displacement of Southern white fears of slave revolt.[23] Such revolts are rare in these novels. Few mention revolts outside of Northern white misapprehensions; even fewer depict them. *Frank Freeman's Barber Shop* (1852), for example, does so somewhat comically to establish its hero's nonparticipation. In *The Planter's Northern Bride* (1854), it is the abolitionist, in that case a Mr. Brainard, who is the brains of the insurrection.[24] Mr. Brainard, and the other abolitionist figures like him, does more than displace this anxiety. His antifamily deviance shores up the sanctity of the plantation family.

Importantly, abolitionists are not a threat alone, but they seize on the generational vulnerabilities of the family as it changes, as a son inherits from his slaveholding father or as a Northern white woman marries into the family. These two plots are particularly effective didactically for they offer a character as a model of acculturation to the plantation values the novel seeks to inculcate in readers. The plantation family is nearly always a broken or incomplete family. Widowers, divorcées, orphaned cousins, unwed aunts, and fatherless sons constitute the family, not to mention the slave-family arrangements that attach themselves to the central white family not as mirroring familial units but as branches expanding out from individual bonds. The incomplete or broken family units of these novels make clear that the only defense of the family is growth—often not in the usual procreative way. The parallel to slavery's national political agenda is striking. Just as proslavery advocates push to preserve slavery through its expansion, so, too, is the plantation family's preservation made possible through annexations.[25]

The complex plot of Maria J. McIntosh's *The Lofty and the Lowly* (1853) demonstrates this point.[26] With many subplots, the primary vehicle for the proslavery agenda is a son-learns-to-run-the-plantation plot. At the outset of the novel, that son intends to marry a cousin who had been adopted by the family. But over the course of the novel, a series of entanglements with Northern capitalists means that such a union would consolidate the family's debt and cause them to lose the plantation. Thankfully, the cousins are not really in love; they must instead marry elsewhere, and a Scottish nobleman enters as new brother-in-law to save the family. Only by its expansion, through marital alliances, can the plantation family survive.

Another common means of familial expansion is suggested in the title of Caroline Lee Hentz's 1854 novel *The Planter's Northern Bride*. If the coming-of-age of the planter's son provides an education in Southern institutions, the Northern bride's relocation to the South provides a vehicle for proslavery acculturation. The problem with Northern brides is always their fanatic abolitionist fathers. In contrast to the postbellum cross-sectional romances of a Southern woman surrendering to a union with a Northern man, these romances stage the national debate about slavery as a Southern courtier winning a bride from the antislavery North. Contrast the courtiers across these proslavery novels, Dr. Manly, Captain Montrose, Colonel Moreland, and Dr. Boswell, with the men of the North, Mr. Frank, Squire Hastings, Mr. Browne, and Mr. Cary. If the latter name effete eighteenth-century Anglo-Saxons to be discarded, the former suggest the heroic masculinity of chivalric medieval Scotch Irish.[27] Abolitionists, hide your Northern daughters. That they are all to be charmed by visiting Southerners is amplified by the novels' comically small global geography. Many have two settings, a New England town and a Southern plantation; everyone who is not in *this* New England town ends up at *this* plantation and everyone who leaves *this* plantation ends up in *this* New England town. In *The Ebony Idol* (1860), an escaped slave seeks refuge in Minden, the very town where the slaveholder's son happens to be a legal apprentice. Fourteen years earlier, a different escaped slave had kidnapped a

plantation neighbor's daughter, who, passed from one adult to another, somehow ends up both also in Minden and engaged to that apprentice, ignorant
that their families are Southern neighbors.[28] In *The Lofty and the Lowly*, two
men who have never met but whose families, unbeknownst to them, have
become entangled are independently and for distinct reasons marooned on
the same desert island in the South Pacific.[29] In *Mr. Frank: The Underground
Mail-Agent* (1853), the planter and abolitionist happen to visit each other's town and plantation, by chance, on alternating trips.[30] The final chapter
reveals that the planter is the abolitionist's long-lost son, risking his marriage
to the abolitionist's daughter, who is, we learn, not his daughter at all but the
long-lost daughter of the planter's adoptive parents.

Some of this is bad writing and some of it fits the comic register in which
certain of these novels operate, but it all advances an argument about the
expansiveness of the plantation family and the existing entanglements that
implicate the North in Southern slavery. In that final example from *Mr. Frank*,
the abolitionist's daughter had told the planter she cannot marry him as long
as he is a slaveholder. The switched-sometime-after-birth ending reverses
their positions and, as she becomes the slaveholder, her principles.[31] In *Uncle
Tom's Cabin*, Stowe shrinks the world so that neutral Northerners might feel
culpable for slavery; the anti-Tom novels stage the world as already shrunk to
increase the proportional size of the plantation family within it and Northern
complicity in the slave system they decry.

Crucially, these novels cast the enslaved population as part of the plantation family, as evident in the avuncular names of various titles. These titles
promise central Black characters, but *Aunt Phillis's Cabin* (1852) is more
about the Weston family than the comic episodes of Phillis and her husband,
and *Uncle Robin in His Cabin in Virginia, and Tom without One in Boston*
has much more to do with Dr. and Mrs. Boswell than Robin or Tom.[32] In
these novels generally, enslaved people work very little, escape and regret
it, lead miserable lives in Northern cities, prove their family bonds, and die
honorably, trying to outdo Uncle Tom's death in rebellion with an apotheosis
of death in loyalty. The deaths of "aunts"—Aunt Phillis in *Aunt Phillis's Cabin*,
Aunt Nelly in *Antifanaticism* (1853), Aunt Dinah in *Frank Freeman's Barber
Shop*, and Aunt Juno in *Uncle Robin*—function as rites of passage for white
characters, marking continuity during the family's transitions.[33]

The plantations of proslavery novels are populated almost exclusively by
children and the elderly to the extent that one wonders who is doing the labor
in these nurseries and nursing homes disguised as farms. While older Black
women are easily integrated into the imagined plantation family as "aunts,"

older Black men as "uncles," and children as dependents of the central white characters, young adults prove a problem for two reasons: they emphasize the labor of the enslaved laborers and, as characters in works of fiction, raise the issues of marriage and sex. Young adult Black women, central figures in antislavery texts like Stowe's, are largely avoided. When they appear, they need patriarchal protection from abolitionist seducers who will whisk them away to prostitution in Northern cities.[34] These novels reject altogether the sexual abuse of enslaved women by enslavers; such sexual relations exist only in the prurient minds of wrong-headed abolitionists. The presumed vulnerability of young women is, however, the same as in *Uncle Tom's Cabin*, though it is abolition, not slavery, that takes advantage of this vulnerability.

Young adult Black men have an even more complicated membership in the plantation family. In these 1850s novels, we never see such relations between masters and slaves imagined as fathers and sons, lest they concede a central accusation from the abolitionist press. Similarly, rarely do we see brotherly language, partly because many slaveholders' sons had enslaved half brothers and partly because fraternal language might imply a fundamental equality. Instead, we see relationships between enslaved men and slaveholders analogized to marriage and romanticized as same-sex intimacy.

Intimacy between Unequals

When, in *The Planter's Northern Bride*, the abolitionist father refuses to allow his daughter to marry a slaveholder, that planter buries his "throbbing temples" in his hands and prepares for an evening of gloomy despair. Albert, an enslaved character who has traveled north with the planter, then "smoothed the pillow under his head, as gently as a woman could have done; then bringing the basin to the bed-side, he bathed his forehead and moistened his hair, till the throbbing veins seemed less wiry to the touch." The narrator explains that this is from no sense of servitude but that "one of Albert's chief delights was to brush his master's hair, and bathe his temples, when suffering from a sick and aching head." Albert's "laying his hand humbly but affectionately on his master's burning forehead" is certainly a familiar act, one that, the narrator states, "might seem too familiar, to those unaccustomed to the caressing freedom of manner often permitted to a favourite slave."[35] Of course, the novel's plot involves the planter overcoming the abolitionist's objections and marrying the bride, but in this meantime of despair, when the planter most suffers from this sort of love fever, the touch of the enslaved Albert soothes his throbbing veins.

The "favorite" slave is one of the chief ways that proslavery novels deal with young adult Black male characters. Not all of the anti-Tom novels contain such characters, some preferring to avoid these complications altogether, but when these characters are included, they often occupy the place of the favorite. Frequently stereotyped as dandies, these young men are a source of both comedy and sympathy. Charles, in *The Cabin and Parlor* (1852), is a "favorite" about twenty-five years old who "gave the idea of weakness of character" with "his attire . . . somewhat dandyfied"; in *Ellen* (1860), "one of the favorite" servants, Jack, "verging upon twenty" is "what is usually termed 'a proud negro.'"[36] This enslaved male dandy is not dissimilar to one featured in *Uncle Tom's Cabin*. St. Clare's enslaved valet, Adolph, with his opera-glass inspection of Tom, his scented handkerchief, and his wearing of St. Clare's vests, follows a stock character in midcentury culture: the Black man putting on airs. His foppish appearance has led several readers to interpret his sexuality and his relationship with St. Clare as homoerotic, but there are no scenes of intimacy to compare with that of Albert in *The Planter's Northern Bride*.[37] Nonetheless, Stowe has deliberately written an enslaved man bodily dependent on the slaveholder. Her intent, beyond comic relief, is to show the tragedy to that dependent when the slaveholder suddenly dies, leaving him to be purchased by a man who says he will "soon have their airs out of them."[38] Charles, of *The Cabin and Parlor*, and Jack, of *Ellen*, also evidence worries about what happens to these dependent men when they lose their master. When Charles's slaveholder dies and when Jack is enticed to freedom by an abolitionist, both men suffer in the North, the former dying of disease and starvation, the latter maimed by thieves. If Stowe uses the dependence of an Adolph on a St. Clare to show the precarious status of the enslaved, these novels offer a more insidious account to make escaping slavery somehow a product of a warped dependence.

William L. G. Smith's *Life at the South* (1852) depicts this dependence even more pointedly.[39] Smith's central character is not a dandified valet, but Smith has his Uncle Tom turn on a kindly master because Tom envies another enslaved man, who he believes supplanted him as the slaveholder's favorite. The novel's plot, in which an abolitionist schoolteacher entices Tom to escape north and, thereby, endure misery in Buffalo, opens with Tom losing a contest to another enslaved man, Hector, over who can hoe corn the fastest. Believing that the slaveholder now prefers Hector to him, Tom begins a psychological unraveling that leads to plotted rebellion and then escape. To contrast Tom's betrayal, Hector remains perfectly loyal, as demonstrated by the slaveholder's test of his loyalty after the race. When the slaveholder offers

Hector freedom, he refuses as if it meant his abandonment. Smith uses a term from phrenology in calling him "the adhesive black," associating him with the part of the brain that produces "intense friendship," that is "susceptible of the highest order of conjugal love, yet bases that love primarily in friendship," as defined in O. S. Fowler's 1849 phrenology textbook.[40] Later in the novel, an abolitionist character's head has what "the phrenologist" would recognize as "the bump of fanaticism."[41] The "adhesive" reference is then clear, that Smith is establishing ardent friendship, in Fowler's terms, as a trait of the enslaved so strong that, in his Tom's case, it brings jealousies that reverse the impulse.

Walt Whitman, notably, uses "adhesiveness" to signal a homoerotic attachment in his "Calamus" sequence of poems, but he was not alone in doing so. An 1836 British medical article with the header "ADHESIVENESS" told of "two gentlemen" who "slept in the same bed" and whose "attachment to each other was so excessive, as to amount to a disease." For Americans like Fowler, as scholar Michael Lynch wrote in "'Here Is Adhesiveness': From Friendship to Homosexuality," the danger of excessive adhesiveness was not that a friendship crossed into homosexuality but that a too-intense friendship too easily turned to jealousy, resentment, and betrayal.[42] Smith's portrayal of a Black male adhesive nature attempted to capture this whole portrait: the kind of devoted, loving friendship to a slaveholder that quickly became jealousy and betrayal. Fowler himself had described "adhesiveness" as one of the qualities that made "the African race as found in America" "extremely attached to their families and the families of their masters, and pre-eminently social."[43] For the proslavery novels where young adult Black men appeared, adhesiveness was a trait that explained both the loyalty of an enslaved man to a slaveholder and the escapes of enslaved men from slaveholders as a perverted product of that same intimacy.

In some cases, intimacy between an older Black man and younger white man resembled paternal care. For example, Sarah Josepha Hale's colonizationist novel *Liberia, or Mr. Peyton's Experiments* (1853) imagined the relationship between the enslaved man Polydore and Mr. Peyton's nephew Philip as a kind of caretaking, in which the "immense black man" protected Philip beginning in his infancy. Through Philip's reading to the illiterate Polydore, first fairy stories and then history and mythology, "a most devoted attachment" developed between them. In the opening chapters of the novel, when there is a never-materialized threat of a slave insurrection, Polydore resolves to be Philip's special protector: "To catch Philip in his arms and escape to the woods with him; for Mas'r Phil was his idol; he loved him as well, perhaps better, than any one in the world."[44] Polydore serves as a father-protector to Philip, whose own father is dead. Polydore, too, was separated from his own family in Africa (his father having been, he later relates, murdered), and he is romantically attached to an enslaved woman, Keziah. He is, however, an inverted father figure for Philip; in the novel's racist structure, Polydore is always childlike, more so than Philip, who tutors him. In fact, Polydore's childlike status is symbolically important in a novel that imagines Liberian colonization in childlike relationship to a paternal United States.[45] *Liberia*, like Cornelius Mathews's *Big Abel, and the Little Manhattan* before it and Mark Twain's *Adventures of Huckleberry Finn* and Joel Chandler Harris's Uncle Remus stories after it, fits the Fiedler pattern of "white boy and his Black companion," often one of paternal symbolism and its inversion.[46] In *Liberia*, this trope, where the child becomes the father figure and the older man the child, establishes the nature of racial slavery between men as a mutually beneficial intimacy of unequals.

The 1861 novel *Old Toney and His Master* takes as its subject the intimacy of unequals between enslaved men and their enslavers. At the time the novel is set, Toney and his master are old, but the novel traces their relationship back to a boyhood attachment: "They had nodded, when boys, around the camp-fire until their heads had touched—the silky ringlets of the aristocratic son of an aristocratic father had touched the wooly, kinky hair of the African boy." The scene repeats in old age, when the pair are reunited after a bandit has murdered the slaveholder's son, with the slaveholder "weeping like a child upon the breast of his slave!" At both moments, the narrator, like that of *The Planter's Northern Bride* naming Albert's familiarity, admonishes a reader who disbelieves this intimacy. "Many can testify," the narrator verifies, that "the love which had existed from boyhood" between slaveholder and enslaved "is not an isolated or an anomalous fact."[47] *The Black Gauntlet* (1860) similarly treats a boyhood intimacy and adult friendship as the enslaved man's "affectionate oneness in all his young master's interests."[48] The narrator of *Old Toney* uses this moment to introduce an antiabolitionist question: "How, then, was it possible to rupture the ties—ties so indissoluble—which existed between such a master and such a slave?"[49]

Not even death can do so, as upon the slaveholder's death Toney learns of the slaveholder's willingness to set him free. For Toney, this pronouncement is such a tragedy that he objects before the lawyer can complete the sentence: "Provided you wish it." During that outburst, Toney expresses a sentiment common among the fictional slaves of the proslavery novels but one that we ought to consider exactly: "*My* master lub me too much to do dat t'ing."[50] The sentiment is not merely the proslavery lie that enslaved people desired enslavement but, corresponding to the romanticized picture of the pair's boyhood and adult attachments, a marshaling of the tropes of romantic male friendship for the proslavery cause. Indeed, the history of the antebellum concept of romantic friendship, discussed in the previous chapter, is incomplete without considering how slavery's proponents put the concept to use. What the proslavery novelists were trying to do—quite feebly when compared to the sentimental power of a writer like Stowe, but trying nonetheless—was to take the abstract rebuttal that enslaved people preferred slavery, narrate it within romance, and embody it in characters' desire.

That desire, in the proslavery novel, is a curious thing, for it rarely takes enslaved men themselves as its object. In a sort of cultural narcissism, proslavery novelists use their Black characters to make their white male inventions the objects of desire. Romanticized intimacies appear through the imagined eyes of the enslaved idealizing his enslaver. In *Toney*, the opening portrait of the slaveholder's son, Langdon, renders him the object of all interest and affection but most of all that of his enslaved male intimates:

> How the neighbors praised him; and how the young and lovely maidens smiled at his approach; while the hearts of many beat quicker, and their cheeks blushed deeper red, becoming incarnadine with the tell-tale taint of love, as he saluted them with the graceful ease of the courtier, but with all the fervor of the ardent devotee at the shrine of youthful beauty and virgin innocence! But O! last, not least, how the humble, the tried, the devoted slave gloried in his young master. How great his homage; how unselfish his love! He could have kissed the ground upon which Langdon trod, and licked the dust from his feet, not through servile fear—no, no!—but through the same spirit of adoration with which he would have licked the polluting dust from the sandals of a Divinity.[51]

That is the crazed self-love of a people who, the same year *Old Toney* was published, would open fire on Fort Sumter and expect European countries to embrace them for it. Needless to say, no evidence indicates that the two enslaved adults and six enslaved children that the author of *Old Toney*, Theodore Dehone Mathews, held as property in South Carolina in 1860 felt any of the affection to the author that he fantasized his slave characters feeling about his fictional slaveholders.[52] With such a fantasy, one could go on endlessly analyzing the displaced narcissism or flipping the imagined subjects and objects of desire here. Mathews displaces it in the love from the enslaved

man to the enslaver, which functions, as Eric Lott describes blackface minstrelsy, as both homoerotic enticement and nonhomoerotic alibi. The "jokey
homoeroticism," as Lott writes, celebrated and, at the same time, ridiculed
the desire for cross-racial intimacies.[53] So, too, does the image of enslaved
men licking the dust from Langdon's feet unite the imagined desire of the
slaves and their debased status within a single fantasy of white self-love.

In this survey of proslavery novels, it is worth noting, as well, what is not
evident. While some proslavery rhetoric accused abolitionists of having an
excessive love for Black people, anti-Tom novels are adamant that slaveholders, not abolitionists, love Black people more. Reactionaries often literalized
that first sentiment, accusing abolitionists of desiring interracial sex: Stowe
was singled out as particularly desirous of Black men.[54] In the novels, abolitionist men are given over to their prurient desire, almost always, however, to
slaveholders' wives. Abolitionists are sexually perverse not because they are
crosswise on gender but as destroyers of marriage. Nowhere does a reader
find what one could expect from reactionaries, the implication that male abolitionists had sexual motives in seducing enslaved men to freedom.[55] Instead,
the proslavery novel operated upon a single dividing line of sexual ethics, the
issue of marriage, and if abolitionist designs upon slaveholders' wives crossed
it, relationships between enslaved men and enslavers were decidedly within
it. Intimacy between men within the plantation family was one of the valorized bonds under siege by the antimarriage threat of abolitionism.

Man and Man!

The most frequent analogy used to typify the relationship between enslaving and enslaved men, beyond paternalism or adhesiveness, was marriage.
For example, in *Frank Freeman's Barber Shop*, the title character entreats a
slaveholder to buy him: "Before Mr. L could finish or prevent, the negro had
stepped forward, and falling on his knees had seized his benefactor's hand!
Then kissing it with fervor, and clasping it against his breast, he solemnly
looked up to heaven and prayed."[56] Novel readers would recognize this type
of scene in many a novel of wooing lovers, rendered with solemnization:
"In that moment the two felt they were knitting into one heart! Colors had
vanished—it was now—Man and Man!"[57] The moment restages an earlier
request with an accompanying illustration that reversed the typical antislavery image of the chained slave supplicating for freedom to a supplication for
enslavement.[58] Readers of sentimental novels would also be familiar with
the image accompanying a marriage proposal. A similar illustration, before

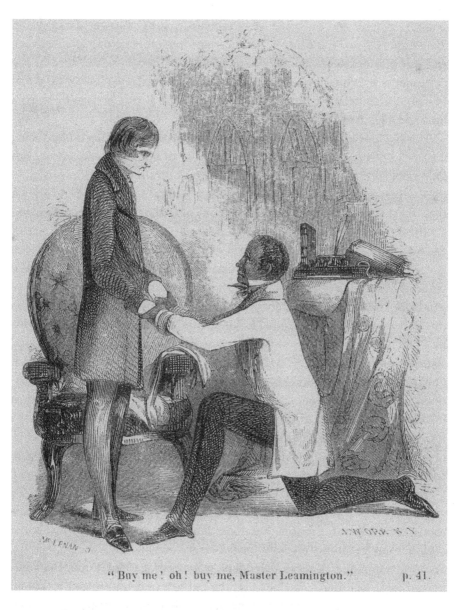

"Buy me! oh! buy me, Master Leamington." p. 41.

Frank Freeman proposes, "Buy me! Oh! buy me, Master Leamington."
Baynard Rush Hall, *Frank Freeman's Barber Shop*, 41. Special Collections,
Princeton University Library.

both the planter and his bride, also resolves Albert's short-term betrayal in *The Planter's Northern Bride*.[59] The marriage metaphor of relations between enslaver and enslaved, as now "Man and Man!," cast enslaved men as the dependents of white husbands in the way those husbands' wives were and rendered their relationship under slavery as natural as marriage between a man and a woman.

For two decades, proslavery speakers and writers had been comparing relations between masters and slaves to those of husbands and wives, with the implication that enslaved men should no more revolt against enslavers than wives against their husbands. In 1832, Thomas Roderick Dew argued that "there is nothing but the mere relations of husband and wife, parent and child, brother and sister, which produce a closer tie, than the relation of master and servant."[60] Scholars of Southern thought have pinpointed Dew's speech as early evidence of a sea change in proslavery thought, from reluctant acceptance of slavery as a necessary evil, as Thomas Jefferson believed, to a positive good, preferable to other systems.[61] So Dew uses the analogy of other domestic relations to attack Jefferson's idea of a slave "hating, rather than loving his master."[62] Proslavery legal scholars, such as Hugh Legaré, Thomas Cobb, and George Sawyer, followed in comparing the master-slave relationship to that of parent-child or husband-wife.[63] The analogy served as rejoinder to abolitionists who cited slavery's abuses: both paternity and marriage contained instances of abuse, but to abolish them would seem ridiculous. Indeed, they highlighted examples of Northern women's criticism of marriage as a means of ridiculing the abolitionist position. That "the same might be applied to marriage" was a consistent proslavery response to antislavery criticism.[64]

Marriage, even more than paternal relations, was a compelling analogy for arguments about slavery as a natural system. Neither slavery nor marriage was natural, according to Enlightenment theories that presupposed a natural state of total freedom. To abolitionists, slavery was an unnatural imposition. So, too, responded slavery's defenders, was marriage. For Cobb, the antebellum legal historian, marriage was the perfect analogy because it was an institution universally accepted as natural while being contrary to the state of nature into which a person is born. Marriage implied a state of unfreedom into which women entered not so much in a free contract of equals but by submission to the natural order of society.[65] When Frank Freeman proposes his own enslavement to a slaveholder and the narrator pronounces them "Man and Man!" readers witness the enslaved character's submission both to the slaveholder and to a presupposed natural order.

Slavery was, some of its defenders argued, an even more natural state than marriage. To Cobb, slavery was "more universal than marriage, and more permanent than liberty."[66] In a footnote, Dew asserts that the bonds of slavery may be even stronger than those of matrimony or paternity, because, he claimed, "hundreds of slaves . . . will desert parents, wives or husbands, brother and sister, to follow a kind master."[67] The novel *The Black Gauntlet* frequently compared the relationship of enslaver and enslaved to marriage, often more favorably. Slaveholders, the novel states in one of its many essayistic asides, are "as a general rule kinder" to the enslaved than husbands are to wives or parents to children. This may be because added to the kindness of patriarchal governance is the interest of *"self-love."* Because enslavers had a financial interest in the health of an enslaved person, the narrator takes as "an undoubted fact, that a *bad* master will take more care of his slaves in sickness and in health, than he will of his wife."[68] Few other narratives put it that way, preferring the pretense that slavery represented a sanctified freedom from the pecuniary interest of wage-labor capitalism and that the bonds within slavery were more noble because they were not dirtied by a profit motive on either side. Compared to the relationships between Northern capitalists and workers, slavery's relations were more natural, intimate, and ardent—bonds, they said, not unlike love.

Within the marriage analogy, slavery accomplished something even more bizarre, as the moment in *Frank Freeman's Barber Shop* indicates: "Colors had vanished—" The statement makes explicit a thread evident in the intimacies discussed above, namely the capacity of the touch between enslavers and enslaved men to obliterate racial distinction. It is surprising to find such obliteration as a positive good for proslavery ideologues. Scholar Tavia Nyong'o has written about how antebellum fantasies of a race-obliterating amalgamation functioned, by mixing desire and fear, to reinforce a nationally imagined race hierarchy.[69] Here is a different version of an antebellum postracial dream, one in which color can disappear and leave just man and man, because the Black man has willfully submitted to a status that had previously been decided by his race. The absence of racial prejudice is possible only through a formalized agreed-upon subjugation: the slaveholder no longer needs racial distinction, because the enslaved man has enlisted in his own enslavement. Racial subordination has vanished, rewritten, through the novel, as the proper emotional attachment between men.

Another proslavery novel, perhaps the most notable of the 1850s, displays the loving intimacy between slaveholder and slave analogized to marriage while presenting a homosocial utopia as preferable to heterosexual marriage. Whether William Gilmore Simms's 1852 *The Sword and the Distaff* ought to be considered among the anti-Tom novels is an open question. On the one hand, Simms wrote to his friend James Henry Hammond that it was "probably as good an answer to Mrs. Stowe as has been published."[70] Beginning with Joseph Ridgely's 1960 essay on the novel as "Simms's first answer to *Uncle Tom's Cabin*," literary critics have read the novel as a proslavery response to Stowe.[71] Certainly it is a proslavery novel and Simms was a proslavery writer, a frequent defender of slavery in the *Southern Literary Messenger* and among the contributors to the 1852 essay collection *The Proslavery Argument*.[72] On the other hand, Simms wrote most, if not all, of his novel before *Uncle Tom's Cabin* was published. Neither its 1852 title, *The Sword and the Distaff, or "Fair, Fat and Forty": A Story of the South at the Close of the Revolution*, nor the revised title of its 1854 republication, *Woodcraft, or Hawks about the Dovecote*, signals a response to Stowe in the usual anti-Tom pattern. Unlike other anti-Tom novels, *The Sword and the Distaff* was a historical romance set in the Revolutionary era and part of a series of Revolutionary romances featuring the same universe of characters that Simms had been writing since 1835: *The Partisan* (1835), *Mellichampe* (1836), *The Scout* (1841), *Katherine Walton* (1851), and *The Forayers* (1855).[73] In the assessment of one sympathetic critic, the influence was the other way around, that "all who may take the trouble to investigate the subject" would see that it was to Simms's work that "Stowe is largely indebted for the materials of her famous romance."[74]

Simms's novel does not read, as do others more firmly in the anti-Tom set, as animated in reaction to an abolitionist threat. This does not make the novel any less proslavery, only less antiabolitionist.[75] Just as some anti-Tom novels are more antiabolitionist than proslavery, Simms's novel is more proslavery than antiabolitionist. As the foremost Southern writer involved in the nationalistic Young America movement discussed in the previous chapter, Simms's literary ambitions extended far beyond the defeat of abolitionism. Though he eventually disdained his onetime ally Cornelius Mathews, his writing, too, demonstrates Mathews's influence, especially in the symbolic primacy of male pairs. The historical setting of *The Sword and the Distaff* celebrates a time before abolitionism developed. Its proslavery argument depends on that historical portrayal, and that portrayal, as for Mathews, is of a nostalgic homosocial past.

As the original title of the novel, *The Sword and the Distaff*, indicates, Simms stages two worlds for his protagonist Porgy, a feminine domesticity in heterosexual marriage to the widow Eveleigh (the distaff) and a male homosocial camp life with his band of deputy officers and enslaved men (the sword). Despite one deputy's exhortations that Captain Porgy needs a wife, the widow a husband, his home some female influence, and the Eveleigh plantation a patriarch, all prove better suited without. As critics beginning with Annette Kolodny have noted, Porgy is patriarch of a plantation in which women are absent except as a metaphor of nature under control.[76] The pages and pages of persuasions for the captain to marry the widow meet a bathetic end when Porgy finally puts the question to her and is refused. His male hangers-on rejoice. The bachelor's paradise had been the plan all along. Aside from one deputy scheming his superior's marriage, all Porgy's men say to one another are declarations of love and promises never to leave one another. The novel ends with Porgy's vow to his men: "I shall live for you only. You could not well do without me; I will not suffer myself to do without you. You shall be mine always—I shall be yours."[77]

At the very center of this homosocial world is the relationship between Porgy and his enslaved cook Tom, about whom Porgy frequently professes his love. "He *does* love you, Captain," Porgy is told. He responds, "And I love him. The old rascal, I do love him. . . . He shall cook for me as long as I'm able to eat; and when I'm not, we shall both be willing to die together."[78] Simms had introduced Porgy as a Falstaff character in his earlier romance, *The Partisan*, always with the enslaved cook Tom providing meals for the gourmand captain. This continues in *The Sword and the Distaff*, where Tom fulfills all the stated needs, cooking and caring, that Porgy is encouraged to find in marriage. The novel demonstrates that Porgy does not need to marry, because he has Tom. In this manner, Simms's Tom repudiates the central argument of *Uncle Tom's Cabin* that slavery is incompatible with domestic life. But Simms does not do so by repudiating the ideal of domesticity; instead he writes slavery—and importantly a slavery between men—as the social organization that enables the domestic ideal. As critic Corinne Dale wrote, "By purging the scene of feminine associations and by renouncing women entirely, Porgy is shown to be domestic, but not effeminate."[79] In this sense, Simms's novel is a different response to Stowe than any of the novels that try to reverse her sentimental values. Simms's proslavery novel attempts to rewrite the domestic ideal without women.

The two most important categories of social organization in the antebellum US South, by a gulf, were the linked categories of race and free or unfree status. The recent scholarly attention on white women as enslavers, most notably by Stephanie Jones-Rogers, makes clear that free status was a more important social marker than gender difference.[80] Simms's proslavery argument was predicated on scrambling these social divisions and celebrating the bonds between men, across differences of race or unfreedom. Slavery, he suggested, was less a marker of inferiority for Black men than it was a system enabling Black men to participate in the homosocial pleasures of male fraternity. Such a view was a fantasy, but that fantasy was a powerful export of proslavery propaganda.

Misreading Male Intimacy in *Benito Cereno*

With representations of homoeroticism between enslaved men and enslavers circulating among proslavery propaganda, we should expect to see engagement with these tropes within antislavery messaging. Although limited, there are some examples of that engagement. During the Civil War, a series of Northern envelope printings mocked the South, often in racist ways, for its dependence on enslaved labor. More indicative of colonizationist attitudes than abolitionist ones, such cartoons faulted Southerners for the role that Black people played in society. At least one envelope cartoon mocked white male slaveholders for intimacies with Black men. "Yancey's Negro Tutor," an envelope produced by Oscar Hampel in Cincinnati, depicts a young William Lowndes Yancey, the South Carolina secessionist, in the arms and between the legs of a large enslaved man, apparently Old Joe. His face snuggled into Joe's, hands gripping the rod—a picture of racial intimacy. The caption, putatively derived from one of Yancey's secessionist speeches defending the nobility of the slave system, reads: "They loved us and shared in our boyhood sports."[81]

The cartoon, of course, resembles two of the most prominent pairs in nineteenth-century American literature: the many images, from the first edition of *Uncle Tom's Cabin* onward, of Little Eva beside or on the lap of Uncle Tom as she reads him the Bible in the arbor, and the idea, which Fiedler put at the center of American literature, of Huck Finn in the loving embrace of Jim. If the former, Robin Bernstein argues, constructs for readers a performance of white, childhood innocence, the anti-Confederate ridicule in the Yancey cartoon depends on substituting a prominent Confederate statesman for a little white girl-child snuggling her large, male Black companion.[82] If the latter represents a dreamt-of return to preracial innocence, the Yancey cartoon makes such racial intimacy the failing of slave society. Its dream may be one of a racially exclusionary society, but the argument here lays bare that the Fiedlerian dream could evolve only out of racial slavery.

The more direct attack on the proslavery propaganda of male intimacy comes from another of Fiedler's practitioners, Herman Melville, in his 1855 novella *Benito Cereno*. By the 1850s, Melville had repudiated the Young America literary circle and its politics. In *Benito Cereno*, he plots a direct reversal of the hierarchies of control rendered in the proslavery novels. If the proslavery novel included slave revolts only in the form of Black male puppets operated by a secret white agency, Melville gives secret agency to the enslaved mutineer Babo playing Cereno like a marionette. The novella of misapprehension

YANCEY'S NEGRO TUTOR.

"They loved us and shared in our boyhood sports, Old Joe, there, whose ivory is displayed at the pleasurable memories of my young pranks, taught me, &c.
Extract from Yancey's Speech at Richmond, 1861.

A young William Lowndes Yancey and his enslaved companion, in place of Little Eva and Uncle Tom. "Yancey's Negro Tutor," an 1861 Unionist envelope printed by Oscar Hampel in Cincinnati, Ohio. MOLLUS Civil War Collection: Patriotic Covers, Harvard Houghton Library.

and misreading is famously best read twice, once along with Captain Delano, whose white supremacist worldview presupposes the impossibility of Black agency, and then again reoriented to all the hidden signs of Babo's secret plot. The motto of the mutineers and the novel, "Follow your leader," is instructive that conclusions follow not the visible evidence but one's presuppositions.[83] Begin with racialized hierarchy in mind and the evidence of dominance and control become symbols of subservience and dependence—follow a different lead and one sees different forces in control.

A similar phenomenon follows when presupposing something homoerotic about the seaman's tale. To readers of *Typee*, *Redburn*, *White-Jacket*, *Moby-Dick*, and *Billy Budd*, it would be more surprising if homoerotic elements were missing from this sea novel, but, following the lesson of *Benito Cereno*, one needs to be prepared to see them. Delano interprets the society on board the *San Dominick* as one of homoerotic relationships, recognizing in Captain Cereno's grief for his lost friend his own losses—"that honest eye, that honest hand—both of which had so often met mine," "a man I loved"—in the homosocial world (as signaled by its name) of his ship *The Bachelor's Delight*. Delano is like a literary queer theorist reading secret same-sex relationships into the story. One relationship that Delano perceives is between Cereno and his servant Babo. After the intimate scene of Babo shaving Cereno, from which an "undesired" Delano exits, he interprets Babo's and Cereno's matching cuts as "sort of a love-quarrel, after all." He is anxious about his own intrusion into the lovers' quarrel, seeing himself and Cereno at opposite ends of the dinner table, "like a childless married couple." Babo stands behind Cereno, a fact that Delano is particularly attuned to, as preoccupied by who is behind whom as the novella is with who is behind it all. The imagery of puppeteering, the "hollowness" of Cereno kept upright by Babo, repeats in the metaphor of Cereno without Babo as "the scabbard, artificially stiffened" and "empty," and suggests, to Delano, the question of who is inside of whom. Suggestive symbols reverberate in Delano's imagination. When another mutineer arrives chained (as a decoy according to Babo's master plot), Babo directs Delano's attention to the symbolism: "The slave there carries the padlock, but the master here carries the key." Delano smiles at this and turns to Cereno: "Padlock and key—significant symbols, truly."[84] Delano's invented homoerotic narrative provides the foundation for his white supremacist conclusions. At moments where the presumed order is most challenged by what he sees, he turns back to the Cereno-Babo intimacy, the symbolic marriage between the pair, which occludes the truth that Babo has captured the ship.

Of course, there is no secret homosexual plot, only Delano's invented homoerotic misprision distracting him and the reader from Babo's mutiny. Melville has deceptively included the very homoerotic energies of the proslavery novels. If those novels propagandized intimacies between men to cultivate sympathy for slavery, Delano, a sympathetic interpreter of these intimacies, is the dupe, falling for the homoerotic imagery and, with it, the proslavery propaganda. What he has missed is what the proslavery propagandists had missed—or displaced by imagining the slaves' love for slaveholders—the "slumbering volcano," that enslaved people did desire to get their arms around their enslavers' necks, just not with affection.[85]

CHAPTER 3

Pretty, Dead,
Young Confederates as
Erotic Emblems of
the Lost Cause

HE CIVIL WAR destabilized and reconstructed conceptions of womanhood and manhood, producing what historians and literary scholars have for three decades termed a "crisis in gender."[1] We might expect, then, to find that the Civil War also represented something like a crisis in homosexuality, but this does not appear to be the case. One difficulty for the historian of homosexuality is that evidence of same-sex sex enters the historical record at moments of crisis, when newfound or intensified attention problematizes same-sex desire.[2] As a result, much of what is taken to be the history of homosexuality is more accurately the history of homophobic repression: the criminal records of the accused or the medical records of the pathologized. The Civil War evidences very little of that history. Instead, evidence from wartime literature, extant soldiers' letters and diaries, medical history, and war reporting show that, amid camp life's intense homosocialization, same-sex desire remained remarkably unproblematized and mostly unremarkable.[3] Within the next two decades, homosexuality would emerge as a remarkable social problem, decidedly linked to Civil War veterans, memory, and social transformations—part of, as I argue in chapter 5, the world the Civil War made. For the war years, however, existing evidence suggests same-sex desire was a mostly stable social element but still recognizable and culturally meaningful, even if not disruptive, especially as crises of gender exploded around it.

The war years saw a distinct proliferation of literature we might expect for a crisis in gender: sensational novels that feature female soldiers dressing as men to fight the war.[4] They present a crisis in gender as mostly superficial, confined to the war, and ultimately conservative. Gender may be performed, within these stories, but it is still a decisive binary. In fact, the costumes' success proves a presupposed difference between genders: with just a moustache "Albert" is now unrecognizable to her fiancé in *The Lady Lieutenant* (1862), and in just a low-necked dress Frances eludes the search for a boy named Frank in *The Rattlesnake* (1862). To employ gender as a disguise—as opposed to supposedly more fluid and less determinative characteristics such as occupation, social class, or regional dialect—is to believe strongly in gender as difference. Once the war is over, these female characters return to traditional feminine appearance and usual marital prospects. Gender transgression remains bound to the war, an oxymoronic symptom of the oxymoron "civil war," so that peace will bring the Constitution as it is and woman as it was.[5]

As scholars of this wartime literature such as Elizabeth Young and Alice Fahs have written, these gender-crossing plots allowed writers and readers to indulge in male and female homoeroticism.[6] Such explorations, from the heroine's attraction to her own male image in *The Lady Lieutenant* to the putatively heterosexual, secretly lesbian kisses all over *The Rattlesnake*, are not necessarily transgressive.[7] There is little evidence in any of these stories of same-sex desire as a source of worry: none of the female soldiers worry about *what it might mean* that, in uniform, they found women attractive; virtually none of the male characters worry about having fallen for what they believe to be a boy soldier. One exception to the rule, Captain Trissillian, in the novel *Remy St. Remy* (1865), comes nearest to the consternations of Thomas Mann's Aschenback or Vladimir Nabokov's Humbert Humbert when driven "frantic" by a boy soldier in his ranks.[8] Despite a few moments of this anxiety, the novel never suggests that such desire means something about the captain, and it is ultimately resolved by the revelation that the soldier is no boy but the captain's sister. None of the homoeroticism in these stories received any public opprobrium for transgressive content.[9] Such lack of self-consciousness about same-sex desire does not indicate widespread tolerance of same-sex sex, but this fact, coupled with the almost total absence of records of misconduct for homosexual activity, indicates that homosexual desire was not a special disciplinary concern during the war effort. The scenes of homoeroticism within these stories indicate less an attention to same-sex as a category of desire than they do a widespread erotic fascination with blurred lines of gender difference. In the popular literature of the Civil War, women are especially attractive when they dress as men and men are especially attractive when they look like girls.

One character type stands out: the girlish-appearing young male soldier. Often, the attractive features of such a character, especially his blushing cheeks, indicate a female character in male disguise. John Esten Cooke's novel *Hilt to Hilt*, for example, contains one story of gender disguise: "A boy of eighteen . . . elegantly clad, and his countenance was one of extraordinary beauty," disappears for much of the book before a reappearance reveals he was a young woman all along.[10] A reader thus primed might expect the same story for one of the two Arden brothers with his near-constant blushing: "He said, with a blush and a laugh," "I thought I saw the youth blush in the moonlight as he spoke," "He looked at me, blushing a little," "Blushing like a boy," "Said the blushing Arden," "And with a quick blush he added."[11] But both Arden boys prove to be male throughout the entire book; they just happen, as we will see with other soldiers in Cooke's writing, to be pretty ones. Similarly, there is a cross-dressing red herring in "Ned Arlington, or Harper's Ferry Scenes," an 1862 story published in the *Southern Illustrated News*. It is an especially notable story, perhaps the earliest casting Black Union soldiers as a sexual threat to white Southern women. The Confederate Ned Arlington, who saves the young women from this threat, is introduced: "He would have given the beholder the belief that he was a female in disguise."[12] Perhaps the story was to extend beyond two issues in the magazine with just that revelation, but, as published, he is male throughout, just attractively feminine.

This character, the feminine male youth, was an erotic category in wartime novels and one that would intensify with Confederate loss. A certain type of dead young Confederate soldier became, in postbellum memory, lionized and eroticized in the same gender-indeterminate descriptions as those of the cross-dressing novels. For many, the appealing form of Confederate nationalism was less the white Southern belle or the goateed colonel but the smooth-faced girl-boy soldier. Of all the Confederate dead, the real-life artillerist John Pelham stood out as an erotic emblem of Confederate nationalism. Not only was his beautified likeness spread widely, but older male officers also announced their intense love for, and the stunning appearance of, the dead young man. Their desire to protect the younger man was at times paternal, but the goal of such protection exceeded a paternal relationship by protecting his sexual innocence. After the young man's death, older veterans (and later Confederate historians) continued to protect his innocence and sexual purity.

Scholars accounting for the sexual components of Confederate nationalism and Lost Cause ideology often put the invented purity of white women at the center.[13] Pelham indicates that the sexual purity of young white men was equally a source of nationalist fantasy.

Innocence and sexual purity enabled dead Confederates such as Pelham to become erotic emblems of Confederate national possibility, preserved in youthful arrested development. As such, the pretty, dead Confederate youth used homoeroticism for the appeal of the Lost Cause. The Lost Cause was a work of collective imagination, with real-world consequences. Like any work of imagination, it had many component parts, and scholars have examined its dimensions in literary romanticism, celebrity, film, religion, memorialization, and sexuality.[14] Portrayals of feminine male youth, cut down on the verge of manhood, formed part of the Lost Cause's erotic appeal. As I examine in a final section, its appeal extends far beyond the end of the war, to the elegiac poetry of Confederate defeat, as well as the elegies of a Northerner like Walt Whitman, and even to the attachment many readers feel to a singular passage in William Faulkner.

Col. John Pelham's Blushing White Cheeks

Alongside the wartime literature involving women disguised as male soldiers, there was no parallel explosion of male-to-female cross-dressing stories. The most famous story of gender disguise was the May 1865 arrest of Confederate president Jefferson Davis. Captured by Union soldiers wearing some piece of clothing (a shawl or cloak) borrowed from his wife, he became, as the story spread in the North, Jeff in petticoats, arrested in a hoop skirt. Cartoons depicting Union soldiers poking at Davis with swords and bayonets while his own dagger dropped to the ground represented, Nina Silber has written, "a metaphorical unmanning of the southern aristocracy."[15] Significant as this particular image may be to the idea of an emasculated Confederate aristocracy, it is hardly the only narrative of male-to-female gendered disguise in the period's politics. Statesmen in dresses, including Republicans Abraham Lincoln and Edwin Stanton and Democrat Thomas Hendricks, were a staple of the era's political commentary, and these depictions, unlike that of Davis, rarely aimed to feminize such figures.[16]

Several accounts, all written decades after the war, narrate male soldiers wearing female disguise positively, as an effective war strategy. One Confederate colonel, Richard Thomas Zarvona, allegedly disguised himself as a "French lady" in order to commandeer a passenger ship and ambush federal steamers.[17] A Tennessee private submitted to *Confederate Veteran* in 1899 a vignette of a visit to friends on the other side of enemy lines with the title "Entering the Union Lines in a Petticoat."[18] Union general Nathaniel Lyons, according to a 1900 source, rode the streets of St. Louis dressed as an old woman in a veil.[19] In a memoir first published in 1926, a Union soldier tried to escape a Confederate prison in a dress.[20] In an 1877 history of guerilla warfare, the Confederate soldier Jesse James convinced a brothel keeper that he was a female prostitute who would bring friends later that night if the keeper invited Union soldiers to be there.[21] Benjamin Stringfellow, a Confederate spy, claimed, in accounts not recorded until the twentieth century, to learn of Ulysses S. Grant's appointment as commanding general by dancing with a Union officer while dressed as a woman at a Union army ball.[22] In all of these examples, in contrast to the Davis story, disguising oneself as female was an ingenious war strategy invisible to the enemy.

Several wartime accounts document army camp dances where men, mostly younger soldiers, dressed as women. These accounts present such cross-dressing events as fairly routine and ordinary. Union captain Thomas Wentworth Higginson, before he became an officer in one of South Carolina's Black regiments, mentioned in a letter to his mother his regiment's all-male dances, in which a young lieutenant "was swept away by the charms of the prettiest of the Sergeants, named Fairweather, & I last saw him winding through the 'Portland Fancy' with her."[23] Another soldier's letter home described a regiment's dance: "Some of the real women went but the boy girls was so much better looking they left."[24] If one story of Civil War masculinity is Davis's feminization, another is that of the youthful, feminine soldiers who captured the attention of their male comrades. No other soldier in the written record appears as captivating to his comrades as the Confederate artillerist John Pelham. Popular mythology of the Civil War remains one of beards, moustaches, and goatees; it is a mythology that crowds out the beardlessness of a Pelham. His feminine features would prove, especially after his death, a potent symbol of the failed Confederate effort.

Pelham's was among the most famous deaths in the short life of the Confederacy. At twenty-two, "the gallant Pelham"—an appellation from Gen. Robert E. Lee that stuck—dropped out of the US Military Academy to fight against his onetime teachers and classmates; two years and 100 engagements later he was killed at Kelly's Ford in 1863. A fellow soldier made sure that a glass window was added to his coffin so that citizens and soldiers could see what his commanding officer, Gen. J. E. B. Stuart, called his "calm sweet face."[25] The *Richmond Sentinel* reported Pelham's funeral as an event for the Confederate nation in the capitol at Richmond, "where many persons 'silently gazed on the face of the dead,' and some tender hand deposited an evergreen wreath" on the metallic casket that held Pelham's embalmed body in his Confederate uniform.[26] For the *Richmond Whig*, the fact that next to the room where the Confederate Congress deliberated, "with the calm of unspeakable peace upon his brow, [lay] the bloody corse of the glorious young Pelham—'the hero fit for song or story,'" provided a daily reminder of the new nation at war.[27]

After his death, Pelham's likeness would spread on photographs throughout the country; one admirer described his face as "all tenderness and softness, as fresh and delicate as a boy's who liked people and who found the world good."[28] Cooke, the author of *Hilt to Hilt*, had served with Pelham in Stuart's brigade as something between an embedded journalist and a poet propagandist. His effusive praise across several volumes about Virginia's "boy defender" is partly responsible for Pelham's posthumous fame. "It was impossible to know him and not love him," Cooke wrote in his fictionalized memoir *Surry of Eagle's-Nest* (1866). "In that light blue eye was the soul of truth and chivalry. The smooth, boyish face was the veritable mirror of high breeding, delicacy, and honor. I never knew a comrade more attractive." Cooke, who frequently slept in a bed with Pelham, remembered him as "a comrade whom I loved, and who loved me."[29]

Cooke had established himself as a Virginia novelist in the decade before the war and earned his unique place in Stuart's cavalry partly on that reputation and partly on being cousin to Stuart's wife. For twentieth-century commentators such as Edmund Wilson, Daniel Aaron, and David Blight, Cooke is an exemplary Lost Cause novelist who translated his war experience into Confederate nostalgia.[30] A master mythmaker, Cooke, through his fiction and nonfiction, became about as responsible as any other writer for the myths of Confederate cavaliers, the pastoral antebellum South, and, through his early biographies, the hagiography of Generals Jackson and Lee.[31] If Cooke's role as purveyor of Lost Cause nostalgia is well established, the recurring role of Pelham, as beloved symbol of that nostalgia, within his work has been less examined.

The deceased Pelham was something of a muse to Cooke, mentioned lovingly in six of Cooke's postbellum books and at least one poem. Like the Arden boy in *Hilt to Hilt*, Pelham's blushing cheeks received Cooke's frequent attention. In *Surry*, Pelham's "color never faded in the hottest hours of the most desperate fighting, but a word would often confuse him, and make him blush like a girl," that "on the slightest provocation, the smooth cheeks were covered with the blush of diffidence." Cooke then contrasts an old farmer's skepticism of Pelham's "beardless face, his girlish smile, his slender figure," with the mettle he would prove, to the entire Confederacy, at Manassas, Sharpsburg, and Fredericksburg: "Such was his record—such the career of this shrinking youth, who blushed when you spoke to him."[32] In *Wearing of the Gray* (1867), Pelham is "modest to a fault—blushing like a girl at times."[33] Cooke's biography of General Lee (1871) includes the famous general pointing Pelham out to a young girl: "'There is the handsome Major Pelham!' which caused the modest young soldier to blush with confusion."[34]

Cooke was hardly alone in claiming Pelham's intimacies. The Prussian officer who joined Stuart's cavalry, Heros Von Borcke, celebrated his own "intimacy" with Pelham in his 1866 war memoirs. To Von Borcke, Pelham's men were "devoted to their young chief" and extended "something of this partiality to him," as Pelham's "dear friend."[35] W. W. Blackford, another of Stuart's soldiers, who during the winter of 1862–63 became "more intimate [with Pelham] than we ever had been before," said of General Stuart, "He liked a handsome man as much almost as he did a handsome woman." To prove the rule, Blackford points to Pelham, "only twenty-one or two years old and so innocent looking, so 'child-like and bland' in the expression of his sparkling blue eyes, but as grand a flirt as ever lived." Pelham's eyes stare back at the reader on the opposite page of Blackford's memoir written around 1896 and published in 1945.[36] By the time of Blackford's writing, that image had made Pelham into an icon of Confederate manhood.

There is nothing particularly Confederate about the most famous image of Pelham as photographed by Matthew Brady in 1858. He was still a student at West Point and dressed as an aspiring Federal military officer. Pelham knew how to strike a pose for a portrait—a Pelham four generations back, Peter, had been a notable portraitist in Boston, known today for a painting of Cotton Mather. Pelham's great-grandfather Peter Jr. had also been a portrait painter, though lesser known than his stepbrother John Singleton Copley, whom the elder Peter adopted. Two generations later the family had moved south and was still wealthy, as Dr. Charles Atkinson Pelham, who sent his son to West Point, owned a large plantation in northeast Alabama. The Brady photograph would have been viewed by few beyond those that Pelham showed it to until his death. Even then, it is unlikely that it had a large reach. As historian Ross Brooks writes, the Confederate photography industry struggled to access materials for printing. That shortage confronted the demand for likenesses of the new national heroes, and the prices for photographs and prints jumped.[37] The end of the war was then a perfect moment for Pelham prints, available in bulk from New York printers eager to meet demand.[38] Pelham may have been a wartime hero, but his likeness became a postwar phenomenon.

Cadet John Pelham photographed, age nineteen or twenty, as Gen. Edward Porter
Alexander remembers him: "A very young looking, handsome, & attractive fellow,
slender, blue eyes, light hair, smooth, red & white complexion, & with such a modest
and refined expression that his classmates & friends never spoke of him but as
'Sallie' and there never was a Sallie whom a man could love more!" Matthew B. Brady,
half-plate ambrotype (1858), National Portrait Gallery, Smithsonian Institution.

Pelham's likeness, visible through the glass of his coffin, circulating in photographs, and read in Cooke's descriptions, marked an absent presence, much like that of Confederate captain William Latané in William D. Washington's 1864 painting *The Burial of Latané*, which depicts grieving white women and enslaved people around an open grave where the Confederate officer's body will be buried. The painting, Drew Gilpin Faust writes, "seeks to define and celebrate Confederate nationalism, identifying the soldier's corpse as at once the source of and meaning for the body politic."[39] Pelham was an equally potent symbol for Confederate nationalism, perhaps in an even more lasting way because his image so strongly signaled a premature death, conjuring the imagined future of the Confederate nation as it lay preserved on the verge of manhood. In an 1863 poem frequently reprinted after the war, James Ryder Randall, the author of "Maryland, My Maryland," continued to celebrate Pelham's beautiful features:

We gazed and gazed upon that beauteous face.
While round the lips and eyes,
Couched in their marble slumber, flashed the grace
Of a divine surprise.[40]

Pelham, dead in 1862 and posthumously promoted to lieutenant colonel in 1863, helps bridge Southern feelings from Confederate nationalism to the Lost Cause.[41] If Confederate nationalism, as Gary Gallagher argues, depended on the home front and the Army of Northern Virginia imagined together, a figure like Pelham, dead at Kelly's Ford and alive in posthumous portraits, accomplished that unity.[42] If, as Anne Sarah Rubin argues, Confederate identity extended beyond Appomattox, uniting the future-looking calls for national independence with the backward-looking memorialization of the defeated cause, the dead like Pelham accomplished that unity too.[43] Rubin, along with James Broomall, has argued for an emotional dimension in the relationships among ex-Confederate men that fostered Lost Cause ideology; in this case, those emotions are located in the face and lips of a striking, young, white twenty-year-old with rosy cheeks.[44] With an appeal mirroring that of Walter Pater's phrase "The ideal of that youth still red with life in the grave," all the what-ifs of Confederate victory appear in the counterfactual blushes of this Confederate twink nationalism.[45]

The desirability of Pelham overlaps, then, with forms of gay male desirability long after, as well as those imagined to exist long before, Pelham's lifetime. Youthfulness, often exaggerated, connects such figures, but so, too, does their status in need of protection. That is to say that Pelham's desirability is not confined to his image but is also part of Cooke's and Von Borcke's and Blackford's and Stuart's desire to keep him with them. In Pelham's case, it is his visible whiteness, his blushing cheeks, and his blue eyes that further exaggerate both that youthfulness and the need for protection. His is a racialized innocence, inviting a companion protector. For Pelham, as for this long-standing form of gay male desirability, whiteness is the necessary precondition of youthfulness.[46] And desire operates as the imagined response to both whiteness and youth calling out, together, for protection and preservation. Pelham's youthful death makes that cry for preservation all the stronger, an erotic analogue to the Lost Cause's paradoxical logic of preserving what was lost into the future.

Preserving the Purity of Pretty Confederate Boys

Pelham is one of several young Confederate officers whose deaths preserved an arrested development potent for Lost Cause ideology. Another was the "boy colonel" Henry K. Burgwyn, a North Carolinian who died on the first day at Gettysburg. Long after Burgwyn's death, a fellow officer would remember the first sight of his appearance: "Young, to be a youth of authority, beautiful and handsome; the flash of his eye and the quickness of his movements betokened his bravery."[47] According to a 1909 article in *Confederate Veteran*, when another officer "reached his expiring friend, 'the boy colonel,'" Burgwyn "gave him a look of love and a tender grasp of the hand," while earning "wreaths of immortality encircling his youthful brow."[48] Burgwyn had apparently come by the nickname when a brigade commander refused his promotion on the grounds that he wanted "no boy colonels," but as the 1985 tome *Boy Colonel of the Confederacy* by Archie K. Davis asserts, he precociously proved that right for promotion among his fellow soldiers.[49] One writing a letter to Burgwyn's parents after his death commented on the deceased's appearance: "When I saw him, his face was as calm & placid as if he were asleep, with no contortion or appearances of pain about any of the features. . . . I believe I knew & loved Harry as well as anyone outside of his family."[50]

Such youthful deaths and such celebrations of the dead young man's appearance are hardly unique to the Confederacy. The Northern counterpart to Pelham's widely circulating image was that of Lincoln's friend Elmer Ellsworth, the Zouave colonel who was killed one month into the war. Like Pelham and Burgwyn, Ellsworth's beauty became a feature of his eulogies, and so too was his intimate relationship with another man, President Lincoln,

whose assassination would come to overshadow Ellsworth's death in Northern memory.[51] The death of Theodore Winthrop may also have represented
a Pelham counterpart in the North; only after his death at Big Bethel in 1861
was his novel *Cecil Dreeme* published, allowing readers to associate the novel's picture of manhood, and romantic male intimacy, with that of the dead
soldier.[52]

Nor are homoerotic descriptions of dead young men unique to Civil War
elegy. Many of the most famous elegies—such as John Milton's *Lycidas* or
Alfred, Lord Tennyson's *In Memoriam A. H. H.*—represent a remarkable
romantic and erotic attention of a male speaker to a dead male friend.[53] Memories of Pelham and Burgwyn follow these patterns in their suggestion that
these deaths were somehow fatalistically preordained as part of a doomed
youth. Burgwyn's quartermaster would write to the fallen soldier's parents
that he had always "felt uneasy whenever [Burgwyn] went into battle" and
that his "forebodings, alas, have proved too true."[54] Burgwyn's 1985 biographer follows in his opening remarks: "One is tempted to say that Burgwyn's
fate in battle was predetermined."[55] What the elegiac writing on Pelham and
Burgwyn adds to these patterns, however, is the political symbolism of the
Confederate nation equally cut down in youth and therefore statically preserved in the images of these young men. In Burgwyn's case, these details
extend to his supposed romantic attachments. There was apparently a young
woman to whom he tried sending gifts during his service. According to
Burgwyn's nephew, she never married and "wore mourning all her life," a
model of conduct for postbellum white Southerners' feelings for the Confederate dead.[56]

Even more than for Burgwyn, the key to Pelham's nationalist meaning for
both the late Confederacy and then the Lost Cause is his preserved innocence. Celebrants have made much of Pelham as Blackford remembered him,
both "innocent looking" and "as grand a flirt as ever lived." All of the flirting
in Pelham biographies, such as in William Woods Hassler's *Colonel John Pelham: Lee's Boy Artillerist* (1960) and Jerry Maxwell's *The Perfect Lion: The Life
and Death of Confederate Artillerist John Pelham* (2011), contrasts Pelham's
shyness among women with his bravery on the battlefield. In a much-told
story from the fall of 1862, Stuart's officers stayed with the Dandridge family near Martinsburg, Virginia, where Pelham flirted with Sallie Dandridge.
Apparently it was a bucolic retreat for the Confederate soldiers on the very
kind of slave plantation, with more than 100 enslaved people forced to labor
and serve them, that they were fighting to preserve. About this episode,
Cooke describes Pelham as "modest to a fault"; Blackford recounts him as

"badly struck" by Cupid's arrow; Hassler has him "sheepish" in responses to Stuart's inquiries about the romance; and Maxwell narrates "Pelham's noted bashfulness . . . slowly disappearing."[57] In all accounts, the scene is like later Confederate nostalgia, an idealized peacefulness of antebellum slave society, with Pelham's bashfulness a crucial part of that world's simple innocence.

Pelham's purity from women is an emphasized feature of his early years as well, from the officer who "complimented Pelham on the neatness and cleanliness of his room, jokingly adding that Pelham had no need of a wife as he could keep an orderly house by himself," to his exceptional role as dancing partner in the all-male dances at West Point, to the letter to his parents in which he wrote, "I have not spoken to a lady since my return. Think I will make a good *Bachelor*."[58] To his West Point classmates he was nicknamed "Sallie," as classmate and future Confederate general Edward Porter Alexander recalled in his 1907 memoir: "He was a very young looking, handsome, & attractive fellow, slender, blue eyes, light hair, smooth, red & white complexion, & with such a modest and refined expression that his classmates & friends never spoke of him but as 'Sallie' and there never was a Sallie whom a man could love more!"[59] I don't compile this evidence to suggest that Pelham's lack of contact with women made him any more homosexually oriented than his classmates—1860s West Point wasn't organized into heterosexual and homosexual cohorts. Instead, it demonstrates that Pelham's classmates and officers were interested not just in him but in protecting his innocence from contact with women who would leave him impure. Pelham's gender expression and his sexuality, during his short life, are entirely unknown. What is known is that after his death, in the period when Confederate propagandists were constructing Lost Cause mythology, they remembered Pelham in gendered and sexualized terms, a beautiful, effeminate boy whom no man could love more. By emphasizing these elements of Pelham's personality after his death, both the veterans who knew him and later biographers put sexual purity at the center of the Pelham mythos, especially his youthful death.

All of the biographies, therefore, narrate Pelham's death as indirectly caused by his straying away from General Stuart to visit a girlfriend, or as Von Borcke puts it, "very anxious to see our lady friends" on "a visit of pleasure."[60] Blackford introduces the series of events with the comment that had any of these events gone differently, "Pelham would not have met his death at that time."[61] But, alas, Stuart did grant Pelham leave to visit a girl about twenty-five miles west of the Confederate camp. Stuart woke the next morning and, signaling the foreboding to later biography readers, regretted granting Pelham such permission.[62] Blackford writes, "General Stuart loved him like a younger brother and could not bear for him to be away from him," so he ordered his return.[63] But, as Hassler writes, "Pelham knew from experience that General Stuart often recalled those close to him for companionships" and had left early enough to be too far to return when Stuart's orders were given.[64] That night, Pelham's date was interrupted by news of a Union attack thirty miles to his north at Kelly's Ford. Pelham did not return to Stuart's camp but joined the fighting, meeting Stuart as he arrived separately from his cavalry. Stuart forgave Pelham's transgression, but fate would not. Hours after the battle, Stuart visited the dying soldier, who would become the namesake for Stuart's daughter Virginia Pelham Stuart. According to a 1908 account of Pelham's death, Stuart sobbed over Pelham's body and "a tear fell on the pale cheek of Pelham."[65] Fifty years earlier, red blushes had been painted onto Pelham's cheeks in the Brady ambrotype of the West Point cadet. Such red paint was a common touch added to the otherwise gray faces in ambrotype; in Pelham's case it matched the blushing cheeks repeated in the written accounts of his life. For ambrotype images of Civil War soldiers, the blushes, as attempts to make the portrait appear more full of life, call attention to the death to which so many were marching. But Pelham's blushing cheeks signal, as well, his famed shyness and his sexual innocence. At the same time, those blushes among the so-described pale cheeks point to a racialized innocence.

Pelham and Burgwyn are not children and are therefore not representative directly of the childhood innocence, raced as white, that Robin Bernstein analyzes in *Racial Innocence*.[66] They are certainly not Harriet Beecher Stowe's Little Eva. Indeed, for a war that did include children in their teen years, they were not among the Civil War's youngest soldiers. But they are not *not* children either in posthumous description, though their youthfulness—as "Lee's boy artillerist" and the "boy colonel"—is a bit exaggerated for college attendees who died at twenty-four and twenty-one, respectively. "Boy" less denotes their accurate age than it makes meaning of their status in Confederate memory. Thus, Pelham's sexualization is not the sexualization of a child but a related phenomenon: using the language of youth and childhood to sexualize an adult man by yoking him to sexual purity and empty innocence.[67] The kind of man to whom, as Cooke did to Pelham, one could say things that would make him blush and then talk about his blushing cheeks forever.

Fitting a frozen perpetual youth, the image of a forever-Confederate-boy has had a long afterlife. In 1905, the United Daughters of the Confederacy erected an exceptionally boyish statue of Pelham at his gravesite in Jacksonville, Alabama. Rare for the peak years of the United Daughters of the Confederacy's monumentation of standard, anonymized Confederate soldiers, the Pelham statue represents a real individual—though not one that resembles the Pelham of photographs. This figure appears about fourteen, ten years younger than Pelham at his death. To one commentator who spent his own boyhood years in the statue's proximity, the cemetery statue "stands with one leg slightly forward, strangely feminine looking, with a plump ass."[68] Jacksonville's Pelham is also rare in depicting a teenage-looking Confederate: with the removal of the "Talbot Boys" statue in Easton, Maryland, in 2022 and "Silent Sam" at the University of North Carolina in 2018, the Sam Davis "Boy Hero" statue at the state capitol in Nashville, Tennessee, still stands, as does Pelham, as a Confederate boy who never grew up.

Their exaggerated boyhood remains exonerating. "Pelham was ambivalent about secession," writes the sociologist Allen Shelton, for whom Pelham is a "doomed Southern knight," "a more muscular embodiment of the Southern Gothic." Shelton's autoethnography, *Dreamworlds of Alabama* (2007), opens through identification with Pelham: "I was ready to be John Pelham," the historical person ("a valiant man," dead at "twenty-six years old [*sic*], still boyish and extremely handsome"); the statue (plump-assed and feminine, with "curls spring[ing] out from beneath his hat"); and the dreamworld figure ("a doorway between this world and the supernatural").[69] Pelham presides over Shelton's lost Alabama world, lost both to him, in a Buffalo exile, and to time. Notably, a world was lost to the Confederates too, but Pelham's arrested development, his perpetual youth, allows for an identification and desire unintruded upon by that history.

Shelton is not alone in desiring identification with a fourteen-year-old Southern boy, as countless readers of a passage in William Faulkner's *Intruder in the Dust* (1948) can attest. At a central moment in the coming-of-age narrative of the novel's sixteen-year-old hero, Chick Mallison, his uncle tells him how a fourteen-year-old Southern boy can preserve perpetual youthfulness by imagining the so-called high-water mark of the Confederacy seconds before Pickett's Charge on the third day at Gettysburg. Citations of Faulkner's sentence in writing manuals, counterfactual histories, and Confederate nostalgia are too numerous to cite: Tony Horwitz did so ironically, Ta-Nehisi Coates did so critically, and Shelby Foote did so perhaps most famously in Ken Burns's 1990 *Civil War* documentary miniseries.[70] The quotation begins, "For every Southern boy fourteen years old, not once but whenever he wants it, there is the instant when it's still not yet two oclock on that July afternoon in 1863."[71] Frequently described as "one impossibly long sentence," it is, instead, only one part of a sentence, a remembered quotation from Chick's uncle, inside a parenthetical, within Chick's stream-of-consciousness about the potential of human action in a world determined by necessity and fate.[72]

The fact that Gettysburg might have turned out differently indicates that destiny is our own to make; that it didn't indicates that efforts to preserve antebellum slavery, exonerate a Black man of a murder charge, or, in the context of Faulkner's writing, achieve racial integration in the South are futile. Gettysburg—in that it could have gone differently but didn't—is for the Southern white boy the ultimate test of human determination against historical necessity, the very question that Faulkner's writing, and for that matter literature, is often after. But that is not how the quotation is often invoked.

Instead, for every grown-up white boy of any age there is a passage in Faulkner that crowns Confederate playacting with the world-historical philosophizing of high literary modernism. Faulkner may well have been one of these boys, but he uses the meditation in *Intruder* to criticize a society in which this particular kind of fantastical retreat from present political problems is possible. That retreat, in Faulkner as well as in Shelton's *Dreamworld*, is not unconnected to an appealing image of a perpetual male youthfulness.

Chick, the novel's focus and eyes, is but a boy. Indeed, the unsettling premise of *Intruder* is how the story of a Black man's trial for a murder he did not commit becomes the story of a white boy's *bildung*. Certainly, for many readers, this is accomplished through identification—what Faulkner has done as well here as anywhere else is portray a boy in whom countless readers see themselves. But literature, especially at its most successful, rarely stops at identification; one of the very themes of literary modernism, and one of the insights of queer theory, is how identification and desire mix.[73] Chick is an updated Pelham, on the verge of manhood, but whose femininity is a more anxious prospect connected to his relationship with, and unpaid debt to, the novel's representative of Black manhood. What makes Chick so compelling as a model of white masculinity is that he is not a man, neither in age nor wholly in his relationship with other men. He is, like the fourteen-year-old boy his uncle imagines, in a state of arrested development.[74] What the failure at Gettysburg accomplished, then, was creating the conditions for a desired perpetual youthfulness, not so that one could be a Pelham but so that one could suspend him exactly as he was, innocent and pure, to rescind, as biographers imagine Stuart desperately tried to do, permission for him to visit a girlfriend so he might stay forever your companion.

The Dead Young Confederate in His Grave

Even more than the Confederate heroines in male disguise, Pelham's image, as the perpetually young, girlish boy hero, suggested a purity that needed protecting. Confederate purity, during and immediately after the Civil War, was located as much in the Confederacy's dying and dead white young men as it was in its white women. Augusta Jane Evans's *Macaria* (1864), a novel locating Confederate nationalism in white women's purity, suggests as much with a late scene in which the novel's heroine cares for a dying Confederate youth who "stands on the verge of manhood." In his final moments, the boy had been stirred back to wakefulness by an older soldier's deluded exclamations in the hospital. The younger man's delusions then go back a few years, as he imagines himself in his old plantation home: "Hush! Jessie is singing under the old magnolia down by the spring. Listen!" The boy dies frozen in that remembered past. His martyrdom is immediately cast in racial terms, as the heroine contrasts his noble soldierly sacrifice with the greediness of enslaved people complaining about the conditions of slavery: "The tenderly nurtured darling of Southern parents, cheerful in the midst of unparalleled hardships, content with meagre rations which his negroes at home would scornfully reject."[75] The dying Confederate youth's cheerfulness amid conditions purportedly far worse than those that caused the war—that is, enslavement—directly employs his image as an argument about who really counts as the Civil War's victims.

After the war, Confederate poetry made such dead youths, once a symbol of optimism for Confederate independence, a symbol of the Lost Cause. Such men are all over the latter half of the more or less chronologically organized *War Poetry of the South*, edited and published by William Gilmore Simms in 1866. Like Randall's "Pelham," which appears in Simms's anthology, poems about the named youthful dead, such as W. Gordon McCabe's "John Pegram" (who was killed in 1865 just weeks after his wedding) or John Thompson's "Captain Latane" (killed in 1862), extol the fair features of the Confederate corpse.[76] Poems to anonymous dead, such as Marie La Coste's "Somebody's Darling," the anonymous "A Rebel Soldier Killed in the Trenches before Petersburg, VA, April 15, 1865," and Henry Timrod's "Unknown Dead," all associate the author or reader with a young woman gazing upon the dead boy she loved.[77] One of Cooke's two poems refers to Pelham; the other surely has Pelham among those implied by "Not on this idle page I write / That name of names, shrined in the core / Of every heart!" The poem, which borrows lines and rhyme scheme from Edgar Allan Poe's "The Raven," has a central conceit in the image of the coffee mug, carried across many a battle, now shattered. The mug's value, first as a "faithful comrade," reveals itself in connection to a soldierly companion whose lips once kissed it:

Those lips this broken vessel touched,
His, too!—the man's we all adore—

That cavalier of cavaliers,
Whose voice will ring no more.[78]

Among the poets in Simms's anthology, Timrod has remained most notable as a national poet of the Confederacy. Along with Simms and Paul Hamilton Hayne, Timrod was anxious to create, during and after the Civil War, an independent Confederate national poetry.[79] His own death at thirty-eight, in October 1867, and his friend Hayne's posthumous hagiographic biography of him have made Timrod a sort of poetic Pelham for the Confederacy, "cut down at their golden prime" but preserved through his verses.[80] Timrod's best-known poem, "Ode Sung on the Occasion of Decorating the Graves of the Confederate Dead, at Magnolia Cemetery, Charleston, S.C., 1867," picks up the themes in many of Simms's anthologized elegies, with martyred Confederates sleeping "sweetly," without proper memorials, as loving women stoop to honor them. Lamenting the absence of marble columns, Timrod's central conceit evokes the image of the Confederate youth as both dead and perpetual. The tears of women water their graves and, in an image suggestive of their perpetual virulence, shafts will sprout from where the bodies lie.[81]

At the same time that postbellum poetry lionized the bodies of the Confederate dead, the South's Ladies Memorial Associations were taking charge of those bodies, moving them from battlefields to burials in hometown cemeteries. For historians Anne Sarah Rubin and Caroline E. Janney, such efforts were highly gendered, both as a public and prominent kind of women's work and as the kind of work that conferred status of proper womanhood upon those doing it.[82] The gender story is complicated, for the imagined innocence and purity of the dead confer those attributes upon the caretakers. That imagined innocence and purity derives, in turn, from the Confederate youth's gendered presentation as decidedly not a man, and not quite a boy, but quite feminine in the beautiful, fair features that persist in death. The dizzying reciprocity between those acts of turn-of-the-century white womanhood, erecting monuments for the Confederate dead, and the objects of those erections, the youthful Confederate dead themselves, resolves itself, quite simply, in the shafts, obelisks, and mass-produced statues of young veterans consecrated across the South.

One such obelisk—stone, white, twenty feet high—was erected for John Pelham by the Anniston College for Young Ladies and United Sons of Confederate Veterans in 1905. In September 2020, the town of Anniston, Alabama, voted to take down the statue, following the murder of George Floyd that summer.[83] Removal of the 1905 Pelham monument received limited opposition within the majority Black town, but men like Pelham have featured prominently in the debate about Confederate memorials elsewhere. One argument would distinguish such young innocent men, "fighting in wars they did not start," from the older secessionist statesmen and slaveholders who started it. "Thinking about John Pelham," one commentator writes citing Stuart's description, "I am reminded that there were young men on both sides of that conflict whose records were 'bright and spotless' and whose careers were 'brilliant and successful' until the war put them to an end."[84] Confederate monuments, so the argument goes, properly honor these young, innocent dead. Pelham's innocence is, however, not with him in the grave but a product of the Lost Cause narratives that pull him out.

This broader appeal is precisely how the Pelham narrative was meant to operate. Crucially, Pelham's appeal is to be universal: "There never was," General Alexander claimed, "a Sallie whom a man could love more." Almost immediately upon his death, Pelham narratives made him the object, as well, of Union officer affections. The *Richmond Whig*, a month after Pelham's death, included an anecdote that a note of commendation had been found in the dead young man's purse, written by a Union officer, "once his companion and friend."[85] This may have been from Gen. George Custer, whose note to Pelham after Fredericksburg is frequently quoted in Pelham biographies: "I rejoice, dear Pelham, in your success."[86] Another Union general, Morris Schaff, in his memoir *The Spirit of Old West Point* (1907), gives a picture of Pelham, "gracefully tall, fair, and a beautiful dancer, and it may well be asserted that Nature was in a fine mood when she moulded his clay." Predicting that "at the last the dew will sparkle brighter on Pelham's memory" than any other, Schaff explains: "Poetry and sentiment, under some mysterious affiliation or charm, seem loath to turn away from great display of courage and sacrifice of life for a principle; most lovingly of all they cherish the ashes of brilliant youth associated with failure. The romance of defeat has more vitality, I think, than the romance of victory,—like, the morning-glory, it blooms freshest over ruins."[87] If Schaff's truism has long helped explain a romanticized Lost Cause, it was again Pelham's image that conveyed that romance to his former combatants.

Just as Pelham's image appealed to Northerners as an emblem of Confederate innocence, so did the image of the dead Confederate soldier in postbellum elegies elicit cross-sectional sympathies. In Travis Foster's analysis, the elegies to the Civil War dead from both sides "enthusiastically celebrate the ability for racial bonds to overcome intraracial differences and heal section division."[88] If such poems in the North and South sympathize over a shared whiteness, what was shared, as well, across such poems was the image of the youthful white corpse. Walt Whitman's postbellum imagery, to take the most notable Northern example, returns to the same images as Simms's anthology. The Endymion-like visions of beautiful Confederate boys sleeping in their graves finds echoes in Whitman's dispatches about convalescent Union soldiers during his work in a war hospital.[89] Whitman wrote about one soldier, "He looks so handsome as he sleeps, one must needs go nearer to him," and about another, "Poor youth, so handsome, athletic, with profuse beautiful shining hair. One time I sat looking at him while he lay asleep."[90] Such sleepiness, perhaps evoking the phrase "slept with me" that peppers Whitman's diary about the young men he met during this same time on the streets of Washington, DC, recalls, with these soldiers, what Timrod calls "a temporary death."[91]

The war turned poetic attention to these Endymion figures. For example, Fitz-Greene Halleck's first poem in over a decade, "Young America" in 1864, features a "young Endymion" sleeping "in quiet heedlessness." Halleck, a poet a generation older than the Young America set—indeed, he was among the European-influenced old guard against whom Cornelius Mathews had rebelled—had long drawn on homoerotic imagery for his verse.[92] In his allegory of national development, three successive figures, a preacher, a soldier, and a female teacher, are each arrested by a fourteen-year-old's (closed) "eye-delighting eyes . . . blue as summer's skies," his "golden ringlets," and his "dimpled cheek." If the first figure represents the nation's Puritan origins, and the third the promise of a mature poetic future, the soldier represents, without direct reference, the ongoing Civil War. Which side the soldier fights for is unclear, but why does he fight? For the esteem of this beautiful sleeping boy. As the soldier rests "beside the slumberer's couch of leaves," he muses, "Ah me! what delight it would give me to wake him / And lead him wherever my life banners wave." The soldier does not but instead wishes that when he dies, "by young hearts like his may the grave be surrounded / Where I sleep my last sleep in the slumbers of fame."[93] The meaning of the Civil War, here, becomes doubly located in young men: the sleeping death of the soldier in his grave and the beautiful sleeping boy who mourns beside it.

Whitman, too, writes the war's meaning between a dead soldier in his grave and the man who leans over it. His closing image in the poem "Reconciliation" is a kiss on the lips of a dead Confederate:

For my enemy is dead—a man divine as myself is dead;
I look where he lies, white-faced and still, in the coffin—I draw near;
I bend down and touch lightly with my lips the white face in the
    coffin.[94]

Whiteness, here, conveys, as it did with Pelham, at least four linked ideas about the Confederate: his innocence, his erotic appeal, his death, and his race. As I began in the introduction, Whitman's most intimate relationship in the period when writing this poetry was with a white former Confederate soldier, Peter Doyle. Whitman's dead Confederates are, however, a more general symbol. Although the soldiers he nursed were of the Union army, Whitman saw Confederate soldiers, wounded and tattered, arriving in Washington toward the war's end. In *Memoranda during the War*, he recalls witnessing some Union officers turning over captured Confederate flags to the war secretary. An officer states that one of the flags had been left by a Confederate youth of seventeen who was killed trying to dismantle a cannon. Whitman conjures, in a parenthetical, the imagined dead enemy: "(Perhaps, in that Southern boy of seventeen, untold in history, unsung in poems, altogether unnamed, fell as strong a spirit, and as sweet, as any in all time.)"[95] The unnamed Confederate youth, like Pelham and Burgwyn, dies arresting all the potential of his strong and sweet future spirit.

For a poet exceptionally attuned to the suffering of others, especially of other men, the fact that Whitman's postbellum feelings gravitate to dead and dying soldiers should be expected. The poet who wrote before the war, "I am the poet of slaves and of the masters of slaves," could incorporate former enemies into his poetic project.[96] But one element that drops out of his postbellum poetry was the concern evident in his antebellum writing for Black Americans. After emancipation, Whitman no longer had a model for Black suffering. For one who had incorporated scenes drawn from abolitionist rhetoric into his verse, and figured himself as the enslaved, this absence transformed the politics of Whitman's poetry. Whitman scholars, Ed Folsom most notably, have tried to account for Whitman's changed racial attitudes after the Civil War by examining Whitman's attitude toward Black Americans.[97] As I suggest throughout this book, his attention, especially his erotic attention, to white Americans may be of equal importance. The victims of the era for Whitman, as much as for the Confederate poets, were men like Pelham, the suffering and dying white male soldiers. This cultural transformation, by which white soldiers replaced enslaved Americans as the chief victims of the era, was a widespread phenomenon beyond Whitman and beyond the war years. With attention to white prisoners of war, it is the subject of the next chapter.

CHAPTER 4

Andersonville
Prisoners of War and the
Racial Competition
of Victimhood

ALT WHITMAN WAS NOT ALONE in turning his attention to the suffering of soldiers. In June of 1864, the front page of *Harper's Weekly* put a new victim of abuse before the eyes of its readers: the naked and emaciated white Union prisoner of war.[1] Unlike Whitman's wounded soldiers, the images are not erotic but sexual in their narrative of abuse, much like the voyeuristic narratives of sexual abuse under slavery that mobilized abolitionists before the war.[2] The startling nudity on the cover of *Harper's* was nearly unprecedented. These images signaled an attention to the bodies of prisoners that would continue for two decades in prisoners' memoirs. Those memoirs would emphasize soldiers' bodies through the loving care and devotion they demonstrated to one another. Indeed, nothing in the canon of Civil War literature comes so close to the Whitman ideal of "manly comradeship," not even Whitman's own wartime writing, than the memoirs of the Andersonville prison camp. The homoerotic descriptions offered political messages, demanding sympathy for the suffering Civil War soldier as a matter of social policy and memory in the decades after the war.

Harper's sensational images of skeletal soldiers with the caption "Rebel Cruelty—Our Starved Soldiers" made a wartime argument to see the war through to Southern surrender. For historian Judith Giesberg, the images of

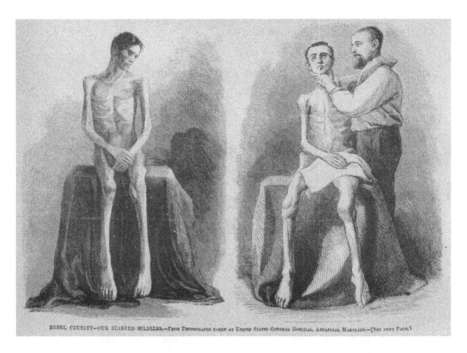

Emaciated bodies of Union soldiers as an emergency call to save those remaining
in Confederate prisons. "Rebel Cruelty," *Harper's Weekly*, June 18, 1864, 385.
Special Collections, University of Mississippi Libraries.

naked prisoners in *Harper's* aimed to provoke "loud calls for revenge against
southern civilians" and Northern desire for "retributive sexual violence."[3]
Almost a year earlier, in July 1863, the magazine printed what might be the
nearest analogue, the scarred exposed back of an enslaved man named Gordon in the article "A Typical Negro."[4] If the sensational image of his brutal-
ized back was one reason to fight the war, the near-naked image of starved
soldiers was reason to finish it. By 1864, Southern atrocity had a new victim
in the Northern imagination to replace the slave: the white Union prisoner
of war.

The prisoners depicted in the magazine were from the Belle Isle Prison
in Richmond, not, as they have come to represent, the Andersonville prison.
In cultural memory, however, "Andersonville," the name of the town nearest to the Confederate prison Camp Sumter, has come to stand not just for
that Georgia prison but for all the Confederate prisons in which Union soldiers were held. For example, John McElroy's 1879 *Andersonville: A Story of
Rebel Military Prisons* narrates his time in Richmond, at Camp Sumter, then
in Savannah, at Camps Millen, Lawton, and Florence. Most of the earliest

prisoners at Andersonville had arrived there from Belle Isle; most survivors were moved to Millen or Florence before their release. For these prisoners, the camps differed by degrees of cruelty: the Andersonville experience became a metonym for the Civil War prison experience.[5]

Conditions at Andersonville justify its place in Civil War memory. Over the course of the fifteen months Camp Sumter operated, 13,000 of the 45,000 imprisoned Union soldiers died of starvation, disease, or gunshot. At its most crowded in August 1864, 31,000 men lived within four walls on a rectangular yard roughly 540 yards by 260 yards. A *deadline* separated the men inside the camp from the wall: those crossing it would be shot. Historians debate Confederate intentions and premeditation in the deaths of these thousands, but Union prisoners themselves, even years after their prison experience, would believe that death there was by Confederate design, carried out intentionally by prison commandant Henry Wirz.[6] Andersonville then became chief among examples of the Confederate crimes that continued to merit punishment years after the war. This chapter's focus is not on the conditions at the prison or on soldiers' experiences there.[7] Instead, this chapter examines the use to which soldiers put this experience in their writing after the war.

One year after the image of starved soldiers on its cover, in June 1865, *Harper's* ran another story and accompanying images on "Rebel Cruelties." By June, Gens. Robert E. Lee and Joseph E. Johnston had surrendered, Jefferson Davis had been captured, and Wirz was awaiting trial, which would take place from August to October. That summer, *Harper's* evidence of Rebel cruelty moved from the stomach to the toes, with images of soldiers gangrenous or amputated at the ankles or, in the case of one pair with interlocked arms, missing six toes between them.[8] The images represented a shift in argument coinciding with the end of the war. While the emaciated soldiers had called for urgent emergency action to save the remaining prisoners before they perished, the maimed soldiers suggested the permanent damage for which the South should pay. That punishment fell exclusively on the prison commandant Wirz, who was executed in November 1865. Wirz was not the only Confederate tried by military tribunals, nor was he the only Confederate executed by a Northern military trial. He was, however, the only one associated with Confederate prisons and the nearest to Confederate leadership to be tried and executed.[9]

In subsequent decades, the story of Union prisoners of war would occupy a prominent place in postbellum culture. The initial prisoner memoirs immediately after the war followed the message of the *Harper's* June 1865 issue to remind readers of Confederate atrocity, as many in the North argued for

The "Siamese Twins," Smith and Churchill, maimed by Rebel cruelty
at Andersonville. Reprinted from *Harper's Weekly* in A. O. Abbott,
Prison Life, 306. University of Memphis Libraries.

more punitive measures for ex-Confederate leaders.[10] Equally, stories of
Andersonville were central to Republicans' voter mobilization. When Republicans wanted to accuse 1872 presidential opponent Horace Greeley of being too sympathetic to the South, they depicted him reaching out for a hug across the Bloody Chasm of the Andersonville dead.[11] Over the course of the next decade, as the potency of such appeals diminished for Republicans against a swelling culture of reconciliation, prisoner-of-war memoirs maintained cultural prominence but for a slightly altered message, one greatly divorced from the war's emancipatory efforts.

Much as the images in *Harper's* represented a replacement of victimhood from the enslaved to white soldiers, the prisoner-of-war memoirs represented an intensifying attention on the white male soldier. They did so not only by emphasizing the suffering of the soldiers at Andersonville but also by focusing their attention on the intimacies between men within the prisons.

As scholars beginning with Jonathan Ned Katz have noted, the methods of survival through the loving intimacies between men look surprisingly homoerotic.[12] Representations of these intimacies sentimentalized the relations between men and directed public sympathies to them. Historians have argued that these memoirs, in the late 1870s and 1880s, were part of a demand to maintain and increase veterans' pensions.[13] Homoerotic portrayal contributed to this message by showing a model of loving care between soldiers for the state to emulate. At the same time, the homoerotic portrayals aided in shifting sympathies away from the enslaved as victims of Southern atrocities to these suffering men. Homoeroticism, and the sympathies it engendered toward these white male prisoners, was then a part of the postbellum revision to Civil War victimhood that made white male soldiers appear to some as the exclusive actors in the drama.

If the Andersonville narrative compels racialized questions about who gets to be the victim of wartime atrocities, that is partly by Confederate design. Indeed, Andersonville is a story of race because Confederate policy and propaganda made it so. Andersonville's deadly overcrowding followed the discontinuation of prisoner exchanges between Federal and Confederate governments. In September 1863, Abraham Lincoln announced that the Federal government would consider Black soldiers as soldiers with rights to exchange equivalent to those of white soldiers. When the Confederate government refused to treat Black soldiers as legitimate prisoners of war, Lincoln refused this exclusion and prisoner exchanges halted.[14] The Confederates then broadcast to Union prisoners that their government was placing the interests of Black soldiers above their welfare. After the war, the Confederate surgeon general ventriloquized Union prisoners as if they "charged their prolonged captivity upon their own Government, which was attempting to make the negro equal to the white man."[15] The point was to make the Union prisoners feel on the losing side of a racial competition of suffering. McElroy described Confederate officers failing to lure defectors through these methods at Andersonville. But suffering's racialized competition would play out in postbellum culture, as the body of the white male soldier overtook the enslaved in memory as the central sufferer of Southern atrocity.

Once they became the central sufferers, the image of prisoner-of-war soldiers was put to further use in reconciliation narratives in the late 1880s and after. Intimacies between men, celebrated in the memoirs, became symbolic of the potential for cross-sectional union. Not only could prisoners and their former guards embrace, but attention on the embrace of wounded men became symbolic of the shared suffering across North and South. That

suffering alone became paramount as the Civil War's primary narrative, elid-
ing the emancipatory aims of the Union's cause.

Who Is the Victim of the Civil War?

Some elements of a plot: A person is captured and held against their will.
There is a semipublic inspection of that person's body by a large group including their captors and others. This person is then in the custody of a sadistic
villain who vacillates between neglect of basic needs and orgiastic delight in
violence. When the person tries to escape to the North, the villain's dogs go
after the fugitive, often with recapture. At long last, the conquering Union
army sets the captive free.

Before the Civil War, such elements were staples of the antislavery novel
and the abolitionist slave narrative. Some may be found in narratives such as
that of William Wells Brown (1847) or in the novel *Uncle Tom's Cabin*; nearly
all are in that work that combined the antislavery novel and the slave autobiography, Solomon Northup's *Twelve Years a Slave* (1853). After the war,
such elements became a staple of the prisoner-of-war memoir, such as *Twelve
Months in Andersonville* (1886). As signaled by the tightened, but parallel,
chronology of Lessel Long's Andersonville narrative, the postbellum memoirs transferred the experience of Black enslavement onto the imprisonment
of white Union soldiers. If the writers of these memoirs drew upon the most
notable public experience of captivity, they equally drew upon the literary
forms of antislavery texts to convey their parallel experience.[16]

In Northup's narrative, he vividly details the dogs trained by slaveholders
to hunt those escaping from slave plantations.[17] Northup's experience added
to a popular cultural image of the escaping slave pursued through woods and
swamps by slaveholders' bloodhounds. Even though the slave trader in *Uncle
Tom's Cabin* does not have dogs with him when pursuing the escaping Eliza
as she crosses the Ohio River, illustrations of that scene would depict dogs
at her heels as she jumps onto the ice.[18] In *Twelve Months in Andersonville*,
Long, an Indiana infantryman captured and imprisoned at age twenty-six,
writes of prisoners escaping from Andersonville being pursued by not just
dogs but the very same dogs trained to catch escaping enslaved people. Long
reminds his readers that "each planter kept a pack of blood-hounds which
were trained to track the negroes in case of attempted flight" and which
"the rebel authorities found . . . equally useful in hunting down refugees and
escaping prisoners during the war."[19] The accompanying image in the book of
an escaping prisoner being hunted by dogs, with the shadowy figures of the

human hunters in the background, recalls the harrowing moments in *Uncle Tom's Cabin* illustrations—in position, in movement, and in the risk dramatized, the prisoner of war has taken Eliza's place.

Slave-hunting dogs retrained to seek escaping prisoners appear in nearly every prisoner-of-war memoir, from the initial crop in 1865–66 through those of the 1880s.[20] Warren Goss's *The Soldier's Story of His Captivity at Andersonville* (1866) included not just retrained dogs but reemployed slave catchers. After Goss fails to escape from a Confederate prison, his captor informs him that he has spent eighteen years in that business and is now receiving thirty dollars for each prisoner caught.[21] Many of these narratives tell of escapees hiding among enslaved people; Morgan Dowling's mostly fictional *Southern Prisoners* (1870) includes a suspenseful scene in which a slaveholder makes "the usual inspection of his slave quarters," in which Dowling is hiding.[22] While such episodes situated escaping prisoners of war within the experience of escaping enslavement, the dogs chasing after them remained the predominant symbol of that shared experience. After Wirz's trial, postcard images of Andersonville's dogs circulated as memorabilia that reminded the Northern public of prisoners' suffering.[23]

At Wirz's trial in 1865, former prisoners testified to the use of dogs to chase down escaping prisoners in the woods of northern Georgia. One prisoner accused Wirz of sadistically ordering the dogs to bite an escapee.[24] The dogs were, however, just one example of the acts of personal cruelty that prisoners charged Wirz with committing. If such cruelties paralleled the capricious cruelties of slaveholders, Wirz took the place of these despots. As the only prominent Confederate officer tried and executed after the war, Wirz came to stand in, as representative or as scapegoat, for the violence of Confederate prisons generally. In a post-trial review, the judge advocate summarized the case against Wirz in a manner reminiscent of Harriet Beecher Stowe's Legree or Harriet Jacobs's debased, demonic slaveholder: "This work of death seems to have been a saturnalia of enjoyment for [Wirz], who amid these savage orgies evidenced such exultation and mingled with them such nameless blasphemy and ribald jests, as at time to exhibit him rather as a demon than a man."[25] For the prosecution, Wirz's villainy entailed the same problems of scale that plagued the antislavery texts between an individual evildoer and a representative of a broader system. Just as abolitionists struggled to make individuated examples of slaveholder despotism representative of a system of slavery, the prosecution aimed to make Wirz the first conviction in a broader conspiracy of Confederate cruelty among all officers, including President Jefferson Davis.[26]

The Andersonville narrative that most aimed for literary status was that of Illinois private John McElroy, who had been imprisoned at age seventeen. Like Long's later narrative, McElroy's *Andersonville* (1879) drew upon antislavery literature, especially *Uncle Tom's Cabin*. Shortly after his capture, McElroy narrated his public examination by the men and women of the Confederacy in ways that his readers would find reminiscent of the slave auction in Stowe and other texts. As the Southern women he stands before stare, comment, and giggle, McElroy "got very red in the face, and uncomfortable generally. Attention was called to the size of my feet and hands, and the usual chorus followed." Before he is made to sing for them, McElroy concludes, "in the minds of these bucolic maidens I was scarcely, if at all, human; they did not understand that I belonged to the race; I was a 'Yankee'—a something of the non-human class, as the gorilla or the chimpanzee."[27] For McElroy, the giggling Southern women, and their comparison of his body to that of apes, puts his own body in the place of the enslaved at the public auction.

The prisoner-of-war memoir also replaced the abolitionist narrative in the period's literary market. After the Civil War, there were some narratives by formerly enslaved people that tracked their experience from bondage to freedom.[28] In quantity, such publications hardly compare to the number of first-person narratives by former prisoners of war between 1865 and the 1880s. These were a staple, as well, of the nation's literary magazines, assembled together in anthologies such as *Prisoners of War and Military Prisons* (1890).[29] This genre, and the descriptions within it, were both cause and effect of the much broader shift of attention from enslaved people to the Civil War soldier. Alongside that shift, veterans became a prominent object of state policymaking.[30] As evident in the images in *Harper's*, it also reflected a shift in the attention to victimized bodies. If enslaved women had been the object of erotic fascination in the antislavery press through their vulnerability to rape by slaveholders, the prisoners of war became sympathetic victims through narratives of their bodily transformations. Attention on white male bodies intensified through an element within these narratives themselves: the men's relation to one another, rendered through their homoerotic intimacies.

Chums at Andersonville

Intimacy between men at Andersonville and other Confederate prisons was a survival strategy. In various ways, scholars have been trying to account for, and even quantify, the effects of that strategy. For example, a 2007 econometric study, "Surviving Andersonville: The Benefits of Social Networks in POW

Camps," analyzes experiences at Andersonville to demonstrate the effect of social cohesion as a survival strategy. The paper analyzes rates of survival in Confederate prisons depending on perceived social networks, such as company and regimental "friends," as well as ethnic and kinship bonds, and concludes: "Both an additional contemporaneous friend and an additional initial friend led to a mortality hazard that was 0.98 times lower."[31] If such quantification would have made little sense to the prisoners, the findings would have been well received. All personal accounts of Andersonville explain means of survival through social networks and organized pairings. The accounts themselves give voice to what it meant to have a social network at a Confederate prison. With nothing to do there but survive, a social network consisted of eating together, resting together, nursing one another, and sleeping together.[32]

Andersonville memoirs substantiate the notion that intimacy between men was a survival strategy, but it was, in those memoirs, plainly more than that. Male intimacies were, contrary to what a later century's perspective might expect, not a homosexual subculture but a nearly universal experience and the structuring principle of organization for tens of thousands of prisoners. A focus on these intimacies, and their sentimental portrayal, intensified after the war, even more so in the memoirs of the 1870s and 1880s. This is a curious fact. To whatever extent male intimacy was a requirement for prison survival, it was a phenomenon that, up to two decades later, prisoners prioritized in the telling of their experiences. No doubt they did so because it was central to that experience. But by emphasizing the loving relations between men, the memoirists were attempting something more than documenting their time at Andersonville. They were also putting their intimacies to use for a political purpose. Memoirs written, in part, to lobby Congress for increased veteran pensions celebrated the loving care demonstrated by one prisoner to another as a model of the care that the government owed to Union veterans. To fully marshal this argument, the memoirs contrasted the total neglect for the welfare of prisoners demonstrated by Confederate officers with the love that Union prisoners showed one another. To modern readers, the homoeroticism might even seem indulgent, but its purpose was to make the readers feel a duty to care properly for these veterans.

To track homoeroticism under the conditions at the Andersonville prison seems indecorous, perverse, or even repulsive. Some homosexual acts should be expected in an all-male prison camp that numbered 35,000 at its peak. At the same time, it would be foolish to presume the camp a site of free love or frequent sex, though not necessarily due to homophobic prohibition, sexual repression, or heterosexual preference. The facts of starvation, disease, weakness, sickness, and madness, stated in all of the accounts, were likely the strongest inhibitors. Moreover, we might expect that some homosexual activity took the form of abuse by prison guards wielding power over prisoners. Two memoirs may imply such abuse: Goss describes a prison adjutant who kept teenage prisoners to sleep with him; Bernhard Domschcke's German-language memoir suggests that some prisoners exchanged favors with guards for better treatment.[33] Documentation of sexual abuse, however, barely registers within the volumes of loving intimacies among prisoners.

With little else to do, sleeping arrangements feature prominently in Andersonville narratives. McElroy, in a lighter moment, remembers organized spooning, including requests from a private to a sergeant, "Let's spoon the other way," with the response "'*Attention!* LEFT SPOON!!' and the whole line would at once flop over on their left sides." But McElroy's playfulness with spooning would turn tragic: "Nightly one of two or three comrades sleeping together would die. The survivors would not know it until they tried to get him to 'spoon' over, when they would find him rigid and motionless. As they could not spare even so little heat as was still contained in his body, they would not remove this, but lie up the closer to it until morning. Such a thing as a boy making an outcry when he discovered his comrade dead, or manifesting any desire to get away from the corpse, was unknown."[34] As this indicates, the men would sleep together in groups: ten was the limit to the tent John Ransom wanted to enter. McElroy's unit began as a fivesome: "The two outside fellows used to get very chilly, and squeeze the three inside ones until they felt no thicker than a wafer. But it had to do, and we took turns sleeping on the outside."[35] In almost every case, these groups were reduced to a pair or revealed themselves to be sets of pairs. McElroy names the foundational unit as "chums." Chums were, McElroy would write, the most important unit of the prisoners' mutual support: "There were thousands of instances of this generous devotion to each other by chums in Andersonville, and I know of nothing that reflects any more credit upon our boy soldiers."[36]

While in McElroy's account the intimacy of these pairs developed in response to the prison conditions and intensified through their needs for survival, the unit preceded the soldiers' capture. In an army camp, the Federal cavalryman "always sleeps with a chum." The pair, rather than sleep with their individual blankets and overcoats, would combine resources to sleep together with more layers.[37] With the staggering death rate at Andersonville, these pairs took on a more life-or-death importance and, as a result, transformed. It was not just that men became dependent, but their self-conception shifted; they identified as the pair, and the pair became the most basic unit of bodily governance.

McElroy narrates a number of chum relationships among the prisoners. One scene that has found a place in histories of US homosexuality involves a Union sailor and his "chicken," a term in Philip Van Buskirk's and others' nautical diaries for the younger sexual partners on shipping and naval vessels.[38] For McElroy, the relationship is "an admirable illustration of the affection which a sailor will lavish on a ship's boy, whom he takes a fancy to, and makes his 'chicken,' as the phrase is. . . . A bright handsome fellow of about fifteen . . . was brought into the Hospital and the old fellow whose 'chicken' he was, was allowed to accompany and nurse him. This 'old barnacle-back' was as surly a growler as ever went aloft, but to his 'chicken' he was as tender and thoughtful as a woman." It is, however, no minority example but representative of the chum relationships that McElroy directly turns to, including his own "chum," whom he found, following this scene, "in a very bad condition." By now, McElroy's fivesome had been reduced to three but would be further reduced with the death of this man: "I lay down beside the body and slept till morning, when I did what little else I could preparing for the grace all that was left of my long-suffering little friend."[39]

McElroy narrates several other examples of chums at Andersonville. There was Ned Johnson, who had been together with his chum Walter Savage for twelve years before Ned lost Walter when their company was captured. Ned's rage to avenge his dead chum becomes suicidal madness as he, surrounded, springs for a guard's pistol to shoot the Confederate. John Emerson and John Stiggall were two Norwegian chums whose "affection for each other" reminded McElroy "of the sworn attachment and the unfailing devotion that were common between two Gothic warrior youths." With Emerson and Stiggall both dying of scurvy, McElroy offered assistance, which was refused because "each seemed actually jealous of any person else doing anything for the other." Chester Hayward "nursed and looked out for George [Hillicks] with wife-like fidelity, and had his reward in bringing him safe through our lines." Another, Bickford, had a partner who died beside him, and he did not move for a week until he joined him.[40] In *Twelve Months in Andersonville*, Long shared a tent with "Charley Weibel, my partner." Suffering from a head wound, Weibel received Long's care as his condition worsened. When Long was transferred out of Andersonville, he recorded, "I was now compelled to leave Weibel for the first time since our imprisonment. Before I left him I took my blanket and fixed him as good a tent as I could, supplied him with water, and there was a young man from Ohio who stayed close to us."[41] The young man took Long's place as Weibel's caretaker until a few days later, when Long was called back to oversee Weibel's death.

The experience at Andersonville of twenty-one-year-old Michigan quartermaster John Ransom included three sets of such relationships, according to his semifictionalized diary written after the war.[42] First, there is George Hendryx, whom Ransom recognized from his company once he arrived in the prison stockade. The following day Hendryx, who was living in a "very good tent, with some nine or ten others," tried to get Ransom a place in the tent. Then, Hendryx "sacrificed his own comfort and lay out doors with me last night and I got along much better than the night before." Five days later, Ransom reported that, with one of the tentmates sent to the hospital, he had "succeeded in getting into the tent with Hendryx." For the next five months, Ransom's was a diary about George Hendryx: Hendryx cooking rations for the prisoners and giving Ransom extra, Hendryx tunneling into the storehouse, Hendryx "foremost in all schemes for freedom," Hendryx resolute in trying again when punished for attempting escape, Hendryx strung up by his thumbs when he gets caught, Hendryx picking fights with the guards and other prisoners and, licked in the fight, "aint so pretty as he was before, but knows more." Hendryx a walking contradiction "who is nothing but a good looking, effeminate boy, fit, you would say, to be going to school, with a mother to look after him, and for not much else. But instead, he is brave, cheerful, smart, watching every chance to get the best of the Johnny Rebs." In April, Hendryx and Ransom attempted an escape together and were caught and returned to their tent within the stockade. When Hendryx was out working at the storeroom Ransom wrote, "Am lonesome since Hendryx went outside." When they were back in the tent together, he wrote about their wrestling, him pinning Hendryx, laughing, and making up after. By June, Hendryx had escaped, and he appears in Ransom's diary only with the refrain "Never have heard one word from Hendryx since his getting away." When Ransom was himself freed, he wrote, "If I had George Hendryx with me now would have a jolly time, and mean to have it as it is."[43]

With Hendryx gone, Ransom's second chum was Battese, "a large full-blooded six-foot Minnesota Indian," whose first name Ransom never learns. Battese took Ransom on to help run the washing business he had established in the stockade as "Battese, Ransom, & Co." When Ransom nearly died from disease, "Battese is an angel; takes better care of me than of himself." Battese created the regimen for Ransom's health, decided against his medical care at the hospital, scrounged for food for the pair, and carried Ransom when Ransom needed to move. While Ransom was in the hospital, Battese was Ransom's near-constant visitor; when absent, Ransom sent Battese notes about his health. "There is no doubt," Ransom concluded, that "he has saved my life, although he will take no credit for it." Transferred away from Battese to a different prison, Ransom was alone but wrote, "Going to be a decidedly cold night, and have 'made up' with two fellows to sleep together." During his lengthy escape he joined a pair of cousins, Eli and David Buck, and they formed a group of three as intimate as the pairs above. Eli scrounged for food; Ransom repaired their clothes; and David was the acknowledged leader.[44]

No other pair, not even Ransom and Hendryx, gets the extended treatment that McElroy gives to the relationship with his foremost chum, Bezaleel Andrews. "Andrews and I," or "Lale" and "Mc," as the unit is rendered, are the final two remaining in McElroy's initial sleeping fivesome. With the scarcity of resources that defined the experience at Andersonville, the pair shared their goods and "retain[ed] possession of [their] little can, spoon, chess-board, blanket and overcoat." They schemed to steal boards and build a new house together, of which McElroy writes, "We were owners of a brown stone front on Fifth Avenue compared to the other fellows." Andrews found a shirt for McElroy; McElroy remarked on finding a silver coin: "I hurried off to tell Andrews of our unexpected good fortune."[45] We might imagine that the scarce resources at Andersonville resulted in two possible ways of living: an individual war of all against all or a sense of collective responsibility. Instead, we find pairs devoted to each other, whose sense of self-protection and responsibility to others outside that unit varied. That relationship structures the plot of McElroy's memoir as, through their time at Andersonville, and through the narrative, they do nothing less than form a life together.

This formation occurs at two levels of language, first, in a patois between the pair—"Andrews communicated to me by an expressive signal, of which soldiers campaigning together as long as he and I had, always have an extensive and well understood code"—and second, in the memoir's narrative. Over the course of that narrative, McElroy's first-person pronoun becomes a unit, "Andrews and I," a unit that overtakes the individuality of the memoir's protagonist. In the final half of the novel, the narrator is "Andrews and I" or "Andrews and me" more frequently than he is "I" or "me." At one point near the end of the narrative, McElroy and Andrews go into "Committee of the Whole Upon the State of Our Stomachs."[46] In the joke, one we imagine within the pair's patois, the role of their pairing as social unit becomes clear: their two bodies as jointly conceived in relation to their survival, a survival rendered as bureaucratic metaphor. That metaphor emphasized the pairs of Union chums as an argument for a suitably caring relationship between government and its veterans.

This state was not permanent; their freedom meant a new crisis disrupting the established social body. Andrews and McElroy struggled at first with "all this radical change in our habits": Andrews "feared that it was rushing things too fast." In their first night of freedom at the Union camp, McElroy feared that proximity to the other Union soldiers risked capture for Andrews and him: "Shivering at this thought, absurd though it was, I arose from our bed and taking Andrews with me, crawled two or three hundred yards into a dense undergrowth, where in the event of our lines being forced, we would be overlooked." On the boat to take them north, they remained inseparable; "Andrews and I found a snug place under the forecastle."[47] But when fully away from Andersonville, they did, in fact, separate. So, too, did all of the chums. The postbellum period represented for nearly all of those who survived a new mode of existence and relation to one another. Many lived far apart, and nearly all of the named survivors would marry after the war and have children.[48] With these afterlives, the Andersonville narrative appears, retrospectively, as a wartime crucible of development, an intense homosociality that gives way to marital maturity.

Andersonville Chums in Reconciliation Culture

For all the literary merit of McElroy's narrative, it is highly derivative of earlier memoirs. McElroy repeats episodes, anecdotes, commentaries, and rhythms of events from the set of 1865–66 prisoner-of-war narratives. Most of these include scenes of intimacy among prisoners, including chums sharing blankets, spooning, and experiencing the death of comrades.[49] Nor are such scenes unique to the prisoner experience. Postbellum efforts to create standard accounts of soldiers' daily lives, such as John Billings's 1887 *Hardtack and Coffee* for the Union side and Carlton McCarthy's 1899 *Detailed Minutiæ of Soldier Life in the Army of Northern Virginia* for the Confederate, both follow McElroy's descriptions of blanket-sharing chums.[50] Clearly the intense homosociality of army life, even for a homosocial society, stood out as remarkable in soldiers' memories. Where McElroy's and the other memoirs of the 1870s and 1880s differ from those immediately following the war is in the sentimental power of these intimacies.

The 1865–66 memoirs celebrate chum relationships as necessary for survival, often in sentimental description. But that sentimentality in these narratives is not reserved for such relationships between friends. For example, the most celebrated intimacy, and tragic death, in Goss's 1866 memoir is that of a young soldier, Willard Robinson, "while lying under the same blanket with his father."⁵¹ The heartbreaking refusal by Confederate officers to let the father bury his son adopts a tone that McElroy would reserve for relationships between chums. Thus, we can track how depictions of male intimacies intensify in the second wave of prisoner-of-war memoirs in the 1870s and 1880s. As the culture of reconciliation took hold, these memoirs became, Blight writes, a "vexing subject," reopening wounds rather than healing them.⁵² For his part, McElroy concluded his narrative with an indictment of reconciliation culture, damning the "maudlin confusion of ideas as now threatens to obliterate all distinction between the men who fought and died for the Right and those who resisted them for the Wrong."⁵³ At the same time, McElroy's narrative had already shifted significantly away from an emancipationist account of the war, toward one that put the bodies of white male soldiers at its center. Moreover, McElroy's male intimacies set the stage for a new iteration of prisoner-of-war narratives, primarily in fiction, in line with the reconciliation spirit.

Homoerotic depictions persisted, less in service of state care for Union prisoners than in service of sentimental reunion. For example, Herbert W. Collingwood's 1889 novel, *Andersonville Violets: A Story of Northern and Southern Life*, narrated the prisoner-of-war experience but in a way, as one review put it, "unmarred by partisan feeling."⁵⁴ "Such stories," claimed another, "go far to banish forever the 'bloody shirt.'"⁵⁵ Born in Massachusetts in 1857, Collingwood was a generation removed from the Andersonville prisoners he fictionalizes.⁵⁶ His novel follows a Union veteran and a Confederate veteran in the years after the war. The Confederate veteran had been dishonorably discharged from the service for refusing to shoot the Union veteran when they were guard and prisoner, respectively, at Andersonville. Because of the dishonorable discharge, his fiancée calls off their engagement and refuses to speak to him. The surviving Union veteran moves south with his wife after the war to take charge of a plantation, where they befriend the ex-Confederate. The Union veteran's wife convinces the ex-fiancée that the ex-Confederate's refusal to shoot was honorable, saving her now husband's life. The fiancée then reunites with the Confederate veteran, and the novel ends with the two married pairs as cross-sectional friends.

The novel begins, however, in Andersonville and sentimentalizes the circumstances of the Confederate veteran's initial heroism. The Confederate guard watches two prisoners, John and Archie, nicknamed the "Babes in the Woods" because the larger soldier was always carrying the "little, delicate fellow, with golden hair and a face like a girl's." John was in love with Archie's sister, but Archie appears to have taken her place: "Archie was just like her—so

John thought as he watched from the shadow. Small and slender, with blue eyes and hair like gold." Archie has promised John that his sister will marry him: "She can't help saying 'yes' for we have been such chums."[57] In a feverish delirium before he dies, Archie asks John to pick for his sister some violets, growing just beyond the deadline. It is while John is in the act of picking the flowers that the Confederate soldier cannot bring himself to shoot him—the sentimentality of the violets contrasting with the violence of the war. Archie's death convinces his sister to marry John. The plot is then of a pattern discussed in the next chapter, where an intense antebellum or wartime male intimacy gives way after the war to one death and one heterosexual marriage. In the case of *Andersonville Violets*, the sentimental power of such a story is narrated within the novel itself, for the later reconciliationist sentimentality hinges on the Confederate soldier having been so moved by this display of male-male devotion that he no longer continues fighting the war.

Former prisoners of war remained a potent reconciliationist symbol for postbellum literary culture. Constance Fenimore Woolson sets her reconciliationist story "Rodman the Keeper" on the hallowed ground of a former Confederate prison in Georgia, obviously referring to Andersonville. She reverses the suffering: it is the Confederate soldier who languishes on the erstwhile prison grounds, the object of a Union veteran's care. Their intimacy, bonding over shared experiences of female betrayal, contrasts with the failed romance-of-reunion plot between the Union veteran and a Southern white woman who cannot forgive him for the defeat of her compatriots, her persistent bitterness a remaining gulf in true national reconciliation. When the Northerner imagines a dead Union soldier admonishing him for crossing the Bloody Chasm to care for a former enemy, he defends himself: "This is merely a question between man and man." Woolson's story suggests that reconciliation is possible only on these terms, not just of individual care rather than national policies but also of the care of one white man for another.[58] As such, Woolson's story responds almost directly to McElroy's; if his evocation of Andersonville intimacies reminds readers that the conflict was between "Right" and "Wrong," her portrait aims to bury that conflict, both the Union and Confederate dead, in the same ground where flowers of reconciliation may bloom.

Even where not directly reconciliationist, Andersonville narratives could serve as an amorphous symbol of an intimate feeling with former soldiers, even for those who had not been imprisoned at Andersonville. For example, throughout the 1890s a man named Ralph Orr Bates would deliver a lecture about his escape from Andersonville. A version of that lecture published by his widow in 1910, titled *Billy and Dick from Andersonville Prison to the White House*, suggested that he had been giving the lecture since 1868. On the inside cover of the book is a request to send money to Bates's widow, Rozella, who, having married Bates after 1890, was not receiving his pension and had payments to meet. The book begins and ends with "unsolicited endorsements" attesting to the veracity of the story and Bates's identity as the titular Billy. A 1951 article titled "The Calvin Bates Fraud" lays to bed any possible claims, demonstrating several errors in the book's chronology and the absence of several individuals named in the book on regimental rosters.[59]

Despite its fabrication, *Billy and Dick* retains as its heroic unit the paired Union prisoners, between whom, randomly chained together by the Confederate guards, "there sprang into existence a friendship and love surpassing the love of woman." Billy and Dick are inseparable in the narrative; following the agreement "that all who got outside should try to escape in pairs," they flee through northern Alabama together and, with the help of an enslaved woman, make it to Ohio. Gen. William T. Sherman is as rapt by the pair's story as postwar culture was by the story of Andersonville: "Towards the close his face flushed with excitement and anger, the veins on his forehead were swollen and his whole nervous organization was strung to its highest tension." Sherman sends the pair, still in rags, to the White House to tell their story to President Abraham Lincoln. Lincoln listens to their story, telegraphs Ralph's father, Calvin, orders the pair washed and fed, weighs each of them personally, walks them to their White House bedroom, visits them in bed, and pinches them while introducing them to Mrs. Lincoln.[60] Of course, *Billy and Dick* is all a fantasy, but what is being fantasized is the intimacy between the head of state and the bodies of these paired prisoners.

Andersonville Chums in the Twentieth Century

The reconciliationist Andersonville story persisted through the twentieth century. There is never just one moment for Andersonville's return to popular attention, but after each major US war, a new story of Andersonville appears in a new genre: a poem in 1928 after the First World War that contemplates Andersonville as a story of national emergence, a novel in 1955 that contemplates the prison camp as a version of the German concentration camp, a Broadway play in 1959 that considers the just-following-orders defense by Wirz in light of the Nuremberg trials, a televised performance of that play in 1970 that reconsiders the same question in light of the US war in Vietnam, and a 1996 made-for-TV movie that returns to the story of national triumph over non-US figures like the Swiss (but truly German) commandant and the immigrant villains in the camp.[61] The story of male-male intimacy persists through many of these iterations.

For example, when Stephen Vincent Benét told the story of the Civil War as one of national progress in his 1928 epic poem *John Brown's Body*, imprisonment at Andersonville is a central scene. Benét's Pulitzer Prize–winning poem attempted an American *Aeneid*, a birth of a nation in which the Civil War perfects the aims of the American Revolution, with the modern North vanquishing a feudal South. John Brown is no hero but a necessary martyr for the progress of the American idea. Andersonville figures as the barbarity of the Southern aristocracy, exemplified by contrasts: "A Georgia belle eats sherbet near Andersonville / Where the Union prisoners rot." Jack Ellyat, one of the poem's Union soldiers, experiences the crucible of national transformation while imprisoned at Andersonville in relation to his fellow soldier Charley Bailey—known as "Bailey" in all other parts of the poem, "Charley" only in the prison scenes or when his lover Soph calls out during an embrace, "Oh Charley!" Ellyat hates Bailey at first, is repulsed by Bailey's assistance and touch, but reconsiders: "Had he ever hated Bailey? It could not have been. / He loved Bailey better than anything else in the world." Bailey's and Ellyat's common care for the other constitutes the Andersonville prison world in the poem. As they weakly lie together in their tent, Bailey first considers carrying the feeble Ellyat out in an attempt to escape. Then, watching the sleeping Ellyat, he "rose with great care. / 'I'll get you some water,' he muttered. 'No, let you sleep.' / He sat down again and stared at the sleeping face."[62] While this doesn't have the same intensity as the memoirs, it is clear that when Benét wanted to convey the intimacy between Union soldiers, he staged the scene inside a tent inside the stockade at Andersonville.

Similarly, when MacKinlay Kantor draws on prisoners' stories for his 1955 Pulitzer Prize–winning novel, *Andersonville*, he too narrates homoerotic intimacies. Drawing from Ransom's memoir, Kantor writes positively that "John Ransom was loved and tended by a mighty Indian from Minnesota named Baptiste, called Bateese by all." Otherwise, he evokes homoeroticism in decidedly negative portrayals. Drawing on the "chicken" relationship in McElroy's memoir, Kantor describes a "mincing" sailor boy and his older protector, who is "far beyond the practice of sodomy." Two other prisoners gossip about "a seaman and his chicken," and their "corn-holing," as a practice of a distinct minority: "I didn't say *all* the sailors. I just said some of them."[63] Hewing closely to the prisoners' accounts to construct his novel, Kantor cannot ignore the homoerotic intimacies, but he rewrites this nineteenth-century homoeroticism as a 1950s version of minority, deviant homosexual identity.

Kantor's novel equally represents a rewriting of the Andersonville story refracted through the Second World War. Kantor remodels the Confederate prison camp as German concentration camps and prison commandant Henry Wirz as a Nazi bureaucrat in the style of Adolf Eichmann.[64] Just as the Nazi version of Wirz represented the novel's postwar update, so must the homosexuality of Kantor's novel include 1950s homosexual predators. Kantor's "homosexuals," a minority of prisoners who threaten the all-male prison camp, are postwar deviants: when "one of the homosexuals crawled close to importune" a sleeping soldier who kicked him, "the homosexual screamed like a frightened spinster and told Edward he was perfectly horrid."[65] Kantor's named-as-such homosexuals, however, read like an alibi for the patent homoeroticism displayed by its central male characters, especially in his plot of cross-sectional reunion.

That plot, like that of *Andersonville Violets* and Woolson's "Rodman the Keeper," relies on the intimacies between a Union man and a Confederate man, a relationship Kantor compares to an interracial marriage. In the woods outside of Andersonville, a Confederate who has lost his right leg meets an escaped Union prisoner who has lost his right arm. The two overcome sectional prejudice to care for each other. To conceal the Union soldier in the woods, the Confederate dresses the Union soldier in his grandmother's clothes and tells his mother that the soldier, Nazareth, is a Black woman with whom he is having an affair. Once the Confederate is able to walk again on a wooden leg, and the Yankee is healed and rationed for a journey north, the pair must part, the Yankee saying as he leaves, "Don't you get too gay, Reb," and the Reb, now alone, "sobbing, momentarily without hope. God damn it, Naz, don't go way."[66] Even with all its 1950s homophobic disavowals, Kantor's symbol of national reconciliation remains the sentimentalized intimacy between cross-sectional soldiers in contrast to the homosexual deviants populating his prison camp.

More recently, the 1996 made-for-TV movie *Andersonville* developed similar themes of national reunion through tropes of male intimacy. This *Andersonville* followed the 1990s surge of popularity for Civil War narratives, beginning with James McPherson's 1988 narrative history *Battle Cry of Freedom*, then Ken Burns's 1990 documentary miniseries *The Civil War* and Turner Pictures' 1993 film *Gettysburg*.[67] Following the success of this film, Ted Turner produced a film about the Andersonville prison camp for Turner Network Television.[68] The movie's initial account of the Civil War follows McPherson's as an abolitionist war against slavery, but the real aim of the film, and what its fans enjoyed most, was its supposed verisimilitude. *Andersonville* included many actors involved in the then-booming hobby of Civil War reenactment, as documented in Tony Horwitz's 1998 *Confederates in the Attic*. Filmed near the site of the actual Georgia prison, with an enormous set built to resemble the prison and with actors experienced as reenactors, the film strives for nothing so much as what Horwitz terms "the quest for the elusive 'period rush.'"[69] As such, political and ideological history drop out in the quest for authenticity and the celebration of Civil War combatants following the principle that as long as they were Americans, they were the good guys. Therefore, the immigrants in the camp are villains to the real American soldiers trying to keep the order, but they are not so villainous as the exaggeratedly German Nazi Wirz. A Confederate officer, played by a sympathetic William H. Macy, even attempts to intervene against Wirz, the foreigner singularly responsible, so the film suggests, for bringing a death camp to America.

Some of the bizarre acclaim among enthusiasts for the film has to do with one conspicuous fact: there are no women in it. Or in a more politic version, as one online viewer review has it, "There are no romantic plot lines or even women in the movie." The review continues, "If you enjoy war films that are not cluttered with cliché romantic plots and are more like buddy films this one is for you."[70] *Andersonville* operates as woman-free fantasy partly through an obliviousness to how gay it appears. Only within the specific 1990s context where male homosexuality seemed definitionally segregated from the kind of male military service represented in the film could the film get away with the touching and head-resting and commitments of devotion between men. That 1990s surge of Civil War content also entailed an intense fascination with white male bodies. Horwitz memorably opens *Confederates in the Attic* by joining the Confederate reenactors in spooning, with the orders called out to turn—a practice clearly derived from Billings's *Hardtack* or McElroy's *Andersonville*. Musing on his first immersion into "hardcore" Confederate reenacting, Horwitz writes, "Eavesdropping on the chat—about grooming, sewing, hip size, honed biceps—I couldn't help wondering if I'd stumbled on a curious gay subculture in the Piedmont of Virginia."[71] For a devoted set of reenactors, verisimilitude involved an obsessive idealization of the Confederate male body, gaunt and rail thin, peaking during a "Civil Wargasm."[72] *Andersonville*, the TV movie, shares with the culture Horwitz describes both the celebrated male intimacies and the fascination with the suffering body of the white male soldier.

That movie has a second conspicuous absence. There are also almost no Black people in the film, with one exception: the film opens with a train carrying prisoners to Andersonville that passes enslaved people at a Georgia plantation. The film's attention moves quickly to the suffering of the white soldiers in the prison and stays with them. The war may have begun to resolve the crisis of slavery; the suffering of the war, however, was felt not by the enslaved but by these white soldiers. The film's attention on the authentic suffering of soldiers, emphasized through the physical contact of these suffering bodies, thus accomplishes the same shift in attention as the images in *Harper's* and the shift from antislavery literature to prisoner memoirs: from the victimized body of the enslaved to the victimized body of the white male soldier.

CHAPTER 5

Chums before the War

HOW TWO VERSIONS OF
HOMOSEXUALITY MADE MEANING
OF CIVIL WAR HISTORY

Y THE SUMMER OF 1866, Republicans were worried about the terms of national reunion. Politicians rallying behind President Andrew Johnson's Reconstruction policies, including amnesty for Confederates and vetoes of the Freedmen's Bureau Bill and Civil Rights Bill, organized a National Union Convention in Philadelphia to build support for the president's allies in the 1866 midterm elections. When the convention opened with the South Carolina governor, James Orr, and the failed Democratic candidate for Massachusetts governor, Gen. Darius Couch, parading with linked arms, Republicans mocked this North-South reunion sentiment as "the Arm-in-Arm Convention."[1] The pages of *Harper's Weekly* caricatured the parade of former combatants alongside improbable animal pairs, such as a dog with a cat and a cat with a mouse.[2] The magazine's cartoonist, Thomas Nast, gave a full page to mock the convention's crocodile tears: one corner depicting "the Spirit of Concord and Brotherly Affection" had the Southern-sympathizing Northern Copperheads and Southern proponents of states' rights locking not just arms but lips on the convention floor.[3]

For Nast, during Johnson's presidency, the image of a kiss between former enemies attacked the worst of presidential Reconstruction policy, a maudlin reconciliation undoing the accomplishments of the war and the sacrifices

Former combatants, North and South, kiss in Thomas Nast's caricature of the so-called Arm-in-Arm Convention, organized to support President Johnson's policies of postbellum reconciliation. Detail of Thomas Nast, "The Tearful Convention," *Harper's Weekly*, September 29, 1866, 617. Library of Congress.

of the Union dead. Such use of an image of same-sex romance to criticize reconciliationist policies was, however, exceptional in the period, especially in contrast to its opposite. In the decades after the Civil War, narratives of same-sex romance between Northern and Southern men aimed precisely for the spirit that Nast's cartoon mocked, the sentimental embrace between men of the North and South.

A novel published a year before the Union Convention, James K. Hosmer's *The Thinking Bayonet*, featured, in a central scene, a kiss between a Confederate soldier and a Union soldier. In a Confederate prison camp, the two men said farewell: "Hands for a moment on one another's shoulders; bearded faces, damp with the rain now falling, coming together under the dark in a kiss." At a college in Massachusetts, the pair had been intimates who, as a classmate wrote, "have a love for one another, almost surpassing the love of women." They broke up over the issue of slavery, when the Southerner returned to his family's slave plantation in Louisiana and the Northerner became involved in Massachusetts abolitionism. The Southerner enlisted in the Confederate army, declaring, "I hate the North . . . and yet the only man I ever loved was a Northerner." Coincidentally overhearing this declaration, the Northerner resolved to fight his onetime friend: "I say it while I love him."[4] The prison kiss was their last. The novel ends with the Southerner, his Confederacy, and their romantic friendship all dead, deaths necessary both for national reunion and for the Northerner's eventual heterosexual marriage.

Hosmer, a Harvard graduate who served as an infantryman in the Union army in the campaign for the southern Mississippi River, narrated the war as the destruction of romantic bonds between white men. The novel's antebellum atmosphere romanticized their nostalgic intimacy, strained equally by their advancement beyond college and by the sectional conflict. Even then, the novel suggested that a paired adulthood was impossible, requiring the Civil War's intervention to end it. The war transformed their intimacy to a thing possible only in the past, ruptured by death and supplanted by marriage.

While antebellum white men celebrated romantic friendship as the stabilizing foundation of the fraternity of white manhood, postbellum novelists like Hosmer imagined these friendships within a developmental framework that moved from youthful intimacies to disunion to adult heterosexuality. In these novels, the Civil War became an event within a trajectory of male development, necessary for the maturation from youthful homoeroticism to adult heterosexuality. Such a framework enabled writers such as Hosmer to navigate incongruities between emotional reconciliation and political reunion.[5] Unlike stories concluding with North-South marriages that modeled emotional reconciliation, stories of romantic friends' disunion oriented emotions toward a lost past. The more intense the intimacies between the two young men, the more the war appeared as the tragic loss of a past that, no matter how desired, cannot return. The closer the men advanced toward the impossibility of a same-sex paired adulthood, the more the war appeared as fatalistically preordained for antebellum society. These novels, then, offered an interpretation of the war as both tragic and necessary.

Hosmer's same-sex romance interpreted the war and its aftermath in opposition to Nast's 1866 interpretation. By treating the war as a tragedy for the relations between white men that is nonetheless necessary for national maturation, Hosmer's interpretation aligns most with that of the early twentieth-century historians of the war and Reconstruction trained by Columbia professor William A. Dunning. The Dunning School is notorious now for its racist presuppositions and for treating the white supremacist enemies of Reconstruction as the heroes of the era, but its chief historiographic innovation was integrating the tragedy of Reconstruction into the postbellum story of national economic development.[6] Hosmer was also an early twentieth-century historian with a significant connection to Dunning. The most influential synthesis of Dunning's interpretation was his 1907 single-volume *Reconstruction, Political and Economic: 1865–1877*, volume 22 in Albert Bushnell Hart's *American Nation* series. For the preceding volumes, Hart wanted, as Dunning wrote for *Reconstruction*, "the standard brief history of the Civil War viewed as a national and not simply a military episode."[7] His choice for writer, then, was a Union veteran turned historian whose Civil War novel's central scene was a kiss between a Union and Confederate soldier. Forty-two years after *The Thinking Bayonet*, Hosmer published *The Appeal to Arms, 1861–1863* and *Outcome of the Civil War, 1863–1865* in the *American Nation* series.

Unlike his 1865 novel, Hosmer's history contains no cross-sectional kisses; nonetheless, his history plays out at grand scale the relationship between his male heroes. Just as the Northerner was taken in by aggressive, radical abolitionist voices, so too was the North led into the war. The Southern aristocrat misperceived his own power from his cotton plantation and launched a misguided effort to defend slavery. Like *The Thinking Bayonet*, Hosmer's history made the war primarily about the intensity of feeling between white men. To be sure, Hosmer's interpretation was not the product of having written the war as a homoerotic disunion, but both his novel and history emphasized the disagreement over slavery as destructive to the happy-but-doomed union between white men while, at the same time, necessary for national maturation. As such, Hosmer's history of the war, volumes 20 and 21 of Hart's series, served as the literal and ideological prequel to Dunning's volume 22.

This chapter covers the roughly forty years for which Hosmer's novel and two-volume history serve as bookends, from war novels that established homoerotic narratives of disunited friends to the Dunning School interpretation in the early twentieth century. During this same period, massive changes to the understanding of sex took hold that introduced a science of sexual perversions and the birth of homosexuality as a pathologized identity. The US doctors and psychologists who developed the field of sexual science in the late 1880s and 1890s drew on the history of the Civil War. Sexologists linked what they saw as the new, increasing problem of urban homosexuality to the social transformations wrought by postbellum development. These developments in sexual science would not only have far-reaching effects in the twentieth century but would also determine the interpretation of the history of the nineteenth. Such effects are clear in the differences between James Ford Rhodes, a Civil War historian writing largely before this science was popularized, and the historians trained by Dunning, who were writing after. Where Rhodes wrote of Union victory as the triumph of sexual morality over a sexual chaos, the Dunning School historians wrote Northern victory as ushering in an era of perverse sexuality. The resulting narrative was a sexualized history of the Civil War's social transformation: the antebellum period and war itself were associated with the sentimentalized romances between men, and the postbellum period was associated with the increasing threat of homosexuality.

Both of these versions of homosexuality were racialized. The sexual scientists of the 1890s categorized homosexual characteristics and racial traits analogously as perversions with overlapping case studies. At the same time, the nostalgic intimacies in Civil War narratives from 1865 to the next century romanticized the loss of the antebellum order of racialized plantation slavery. As in the film *The Birth of a Nation*, discussed in the introduction, these two homosexualities were triangulated with the figure of the Black male rapist, a figure itself developed by sexologists' interpretations of Civil War history.[8] Like the nostalgic depictions of plantation slavery itself, the chums' youthful antebellum romance contrasted the deviant sexualities of postbellum society. What these narratives achieved, perversely, was the linking of a lost homoeroticism with the Confederacy's Lost Cause as a sanctified, longed-for past that cannot return.

Two College Friends in Postbellum Literature

Postbellum romantic friendship novels, such as Hosmer's *The Thinking Bayonet*, continued the long-standing American tradition of presenting intimate male friendships as emblematic of a gendered and racialized imagined national identity. During and after the Civil War, narratives of ruptured intimacies between white men were one way that postbellum culture grappled with the "imagined fraternity of white men" after disunion.[9] Hosmer's novel commences a distinct rise in the use of disrupted male friendship as a feature of fictional plots from the Civil War to the end of the nineteenth century. These novels, as literary scholar Axel Nissen accounts for them, not only share the feature of an intimate, eroticized relationship between two male characters but also treat the rupture of these friendships as the primary problem for the plot's resolution. Nearly all of the novels Nissen documents from 1861 to 1895 end with the end of the friendship, by death, marriage, or, frequently, both.[10]

As such, these novels were drawing on the predominant understanding of how male-male intimacy operated, a developmental model in which an intense youthful intimacy gave way to marriage to a woman.[11] That marital ending resembles the postbellum narratives examined by Nina Silber and others, in which marriage, often cross-sectional, sentimentalized national reunion. But Hosmer's novel, and the broader set of disrupted romantic friendship novels of which it is an example, adds to the story of national progress the deeper sadness of a lost romance. The homoerotic nature of that romance, within the developmental framework, made its rupture inevitable. The trajectory of male development required a Civil War for the inevitable death of one friend and the inevitable heterosexual maturity of the other.

These novels, then, are less about exploring the status of male-male intimacy and sex than they are using homoeroticism to make a political argument about the postbellum United States. As such, the Civil War looms large in novels of romantic friendship, and romantic friendship is an especially prevalent trope in postbellum novels.[12] For the literary realists among these novelists, a romantic friendship's dissolution allowed for meditation on the generic transition from romanticism to realism.[13] For example, William Dean Howells's 1874 novel *Private Theatricals* narrates a separation of minds from the union of two Union army veterans, romantic friends who became attached and laid the seeds for their disaffection during the war. The scenes of their unraveling friendship are also the most intensely homoerotic scenes in the novel. The comrades' previous wartime attachment becomes its own argument for a resentful shame between them, as one reflects, "A stifling recollection of the delicacy, passing the love of women, with which they have always treated each other smote upon him."[14] The romantic friendship appears to contain its own self-destruction, as if, in the light of Howells's realism, a romantic friendship could not survive the war. But the death of romantic friendships in novels did not correlate with their absence from fiction—much the opposite. Romantic friendships are most prolific in the fiction of this postwar moment because narrating romantic friendship's destruction exemplifies a novel's realist orientation.[15]

Postbellum novels of ruptured romantic friendships also provided an interpretation of the war as an event simultaneously personal and national. An early example, Mary Jane Haw's *The Rivals*, written in 1864 when Confederate victory still seemed possible, used the rupture of two Virginian male intimates, compared by West Point classmates to the Biblical intimates "Jonathan and David," as allegory of Confederate independence. Introduced with arms around each other's necks "in the familiar and affectionate manner so common to boys who are particular friends," they, like the friends in Hosmer's novel, split with the war.[16] After invading his homeland, the Unionist friend dies regretfully, a regret the author hopes will stand in for the Federal war effort. The Confederate survives, forgives his dying friend, and marries a woman for whose affection the pair once rivaled, predicting the breakup and independence that would constitute Confederate success.

Immediately after the war, two other Confederate-aligned novels, Augusta Jane Evans's *St. Elmo* (1866) and Sidney Lanier's *Tiger-Lilies* (1867), employ the dissolution of romantic friendships to make sense of Confederate defeat. Though Evans would remain a Confederate partisan after the war, her novel used the memory of a romantic male pair as an allegory for forgiving the men who led the Southern states into a "fratricidal war." That the killing of one friend by the novel's eponymous hero in a duel followed the intensity of passion between them (as he says, "There was not a dream of my brain, a hope of my heart which was not confided to him. I reverenced, I trusted, I almost—nay I quite worshipped him!") exonerates St. Elmo's moral status in the eyes of the novel's heroine.[17] St. Elmo's personality transforms in the novel from the passion of that romantic friendship to an embrace of a sober heterosexual partnership, through which the novel narrates the development of the Southern men who started the failed war as they mature away from intense wartime passions. Lanier's *Tiger-Lilies* uses the end of a male-male intimacy as representative of the social transformation wrought by the war. Lanier's novel demonstrates the same trend of Civil War transformation of literary style from the overwrought, florid, prewar romanticism into a terse, plain, postwar realism. A romantic friendship in which two men fall in love "with the ardor of a friendship-at-first sight" forms part of Lanier's romanticized antebellum atmosphere, one that gives way, in the final third, to the war realism of bodies "emaciated to a skeleton" and an atmosphere in which romanticized friendship is no longer possible.[18]

If disunion between romantic friends was a way for realists to write about how the war had transformed society and for Southern writers to make sense of Confederate defeat, the Union veteran Hosmer used the plot to explain victory—both the rupture that precipitated it and the violence to Southern whites it required—as an inevitable development. The title phrase, "thinking bayonets," had, during the previous year's presidential election, described how the experience of the war solidified soldiers' support for Lincoln and the war effort. The thinking in the novel is that of Herbert, the Union soldier hero, as he philosophizes on the justifications for war. The evocative title has been a focus of the little scholarly treatment the novel has received. Because of that focus, and because of the novel's convoluted epistolary style, its central same-sex romance has not received attention.[19] But that plot, too, addresses the themes in the title, for, in committing to war, Herbert must justify war against "the same dear warm heart that he was when we slept together when we were boys." Following the common abolitionist argument that slavery degraded the slaveholders, Herbert resolved to fight the man he loved, treating antislavery politics like an intervention to a Southern beloved: we are confronting you about slavery because we love you.[20]

Herbert's war experience represents an extended crisis in the transition of his romantic interest from Claiborne to his eventual wife, Leonora. Leonora and Claiborne were two of three love interests for Herbert. After his disunion with Claiborne and a failed early romance with Leonora, Herbert fled west and became a coal miner. There he met a third-best companion on top of him in a narrow mine shaft. Herbert wrote about the man whom he had taken "in place of Claiborne and Leonora" that "I may enjoy sometime getting my arms about his neck, as I used to with Claiborne."[21] These three potential partners for Herbert, far from divided into heterosexual or homosexual orientations, are treated as equal options. But Herbert's old affection for Claiborne persists during the war, returning most forcefully during their farewell kiss in the Confederate prison camp. Having leveraged his proximity to Claiborne in order to escape the prison and return to his regiment, Herbert soon engages Claiborne in the final battle scene. Claiborne shoots Herbert in the groin but is captured and thrown from a third story to his death following an argument about slavery.

As the war experience intensifies the commitment of Lincoln's thinking bayonets to the war effort, so does Hosmer's combat and injury intensify his commitment to Leonora and, with her, a family unit upon which the national future depends. While that marital ending is moralized, it is not moralized in contrast to Herbert's homoerotic relationship with Claiborne. Instead, the chastening and purification at the end of the novel, emphasized by the suggestive imagery of Herbert's injury to the groin, stands in opposition to revelations about Claiborne's sexual contact with enslaved people. When occupying Claiborne's family's plantation, Herbert discovers not only that Claiborne had been having sexual relationships with enslaved women but also that, because his father had been guilty of the same crime, Claiborne's interracial relationships are incestuous. Claiborne's crime is not merely interracial sex but the threat of an impure contagion (similar to Van Buskirk's attitudes about a white Southern object of his desire, as discussed in the first chapter), and Herbert's heterosexual union purifies the racialized sexual exposure of Claiborne's connection to slavery. In the end, the object of the Civil War was to cure Claiborne's sexual immorality and to sanctify the memory of Claiborne and Herbert's relationship against threats of racialized sexuality.

Homer White's 1873 novel *The Norwich Cadets* follows Hosmer's premise, albeit with less physical affection between its cross-sectional "chums." Tom Lyon, from Vermont, "a staunch republican and anti-slavery man," and Bill Wolfe, from Georgia, "a Breckinridge democrat and pro-slavery man," are "inseparable companions" and "devoted friends" at the Norwich University military academy. Their "very close fellowship" and "strong bond of union" is tested when Wolfe follows his state of Georgia and joins the Confederate Army. In their first encounter as combatants, the pair lowers their swords as respective comrades sweep them from the field. Like Herbert in *The Thinking Bayonet*, Lyon finds himself imprisoned in a Confederate camp, visited by his old school chum. Instead of a kiss between the pair, Wolfe brings along his sister, and, signaling the war's transformative power, Lyon feels himself "transferring his affection from the brother to the sister."[22] *The Norwich Cadets* differs from the other postbellum chum narratives in that it keeps both heroes alive at the war's end, though each is presumed dead at different points in the narrative. In a decidedly racist story line, an enslaved man, Caesar, demonstrates his devotion to both his former enslaver and his enslaver's chum when nursing both back to health. With the war over, Wolfe mostly shrugs off Confederate defeat—little of his world appears changed. Caesar returns, willingly, to the role of dependent. Wolfe's sister marries his best friend. He and that friend become partners, opening a law firm together. Like the other chum narratives, the romantic friendship transforms with the war into a heterosexual union; instead of one chum's death, their friendship persists in the form of a professional partnership.

Frederick Loring's *Two College Friends*, published two years before *The Norwich Cadets*, is perhaps the most patent in its homoeroticism. Named upon its discovery in the 1990s as "a gay Civil War novel," it tells of Ned and his "chum" Tom, who leave Harvard to enlist in the Union army.[23] Their regiment engages Stonewall Jackson's army, and the friends, an unconscious Tom and a conscious Ned, are captured as prisoners. Ned escapes, carrying Tom back to Union lines, then returns himself, out of honor and obligation, to Jackson, to give up his life, he says, in recompense for Tom's. In contrast to *The Thinking Bayonet*, *Two College Friends* illustrates homosexuality's nineteenth-century evolution. Whereas male and female partners are equal alternatives for Herbert's companionship, Ned's love for Tom is cast as an exclusive alternative to heterosexual marriage and a lifelong orientation predetermined by traits within Ned. What stands out in the presentation of Ned's sexuality, through Ned's anxiety about a heterosexual adulthood for himself ("I wonder if I shall ever care for any woman as much as I do for Tom") and for Tom ("I never will go near his wife—I shall hate her"), is Ned's sense of an impossibly doomed future.[24] It is this sense—the impossibility of a future without or with Tom—that makes Ned's sacrificial death necessary to the plot and the Civil War necessary insofar as it resolves the crisis of his sexuality.

What is most surprising, however, about *Two College Friends* is not its clear homoerotic content—no one comes to the novel now unless directed to it as a gay text—but how strongly Ned flirts with switching sides. His stated admiration for the enemy general makes Ned think he might join "Stonewall Jackson, and learn how to fight." What accounts for this nonpartisan sentiment? His love for Tom, not the Union, was always the cause for which he fought. When Jackson asks Ned why he deserted the Union in order to return to Confederate punishment, Ned responds, "I have only one person in the world to care for: I have no family, no relatives, only this one friend"—or, no other soldiers, no army, no Union, and certainly no emancipatory cause. As in postwar cross-sectional romances, a higher law of sentimentality has supplanted the politics of sectional antagonism. In Loring's homoerotic romance, however, it is not a postwar conciliation but a wartime breakup, emphasizing the impossibility of sustaining the antebellum order. As others die to make men free, Ned dies to ensure another man lives to marry and have children. What has been celebrated by present-day readers as wartime gay male affection is more accurately about the impossibility, in adulthood and after the war, of gay affection. The final scene of the pair's now elderly professor gazing out the window, quoting the last letter that Ned sent before he died—"In such a season and at such a time . . . if ever I can be on earth

again, it is there I should wish to be"—writes the antebellum period as a time
when Tom and Ned's love was possible.[25]

Nostalgia sanctified depictions of male-male intimacy throughout the
final decades of the nineteenth century, but so too did the status of characters
and writers as soldiers. As discussed in the previous chapter, one prominent
site of postbellum soldierly romance was the genre of semifictionalized prisoner-of-war memoirs. As we have seen, John McElroy's *Andersonville*, John
Ransom's *Diary*, and Ralph Orr Bates's *Billy and Dick from Andersonville
Prison to the White House* all deployed male-male intimacies to make the
case for government support for veterans, while Herbert Collingwood's novel
Andersonville Violets cultivated cross-sectional sympathies through a prison
love story in which one male prisoner has replaced his sister as the object of
his comrade's affections. This trope of male-male intimacy between Civil War
soldiers had a staying power through the nineteenth century even as scrutiny
of sexual behavior increased.

Intimacies between men were, for at least a few decades, exempt from the
dramatic postbellum rise in state efforts to criminalize sexual activities. Pornography, contraceptives, and female prostitution were all objects of scrutiny for anti-vice champion Anthony Comstock, but sex between men largely
was not. As Judith Giesberg has written, young men—Civil War soldiers in
particular—were the imagined subject, not object, of Comstock's efforts.[26]
Far from something to guard against, intimate male friendship remained an
ideal, one that served as protection from pornographers and prostitutes. For
example, Comstock's most significant mentor, the Christian moralist Henry
Clay Trumbull, was also a celebrant of male intimacies, as evident in his
1891 book *Friendship the Master-Passion*, a compendium of the best that
has been said about friendship with a focus on those models now familiar
to popular gay histories: Damon and Pythias, David and Jonathan, Achilles
and Patroclus.[27] When Edward Carpenter published a similar anthology of
friendship a decade later, he did so to advocate subtly for acceptance of same-
sex desire.[28] Trumbull could draw on more than ancient models. His 1865
book *The Knightly Soldier* celebrates "the peculiar and rarest intimacy" he
developed with a fallen Union comrade, Henry Ward Camp. Trumbull himself enters as a character in the third person in the biography, arriving just
after Camp remarks in his journal, "How I should enjoy the right fellow for a
chum!" Three pages later, "in a midnight talk," he and Trumbull "opened their
hearts to each other, and entered upon that life of peculiar oneness which
was so marked to all who, thenceforward, saw them together. Like Jonathan
and David . . . the soul of the one was knit with the soul of the other" and

"each loved the other as his own soul."[29] Comstock's attempt to criminalize sexual behavior was not in hypocritical opposition to his mentor's celebration of intense, romantic male intimacies. Instead, for men like Comstock, the innocence of male intimacies, and association with the period of wartime youthfulness, separated them from criminal (mostly female) sexuality as the innocent, sanctified stuff of a bygone era.

The Civil War among the Sexologists

The sexual science that developed in the 1880s began not as a continuation but as a critique of efforts like Comstock's to criminalize sexual activities. The animating spirit for the set of doctors writing about sexual behaviors, both in Europe and in the United States, was to treat aberrant sexual behavior as a social disease, better met with medical remedies than criminal punishment. One of the first doctors in the United States to advocate medical treatment for "pederasty," his catchall term for male-male sex irrespective of participants' ages, was William Alexander Hammond, the former Union army's surgeon general from 1862 to 1864. In that role, Hammond launched both the Army Medical Museum and the plan for publishing the *Medical and Surgical History of the War*, instituting the methods of data collection through which the war produced new medical knowledge.[30] After the war, Hammond established a private practice for neurology in New York City, where he treated male impotence for many veteran patients as both a physiological and mental disorder.[31] In *Sexual Impotence in the Male* (1883), Hammond cataloged his treatment of sexual dysfunction, as well as "cases of sexual inversion in which the subjects were disposed to form amatory attachments to other men."[32] Only after the war, during which Hammond never mentioned same-sex sexual behavior as a problem of army hygiene or soldiers' well-being, did this problem of male sexual life present itself to Hammond.

Why was same-sex sexual behavior a problem for a doctor like Hammond at the same time that Comstock apparently took no notice of it? One answer is that male patients, and sometimes their families, were coming to the doctor to remedy failures in reproductive and class expectations. Operating a cash-based practice, Hammond's clients tended to be wealthier New Yorkers. A patient experiencing same-sex desire was typically, in Hammond's words, "a graduate of a college, of an aesthetic turn of mind," "well educated, had travelled extensively, and had ample means at his command," and from a family "of the highest respectability." In one case, absence of heterosexual desire would have little effect on a patient's well-being, except that if he did not have children some family property would, upon his death, go partly to "strangers" and partly to "certain charitable institutions."[33] Thus, in the postbellum decades, same-sex sexuality did not emerge as the problem it would become, of urban vice, but emerged, instead, when men began seeking medical solutions to the sexual issues preventing them from achieving class expectations for marriage and family.[34]

It was the Civil War experience, however, that led doctors like Hammond, and then also his patients, to believe that this kind of problem was within their power to remedy. "The Civil War," as Randall Knoper writes, "with its mysteries of nerve injuries, battle fatigue, and what would later be called shell shock, all beyond the grasp of anatomical explanation, gave impetus to the emergence in the 1860s and 1870s of neurology as a specialization of psychology, which had itself been newly consolidated as the science of mind."[35] When Hammond, a founder of neurology, was faced with the nonanatomical problem of "sexual inversion" he treated it as a problem of the mind. Influenced by the French neurologist Jean-Martin Charcot, Hammond treated men by applying a cauterizing iron to the nape of their neck in order to jolt their brains out of debilitating habits. Hammond also, predicting the later emergence of a sexual psychology, recommended exercises of concentration, especially on complex mathematics, as a remedy for perverse sexual desire. For Hammond, the problem of pederasty, though "distressing and disgusting," was not criminal but medical, less a social problem than one for an individual's procreative capacity.[36] Like his fellow former Union officer Comstock, Hammond contributed to an emerging regime of sexual restriction and control while being motivated by a profound concern for the welfare of the young men with whom he served.

When European sexual science arrived in the United States in the 1880s, its catalog of perversions found ready application in Hammond's case studies. Nearly every text of early US sexology cited by historians of homosexuality would, in turn, cite the former surgeon general. Two University of Chicago sexual scientists who cite Hammond's work, urologist G. Frank Lydston and psychiatrist James G. Kiernan, occupy a prominent place in the US history of homosexuality. Kiernan's 1892 essay "Responsibility in Sexual Perversion" documented the earliest use of "homosexual" in the United States. Lydston's 1889 comment that "there is in every community of any size a colony of male sexual perverts; they are usually known to each other, and are likely to congregate together" is widely anthologized as one of the earliest US references to gay communities.[37]

Kiernan and Lydston also evidence the fact that, as historians Melissa Stein and Siobhan Somerville have written, racialized and sexual science were not separate but the same science being written by the same scientists, allied with the period's other social sciences to justify racial segregation.[38] Kiernan's theory of sexual perversions relied on a hierarchy of racialized traits; Lydston would directly apply that theory of perversions to racist theories of US society in *Sexual Crimes among the Southern Negro* (1893), his enthusiastic response to a request by the president of the American Medical Association, Hunter McGuire (formerly a Confederate army surgeon who had amputated Stonewall Jackson's arm at Chancellorsville), to explain "the sexual perversion in the negro of the present day."[39] The idea that the rape of white women by Black men represented a vast and increasing social problem had been an 1880s invention, developing alongside theories of sexual perversions.[40] In his later volume *Diseases of Society* (1904), Lydston, drawing on Kiernan's theory of homosexuality as a confused, uninhibited form of sexual hunger, argued that "the mutilation of women by rapists, black or white, and especially the former, are phases of the same form of perversion in which atavism results in confusion of sexuality with the parent instinct of hunger."[41] It would be wrong to conclude that scientists like Lydston saw Black sexuality as a homosexual threat, but because homosexuality was not explained through a gender-inversion model, the gendered object of desire did not pose an obstacle to linking hypersexuality and homosexuality as similarly confused forms of sexual desire. As Stein has written, Lydston's recurrent object of analysis, a "mulatto hermaphrodite," demonstrated, to him, a web of nonnormative confusions of race, gender, and sexual desire.[42]

At the same time, Lydston found the causes of Black sexual crime in Civil War history. Blaming "the National government" for "the degeneracy and crime of the Southern negro" and the Republican party for "the colossal wrong inflicted upon" the South by "giving the recently freed negroes the elective franchise," Lydston claimed that the "sexual furor" of Black men was especially prevalent "in states cursed by carpet-bag statesmanship."[43] For the claim that "carpet-bag government" was "a very powerful factor in destroying negro respect for law and order in the South," Lydston cites James Pike's 1874 *The Prostrate State: South Carolina under Negro Government*.[44] Pike's racist account had focused on corruption and his assessment of Black unpreparedness for governance, but the book made no reference to sexual behavior.[45] While Kiernan was a self-described Jefferson Democrat, Lydston was more idiosyncratic about his politics—later in life, he would attract controversy for his belief, evident as early as *Sexual Crimes*, that race-mixing might be a remedy to the problem of Black sexuality.[46] In his lifelong attention to criminality, Lydston, unlike Comstock, saw the solution to vice in medical treatment more than criminal law.[47] In his nonmedical writing, such as the comic volume *Over the Hookah: Tales of the Talkative Doctor*, Lydston wrote Southern sketches with childish Black adult characters speaking an invented dialogue characteristic of Joel Chandler Harris's Uncle Remus tales. Lydston's racism is then not merely typical of the era's scientific racism but also typical of the distinctly post-Reconstruction racism in postbellum plantation fiction.[48]

Lydston's belief that Black sexual crime had been increasing since emancipation matched his belief that "typic male sex perverts have so increased in numbers that they have formed large colonies with well-known resorts."[49] Sexologists recognized that sodomy was not itself new, but, as a commentator wrote in 1900, once "restricted to a great extent to soldiers, sailors, miners, loggers, campers, and others whose occupations separate them for the greater share of time from women," sodomy was "becoming quite common in our large cities, where this condition does not exist."[50] Seeking to explain why, as Lydston claimed, "sexuality-fostering influences—i.e. features of environment that excite psycho-sexual erethism—were more "abundant and potent . . . in great cities," sexologists theorized that homosexuality was connected to advancing urban civilization.[51] The fact that, as physician William Lee Howard argued in "Sexual Perversion in America," perversions "correlated with the cycles of civilization" indicated that "the influence of wealth gradually brought about luxury, luxury vice, and vice degeneracy."[52] Fears about the new problem of homosexuality united apprehensions around Gilded Age wealth, luxury, and urbanization. By 1912, the *Journal of the American Institute of Criminal Law and Criminology* would summarize as "generally accepted" the syllogism that as "degeneration is the fundamental cause of homosexuality" and "as man advances in civilization degeneration increases," then "homosexuality is a distinct manifestation of degeneration [and] a direct product of our culture."[53] Ten years later, in transatlantic correspondence from an American doctor to British sexologist Havelock Ellis, a shorthand had developed: homosexuality was "a penalty of civilization."[54]

Historians of homosexuality have also connected the formation of gay and lesbian communities to postbellum urbanization. The insight that, as John D'Emilio has written, "during the second half of the nineteenth century, the momentous shift to industrial capitalism provided the conditions for a homosexual and lesbian identity to emerge" would have found ready agreement among turn-of-the-century sexologists, who would have called "the shift to industrial capitalism" the progress of civilization.[55] This shift was as connected to the transformations wrought by the Civil War and Reconstruction as any postbellum phenomenon. Northern cities were emphasized, but Southern cities were under threat insofar as they had begun to resemble Northern cities. Writing about nervous diseases that included sexual perversions, neurologist George Beard suspected in 1884 that "since the war there has been among the whites of the South an increase of functional diseases," especially where he saw "a commercial activity" comparable to Northern cities.[56] For Beard, this urban-rural distinction applied just as much to the country's Black population, as he contrasted African Americans who lived "among the strong, healthy farming population," where "nervous diseases do not exist or exist but very rarely," with those "in the great cities, especially since emancipation," where insanity was more prevalent. If homosexuality was a problem connected to the victories of Northern industrial and commercial life, then the remedy was clear: a return to a more agrarian life. "Those who live out-doors and have well-balanced constitutions of the old-fashioned sort are not annoyed by sexual desire," Beard wrote, "to the same degree as the delicate, finely-organized lads of our cities and of the higher civilization."[57]

Beard and Hammond's fellow neurologist Silas Weir Mitchell had similar advice for men suffering from the effects of urban, industrial life: escape the effeminizing effects of civilization by going into nature in the West. The proposed rugged "West Cure," as Anne Stiles writes, was a decidedly homosocial camp life especially rehabilitating for men with homoerotic aesthetics like the poet Walt Whitman and the painter Thomas Eakins.[58] As Stiles notes in another essay on Mitchell, he was also the author of a homoerotic Civil War novel following the style of *Two College Friends*. Mitchell's *Roland Blake* (1886), a novel primarily about whether shame over past actions determines one's present psychology, includes a romantic friendship between two soldiers a world apart from the betrayals, blackmails, and double-dealings that are the source of other characters' shame. The male-male romance is in the background, and it features neither a wartime disunion nor the death of one friend but otherwise tracks the pattern of male antebellum intimacies giving way to the hero's postbellum heterosexual marriage.[59] Mitchell's novel demonstrates that among medical professionals, two versions of homosexuality were developing: one the innocent rustic camaraderie between men especially connected to nature, and one pathologized as a medically scrutinized, effeminate type. Male-male attraction itself remained less a problem than a gender performance imagined as linked to urban, industrial life.

For many commentators, dividing old-fashioned male intimacies from new pathologies was racialized, with Black sexuality and urban homosexuality seen as intersecting problems. While Lydston had believed that Reconstruction governments had caused Black men in Southern states to be more sexually deviant than counterparts who lived in or moved to Northern cities, others, following Beard, believed that cities increased Black sexual immorality. The hysterical 1893 complaint by psychologist Charles H. Hughes of a "lecherous gang of sexual perverts and phallic fornicators" among Black men in Washington, DC, some of whom were "employed as subordinates in the Government departments," combined homophobia, racism, and an attack on the Republican governmental policy of employing African Americans as clerks in federal departments.[60] One school of thought, held by Havelock Ellis's American correspondent, suggested that homosexuality was "far more prevalent among" Black than white people.[61] An apologist for homosexuality writing under the pseudonym Xavier Mayne, with a universalist belief in widespread similisexualism (his term for homosexuality), claimed, "The American negro has ever been similisexual."[62] This racialized view matched the long-standing view in sexual science, from Kiernan on, that nonwhite people, insofar as they were at an earlier stage in an evolutionary model of civilization, were more prone to sexual deviance and homosexuality.

Postbellum sexual science appears, then, as more than a bit incoherent. It held two paradoxical views of homosexuality: a white supremacist theory of civilization saw nonwhite people more prone to homosexuality because they were developmentally behind those of European descent, while homosexuality was also said to be the symptom of advanced civilization.[63] The American correspondent in Ellis's *Sexual Inversion* offered as a solution to this paradox: "Perhaps, however, the Negro, *relatively to his capacity* is more highly civilized than we are."[64] Add to that the convoluted logic by which a racist preoccupation with protecting white womanhood saw a grave threat in Black male homosexuality. The effects of the Civil War, for sexologists, could cut across these paradoxes. From either direction, they imagined the Civil War added to the problem of Black sexuality: by removing the positive checks that white slaveholder control had on the innate, primitive traits of Black Americans or by bringing Black Americans, through urbanization, into the dangers of advancing civilization. In either case, sexual scientists viewed Black sexuality as determined, to a great extent, by white influence and control. For social scientists, the final object of studying Black sexuality was not diagnosing permanent racial traits but determining how white society should act to respond.

Turn-of-the-century racism most obsessed with the figure of the Black male rapist, such as in Thomas Nelson Page's novel *Red Rock* (1898) or Thomas

Dixon's *The Leopard's Spots* (1902), did not identify the threat of Black sexuality as homosexual, but it did follow the sexologists' explanation in portraying Black male characters with an insatiable sexual appetite. Dixon's novel, which presented Black men as unable to change their propensity to rape (as unable as a leopard is to change its spots), also invoked a book curiously similar to the sexological texts. The novel's white Republican villain, attempting to seduce another man's wife, presents her with a book that he read in medical school that "could scientifically demonstrate the purely physical basis of love." She summarizes the unnamed book's argument back to him in what amounts to a paraphrase of Kiernan: "The first elemental passion, hunger, has for its end the preservation of the individual; while love finds its fulfillment in the preservation of the species." She uses this distinction to dismiss his overtures, explaining that her character "is in the soul; [his] in the appetites."[65] Central to this plotline, the book of sexual science also justifies the novel's worldview: the presentation of Black characters as having capacity only for sexual appetite opposes the purity of rational love in the white characters' romance. That romance, between the novel's white hero and heroine, stands for the preservation of the white species, threatened by the sexual hunger of Dixon's Black characters. Dixon's historical narrative, however, emphasizes this problem not as static but as determined by white actors: the white Republican villain has unleashed the problem of Black sexuality, and white characters like Dixon's heroes can, with appropriate effort, bring it back under control. When D. W. Griffith adapted Dixon's dramatization of the novel and its sequel *The Clansman* (1905) for *The Birth of a Nation*, he dropped the sexological book from the story but supplemented the heterosexual white romance of Dixon's novel with another, between Tod and Wade, which contrasted just as well the scientists' etiologies of sexual hunger.

Thus, for white reactionaries, what appears as a set of nonequivalent threats—Blackness, homosexuality, urbanization, industrialization, and modernity—formed a singular attack on a society valorized as white, agrarian, and traditional. Black sexuality and homosexuality both appeared as products of developments inaugurated by Union victory: emancipation, industrialization, and urbanization.

Sexology among the Civil War Historians

US sexual science, formulating theories in reference to the recent Civil War, would, in turn, change the way the history of the war was written. As that science developed, and before its influence spread, the history of the Civil War already had an implied sexual morality. James Ford Rhodes, the period's most prominent Civil War historian, had begun writing history after amassing a fortune as an industrialist. His seven-volume *History of the United States from the Compromise of 1850*, published from 1893 to 1906, told that history as a national triumph over two evils: slavery and Reconstruction. Rhodes's history of sexual morality matched his indictment of slavery and Reconstruction. Adopting the view of Harriet Martineau and other abolitionists, Rhodes wrote slavery as an institution of immoral licentiousness, in which slaveholders created a sexual market for enslaved women.[66] One explanation for the national victory over slavery, then, was the considerable sexual morality of white Americans, due primarily to white women's discretion and white men's work ethic. That triumph became blemished by the sexual immorality of the Reconstruction era. First, Union victory in Northern cities caused a period of "extravagance and luxury" in which morals declined. Then, Reconstruction-era corruption included sexual immorality: "A bureau of the Treasury Department," Rhodes wrote, "made a house of seduction and prostitution."[67] The historian racialized corruption and sexual immorality, while linking urban Black unrest to sexual violence. But national sexual morality would triumph over immorality, in Rhodes's account, as surely as Redeemer governments triumphed over Reconstruction politicians. While he introduced some of the same themes as the sexologists, linking urbanization, vice, and racialized sexual violence, Rhodes did not arrive at the same conclusion that tied the advancement of civilization to sexual immorality. Instead, the Northern industrialist saw national progress and sexual propriety as twin victories of the nineteenth century.

Rhodes's history, as David Blight has written, was widely celebrated by white Northerners and Southerners for its fairness to both sides. One of Rhodes's chief Northern celebrants was his fellow businessman historian Charles Francis Adams. In Blight's analysis, Adams took Rhodes's white supremacist history a step further: his status as a Union veteran and a member of the most famous Massachusetts family made his defense of secession, his minimization of slavery, and his celebration of Gen. Robert E. Lee more influential.[68] Adams's *Some Phases of the Civil War: An Appreciation and Criticism of Mr. James Ford Rhodes's Fifth Volume* was much more appreciation than criticism. Its criticism narrowed on the single-minded way that Rhodes took slavery as the cause of the war. Adams argued for an adjacent cause: that Southerners, misperceiving the political and economic power of cotton, had buoyed their separatist confidence with the belief that the cotton industry would compel European support and compete favorably with Northern industry.[69] (Such a view shifted the most crucial Civil War battle to European diplomacy, where Adams's father had succeeded in preventing the English alliance with the Confederacy.) If Adams disagreed slightly with Rhodes's phases of Civil War history, he appears to have been more in line with Rhodes on the national development of sexual morality. His 1891 pamphlet, titled in the same pattern, *Some Phases of Sexual Morality and Church Discipline*, examined the sexual behavior of colonial New England and concluded that sexual morality had, by the end of the nineteenth century, remained the same or improved slightly.[70] The sexologists writing in that same decade would disagree in full. But for the two Northern industrialists turned historians, the development of industrial capitalism in the second half of the nineteenth century represented two positive developments: one for a reconciliationist spirit over sectionalism and one for improvements in sexual morality.

The historians trained by Dunning, in revising Rhodes's and Adams's Civil War histories, reversed this narrative of sexual morality. While Rhodes's histories were contemporaneous with the emergence of US sexual science, Dunning's students published theirs in the subsequent decades, from 1901 to 1924. Unlike that of Rhodes, the intellectual origin of the Dunning School, like that of the new sexual science, was the US-German cultural exchange of the late nineteenth century.[71] In general, Dunning's students differed from Rhodes by providing more excuses for white Southern slave society and more faults for Reconstruction policymakers. Where sexual behavior and morality appear in Dunning School histories, they share the perspective of the sexologists. While Rhodes saw the triumph of sexual morality over Reconstruction, Dunning School historians saw the sexual trends of Reconstruction, rooted both in urbanization and Black empowerment, as part of late-century trends toward increasing urban and Black sexual vice.[72]

Dunning School historians treated these trends within a central theme of their histories, familiar to the sexologists: the contest between agrarian and urban society. William Watson Davis, building on Rhodes's characterization of Southern states as "but a farm," would characterize the Civil War and Reconstruction in Florida as "a profound revolution in a sparsely settled and distinctly rural region."[73] Walter Lynwood Fleming characterized the antebellum South as having "no city life, and country and town were socially one." These historians cited, as one of Reconstruction's chief products, the migration of emancipated people to cities, which, in their view, combined, almost logarithmically, the problems of Black and sexual immorality.[74] It was James W. Garner, the Mississippi historian treated by W. E. B. Du Bois as more moderate than the rest, who most theorized urban crime as a failure of

Reconstruction policy. Garner criticized white policymakers in Mississippi for "prohibiting the freedmen from renting land outside of towns and cities." This policy drove freed people into urban spaces, where, according to Garner, "they must suffer from idleness, vice, and disease."[75]

The distinction between agrarian and urban communities in the Dunning School Reconstruction histories must be contextualized within their shared experience as graduate students from tiny Southern towns living in New York City. Dunning's students are a much-generalized group. Their ideological biases have been attributed to the fact that nearly all of them spent their childhood in plantation-like settings in the South.[76] Dunning was no fan of Reconstruction, but it was his students who supplemented his interpretation with nostalgia for antebellum society. Certainly, consensus developed among them within the classrooms at Columbia University, but equally important as their rural upbringing to their collective bias is their shared urban experience between the 1890s and 1910s in a particular place in Manhattan. For most, the primary urban experience of their life would be the short time living near Columbia. Except for Davis, who lived in a Columbia dormitory, all of those who went on to publish Reconstruction histories lived in buildings east (Fleming and Ulrich Phillips) or north (Charles Ramsdell, Joseph G. de Roulhac Hamilton, and Garner) of campus. The residences north of Columbia—Ramsdell and Hamilton on 123rd Street, Garner on 125th and then 115th Street—put them a few blocks from the Harlem blocks at 130th Street and above, which were developing into one of the country's most prominent Black neighborhoods.[77] Within the next fifteen years, as historians Eric Garber and George Chauncey have written, a prominent and much-discussed gay subculture developed, with Southern-oriented clubs from 130th to 138th Streets.[78] To be sure, that proximity, in space and time, does not indicate the Dunning students' attendance. But they did collectively theorize the effects of urbanization on a rural, racialized society while living in a city, very near to a developing Black neighborhood that was becoming notorious for its sexual communities.

Garner, who had also studied at the University of Chicago in the late 1890s, would make the problem of urban vice an area of his scholarly research and professional writing. In 1910, as a political science professor at the University of Illinois, Garner was the founding editor of the *Journal of the American Institute of Criminal Law and Criminology*, cited above for its 1912 "Homosexuality and the Law" article. The journal's earliest issues reflected the influence of the new sexual science, with a mission, written by Garner, to advance "the scientific study of crime" and contributions by Lydston and other sexual scientists.[79] One essay under Garner's editorship asked whether the recently established view of congenital homosexuality implied a more widespread congenital criminality.[80] Garner's own writing occasionally treated these topics, though not with as much attention as his journal gave them generally. In one early review on proposals to sterilize criminals, Garner quoted at length a case study from a proponent for punitive sterilization. The subject, who was sent in his youth to "the negro reformatory for incorrigible boys," had been, according to that institution's superintendent, "a past master in sodomy and masturbating." After leaving the school he had been arrested for burglary and continued to take "the lead in sodomy and kindred deviltries" until he was sterilized by vasectomy. According to the proponent, this rendered the subject "a strong, well-developed young negro, well behaved, and not a masturbator or sodomist." For his part, Garner concluded that there was still disagreement among the medical authorities and criminologists about punitive sterilization.[81] Garner's career demonstrates that just as the period's sexual and racial sciences overlapped, its professional historians overlapped with the sexology-inflected social sciences.

Hosmer, as a Civil War historian, is largely forgotten between Rhodes and the Dunning School, but he is the historian who connects them. From his position as director of the Minneapolis Public Library, he had corresponded with both Rhodes and Adams about their histories. He wrote frequently to Adams—he remembered him from college (Hosmer was Harvard class of 1855, Adams 1856)—about how much he would depend upon Adams's writing for parts of his Civil War history. Hosmer would not go as far as Adams in defending slavery or glorifying General Lee, though he would write to Adams his agreement that it had been "altogether natural" for young white men of the South to follow Lee, for they "made a noble fight animated by a pure and manly purpose."[82] Hosmer's most substantial revision to Rhodes's history was in adopting Adams's view about the importance of cotton, or really the Southerner's cotton-rooted misperceptions of his own power. Whereas for Rhodes slavery was a great evil in need of elimination, for Hosmer slavery was another aspect of the Southern delusion by which white Southerners tragically misperceived their status. Northern abolitionists were, however, the more direct cause of the strife—just as Northerners were at least as responsible as Southerners for slavery.[83] Enslaved people, absent from Hosmer's novel except as a component of Claiborne's sexual immorality, are, in the history, "awaiting quietly in their cabins the impending deliverance." It is the Southern aristocrat, like Claiborne, who is to be improved by the war. Enervated by reliance on slave labor, he finds that "emancipation took from his shoulders a great burden." The North was also improved, as Hosmer quotes Rhodes quoting Francis Parkman that the war was an event in the "well-balanced development of nations, as of individuals." Hosmer concludes that the Civil War was "worth all it cost in blood and treasure," because by the time of his writing, "among the nations of the earth, there is not one whose foundations seem more stable."[84] This set Dunning up perfectly.

In the preface to his Reconstruction volume, Dunning laid out what would be an animating paradox for his followers' interpretations: the period both contained a "scheme that threatened the permanent subjection" of Southern whites "to another race" and was "a step in the progress of the American nation."[85] The emotional valance of this narrative, and the chief difficulty for Dunning's students, was to balance the sense of loss of the antebellum world with the inevitability of national progress. In that sense, Hosmer's novel more than his history sets the emotional stage for the progress narrative of the Dunning School—the death of Herbert and Claiborne's intimacy was inevitable and necessary no matter how longingly it is looked back upon.

Nostalgia for a Homoerotic Past

The narrative in Dunning School histories that Reconstruction ushered in sexual immorality made the depictions of antebellum sexuality, the prewar intimacies in the romantic friendship novels, only more appealing. As the vision of professional historians at the beginning of the twentieth century became more rose-colored about antebellum society, images of male intimacy persisted as a way to typify that bygone time. For example, one of the most popular historians contemporaneous to Dunning's students was Union veteran Morris Schaff, who, like Hosmer and Adams, wrote with sympathy for the Confederate cause in works such as *Sunset of the Confederacy* (1912) or *Jefferson Davis: His Life and Personality* (1922).[86] Schaff's 1907 memoir of schooldays at the US military academy, *The Spirit of Old West Point 1858–1862* (mentioned in chapter 3 for its nostalgic portrayal of John Pelham as emblem of the Lost Cause), remains his most notable work due to persistent interest in the war's central personalities. Celebrated among contemporary historians, Schaff's memoir also found an enthusiast in defender of homosexuality Xavier Mayne. In his 1908 *Intersexes*, Mayne wrote of Schaff's memoir, "Especially in its elegiac passages, it is eloquent of the homosexual thrill in young hearts that beneath uniforms can beat so passionally for each other."[87] Mayne's *Intersexes* was privately printed in Rome; it is unlikely that Schaff saw Mayne's appraisal of his book.[88] Nonetheless, Mayne's commentary on

Schaff indicates how the emergence of homosexual identity shared a world with Civil War memory.

What Mayne noticed in *The Spirit of Old West Point* was Schaff's delicate attention to the appearances of his onetime chums, which had a pattern of description: the color of a friend's eyes, the color of his hair, the flush of his cheek, where and when he died in a Civil War battle. A few friends, in addition to Pelham, stand out, including Schaff's Southern roommate, from whom he was to be separated by the institution's practice of rooming by companies, which were arranged by height. In order that they might stay together, Schaff stuffed papers in his shoes when his height was being measured so that he could remain in his roommate's company. Another intimacy was with a student who roomed on the floor above him, who "would come down into my room or I would go up into his, and there night after night we would ramble from topic to topic as two little idle, barefoot boys might ramble along an old dusty road toward a schoolhouse among the fields."[89] Schaff's tone is deeply nostalgic; his primary method for cultivating that nostalgia is romanticizing these lost collegiate intimacies.

The tragedy of the war would come for these intimacies as the spring of 1861 arrived. Schaff's image on the eve of war, with tremendous emotional power, is of his classmates dancing in pairs. Schaff waxed:

> Down in the little battalion of cadets we were only vaguely conscious of the nation's crisis; though to those of us who had Southern roommates every little while it drew near and we caught glimpses of its dark menace. . . . During release from quarters, when the recitations of the day ended, some would take a stroll around Flirtation Walk—beautiful and solemnly elevating, as through trees and from open spaces the eye fell on the river in the fading light of day, on the snow-covered, skyward-tending landscape and the worshiping hills—all waiting in religious peace, for the coming of the night—how I should love to ramble along it once more!—a few would go over to the inspiriting silence of the library; a small number, poor victims of athletics, would wrestle with parallel bars, etc. in the gymnasium; but the larger number would congregate in the fencing-hall and dance to music by members of the band. How often I sat with Comly—for dancing was not among our accomplishments—and watched the mazing couples, Rosser and Pelham, "Cam" Emory and Ames, Chambliss and Hoxton, Kent and Beaumont, Haines and Cushing, Dearing and Gillespie, Dupont and Farquhar, and many, many others! Yes, that was the way we were passing the time in that January of 1861, on the verge of the Civil War.[90]

Even for readers in 1907, the names of James Dearing, a Confederate killed the day before Lee's surrender at Appomattox, Alonzo Cushing, killed at Gettysburg, and of course "the Gallant Pelham" would conjure a past that cannot return.[91] For Mayne, the defender of same-sex romance, what stood out was the "manly similisexualism of psychic quality [that] pervades the record." He predicted that the West Point history would make "a peculiarly subtle appeal," though its homosexual accents "may not be intelligently appreciated."[92] The nostalgic homoeroticism, for Mayne, stood in contrast to the antihomosexualism against which his book defended. That opposition, between the old homoerotic intimacies and the new problem of homosexuality, was partly how Schaff achieved his nostalgic tone and, with it, his reconciliationist message.

By the early twentieth century, these two versions of homosexuality—the innocent homoeroticism of the past and the deviant homosexual identity of modernity—operated together to make meaning of the war. Only a few years after Schaff's West Point nostalgia, another pair of mazing young soldiers hugged, embraced, and seemingly kissed in *The Birth of a Nation*. As I wrote in the introduction to this book, the innocence of the chums' sexuality relies on two oppositions: one to the criminal Black sexuality that threatens white society within the film and one to the problematized homosexual identity experienced by the two actors. The lives of these actors, as well as Mayne's contemporaneous reading of Schaff, demonstrate the overlap in the early twentieth century between Civil War memory and an emerging homosexual identity. So, too, may the career of sculptor Moses Ezekiel, a Confederate veteran whose studio in Rome produced among the most prominent memorials to the Confederate cause. His biographer, citing his relationship with German painter Fedor Encke as that of "lovers," labels him "homosexual."[93] Homoerotic imagery infuses his work as well, including his most famous sculpture, the monument to the Confederate dead formerly at Arlington National Cemetery, *The New South*. Beneath a Minerva figure is a series of thirty-two figures in relief that both aims to represent the Confederate cause and has "the leading purpose," the chairman of the monument's organizing committee wrote, "to correct history."[94] Such corrections include an enslaved man, inspired by Thomas Nelson Page's story "Marse Chan," devotedly following a Confederate soldier to battle and an enslaved woman, as a stereotypical "mammy" figure, receiving a war-going soldier's infant to care for while he's away.[95]

Ezekiel's celebration of the Confederate effort, as well as his white supremacist inclusion of Black figures, operates alongside his homoerotic imagery.

Two narratives at work in Confederate memorialization: the intraracial intimacy of
a Confederate soldier pair and the racist fantasy of a Black Confederate soldier.
Detail image of frieze, *The New South* (Confederate memorial) at Arlington National
Cemetery. Moses Ezekiel (1914). Removed from Arlington Cemetery in 2023. Photograph
by Tim Evanson.

Among the figures in the Arlington memorial's relief, an engineer-soldier
throws his arm around a sailor as they stride together; a muscly blacksmith,
in a sleeveless shirt so thin that he seems to wear no shirt at all, newly fash-
ioned sword between his legs, says farewell to a wife caressing his triceps;
and one soldier's hand grasps the arm of a striding comrade as they march.
This final set stands before the now notorious image of an enslaved man par-
ticipating in this Confederate march. As several historians have written, that
image, of a Black man's loyalty to the cause of his own subjugation, is a racial
fantasy.[96] So, too, is the pair before him. This chapter has suggested that we

should see these two fantasies, one of intraracial white male intimacy and one of racial subordination, together, the first cultivating sympathies that justify the second. For Ezekiel, such images were meant not only to commemorate the Confederate cause but also to foster a spirit of national reconciliation. For many, they did just that. The Republican president William Howard Taft, for instance, was pleased that Ezekiel, though a Democrat, had been the one chosen for the Confederate monument at Arlington. President Taft appreciated the power of Ezekiel's sculptures to create cross-sectional fraternity, to inspire the veterans of North and South to join together. According to Taft, photographs showed Northern veterans and Southern veterans visiting Ezekiel sculptures and "fraternizing together . . . arm in arm."[97]

CHAPTER 6

Corruption, Ingenuousness, and Manly Honesty

HENRY JAMES'S ATTRACTIVE
WHITE SOUTHERNERS

IN THE PREVIOUS CHAPTER, I argued that postbellum culture mapped two contrasting versions of sexuality onto the Civil War's social transformations: the modern, pathologized sexual identities of the postbellum present against the innocent male homoeroticism of the antebellum past. No work so thoroughly contemplates Civil War memory through opposing sexualities as Henry James's *The Bostonians* (1886). The battle between Basil Ransom and Olive Chancellor over Verena Tarrant is at once a battle between the antebellum South and the postbellum North, between Mississippi and Massachusetts, between conservatism and progressivism, between past and present, and between something like heterosexuality and something like homosexuality. As an emblem of the latter, Olive's very nature appears like a case study from the previous chapter's sexologists: "perverse," "so essentially a celibate," and "visibly morbid." The narrator repeats that word five times in introducing her: "It was plain as day she was morbid."[1] If, as Annamarie Jagose has written, such terminology drew from the period's "developing sexological vocabulary," James, like the sexologists, made Olive's nervous disorders a product of modernity: "There was something very modern and highly developed in her aspect; she had the advantages as well as the drawbacks of a nervous organization."[2]

If Olive suggests a modern, postbellum problem of pathologized homo-sexuality, what of her rival Basil Ransom? On the one hand, he represents the heterosexual imperative; Verena must surely choose him over Olive, as a youthful romantic male friendship must end. On the other hand, it is the narrative as James constructs it, not Verena, that orients the reader toward Ransom's attractiveness: the way he appears on the opening pages as "a strik-ing young man" with "magnificent eyes" of "smouldering fire," the way he wins the affection of Boston's ladies while ironizing them, the way he makes "the staircase groan" and the Cape Cod hotel rattle when he descends it.[3] As Eve Kosofsky Sedgwick asked, how does Olive's desire for a girl like Verena parallel the "ventriloquistic, half-contemptuous, hot desire of Henry James for a boy like Basil Ransom"?[4] James eroticized Ransom through both his connection to the antebellum Southern past and his status as a still-young, though defeated, Confederate veteran. More than that, Ransom's homoerotic attractiveness derived from associations James assembled between this Con-federate veteran and the Union dead of James's own eroticized past. *The Bostonians*, then, returned to these same contrasting homosexualities: the eroticized intimacies between men of the past and the pathologized sexuali-ties of postbellum modernity.

Ransom is one of many white Southerners who populated postbellum culture. They appeared in a few standard forms. One type was old, often infirm, emphasizing the Confederate veteran's status as out of place in the modern world.[5] Another set was young, or at least youthful enough to appear marriageable to Northern ladies. Nina Silber has attended to these plots as a subsequent stage in the cross-sectional marriage formula, one in which the white South reasserts its manhood by wooing Northern white women into Southern sympathies.[6] The period's plots were, as scholars since Silber have written, more complicated than this formula suggests, with North-South heterosexual romances balanced by gender-reversed pairs and supplemented by intra-Southern weddings.[7] Across this ideological diversity, a related phe-nomenon stands out: postbellum novels spend considerable time demon-strating, examining, explaining, or criticizing the attractiveness of white Southern men.

Attractive white Southerners, such as Ransom, offered a useful figure for postbellum politics. In addition to this "striking young man," postbellum readers found a man of "great attraction," the Confederate veteran John Car-rington, in Henry Adams's *Democracy* (1880); a "handsome, soldierly man," Confederate officer Col. George Selby, in Mark Twain and Charles Dudley Warner's *The Gilded Age* (1873); and a "noble" and "brave" Confederate veteran with a "finely-chiseled head and face," Hesden Le Moyne, in Albion Tourgée's *Bricks without Straw* (1880). All of these men were precisely thirty years old.[8] The white Southern aristocrat, the antebellum cavalier, and the Southern Confederate became, in postbellum culture, a distinctly usable type. Indeed, when the erstwhile Southern Whigs wanted to make their take-over of state governments a "Redemption" of the Old South, they grew, as C. Vann Woodward ironizes them in *The New South*, the little goatees and moustaches of the imagined antebellum aristocrats.[9] When Owen Wister wanted to romanticize the heroic masculinity of the West, his "slim young giant, more beautiful than pictures," was a Virginian, who himself woos a Yankee schoolteacher in Wyoming, repurposing the chivalrous attractiveness of the Old South.[10] These postbellum stories were all quite different from one another. The romances they staged for white Southern men allegorized dif-ferent postbellum politics, but they all used the attractive appearance of these Southerners to contemplate links among male attractiveness and the era's key political concepts, honesty and corruption.[11]

This chapter explores the status of the attractive white Southerner, espe-cially the Confederate veteran, in the postbellum Northern imagination. In contrast to preceding chapters that survey a broader swath of the period's writing, this chapter sustains a deeper attention on a single author, Henry James. Among the novelists mentioned above, James may be an unlikely choice for exploring postbellum US politics. Not only was James mostly in Europe from 1870 to the end of his life, he also avoided, with some effort, discussion of US partisan politics. His political aloofness, the expansiveness of his thought beyond partisan camps, not to mention the obscurity of his prose style means that one might as easily pick James up and place him in a political category as a hippopotamus would a pea. And yet, James may still be taken as an ideological representative, and an exceptionally insightful one, who can serve as both an example and an analyst of a political orientation consequential to the end of Reconstruction: mugwumpian liberalism. James embraced the mugwump values that separated virtuous culture from vul-gar politics. His aversion to political commentary may be, then, even more quintessentially mugwumpian than that of an outspoken mugwump like his friend Henry Adams. Indeed, by examining James—far away both intellec-tually and geographically from the partisan politics of US Reconstruction—I aim to explore how deeply this strand of Southern sympathizing saturated Northern liberals' views.

At the same time, no other writer gets at the links between male eroticism and political thinking better than James. Homoeroticism in James's writing illuminates the appeal of the young, white, male Southerner in the eyes of Northern liberals. Queer studies scholars, Sedgwick most prominently, have described how James eroticizes the past, figured as a younger man.[12] Forty years earlier, historian C. Vann Woodward noted that the novelist, like other mugwump writers such as Adams, employed a young Southern man in *The Bostonians* as spokesman for criticism of Gilded Age corruption.[13] To put Sedgwick's and Woodward's observations together: James's critique of post-bellum America used an eroticized figure, the young white Southern man.

That sexualized political ideal tells us more than James's individual polit-ical orientation. James's attentiveness to what makes young men attractive directs us to a representative strand of political thinking for postbellum lib-erals. For liberal men, the character of male electoral candidates became more important than partisan agenda. In 1876, representing that liberal and eventual mugwump perspective, Twain would remark, "Platforms are not the essential things now—men are."[14] The primacy of political character rep-resented for liberals both an ideal of the honest man and a fear that with-out tests of character, political power would consolidate in the hands of the wrong men: corrupt leaders, such as a party boss, or mobs of interest, such as industrial workers or Black tenant farmers. From this liberal perspective, democracy was a problem, one of interested individuals who might subvert the public trust, or of interested groups who might subvert the key freedoms of labor and trade. "Liberals," as the historian Richard White writes, "bereft of other ways of ordering politics, fell back on character."[15]

But how was one to evaluate character? Postbellum novelists often artic-ulated the problem through the attractiveness of male lovers, which could disguise or reveal a man's honesty. Postbellum electoral politics, especially in the contest over liberal voters, equally returned to male appearances. Cam-paigns for president during this period were preoccupied with "honesty," but evidence for or against a candidate's "manly honesty" arrived through his attractive, manly appearance or his unattractive, unmanly appearance.[16] Within this sexualized politics of honesty and manhood, the character type of the marriageable young white Southerner emerged for mugwump liberals as a romantic and political ideal, one whose connection to a defeated past cast him as an attractive, honest alternative to the corrupt present. No such Southerner won the presidency in the second half of the nineteenth century; nonetheless, this political character shaped national sympathies. It was to his attractive appearance that Northern liberals wanted presidential candidates to direct their sympathies.

James's contributions to the period's stock of young white Southerners, by conflating male appearance and political character, help explain connections between two crucial components of Northern liberal ideology. Those liberals were against, first, corruption and, second, continuing Reconstruction policies of federal intervention in Southern states. Why did Northern liberal perceptions of corruption correspond to a retreat from Reconstruction efforts? What counts as corruption, as the historian Richard White suggests in an essay of that title, depends on its selective definition through the inclusion of certain exchanges of power and the exclusion of others. Corruption is a matter not just of legal definition but also of cultural production, through which the *what* of corruption consolidates into the *who* of corruption.[17] Postbellum liberals were particularly susceptible to how Reconstruction's opponents linked corruption to Black political participation. Epistemologies of sexuality also constructed the meaning of corruption, especially in white reactionaries' portrayal of Black voters and Black-elected legislatures.[18] If villains of public corruption are constructed through cultural narratives, so, too, are the supposed redeemers. In other words, political thinking consists of not merely caricaturing one electoral or policy option but also cultivating sympathy for its alternative.

For James, corruption's opposite was ingenuousness, a quality he found particularly attractive in men. His writing is full of eroticized male ingenuousness, frequently that of Southern white men. Kenneth Warren, in his study on the postbellum realists and race, asks why James's critique of commercialism and corruption in *The American Scene* did not also critique American racism.[19] One answer is that James's critique of the corrupt present was already racialized because it came with a sympathetic alternative, the defeated protagonists of the Old South. For James, the failed, delusive, striving endeavor to preserve racial slavery within a modern world exemplified this quality he found attractive in men, ingenuousness. The desirous observation of male ingenuousness, we will see, was also central to James's thinking about homoeroticism itself. The homoerotic appeal also helps explain James's remarkable shift, alongside that of his liberal friends, from the wartime sympathies for Black Americans to postbellum feelings of tenderness.

James was aware of his own shift of sympathies in the decades following the Civil War. "Our sympathies," James would later recall of his family in the 1860s, "were all enlisted on behalf of the race that had sat in bondage."[20] His father had been an abolitionist, who criticized the seceded Southern states in a July 4, 1861, oration for their "dirty and diabolical struggle . . . to give human slavery the sanction of God's appointment." James's two younger brothers fought as officers for two of the Union's Black regiments, the Massachusetts Fifty-Fourth and Fifty-Fifth. He and his older brother William applied in 1863 to work with Federal relief efforts among refugeed freed people.[21] By 1898, however, James, commending William A. Dunning's essays on Reconstruction, described the Civil War as the tragedy of "the romantic idea" of states' rights, which had been "among the proud things of the earth" and were "the protagonist of the epic."[22] Observing Richmond, the onetime Confederate capital, in the 1907 travel memoir *The American Scene*, James sympathized with antebellum white Southerners as "such pathetic victims of fate . . . that I found myself conscious on their behalf of a sort of ingenuity of tenderness."[23]

The next section explores James's eroticization of male ingenuousness, a quality he connected to the defeated Confederate project of preserving slavery. That quality made a young man attractive and an emblem of an eroticized, honest past. Like his liberal friend, Henry Adams, James deployed the figure of the honest past, the defeated young Southerner, as a critique of corrupt politics. A middle section turns to postbellum presidential politics, with its attention on the masculine appearances through James's eyes. While that section focuses on how James connected masculine appearance to political honesty, it also provides an overview of the period's electoral politics of *manly honesty*. His commentary on presidential elections, in his letters, informs the mugwumpian politics within his novels. In the final section, I return to the young Southerner as critique of corrupt politics, analyzing why Basil Ransom wins this restaging of the Civil War conflict, or what makes this defeated Confederate attractive. That attractiveness, in both Ransom's appearance and his connection to an honest past, oriented the sympathies of a Northern man like James to the antebellum white South.

James's Ingenuous Virginians

The Virginian cavalier of John W. De Forest's 1867 novel *Miss Ravenel's Conversion from Secession to Loyalty*, while a Union soldier and not a Confederate veteran, fits, and might even inaugurate, the pattern of postbellum attraction to white Southern masculinity. For De Forest, Colonel Carter's attractive cavalier masculinity disguises his corruption, both in defalcating military equipment and in having an affair with the corrupt Miss Larue. The lesson, for Miss Ravenel, is to distrust such attractive male appearances in favor of the plainer but more honest New Englander Captain Colburne. It is a lesson missed on James, who preferred the Virginian cavalier to the sober representative of his own region. In an 1867 review, James complained that Miss Ravenel had replaced the Southerner Carter, "this handsome officer with his thirty-five years, his ruddy-bronze complexion, his audacious eye, his mighty mustachios, his easy assurance," with the Northerner Colburne, "a good fellow as well as a good man, but a little colorless, commonplace, young, and on the whole of no consequence."[24] With this take, James does a lot of work to miss the point of *Miss Ravenel's Conversion*, that the country should prefer the model of practical Yankee masculinity to impetuous Southern chivalry. Even in this review, James mixed appearance with personality in the character of the romantic Virginian—"eye," "mustachios," "ruddy-bronze-complexion" signaled the audaciousness and "easy assurance" that would typify James's Southern men.

Ingenuousness—what James, in contrast to present-day distinctions between the two terms, often calls ingenuity—was, for him, a defining feature of Southern character. His feeling on behalf of Southerners in *The American Scene*, "ingenuity of tenderness," echoes a contemporaneous theological description of the ingenuous capacity of God or a parent to see always the good in their children, the opposite of fault-finding.[25] Moments after expressing this feeling for white Southerners, James meets one, "ingenuous," "eager," and "exhaling a natural piety." The "gallant and nameless, as well as a very handsome Young Virginian" embodies those earlier reflections on Richmond, in which the Old South became the "hugest fallacy": the absurdity that a slavocracy might endure within modernity demonstrating a romantic delusion that required "an active and ardent propaganda," a rewriting of history and a remaking of culture.[26] This romantic striving against the forces of modernity made the defeated Southerners appear to James as ingenuous, even foolish, objects of James's sympathy. Ingenuousness established James's young men as admirably disconnected from the present and attractively connected to the past—often to the Civil War and Confederate defeat. In *The American Scene*, "ingenuity" is a quality of both observer and observed, the source of James's tender feelings for white Southerners and, elsewhere in James's writing, both an experience and structuring framework of homoerotic desire.

"So much the kind of Southerner I had wanted," James recognized the young Virginian as "a lively interest of type." He compares the man, "for all the world like the hero of a famous novel," to the protagonist of Wister's *The Virginian*, who brings an Old Southern heroism to Wyoming. James delights in the young man's brazen declaration about the "old, unhappy, far-off" Civil War battles that, "oh, I should be happy to do them all over again myself!" James can understand the young Southerner's anti-Northern prejudice, without which "his consciousness would be poor and unfurnished." Consistently, the outward appearance of poverty signals the inner inexperience of James's ingenuous young men and wins James's sympathies. The anti-Black prejudice that adorns the bare walls of such a consciousness also finds the narrator's sympathy. As Sedgwick notes with Ransom, James's attraction to these young Southerners does not respect their intellects: it is, she writes, a "half-contemptuous, hot desire." He listens to this young Virginian, "fair, engaging, smiling," as he tells of the violent acts he would do to Black Southerners, offering a playful, though ironic, parenthetical of his and James's affiliation across regional difference: "(Ah, we had touched on some of these!)"[27]

A few pages earlier, James narrated sympathy with white Southern racism generally. The white Southerner's fearfulness toward the Black American must be "understood at a glance," James explains, considering "how much he must loom, how much he must count, in a community which, in spite of the ground it might cover, there were comparatively so few other things." Reflecting on his own view of Black Americans at a railway station in Washington, DC, James's impressions at Richmond lead him to feel alongside white Southerners "the thumping legacy of the intimate presence of the negro."[28] Tellingly, the narrator's interactions with the young Southerner begin as they gaze mutually upon a preserved Confederate artifact: James narrates how his impressions of Richmond lead him to share white Southerners' racism.

Importantly, he does not presume to share that racism under the rubric of a mutual white identity but, instead, by interrogating and sympathizing with an alien consciousness. We should doubt that white Northerners were as a whole, as James claims, "preaching, southward, a sweet reasonableness" against the Southern white treatment of Black citizens, and doubt that such reasonableness was itself free of distinctive Northern racism. But, in this reflection, James presumes a difference between Northern and Southern whites on race, and presumes, as well, that Northern admonitions must be checked through sympathizing with how white Southerners have been, before and after the war, imprisoned by the question of race and a Black population. Racism, in the case of the handsome, young Virginian and white Southerners generally, is attractive precisely because James sees in it a reaction to material and intellectual poverty. With their present poverty, foolhardy Richmond and the ingenuous young Virginian send James into an attractive past that serves, he writes, as "food for sympathy."[29]

For all that has been said of James's innocent female ingenues, it is the ingenuousness of young men that helps us map homoeroticism within his writing. For example, at one of the moments in *The Ambassadors* (1903) in which exposure to Little Bilham's homosocial Parisian world seemingly opens, for the hero Strether, a new world, Strether celebrates, repeatedly, Bilham's "ingenuous compatriots": their "enthusiasm and execrations that made him, as they said, sit up; he liked above all the legend of good-humoured poverty, of mutual accommodation fairly raised to the romantic." About "the ingenuous compatriots," he liked as well their "candour" and that "they were red-haired and long-legged, they were quaint and queer and dear and droll; they made the place resound with the vernacular."[30] If the quality of their "admirable innocence" casts a spell on Strether, it mirrors the charming "impudence" that James reads (as Sedgwick noted) in his own slightly younger self writing *The Ambassadors*, as well as the infectious quality of Chad's cheery "knowing how to live" that made the one, Strether, imparting knowledge to him become, "not only with proper cheerfulness but with wild native impulses, the feeder of his stream." One could hardly conclude that James thought ignorance bliss, and yet, about the Thomas Gray poem from which that aphorism derives, James connected the "ecstasy of the ignorance attending [the artless schoolboys]" to the writing efforts of his younger self.[31]

Youthful, masculine striving, especially in willful ignorance of the odds stacked against it, is what James found attractive. In a personal letter to Hendrick Anderson, published in *Dearly Beloved Friends: Henry James's Letters to Younger Men*, James extols Hendrick's brother as "so young & so ingenuous, on that great fierce battlefield, or tropical artistic wilderness of Paris; but on the other hand, with the evident beauty of his nature & seriousness of his inspiration, he makes one *believe* in him." James then maneuvers to address the more beloved Hendrick: "Part of what I liked in him, too, was *you*, to whom his resemblance of look, tone, voice, expression is at moments extraordinary. He brought you back to my side."[32]

Ingenuousness is not merely an attractive attribute, but it also fits the overall Jamesian treatment of male homosexuality. A second consciousness, such as God, a parent, or in James's case an older man, is necessary to apprehend youthful inexperience tenderly. The experience of a homoerotic perception, by one with knowledge of one without, governs the experience of homosexual desire itself as a problem of self-knowledge. Kevin Ohi concludes *Henry James and the Queerness of Style* by reflecting that consciousness's belated relation to living, which constitutes the style of *The Ambassadors*, also structures homosexual self-knowledge: the moment of self-recognition producing its own pre-knowledge past.[33] Even in abstraction, James is never one to empty an embodied experience, like desire, of its content. Instead, he frames homosexual self-knowledge within his homosexual experience, that is, desiring ingenuous younger men from the vantage point of knowledge.

If ingenuousness observed both exemplifies and structures homoeroticism in James's writing, it is a curious fact that he maps this phenomenon directly onto the experience of the Civil War. His most direct commentary on the kind of change that the Civil War wrought comes in his 1878 critical biography of Nathaniel Hawthorne, where he contrasts Hawthorne, who died in 1864, with the post–Civil War Americans who had "eaten of the tree of knowledge." The war, James wrote, was "an era in the history of the American mind" that rendered the postbellum American, "without discredit to his well-known capacity for action, an observer." Viewed from that postbellum consciousness, Hawthorne's appeal was his ingenuousness. The author's "faith . . . was a simple and uncritical one, enlivened with an element of genial optimism," and in him, the recognition of the country's "problems to solve was blissfully absent." Those problems were, namely, slavery, and James locates Hawthorne's ingenuousness in his "sympathetic" portrait of a Northern defender of slavery, Franklin Pierce, receiving "obloquy" from abolitionists.[34] When James returns to the Civil War in his Dunning review of 1898, he similarly laments the consciousness that went extinct with both the war, "trampled in the dust of battle," and Reconstruction, "stamped to death in angry senates." "There never can be again," he writes, "the particular deluded glory of a Virginian or a Carolinian, or even a son of Massachusetts or Ohio." As with Hawthorne, James's Northern examples might distract from what was, within the war, the Southern concept: "The fond, old figment of the Sovereign state."[35]

Three years before he published *Hawthorne*, James depicted ingenuousness and its observer through the doubled male protagonists of his novel *Roderick Hudson*, a pairing, within the novel, also connected to the Civil War. After his older brother Stephen died fighting for the Union, Roderick had, he says, to "fill a double place." Roderick does not, however, fill this second place; another Union veteran, Rowland Mallet, whom James would call the novel's central "consciousness" in his 1907 preface, does.[36] The novel resolves the problem of the war-wrought doubled consciousness through one man appreciating another's ingenuousness, a pairing many readers have seen as homoerotic.[37] What attracts Rowland to Roderick? Robert K. Martin suggests it is Roderick's Virginian appearance as "a rather shabby cavalier, symbolically associating him with the florid Romanticism of the American South."[38] Roderick's romantic striving—the mismatch between his ambition and circumstances—inspires the more experienced older man, like James to Hendrick's ingenuous brother (or Strether to Chad), to believe in him.

Roderick's honesty is questionable, but his pleasing appearance disguises his dishonesty. After remarking that a man, especially one engaged to be married, who unsuspiciously welcomed another unmarried woman's flirtations, must be a "fellow of remarkable ingenuity," Rowland asks whether to the moral questions Roderick "should have it at his command to look at you with eyes of the most guileless and unclouded blue and to shake off your musty imputations by a toss of his romantic brown locks?"[39] The young man's pleasing appearance and guilelessness substitutes admirably for candor. That appearance, Roderick's romantic striving, his Virginian background, and James's explorations of the Civil War's effects on American consciousness all suggest that the appeal of one like Roderick is an ingenuousness untouched by the war. If, as James writes in *Hawthorne*, the postbellum American had tasted "of the tree of knowledge," he knows it by holding in his sympathetic view the ingenuous young Virginian.

James and Adams View Washington from Mount Vernon

James's use of male ingenuousness is then another version of a story now familiar in this book: the postbellum eroticization of the antebellum past. Such a framework makes the Civil War a crucible of sexual development, exactly as countless commentators have described James's war years. The dubious biographical accounts of James's accidental castration or a sexual awakening with a sleeping veteran awkwardly literalize the trend in James scholarship that reads his Civil War memory, both personal and political, as a transformation of masculinity and sexuality.[40] In Peter Rawlings's account of how James uses the past, the events of the Civil War divide the present from a past in which James assimilates his own sexual self-development, the war-wrought national transformation, and coded homoeroticism. Such erotic associations with the past appear frequently, as Rawlings explores, in *The American Scene*, James's account of his North-to-South trip that reads as a journey from a personal to a public past.[41]

In one prominent example, James explores that public past in a potent Virginian setting, George Washington's Mount Vernon plantation home. There, James experiences what he calls a "fantastication" of the past, embodied as a young man delivering recovered wealth to the present: "The slight, pale, bleeding Past, in a patched homespun suit, stands there taking the thanks of the bloated Present—having woundedly rescued from thieves and brought to his door the fat, locked pocket-book of which that personage appears the owner. The pocket-book contains, 'unbeknown' to the honest youth, bank-notes of incredible figure, and what breaks our heart, if we be cursed with the historic imagination, is the grateful, wan smile with which the great guerdon of sixpence is received." Here James's abstract Past assumes a male body in the same pattern of his ingenuous young men: impoverished but "honest," offering a naïve, "grateful, wan smile," ignorant that he has been shortchanged in recompense for his heroism. James's sympathies—"what breaks our heart"—are clear. In subsequent sentences, the personages are clarified: the young past is "Washington," the Virginian first president; the "pomp and circumstance" of the Present is "Government." The political commentary then becomes clear: the corrupt present has stolen wealth from the honest past, represented as a poor, honest youth of the erstwhile Southern aristocracy.[42] With James's famously obscure prose, it is a remarkably complex allegory, but one that represents a standard political complaint about a corrupt government and a redemptive past—indeed, the same mugwump complaint for which his friend Henry Adams had made use of Mount Vernon in *Democracy*.

In that novel, parallel to James's preference, Adams reversed De Forest's romantic formula and its political meaning. Adams's heroine, the widow Madeleine Lee, nearly marries the corrupt Illinois senator Silas Ratcliffe (from New England) before coming to her senses, the ending implies, and choosing the honorable Virginian lawyer John Carrington. The love plot of *Democracy* mirrors its political message, that the United States should spurn a corrupt Republican government and fall in love again, though late in life, with what remained of the Southern planter aristocracy. Ratcliffe is not merely a Northerner but a corrupt one.[43] According to Carrington, the worst was in "what Ratcliffe represented": "universal suffrage" and the much-despised word of the book's title, "democracy." *Democracy* may confine its satire to the national representatives of Washington, but its indictment spreads as well to those who sent them there, the people's majority. Not only did they elect Ratcliffe, but they would prefer him as a lover. By the end of the novel, Mrs. Lee, who has repudiated Ratcliffe, indicts them by an imagined referendum. "The bitterest part of all this horrid story," Mrs. Lee writes to Carrington, "is that nine of ten of our countrymen would say that I had made a mistake."[44]

The remedy for corruption, then, is not a policy or rule but a better character. That character is the Virginian Carrington. Upon meeting him, Mrs. Lee appreciates him as "a type": "My idea of George Washington at thirty." He functions as the ideal alternative to the corruption of Washington's residents, just as George Washington's home at Mount Vernon does to that city. A central scene brings him to this native place—his family had been on friendly terms with that first president—while the city dwellers feel shamefaced, unable even to breathe the pure air where honest Washington once lived. Mount Vernon forces the contrast between the honest, antebellum past and the corrupt present. While Ratcliffe states that Washington could not survive among the money-fueled politics of the present, Carrington defends his fellow Virginian: "Mr. Ratcliffe means that Washington was too respectable for our time." When the heroine asks, "Was he the only honest public man we've had?" the Virginian answers, "One or two others," presumably those who owned plantations nearby.[45] At the time he was writing *Democracy*, Adams was working on histories of the presidencies of two such Virginian planter presidents, Thomas Jefferson and James Madison, whose example Adams saw as redemptive for postbellum politics.[46] Southern planter politicians could be models of public virtue for Adams, regardless of that class's ability to transcend political self-dealing and profit seeking through their holdings in land and enslaved people.

Adams's longing was for that past of national male friendship, celebrated, as I wrote in chapter 1, in Washington's farewell panegyric to "fraternal affection." Male fellowship once transcended section and politics, symbolized by tickets and cabinets: Adams's great-grandfather as Washington's vice president; Jefferson as his great-grandfather's; his grandfather as James Monroe's secretary of state; and John C. Calhoun as his grandfather's vice president. Politics had, in the youngest Adams's opinion, ruptured this spirit of fellowship. His grandfather's loss to Andrew Jackson had meant appointments due to political affiliation rather than the merit that had long disproportionately qualified men named Adams. For the postbellum Adamses, Henry and his brother Charles Francis, no Southerner symbolized the classical virtues of those previous generations more than the son of one of Washington's foremost soldiers who had married a great-granddaughter of Washington's wife: Robert E. Lee.

Carrington is attractive through his association with both Washington and Lee. At the cemetery at Arlington—before the seized estate of the Lee family, inherited from Washington's stepson, and once called Mount Washington—Carrington inherits the Lee mythos: a Union man, never a true supporter of slavery, he had fought with the Confederacy but "never . . . with enthusiasm," only in loyalty to his state. The cemetery for Union soldiers and the confiscated property of the Lee family were "reasons which made a visit to Arlington anything but a pleasure to him."[47] Mrs. Lee is absent, but her sister models for the reader an overflowing of sympathy for the mopey Confederate veteran. The scene achieves an important communion among a set of men: the Union dead buried at Arlington, the melancholy Carrington himself, and the dead Confederate hero distantly related to the object of Carrington's affection. As such, Carrington is both attractive and opposed to Ratcliffe's corruption, but that attractiveness and opposition are together linked to a Civil War past and his defeat.

Reading Adams with comparison to James reveals the centrality of a white Southern man's attractiveness to Adams's presentation of postbellum politics. Reading James with comparison to Adams reveals the political argument of James's homoeroticism. James, meditating on the same Mount Vernon setting as Adams, also uses the past to redeem present politics. For James, of course, the past is more than partisan commentary. His image of the past, as an ingenuous young Virginian, is obscurely connected to the convulsion of the Civil War, the delusion of a slavocracy, a sense of premodernity, and the writer's own sexual self-development. But the present, in contrast to all of this, is corrupt government. The past, for James, as for everyone, is never merely the past but also a commentary on the politics of the present.

James's Mugwumpian View on Presidential Politics

James left the United States for Europe a month before Ulysses S. Grant's inauguration as president, and it is unlikely that he voted in US elections after 1868. His deliberate effort after the 1860s to keep US politics out of his field of vision evidences his belief that politics corrupted culture. That belief is itself political and one widely shared, in the postbellum era, by mugwump men. In naming James foremost in *American Snobs* (2021), Emily Coit presents a picture of an antidemocratic and reactionary James (notwithstanding the fact that critics used his writing for democratic and progressive claims). For Coit, James's conservatism derives in part from his reactionary response to the project of an earlier, less conservative transatlantic liberalism committed to cultivating subjects for democratic participation.[48] When we examine James's political thinking within the US national context, his distinctly mugwumpian views take shape.[49]

Henry James, unlike his brother William, was never a self-proclaimed mugwump, though the Jameses exemplify the classic definition of the mugwump type: the children of antebellum old-money elites who saw their power waning as that of commercial and industrial leaders increased.[50] Importantly, James's American friends, correspondents, and editors—indeed almost the entirety of his connection to the United States while in Europe—were politically active Liberal Republicans and mugwumps. In 1870, the second year of Grant's presidency, James returned to Cambridge, where he befriended Henry Adams. When he returned to Europe a month before the Liberal Republican Convention in 1872, his friendship with poet James Russell Lowell deepened. One of James's primary correspondents during this time was the writer and future Harvard president Charles Eliot Norton. James's primary outlet for writing was the magazine the *Nation*, edited by his friend E. L. Godkin.[51] These men were prominent Grant critics, with Adams and Godkin active in organizing the 1872 Liberal Republican Party.[52] By the end of Grant's first term, James agreed with their assessment of the Grant administration. "Our government," he wrote to a friend, "is not doing things handsomely."[53] By the end of the second term, continuing to see presidential politics in terms of appearance, James would respond to the resignations of Grant's war secretary and private secretary for respective scandals: "The news we get from America seems of course hideous."[54]

James's sympathies were with his Liberal Republican friends, and he shared their disappointment when their convention nominated Horace Greeley, who James predicted would "carry but a small fraction of the country." Indeed, the Liberal Republican alliance with the Democrats against Grant solidified the president's base of Union veterans and Black voters, while Greeley's past positions, at odds with Liberal Republican goals, allowed Grant to claim elements of that platform as his own. The result was a sound defeat of Liberal Republicans' attempted ouster of Grant, but, as James wrote about the movement, "it is not a pure misfortune however that it should be forced to await a stronger maturity."[55] In this prediction, too, James proved right. Versions of the Liberal Republican Party platform spread across the country, often under the banner of Reform, weakening Republicans' electoral strengths and helping Democrats win a congressional majority in 1874. By 1876, the Republican standard-bearer, Rutherford Hayes, had moved much closer to the Liberals' position on civil service reform and Reconstruction, while Democrats, evidencing that both parties sought reform-minded votes, nominated the Reform-aligned Samuel Tilden.

In this competition over the former Liberal Republican voters, that election's watchword became "honesty." At Hayes's nominating convention, Republicans opened with the declaration "All we want is a man, in the first place, who is honest."[56] Democrats, at their convention, aimed to do one better: their candidate must not only be "intrinsically honest" but also "the cause of honesty in others."[57] Democrats were single-minded in making Hayes appear connected to Republican corruption. Republicans assailed Tilden's unattractive appearance as thin and sickly.[58] Most savagely, Republican stump speaker Robert Ingersoll mocked Tilden as "half a man, half a pair of scissors."[59] Ingersoll also lampooned Tilden for being a bachelor, insults that recent commentators have treated as accusations of Tilden's homosexuality.[60] Certainly Ingersoll alluded to abnormal gender behavior: "Any man . . . surrounded by beautiful women with rosy lips and dimpled cheeks, in every

dimple lurking a cupid, with coral lips and pearly teeth and sparkling eyes—
any man that will push them all aside and be satisfied with the embraces of
the Democratic party, does not even know the value of time." But the final
part of that comment, Tilden's preference for a political over a husbandly
or paternal life, was a more important attack than insinuating secret sexual
behavior. Ingersoll's primary goal was to connect Tilden to the most recent
bachelor Democratic president, James Buchanan. A section of an Ingersoll
speech, which, when printed, bore the title BEWARE OF BACHELORS, began:
"Then there's Buchanan; an old bachelor, and, for God's sake, never trust
another."[61] The attention paid to Tilden's thin appearance and his bachelor
status were meant to undercut his honesty and reform credentials. It was
not wholly successful: Tilden won more votes than any previous presidential
candidate and 200,000 more than his opponent, Hayes.

From London, James was eager for news of the close presidential election.
His interest in the election did not, however, indicate a preference between
the two candidates embracing reform. To a female friend, he lamented that
he could not delegate his ballot to her.[62] The one interest James appeared to
have in electoral outcomes was a mugwumpian one about government personnel. He often worried that the appointment of his friend James Russell
Lowell as minister to the United Kingdom made the acclaimed poet a mere
"sport of fortune" to the electoral whims of American democracy.[63] A worse
danger arrived in the 1876 election. Tilden's popular vote victory and contested Republican electors in three states that would give Hayes an Electoral
College victory could not have been worse for James, who feared, in a letter to his sister, agitation and violence arising from the political chaos.[64] The
desire to keep the national peace trumped partisanship for liberals, who saw
nothing to gain and much to lose from political strife. When that crisis was
averted by negotiations that appeared to bring the president-elect, Hayes,
even more toward a posture of sectional reconciliation, James wrote to his
mother, "I hope the land under him will revive." He underlined the next line:
"*Do send me his portrait.*"[65] As eager as he was for political news, he was as
eager for presidential portraits.

Almost the entirety of James's assessments of US presidential candidates
refer to their appearances. James would also press his sister for a Hayes portrait and, four years later, a portrait of successor James Garfield.[66] About
Garfield James would write, "I like his face, which though, I think, peculiarly 'self-made,' is pleasant, & manly in expression, much more potent than
Hayes's."[67] James's assessment matched the electoral outcomes; Garfield was
more potent than his predecessor by about 400,000 more votes. Garfield was

an exceptionally skilled political character, one who managed to enthuse both a Republican base and potential liberal defectors. What is most remarkable about Garfield—given that he had been a partisan Republican operative, been implicated in a railroad corruption scandal, and advocated stronger support for Reconstruction efforts and Black voters—was how he retained support from the mugwump-type voters who would defect in 1884. His decisive 1880 electoral victory bucked the trend of Republican defections. Considering that trend of liberal defections to Democrats, Garfield's victory—the only Republican candidate between Grant in 1872 and William McKinley in 1896 to win the popular vote (or Henry Adams's vote)—may be more the outlier than Cleveland's Democratic victory four years later.[68] The reasons for Garfield's support among liberals, as James suggested, were mostly superficial: the mugwump-type voter saw himself in the hyperliterate former college president who expressed support for (but not a lot of action on) civil service reform.

James's attention to the portraits of these candidates, though superficial, matched the campaign's own argument. The Garfield campaign made much of the candidate's attractive physical appearance. A Garfield supporter, summarizing the candidate "in one word," chose "his thorough *manliness*," meaning that he had both "the figure of an athlete" and "no lines of craft or cunning." Garfield campaign biographies contrasted his attractiveness—"endowed by nature with a grand physique" and "prodigious strength of muscle in the arms"—with a feminized portrayal of his opponent, Winfield Scott Hancock. Democrats celebrated Hancock as exceedingly handsome, while Republicans lampooned him as exceedingly vain. The publicized rumor that Hancock wore a corset doubly feminized the candidate in both feminine attire and a deceptiveness that contrasted Garfield's "robust physique and open countenance."[69] Campaign materials in postbellum elections did not just harp on "honesty" but, in particular, the amorphous value of "manly honesty." Competing for the Liberal Republican voters, campaigns evidenced their candidates' "manly honesty" through their appearance. A "manly honesty" was a quality, liberals accepted, that one could see in the candidate's face. James appeared to believe that corruption or attractiveness were visible in a campaign portrait.

The year after Garfield's inauguration, James visited Washington, with Adams and his wife as tour guides. Garfield was dead, and the White House was, James wrote, "shrouded in gloom."[70] That the delusional person who assassinated Garfield did so because he believed his politicking for Garfield had earned him a federal job only added to the liberal call for reform of federal appointments. While in Washington, James met Garfield's successor, Chester Arthur, whom he liked, despite Adams characterizing the Arthur administration as "the centre for every element of corruption, south and north."⁷¹ In several letters, James characterized the new president as "an agreeable, 'personable' man, with an evident desire to please," and "a good fellow—even attractive," with "a well-made coat & well-cut whiskers" and "a more successful physical development than is common here (in the political world)." Politics was corrupting, physically as well, in Washington, though Arthur managed to avoid a sickly appearance. Sticking to appearances, James qualified that Arthur "did not reveal to me any of the secrets of his policy—so I can't characterize him as a ruler & administrator."⁷²

Despite his access to political power, James adopted the perspective of an outside observer when his DC visit became material for the 1884 story "Pandora," which examined Washington society through the ingenuous eyes of a German diplomat. That perspective allowed for mugwumpian themes on the presidential "distribution of spoils" and for a couple modeled on the Adamses joking about a party, "Let us be vulgar and . . . invite the President." Even the frequent Jamesian theme of the spectacle of the self-made woman turned to mugwumpian critique when the novel's closing scene revealed that she used her newfound power to secure her businessman boyfriend a foreign appointment from the president. That the president might be giving jobs out for qualifications other than merit was just the kind of corruption mugwumps were worried about; even worse would be jobs in exchange for female flirtations. James's mugwump story, as in *The American Scene* and Adams's *Democracy*, contrasts the federal city with Mount Vernon. The German protagonist finds Washington's home charming in its modesty; the new American woman is too savvy and cynical to understand, as the foreigner does, the Washington ideal. "You Germans," she muses, "are always in such awe of great people."⁷³

"Pandora" was published in June 1884, the same week that James Blaine received the Republican nomination, and in the *New York Sun*, the same paper in which Charles Dana would first call Republican defectors from Blaine mugwumps. Blaine had won the nomination through decades of attrition, becoming virtually the last man standing of the various contestants in the past two decades of Republican nominations. The Republican argument was that no man was better prepared to be president than the former Speaker of the House, secretary of state, and now historian of Congress. But history would be what hurt Blaine as his two decades of political experience attached him to many of the Republican scandals of the era. James would, four years later, apply the same description he had used for the Grant administration

1884 Republican presidential candidate James G. Blaine exposed as a prostitute of the public trust. Bernhard Gillam, "Phryne before the Chicago Tribunal, with apologies to J. L. Gerome," *Puck*, June 4, 1884, 216. Library of Congress.

upon "the hideous Blaine."[74] In an 1884 cartoon in the Democrat-aligned magazine *Puck*, political scandals were also written on Blaine's body, with the candidate stripped and exposed before Republican leaders, in parody of Jean-Léon Gérôme's 1861 painting of the Greek Phryne stripped and exposed before her jury in ancient Athens. Meanwhile, Cleveland's own sex scandal during the 1884 election—allegedly buying the silence of a woman he had impregnated—did not tarnish his reputation for *manly honesty* as Blaine's political scandals had. To mugwumps, far better to have the public rectitude and private immorality of Cleveland than the private rectitude and public immorality of Blaine—the sex scandal preferable to the image of Blaine as prostitute of the public trust.[75]

A Blaine presidency would not have meant the return of Grant-era Reconstruction policies. Blaine had opposed removing political disabilities from Jefferson Davis, as well as withdrawing Federal troops from Southern states, but as Speaker of the House, he had moderated a more robust Federal intervention.[76] Cleveland's victory, after years of diminishing Reconstruction efforts, meant, more than that, its reversal, especially in executive agencies where Reconstruction enforcement had been located, such as the attorney general's office and the Department of the Interior. Cleveland installed a Confederate senator in the former and a Confederate veteran in the latter.[77] Mugwump defection alone hardly explains Cleveland's victory, but it was significant in the 1,000 votes that gave Cleveland New York State and the election.

James's Usefulness for Roosevelt

Back in London, working on a novel tentatively titled *Verena*, James had very little to do with the mugwump defection, but you would not know that listening to the anti-mugwump speeches of Theodore Roosevelt, who treated the novelist as a totem of mugwumpery. Though Roosevelt shared the background of the typical mugwump (Harvard education with an old-money, philanthropist father), he remained a Republican loyalist and defended candidate Blaine in 1884 in a speech to the Brooklyn Young Republican Club. Portraying James as "ornamental, but never useful," Roosevelt found the novelist quite useful as an example of mugwump masculinity. He attacked James as bearing "the same relation to other literary men that a poodle did to other dogs." He continued that James in particular and mugwumps in general were "possessed of refinement and culture to see what was wrong, but possessed none of the robuster virtues that would enable them to come out and do the right."[78]

Various scholarship has taken Roosevelt's attack on James as being essentially about the contemplative life of a writer, or imperialism, or male gender performance, or homosexuality. Over the next several decades, Roosevelt would continue to develop this contrast between his masculine performance and an effete critic like James, most famously in his 1910 "Man in the Arena" speech. His evolution during that time into a champion of aggressive US imperialism and the evolution of many prominent mugwumps, including William James, into critics of US imperialism has led scholars to read the earlier gendered attack on Henry James within the politics of Roosevelt's imperialist masculinity.[79] During the 1884 presidential campaign, however, the dispute was less about imperialism than it was about whether long-standing loyalty to the Republican Party should win over the criticisms of character. Their disagreement was primarily about whether Republican voters ought to stick with the Republican Party and vote for Blaine in 1884.

Roosevelt's gendered attack on James was part of a broader phenomenon of politics and sexuality beginning in the 1880s, as Kevin Murphy explains, in which Republican loyalists treated the defecting mugwumps in terms drawn from the emerging sexual science: "political hermaphrodites" or a "third sex."

Certainly for party loyalists there was an easy binary-based analogy between switching parties and switching genders that may go a long way to explain the mugwumps' centrality to this rhetoric, though mugwumps were neither its first nor its last target. Murphy shows how the deployment of this political rhetoric mingled, as both source and product, with the emergence of pathologized identities in the final decades of the century.[80] Like many a homophobic insult, and like most things with Theodore Roosevelt, the speech also revealed the speaker's insecurities—though more political than gendered. As the *New York Times* reported, Roosevelt was justifying "himself for supporting Blaine after opposing him in convention." Roosevelt aimed to transport his audience back to the recent past, recasting the 1884 election within the Civil War and Reconstruction struggle. His was the party of Lincoln; the Democratic vice-presidential candidate, a onetime opponent of the Lincoln administration in the Senate, was an insult to those loyal to the Union. Roosevelt alluded to the Democrats' voter suppression "in a certain section of the country," meaning among Black voters in the ex-Confederate states.[81] Mugwump defection, to Roosevelt, betrayed the Union war effort and demonstrated a sympathy to the Confederacy and Democratic South. These facts complicate the gendered attack. As risky as it is to say, Roosevelt's criticism of James within the politics of the 1880s was not without some merit: after all, the son of an abolitionist, the brother of officers in Union Black regiments, was not a Republican voter.[82]

James would criticize Roosevelt most directly fourteen years later in the same article in which he commends Dunning's history. In 1898, James wrote eleven "American letters," each examining two or three recently published books by American authors. As reviews of contemporary books, the pairings were less determined by a plan of comparison than by whatever James happened to be reading.[83] Nonetheless, the essay implies one contrast between Roosevelt's vacuous American nationalism and Dunning's "fond, old figment of the Sovereign state," while naming another between the "lucidity" of Dunning's *Essays* and the "puerility" of Roosevelt's *American Ideals* (1897).[84] To the extent that James can praise Roosevelt, it is for mugwump reasons: Roosevelt's criticism of New York machine politics and work on the Civil Service Commission within President Benjamin Harrison's administration. But, once more, James's and Roosevelt's argument is about criticism, action, and honesty. For Roosevelt, the honest American is unencumbered by criticism. James, mocking Roosevelt, finds such an American to be unencumbered by a mind. In accusing Roosevelt of philistinism, James retains his mugwumpian skepticism of democracy. The review's title is "Democracy and Theodore

Roosevelt," and James is critical of both. When Roosevelt argues that an educated man who enters politics should free himself of his critical orientation or
find himself "upset by some other American with no education at all," James
responds that rather than "barbarize" the educated man, society should "civ-
ilize the upsetter." In the 1898 article, then, James confirms the mugwump
views for which Roosevelt had criticized him in 1884.

How did James respond in 1884 to Roosevelt's attack that a defective
gender identity caused a perverted sympathizing with the wrong side of the
recent North-South conflict? On the one hand, near silence: about "Roosevelt's allusion to, or attack upon, me in his speech," James wrote to a friend,
"I have heard nothing, & know nothing, of it."[85] On the other hand, two years
later, he published *The Bostonians*, a novel about the problems of gender,
postbellum North-South sectionalism, and as may critics have written, the
problem of sympathy itself.[86]

Homoerotic "Tragic Fellowship" in *The Bostonians*

Sympathy appears with remarkable frequency in *The Bostonians*. The novel
insists, when both narrator and characters use the term, that it is a feeling
one primarily has not for people but for ideas. The novel's chief lesson in
fictionalizing postbellum US politics through a love plot is that objects of
political sympathy are not abstractions but embodied figures. As the novel
opens, Olive warns Ransom, "If you are not in sympathy"—meaning to her
political ideas—"perhaps you had better not come" to hear the speeches at
Miss Birdseye's. Ransom responds, "In sympathy with what, dear madam?"
pointing out that if there is to be a political debate, there will be two sides,
"and of course one can't sympathise with both."[87] In that problem is the challenge of the novel, both for Verena, who must choose between Ransom and
Olive, and for the ambivalent narrative voice that redirects readerly sympathies alternatively to these rivals.

The rivals, of course, restage the Civil War. Early on, in celebrating his
own "good cause," Ransom alludes both to "the great Secession, and by comparison, to the attitude of the resisting male."[88] Ransom and Olive's Civil War
combat is more than metaphoric: in postbellum society they are partisans
still hostile after national peace. The feminists, on whom Olive and her peers
are modeled, saw their effort for expanded rights as continuing the wartime revolution. They felt betrayed that Republican allies, especially in the
gendered language of the Reconstruction amendments, had used their support for emancipation and Black suffrage only to abandon efforts for female

suffrage.[89] For his part, Ransom is extreme in the other direction, a conservative pulling back progress not merely to 1860 but by three or four centuries in the estimation of a reviewer of one of his essays.[90]

If *The Bostonians* restages the Civil War, the contest over Verena inverts the war's outcome—the South wins and Olive loses—and reverses the lost-cause feelings the war produced. One cannot close *The Bostonians* without feeling that there is indeed a Lost Cause, a fight made worthy by the odds stacked against it, but it belongs not to Ransom but to Olive Chancellor, whose last name alludes to the war's most significant Confederate victory. Near the end of the novel, when Verena flees from her coastal vacation town, Ransom decides against pursuing her, proving "to himself how secure he felt, what a conviction he had that however she might turn and twist in his grasp he held her fast."[91] Gen. William T. Sherman made the same decision in marching to the sea from Atlanta rather than pursuing Confederate John Bell Hood. In an 1864 letter, published in subsequent histories of the war, Sherman explained, "To pursue Hood is folly, for he can twist and turn like a fox and wear out any army in pursuit."[92] At that point, the war's outcome was decided, though it had not yet ended. To postbellum Confederates, that sense extended backward, as if their defeat had been lost before it started. Olive, at this point in the narrative, "too weary to struggle with fate," recognizes the inevitability of her defeat, that there was no help in a flight to Europe, that the forces aligned against her were not just Ransom as an individual; rather, "women had from the beginning of time been the sport of men's selfishness and avidity."[93]

The South wins in *The Bostonians*, because of the necessary logic of events, that Verena, as Ransom tells her, was "made for love"—not for Olive but for him.[94] Olive's pull on Verena, whether intended by James to be read as lesbianism or something just shy of it, was against a strong normative force, what would be called, a century later, compulsory heterosexuality. Southern victory, in James's hands, is the foreordained outcome, like marriage between a man and woman, to which a delusion, like a Boston marriage, must naturally revert.[95] As for ex-Confederates the ex post facto feeling that their cause had been doomed became an inexhaustible source of sympathy; so, too, have many readers of *The Bostonians* found their sympathies drawn to Olive and her defeat. James scholars over the decades, especially those exploring his affinity for queer subjectivities, have read a sympathy on the part of the author with Olive.[96] If so, that sympathy mirrors what *The American Scene*'s narrator feels toward Confederate Richmond, toward a mind "in the very convulsions of perversity—the conception that, almost comic in itself, was yet so tragically to fail to work, that of a world rearranged."[97]

If Olive's loss is preordained, Ransom's victory remains the novel's key question—and ultimately its political argument. Many critics have explored how Ransom represents an imagined South—a chivalrous antebellum South, an emasculated postbellum South, or an altogether misrepresented South.[98] As this attention to Ransom as a representative Southerner demonstrates, one primary object of the novel's political thinking, where James refuses to disentangle politics and sexuality, is to ask what makes this young Southerner attractive to the Northern Verena, to James, to the reader, and to Northern white liberals. Had James been a different writer, one whose inquiries into human psychology were more aimed at neuroses and crises, we could imagine the question at the heart of this novel posed through a davening Verena, repeating, *I don't love the South. I don't. I don't love it.* Instead, James explores Ransom's attractiveness through his masculine, honest appearance and through a homoerotic connection to a remembered Civil War past.

What makes Ransom attractive? First—and most of all—it is his appearance. His introduction, following the pattern of James's young Southerners, emphasizes the mixture of poverty and a pleasing face: "As poor as a young man could look who had such a fine head and such magnificent eyes." The narration insists that his male rival for Verena, the young Henry Burrage, is as, if not more, conventionally handsome, but if we are to take Olive's calculations, that men are "good-looking" in reverse proportion to their acceptance of new truths, Ransom is by magnitudes of conservatism the most so.[99] That conservatism undoubtedly forms part of the appeal, linked, as Judith Wilt suggested, to an eroticization of patriarchal control.[100] He is young (the narrator repeats this fact) but no longer ingenuous. Nonetheless, he bears a distinct relation to Confederate ingenuousness. His family had "tasted of all the cruelty of defeat" when they "lost their slaves, their property, their friends and relations, their home," but now, as Verena hears his views on slavery, he was no "more tender to that particular example of human imbecility than he was to any other."[101] Thus, Ransom occupies the Jamesian view uniting the ingenuousness of the past with its present observation.

The Civil War past comes back in the "I'll Take My Stand" posturing of the novel's final scene: Ransom, compared in the theater to John Wilkes Booth, is alone against confederate enemies, the onetime abolitionist Olive, the profit-seeking event manager, the intrusive reporter, and Verena's father, compared at the opening to "the detested carpet-bagger."[102] Verena's tears, as she is whisked away, make the ending famously ambivalent, but one thing that is not ambivalent is the opposition between Ransom and those now deceiving the audience about the night's proceedings. Each encourages Verena to speak, but each for secret, self-interested reasons: Olive to keep Verena her own; the event manager, the reporter, and Verena's parents to profit from her speech. Ransom, too, is self-interested, but he is, in contrast to their deceptiveness, honest about his interest.

As several scholars have written, engagement with the Civil War past occurs not merely within the novel's pages but also in its context, especially that of the magazine in which *The Bostonians* was first printed. Barbara Hochman points to the reconciliationist writing that accompanied the novel's serialization in the *Century*, especially the series "Battles and Leaders of the Civil War" celebrating the heroes of both sides of the conflict. The spirit of reconciliation in the 1880s was not merely a popular cultural feeling, but a decidedly political one—that is, it was not unanimous but a feeling around which a political group organized and mobilized. Richard Watson Gilder, the *Century* editor who promoted the "Battles" series and published *The Bostonians*, was among the most prominent mugwumps and supporters of Grover Cleveland. For Gilder, the use of a Civil War past—whether in "Battles" or in *The Bostonians*—helped cultivate reconciliationist feeling not merely for its own sake but for a distinct political project. The *Century*, as Mark Noonan explains in his case study on the magazine in the 1870s and 1880s, aimed for a larger political project of cultivating liberal values broadly, where sympathies for defeated Southerners were one prominent component.[103]

The novel's most notable shift of sympathies toward Ransom occurs through his connection with the Civil War past. It also happens outside of Verena's view, between Ransom and other men. In that scene, central both to the novel itself and to Ransom winning readerly sympathies as a substitute for Verena's, Ransom reads the names on the memorial of Harvard students who died in the Union army and then returns, once Verena has stepped outside, to "read again the names of the various engagements at several of which he had been present."[104] The scene, similar to Adams's Confederate veteran reminiscing at the national cemetery for Union dead, situates Ransom within what James would later call that "tragic fellowship."[105] For Ransom, "the simple emotion of the old fighting-time came back to him, and the monument around him seemed an embodiment of that memory; it arched over friends as well as enemies, the victims of defeat as well as the sons of triumph."[106] What changes the reader's perception of Ransom has nothing to do with Verena but everything to do with his connection to the young men of the Civil War past. That fellowship, as Susan Ryan has argued, privileges a communion of feelings between men over that between men and women. The scene's emphasis of, she writes, "the homo-affective, perhaps even homoerotic elements of postwar reunion" connects the young Southerner to the memories of young men from James's own prewar past.[107]

The Bostonians does not mention directly any of the inscriptions within Harvard's Memorial Hall, but many of the names that Ransom reads would have been those James knew personally. James had watched CABOT JACKSON RUSSEL, 18 JULY 1863. FORT WAGNER depart for the war alongside his brother Wilkie. Both Cabot and Wilkie were missing after the battle of Fort Wagner. It was Cabot's father who found Wilkie in an army hospital and brought him back to the James family when his own son was dead. In his 1914 autobiography, James remembers Cabot's departing face: "Dark-eyed, youthfully brown, heartily bright, actively handsome, and with the arrested expression, the indefinable shining stigma."[108] These same attributes, midway between that departure and its recollection, characterize Ransom's attractiveness, his "dark, deep, and glowing" eyes "with their smouldering fire," "thick black hair, perfectly straight and glossy," and "deep dry line, a sort of premature wrinkle, on either side of the mouth."[109] Ransom would also have seen, a few tablets over from Cabot, WILLIAM JAMES TEMPLE. 1 MAY 1863. CHANCELLORSVILLE, who exemplified, for James, "young confidence in a glory to come." As James remembers his youthful death, "his appearance and my personal feelings about it live for me again."[110]

On that same tablet, Ransom would also have seen AUGUSTUS BARKER. 18 SEPTEMBER 1863, James's cousin Gus. A few years earlier, in a formative erotic moment also remembered in *Notes*, James had walked in on "the beautiful young manly form of our cousin Gus Barker . . . perched on a pedestal and divested of every garment . . . the gayest as well as the neatest of models." The model being painted by his brother William was, James writes, his "first personal vision of the 'life,'" meaning a nude model but suggesting at the same time a sense of his vocation (or possibly orientation), as different from his brother's, which James then renders, suggestively, as "pocketing my pencil." James kept the painting of the nude Barker for the next fifty years, which was, by 1914, "to speak for the original after his gallant death, in sharper and finer accents perhaps than aught else that remained of him."[111] If Ransom reading these names within *The Bostonians* establishes a "tragic fellowship" between himself and the Union dead, these names of the dead were, for the novel's author, not abstractions but remembered bodies, the very male bodies that had been the object of early erotic fascination.

The eroticized "tragic fellowship" also responded to Roosevelt's attack. Roosevelt, in no less an emotional appeal, constructed a fellowship between

the Union dead and the present Republican political project against former Confederates and contemporary Democrats. James, instead, brought
together the Union dead and the former Confederates to represent a longed-
for past, opposed to present politics. If Roosevelt attempted to paint such
Southern sympathizing as a deviant, hermaphroditic gender performance,
so, too, did James set a masculine homoerotic fellowship against perverse
female sexuality. The two men agreed that society's feminization represented
a danger to the present; where they disagreed was in the use of the Civil War
past. For Roosevelt, that past struggle was allied with the present Republican
struggle, including against the disenfranchisement of Black voters; for James,
the former antagonists of the past, white men of the North and South, were
allied, as a celebrated past, against the corrupt present.

Roosevelt's coalition lost the 1884 election. The winning side indeed represented a coalition of past and present. A Cleveland biography had predicted
that, with his victory, "the 'rebel yell' will at length be heard on the heights
of the Capitol of the United States, but only in expression of patriotism and
heart-felt joy of prodigal sons, who, after twenty-five years of political exile,
realize at last their full restoration to the Union."[112] During that period, their
fictional counterparts had hardly been exiled from literary fiction. Cleveland
installed some of the models for these fictional Confederate veterans at the
highest levels of government. One, the Mississippian Lucius Q. C. Lamar, was
appointed secretary of the Interior and, three years later, a Supreme Court
justice. At the time of *The Bostonians'* publication, Lamar would have been
among the most well-known Mississippians, and James intimated that Lamar
was a model for Basil Ransom. When he heard of Lamar's "appreciative judg-
ment of my rather reckless attempt to represent a youthful Southron," James
mentioned that Lamar was "one of the few very Mississippians with whom I
have had the pleasure of conversing."[113] Lamar had been a US senator since
1877, but he was most notable for a speech that he gave, as a Mississippi congressman, after the death of Massachusetts senator Charles Sumner in 1874.
At the end of the speech, Lamar made the dead abolitionist partisan rise up
from the grave, seemingly alongside the Union and Confederate dead, with a
message to the living: "Would that the spirit of the illustrious dead, whom we
lament to-day, could speak from the grave to both parties to this deplorable
discord, in tones which would reach each and every heart throughout this
broad territory: 'My countrymen! *know* one another and you will *love* one
another.'"[114] As in the scenes at the Harvard memorial for the Union dead in
The Bostonians, at Arlington Cemetery in *Democracy*, at Stonewall Jackson's

camp in *Two College Friends*, and at the prison camp in *Andersonville Violets*, as with Schaff's memories of Pelham in *The Spirit of Old West Point* and in the poems of Whitman's *Drum-Taps* with which I opened this book, Lamar made the message of the dead men from the past one of reunion and love between countrymen.

The Sexuality of Historiography and the Premodern South

WO UNSYMPATHETIC READERS of Henry James were the historians Charles and Mary Beard. In *The Rise of American Civilization* (1930), they accused James of fleeing "from the land of prosperity for the purpose of sketching the etiquette of dying ages." If the central thesis of their second volume of American history was that in the nineteenth century's latter half one economic system, industrial capitalism, conquered another, agrarian feudalism, James—by renouncing American citizenship to become "a subject of King George"—was the trend-proving exception, a cultural reactionary to the social transformation. For the Beards, James's status as "the grandson of a millionaire" allowed him to enjoy "luxurious leisure" enough to "evolve a meticulous and fine-spun style, one so vague and so intricate" that even his brother, they claimed, urged him to be more straightforward.[1] The fact of his self-exile, taking with him an abstruse style so at odds with modern efficiency, underscored the victories for American industrial progress.

For Richard Hofstadter, James, or rather the Beards' treatment of James, was also exemplary, but of the tendencies of "the progressive historians" (as Hofstadter's 1968 book-length work of criticism called the Beards and their contemporaries) to squeeze historical interpretation into the foreordained conclusion that ideas directly represent economic interests. Hofstadter criticized Charles Beard, alongside literary historian V. L. Parrington, for his parallel condemnation of James, whom, Hofstadter suggested, they read neither very closely nor with "enough detachment even to see the necessity of being fair."[2] Certainly, Hofstadter was on to something, given how James's *American Scene* predicted the Beards' narrative of the Civil War as an inexorable clash between forces of past and present.[3] More to the point, Hofstadter saw in Beard and Parrington the "characteristic American male reproach of absorption in the effeminate and the unreal that had so long been made against men of complex and delicate sensibility."[4] Without the terms for it, Hofstadter accused historians not merely of a homophobic reaction to James but of being led by homophobic bias to write bad history.

Hofstadter's point was that historians' interpretations are colored by their own experience with masculinity.[5] We should take Hofstadter's premise seriously and extend it—to what extent does historical interpretation depend on historians' own experience with homosexuality? If epistemologies of sexuality structure the thinking of an entire culture, in addition to a same-sex-desiring minority, as Eve Kosofsky Sedgwick established, then we should expect such thinking to inform historical interpretation.[6] For historians in the twentieth century, a century in which the crises of identification with one of two categories of sexual orientation, homosexual or heterosexual, dominated a great deal of thought, this may be especially true. The fact of sexual orientation—whether heterosexual assertion or the specter of nonheterosexuality in oneself or others—bore down upon the life of the twentieth-century historian. Their works of American history have, hidden beneath the surface, this queer character, secretly pulling at the strings.

I don't mean to suggest the twentieth-century historian as closeted away, working out his sexual identity by tracing General Hancock's maneuvers at the First Battle of Deep Bottom. Instead, I aim to take up Hayden White's thesis in "The Historical Text as Literary Artifact" that what the historian does to historical events is charge them "with the symbolic significance of a comprehensible plot structure."[7] White brought the literary critical method of genre analysis to bear on historiography, but literary methods extend beyond form, even to that late-century export of English departments, queer theory.[8] Foundational texts of queer studies have shown that the emplotment of sexuality, too, was part of a narrative's symbolic significance.[9] If we take historical narratives as literary artifacts, these artifacts reveal themselves dependent on timebound presumptions about sexuality, on categorical divisions between normal and queer.

We already have, to be sure, robust methods of queer history: recovering the lives of same-sex-desiring people and gender-nonconforming people in

the past, excavating the architecture of categories of sex and gender, and identifying modes of resistance to overlapping regimes of oppression. For much
of the twentieth century, historians saw such work with suspicion, accusing
practitioners of being too influenced by presentist sexual or gender identity
to see the past clearly. But, we can now see, these homodox historians were
themselves performing similar maneuvers, of identifying queerness in the
past, and no less motivated by presentist self-conception and identity. "Just
as the historical constructs the sexual," Susan Lanser writes in *The Sexuality
of History*, "so too does the sexual construct the historical, shaping the social
imaginary, and providing a site for reading it."[10] If those readers, as writers of
history, are informed by their own thinking about sexuality, then we might
suggest that history writing entails epistemologies of sexuality.

Where are the epistemologies of sexuality within the interpretation of
American history? Not at the margins but in the very central questions of
historical interpretation. Within the history of US imperialism, were the
filibusters explored in the first chapter—those private invading armies of
the 1850s—consistent with or aberrant to the current of US foreign policy?
Writers taking up the latter thesis have emphasized the queerness of figures
like William Walker, while accounts of male sexual desire have long been the
explanation for private invading armies. Meanwhile, in historical biography, representative, moderate men and their eccentric, radical counterparts
become refracted, as in the case of Abraham Lincoln and Charles Sumner,
through assertions of sexual biography. Even the status of the antebellum
South, itself, has been written through a sexualized interpretation, conflated
with homoerotic nostalgia for an imagined premodernity. The myth of the
premodern South—that it stood before and in opposition to the forces of capitalism, industry, progress, and the modern world itself—took hold because it
was desirable.[11] It was desirable not merely in the sense that it justified white
supremacist political resistance but also as an eroticized orientation to the
past as a worldview and way of living.

Filibustering Men

The chief question for historians and commentators on Walker and the US
filibusters has been whether their efforts to invade and conquer foreign countries has been within, or aberrant to, the tradition of US foreign policy and
imperialism. That interpretation decidedly overlaps with a presentation of
Walker's sexual and gender identity. Those who seek to cast Walker's imperialism as a significant deviation from American norms emphasize Walker's "sexual disorder" and his tendency to keep "the slimmest and most

girlish-looking young devils" as aides-de-camp, while explaining his invasion of Nicaragua as compensation for sexual dysfunction.[12] Literary scholar Brady Harrison has noted that, especially in a Cold War context in which the United States aimed to project itself as a benevolent aid to, rather than clandestine invader of, other nations, Walker's "effeminacy and homosexuality come to signify both disloyalty to the nation, *and* masculine failure."[13] Meanwhile, for historians who situate Walker's imperialism within American norms, most notably Michael Gobat, any mention of Walker's extranormative sexuality or gender disappears from the story.[14] Gobat's dequeering of Walker's imperialism is persuasive; my own twenty-first-century view of homoeroticism's potential congruities with US imperialism led me to my conclusions in chapter 1 that Walker's decidedly homosocial, and even homoerotic, appeal was quite normal for a popular imperialist project.[15] Nonetheless, Walker's queer status in history depends less on the facts of his life than on where he fits within historical interpretation.

Nearly every historical account explains the filibusters' appeal, in part, through male attraction. Naming a central motif, Charles Brown opens *Agents of Manifest Destiny* with "two attractive men," Francisco de Miranda and Aaron Burr.[16] The latter, as prototypical filibuster for his 1807 plot to invade Mexico, inaugurates filibustering's explanation through male seduction. That Burr had a seducer's hold on his young male supporters was, Nancy Isenberg documents, an accusation within his lifetime, levied directly by prosecutors at his trial for the Mexico invasion conspiracy.[17] Personal magnetism would become, for other historians, a standard explanation for why young men would follow an attractive filibustering man. How else to explain this queer practice (of invading Nicaragua) than by naming it a queer practice (of male homoeroticism)? That a military leader's personal charisma bleeds into eroticism may apply here as much as anywhere, but the emphasis with filibusters on male seduction was a way of implying their abnormality and deviance.

Walker is doubly, if not triply, queer: not only did this man seduce his male followers, but he was not even a real man. His story is an invert's inversion. As such, it opens up for Walter Johnson's magisterial account of slavery's racial capitalism a way of thinking through the inversions by which material processes become abstraction. Walker's innate masculine failures, near the end of *River of Dark Dreams* (2013) add to Johnson's method of analyzing the "interlinking of material process and cognitive experience" that defines his historiographic approach. It is an approach to racial capitalism that originates in the material conditions of slavery in the Mississippi Valley and extends to the slaveholder's ambitions for empire, global trade, and white supremacy. That interlinking, both between racial slavery and global capital and between material processes and cognitive experience, depends, for Johnson, on contradictions, inversions, and overcompensations that ultimately mask the origins of abstractions—slavery, capitalism, whiteness, agency, power—in material conditions. And so, like an allegory, Walker enters as a fantastical embodiment of masked contradictions: the "effeminate" boy, "an unconvincing man," "withdrawn to the point of shyness," as the avatar of filibustering's "sexual self-assertion" and its "imagery of sexual conquest." It makes Walker's life "a sort of white-supremacist fairy tale," Johnson writes. "His early life of incomplete, ineffectual masculinity offered a parable of whiteness overcoming the limitations inherent in its unlikely vessel, of a boy made man through imperialism and slavery, of manifest destiny's homunculus become a dictator in Central America." Johnson builds skillfully on a few decades of gender analysis, to put masculine self-conception—where it should be—at the very crotch of imperialist ideology. And yet, Walker's fairytale status within Johnson's narrative transforms Walker's unmanliness and sexual inadequacy into something at the superstructure's base, as real as the "bare-life processes," the "animal energy, human labor," "grain, flesh, and cotton," which it was not.[18]

The case of Confederate soldier John Pelham, presented in chapter 3, offers biographical overlaps with Walker's without the sexual-imperialist overcompensations. Pelham was also celebrated, as Johnson writes of Walker, as "a beautiful boy making his way through a man's world, with the heart of a lion concealed in his breast."[19] Pelham would be lionized not because he overcame his effeminacy to be a martial man penetrating virgin lands but because his virginal innocence required the project of protecting white supremacy. Returning to Walker's unmanliness with Pelham's model in mind raises a terrifying question: What if imperialism were a project of bottoms, as well as tops, and not just to overcompensate for being bottoms? Isn't the language of conquest just as much one of accumulation, absorption, and extraction as it is penetration? In a crucial passage from Walker's *War in Nicaragua*, whose sexual imagery Johnson explores, the "graceful cone" of the volcano Omotepe rises from Lake Nicaragua. "The appearance of the volcano," Walker continues, "was so much that of a person enjoying a siesta, the beholder would not have been surprised to see it waken at any moment and throw the lava from its burning sides. The first glimpse of the scene almost made the pulse stand still."[20] If a sexualized image, isn't it one where the Nicaraguan landscape, if wakened by the filibusters, bubbles over hot liquid from its cone while the filibusters' pulse stands still as they take it in? The psychic pleasure of filibustering here may not be desexed, exactly, but devirilized, a metaphor more polymorphous than male ejaculation.

Doubtless, imperialist ideologies enmesh themselves within masculinist ideologies of sexual conquest and sexual violence. But when stories of masculine identity outside the formula by which imperial invasion equals heterosexual penetration come back by Freudian inversion to that same formula, we risk being led to conclusions about gender's meaning, not by the historical evidence but by theories of a transhistorical experience of gender. Johnson's work admirably turns to psychoanalytic tools for historical explanation, but the value of such tools, as Joan Wallach Scott writes, comes in reading "the unforeseen and the unknown" and not in reading "diagnostically" with "categorical explanations and reductive causalities."[21] Johnson's Walker is not merely diagnosed but reduced to a "fairy tale" structure, whose moral is that effeminacy can mean only one thing, castration, which can lead to only one thing, invading Nicaragua.[22]

I treat Johnson's nuanced understanding of Walker's masculine identity here precisely because, even in its complexity, we can find the historian's presumptions about sexuality determining interpretation. In a personal essay, Johnson movingly laid out an understanding of masculinity and homoeroticism, in which guns, violence, and whiteness overcompensate for same-sex love.[23] Johnson offers astute analysis of how these ideologies operate today, but the framework for his late twentieth-century upbringing, in which same-sex eroticism gets sublimated into gun culture, is notably similar to Walker's mid-nineteenth-century sublimation of masculine failure into Nicaraguan invasion. We ought to be skeptical that such sublimation operated so similarly, as a universal structure, across two centuries.

For twentieth-century historians, writing with far less nuance than Johnson, a schoolyard equation of homosexuality and abnormality had to be, alternatively, overcome or leveraged to make a historical argument. For example, confronted with the collegiate homoeroticism between future South Carolina statesmen Thomas J. Withers and James Henry Hammond, biographer Drew Gilpin Faust dismisses the language of "poking and punching a writhing Bedfellow with your long fleshen pole" as "hardly referring to overt homosexual behavior." Faust conjectures that Withers, "who would later become a prominent state jurist," was "concerned here less with the question of sex than that of power." Faust's biography aims to make her man a, if not *the*, representative white Southern patrician; Hammond's ideological differences with other Southerners, including Confederate leaders, must be elided and his homosexual behavior must be excluded to retain the representative normality of her subject to a presumed-as-straight historical audience.[24] Meanwhile, the case of Confederate secretary of war Judah P. Benjamin has proceeded in the opposite direction. To accentuate the Jewish Benjamin's difference from other

Confederate leaders, and to insinuate additional layers to his special culpability for the Confederacy's failure (thereby exonerating others), twentieth-century biographers implied his homosexuality and gender deviance.[25] With the sexualities of Civil War biography, as in those of two of the era's central Republican personages, Abraham Lincoln and Charles Sumner, there are two sides to the coin, both a homophobic exclusion and a queer inclusion, with ideological interpretation proceeding through the use of that dividing line.

Two Versions of Homosexuality in Civil War Biography

Questions about the sexuality of Lincoln and Sumner have tended to focus on the unanswerable and anachronistic "Were they gay?" There are, however, more pressing historical and political questions: Why—for what political purposes—was Sumner's sexual identity interrogated and Lincoln's relationships with other men romanticized?

Lincoln's story is familiar. In 1837, he walked into a store in Springfield, Illinois, and promptly moved in with the proprietor, Joshua Speed, with whom he would share intimate feelings, affectionate letters, and a bed for the next four years. Their relationship was in the model of antebellum romantic friendship, perhaps paradigmatically so, as Jonathan Ned Katz posits by opening *Love Stories* with the pair.[26] But, as I write in chapter 1, even the question of when Lincoln was seen to have close friends needs historicizing. No friends—not Speed who voted against him, not law partner William Herndon who was kept hidden, not campaign manager David Davis who detested him personally—played a public role in Lincoln's 1860 campaign as emblem of the self-made, self-taught man. It was not until Lincoln's death, and the outpouring of grief among his friends, or even much later, that his public image became associated with male friendship.

The Speed-Lincoln friendship received new attention beginning in the 1880s with the biography written by Lincoln's onetime secretaries John Hay and John Nicolay. Writing in installments for the *Century* (which under mugwump editorship continued its reconciliationist tone), Hay and Nicolay treated Speed as the "Pythias" to Lincoln's Damon, the "Pylades" to Lincoln's Orestes, possibly the only "intimate friend that Lincoln ever had."[27] Lincoln-Speed was a perfect symbol for reunifying the nation through a romance of white male intimacy. Speed was not merely Lincoln's best friend; the plantation owner's son was also his best cross-sectional friend. By their 1837 meeting, Lincoln had been in his second term as an antislavery politician in the Illinois legislature; by 1865, Speed still held enslaved people as property. Their friendship, for those celebrating national reconciliation decades later, made Lincoln a model of sentimental affection conquering sectional ideology. A 1905 article concluded a vignette of the pair's first encounter with "From that day on, it was Damon and Pythias again on the banks of the Sangamon."[28] By 1926, Carl Sandburg portrayed Lincoln and "his Kentucky chum" as having "a streak of lavender and spots soft as May violets." The hints of homoeroticism made Lincoln-Speed a symbol of cross-sectional national unity.[29]

More consequential than the question of whether Lincoln and Speed had a sexual relationship is what political work the memory of Lincoln's male affections accomplished. In *We Are Lincoln Men* (2003), historian David Donald demonstrated that while forcefully denying that Lincoln could have been gay. Donald quoted the psychoanalyst Charles B. Strozier to assert that homosexuality would have made Lincoln different: "A bisexual at best, torn between worlds, full of shame, confused, and hardly likely to end up in politics."[30] (History has shown Strozier's descriptors to be, far from disqualifiers, often a résumé for politics.) Donald, citing Katz's discussion of prehomosexual male intimacies, differentiated the Lincoln-Speed relationship from homosexuality. "In these still primitive, almost frontier, days in Illinois," Donald wrote, "it was anything but uncommon for two or more men to share a bed."[31] Donald's logic, that it cannot be homosexuality if everyone is doing it, rebuts the idea that Lincoln had any minoritarian self-conception as differently oriented from other men. As Donald's frontier myth indicates, Lincoln and Speed are representative of a lost prehomosexual paradise, where, depending on one's view, male intimacy is unsullied by homosexuality or male-male sexual contact is unburdened of homosexual definition.

Decades earlier, Donald interpreted Charles Sumner's sexuality very differently. In a footnote to his second volume, he denied that Sumner experienced "an overt homosexual relationship" but proceeded with insinuation that Sumner was "by choice and by temperament a bachelor," with "a passive, essentially feminine element." In the story of some onetime girlfriend and a broken engagement, Donald saw a recognizable "myth, perhaps started by Sumner himself to explain his unwed state." About Sumner's rumored impotence after his failed late-in-life marriage, Donald wrote, "If there was impotence, it was not physiological," and called it "psychic impotence."[32] Even from the first volume, which had less statement and more insinuation than the second, contemporary readers did not miss the point. Historian Charles Crowe summarized the book's "images of emotional impotence, latent homosexuality, and the sick escapism of a man who fled from his own neuroses into reform politics."[33] In a review in *Dissent*, Fawn Brodie commented on Donald's psychoanalysis of Sumner's "latent homosexuality" as betraying "a pervasive distaste for Sumner and an absence of respect for his cause."[34] These commentators recognized that

Donald used Sumner's supposed latent homosexuality to imply that Sumner's adherence to racial equality was psychologically disturbed.

Donald's presentation of Sumner as a latent homosexual was intentional. It was even briefly an example of how to use psychoanalytic tools in writing history. A how-to book of effective history writing, *The Modern Researcher* by Columbia historians Jacques Barzun and Henry F. Graff used Donald as an example of how the historian might draw upon the lessons of Freud. "In the writing of history, to take one example," they write of psychoanalysis, "its use enables the writer of a forthcoming biography of Charles Sumner, Professor David Donald, to account for his subject otherwise than as an 'odd fish' by disclosing in him the patent evidences of a repressed homosexuality." The sentence appeared in early editions of Barzun and Graff's 1957 book. In subsequent printings that year, the sentence was replaced with a citation to G. Wilson Knight's 1952 biography of Lord Byron, possibly on the insistence of Donald himself, who is thanked in the book's acknowledgments, perhaps embarrassed at having his method so outed.[35]

Donald's interpretation of Sumner has stuck. For example, a 2004 biography of Henry Wadsworth Longfellow contrasted the poet's presumed heterosexuality with his friend Sumner: "Sumner probably was gay . . . [but] both his intense absorption in reform politics and his compulsive art collecting suggest a sublimation of the erotic side of his psyche."[36] In 2017, Ron Chernow contrasted Sumner with his biographical subject Ulysses S. Grant as "a cold, humorless bachelor, [who] sashayed around Washington with his walking stick, glorying in his self-importance."[37] Poor Sumner—the slave power's chief legislative opponent for more than a decade, nearly beaten to death for his abolitionism, and ridiculed by historians because his speeches against slavery were a little much and went on too long. If only, following this logic, the Senate had more closeted men in 1852, they could have overturned the Fugitive Slave Law.

Much of Donald's career was spent marking the opposition between Sumner and Lincoln, with his strong preference for the latter. In one of his most notable—and most historically inflammatory—statements, written between the first and second volumes of the Sumner biography, Donald suggested that Lincoln somehow saved the abolitionists from their own fanatical psychosis: "The freeing of the slaves ended the great crusade that had brought purpose and joy to the abolitionists. For them Abraham Lincoln was not the Great Emancipator; he was the killer of the dream."[38] It is because of Lincoln's more moderate politics that Donald found him, though an exceptional leader, a normal man, and because of Sumner's radical politics that Donald found him more than an odd fish. He put them in opposition to each other through accounts of their sexuality, and these accounts follow the two versions of homosexuality described in this book: Lincoln, with his male intimates, moderate on racial equality, in that premodern and prehomosexual frontier air; Sumner, a city dweller, gender-inverted and sexually confused, radical on racial equality, a homosexual. When it comes to homosexuality and history, Donald's orientation toward homosexuality mattered more than Lincoln's or Sumner's supposed sexual orientations. Sumner could look, to Donald, frighteningly modern, not unlike the activist political creatures of his present. Donald's longing for a not-gay Lincoln was a longing for a moderate Lincoln and a longing for those "primitive frontier days" of premodernity.

The Homoerotic Appeal of the Premodern South

For late nineteenth-century Northern liberals, the view of a premodern South was a great source of sympathy, one that contributed to the Old South's nostalgic appeal. Certainly, the idea that the Old South stood opposed to the forces of modernity held a long-standing appeal to white Southerners, one that would only increase in the twentieth century. For white Southerners, the notion of a premodern South was a presupposition for academic and political conclusions. Southern social scientists of the 1930s and 1940s, such as Howard Odum and Wilbur Cash, diagnosed Southern society as lagging behind modernity, while the essayists in *I'll Take My Stand* (1930) defended Southern agrarian society against what they saw as Northern-directed modernization toward industry and commercialism.[39] In the case of Southern reactionaries across the twentieth century, fear of sexual threats formed part of their perceptions, the fear that reforms coming South brought with them interracial sex, expanded public power for women, or, eventually, gay rights. But the two stories of sexuality persisted as well, and one lasting appeal of the antebellum South was also sexual, the long-gone freedom of intimacies between men.

The notion of a premodern South was not a narrative of sexuality pure and simple, but the story of sexuality bolstered a historical interpretation that portrayed the Civil War as a clash between a feudal, agrarian past and a capitalist, industrial present.[40] Mark Twain, for one, allegorized the Civil War that way in *A Connecticut Yankee in King Arthur's Court* (1889). Even more famously, *Huckleberry Finn* imagined the world outside of civilization as a site uniquely romanticized for nude male bonding. As I've written, late nineteenth-century sexologists and historians posited the Civil War's effects on US society as exacerbating tendencies toward new dangerous behaviors, both the racialized threats of Black male sexuality and those of urban male homosexuality. At the same time, as in *The Thinking Bayonet, Two College*

Friends, or *The Birth of a Nation*, narratives that left homoerotic intimacies dead on Civil War battlefields reconstructed the antebellum past longingly as a time when innocent same-sex romance was possible. Literary scholars Michael Bibler and Tison Pugh have demonstrated twentieth-century white male homoeroticism to have been an orientation to the past—a plantation past imagined, as in Twain, as also a medieval one.⁴¹ That such homoerotic nostalgia coexisted with the view that traditional, agrarian Southern society was besieged by the dangerous sexualities of urban modernity presents the same paradox as in *The Birth of a Nation*. That paradox is equally evident in the widespread twentieth-century stereotypes of the South as a site of homophobic intolerance, but one that will also treat any traveler penetrating too deeply among the backwoodsmen to sodomitical misadventure. If the South has long been a premodern problem, its problems have included both a resistance to queer forms of life and the persistence of queer forms of life that, drawn from the past, haunt the present.⁴²

Looking backward, the antebellum past's agrarian ideals could also entail erotic intimacies between men, masking the antebellum agrarian past's basis in racial slavery. For many men, even those born much later than the Civil War, a national youth could resemble their own youth, where intense homosociality included same-sex intimacies, desires, and sexual behaviors. For some white Southerners, the homoerotic past was just one more aspect of the antebellum period's appeal.

For the early twentieth-century Mississippi poet William Alexander Percy, the past permitted exploration, his biographer writes, of "the relationship between nostalgia and the erotic."⁴³ The son of a segregationist senator who owned sharecrop and peon labor plantations in Mississippi and Arkansas, Percy was of the Mississippi Delta aristocracy. He had occasional roles in public administration, such as when his father appointed him refugee commissioner during the disastrous 1927 Mississippi River flood, but his life's project was his poetic work, which echoed classical and medieval forms and consistently indulged homoerotic imagery. Three frequent images were the Virgilian shepherd boy ("lovelier than the youthful day / More beautiful than silver, naked Ganymede!"), the Whitmanesque clinging comrades ("frail delight as in the days / We clung together here . . . / O comrade mine"), and the elegiac yearning for the dead young soldier:

> Yet what have all the centuries
> Of purpose, pain, and joy
> Bequeathed us lovelier to recall
> Than this dead boy!⁴⁴

Percy used medieval romance to imagine his homoerotic nostalgia. The dramatic poem "In April Once" situates a male romance within a thirteenth-century Florentine civil war. A soliloquy from the poem was published, possibly following Percy's submission, in the anthology of homoerotic poetry *Men and Boys* in 1934. About "In April Once," his friend William Faulkner—one to talk—said Percy "suffered the misfortune of having been born out of time." Faulkner continued: "The influence of the frank pagan beauty worship of the past is heavily upon him, he is like the little boy closing his eyes against the dark of modernity which threatens the bright simplicity and the colorful romantic pageantry of the middle ages with which his eyes are full."[45] For Percy, that turning away from "modernity" was sexualized, for it was in the past's "romantic pageantry" that he found his homoerotic imagery. Crucially, Percy's romantic past connected to the past of his own South, through imagined links of latitude, climate, and relative geography—that the Mediterranean was to Europe, the South. By "the South," Percy most frequently means the Mediterranean, though he blended it, both ancient and medieval, with his own South. In a poem like "Greenville Trees," contemplating southern soldiers on their way to fight in World War I, the medievalism of "Crusaders, knights, and troubadours" represented his Mississippi town.

Percy is most notable in literary history for his 1941 memoir *Lanterns on the Levee*, which celebrates his family's brand of racial paternalism, and for his influence on the young white poets at Vanderbilt publishing the literary magazine the *Fugitive*.[46] In 1930, these Fugitives, as they would call themselves, published essays defending an agrarian, premodern South against Northern, industrial modernity in *I'll Take My Stand*. Unlike Percy, these writers mapped a history of sexuality onto their oppositions by suggesting, as had the postbellum sexologists, that Northern industrial society was the source of sexual immorality and urban expressions of gender and sexuality were poised to obliterate the traditional nuclear family.[47] But even among such homophobic prejudice, the old appeal of the premodern South as a place of homoerotic male intimacies held out.

The final essay in *I'll Take My Stand*, by poet and novelist Stark Young, offered another defense of Southern traditionalism as an escape from Northern morality. To Young, Northern conquest threatened the varieties of Southern life, its freethinking, anticommercial ways of living. Young offered a notable example, that of the dean of a New England college "complaining of the lapses of the students on some matter about which he preached continually."[48] The unnamed lapses, which for Young exemplify puritanical reform's failure to change traditional behavior, might be any possible undergraduate offense—tardiness, work ethic, alcohol use, or any peeve of a petty-tyrant dean. Eight years before the essay's publication, Young had his own run-in with a university administrator when his Amherst College colleague, the poet Robert Frost, asked the college president to fire Young for his immoral conduct in attempting to seduce male students.[49] Frost's campaign against Young appears to have been connected to the homosexual activities of Amherst fraternities, described by undergraduate Gardner Jackson.[50] Whether Young was referring to these incidents in his account of a puritanical New England dean is unknown, but Young would have seen Frost's attitude as characteristic of Northern reform ambitions failing against traditional cultural practices. If the tragedy that American culture had been captured by Northern industrialists represented, for the Fugitives, the deviant sexual types threatening the traditional family, that tragedy, for Young, appeared in the moral dictates that would obliterate the varieties of Southern male living.

The two most famous New England undergraduates indulging in the homoerotics of half-naked storytelling in their dorm room do so by remembering, or becoming, the homoerotics of two, parallel, in-love Confederate soldiers. Quentin and Shreve, at Harvard in 1909, and Henry and Bon, at the University of Mississippi and then in the Confederate army, map same-sex romance upon both ends of this period, from past to present, from Mississippi to Massachusetts.[51] In *Absalom, Absalom!* (1936), Faulkner puts the indulgent, homoerotic backward looking of a Percy or a Young at the very center of the story of the South, the US landscape of racialized sexuality, and the project of literary modernism. The Harvard roommates, within a world of problematized homosexual identity, look backward to a Confederate pair, Bibler writes, as an "earlier model of the homoerotic relationship they share with each other." In the plantation past, he continues, they find a "loophole in the taboo against homoeroticism" within their postbellum present. The novel, then, "imagines that while there was a time when the southern plantation made it possible for white men to love each other openly and without challenge, one tragic outcome of the Civil War is that this queer possibility no longer exists."[52]

More than a loophole that Quentin and Shreve find in the past, Faulkner is engaging with a cultural tradition of male homoeroticism within Civil War narratives.[53] That tradition has been the subject of this book. When, at the war's end, one college chum (Henry) kills the other (Bon)—as told by two college chums (Quentin and Shreve)—Faulkner has reanimated the trope of the Civil War death of male intimacy. Homoeroticism is not, however, among the successive discoveries—Bon's mixed-race female lover, Bon's sibling status to Judith and Henry, Bon's Black ancestry—that explain why Henry shoots Bon but is, instead, undiscoverable as an acknowledged structure of this story and its characters' lives. Crucially, it is not Quentin and Shreve who invent Henry and Bon's love, and the possibility of sex, but Quentin's father who insists on it in the novel's fourth chapter. (Just as it is Mr. Compson who first suggests the possibility of sex between Quentin and Shreve by ventriloquizing Bon contrasting, for Henry's sake, the ceremony of "marriage" to "a ritual as meaningless as that of college boys in secret rooms at night.")[54] Quentin and Shreve reinhabit a narrative that precedes them.

That narrative tradition may well be why "neither Henry and Bon, anymore than Quentin and Shreve, were the first young men to believe (or at least apparently act on the assumption) that wars were sometimes created for the sole aim of settling youth's private difficulties and discontents." One thwarted potential, even, is a story very much of this book's chums: Henry wounded, desiring death, directs his best friend/brother to go marry his sister, saying, "Let me die! I wont have to know it then."[55] As if Henry's death would resolve their homoerotic intimacy as well as the problems of race and incest too—exactly what Claiborne's death accomplishes in *The Thinking Bayonet*. But Henry lives, outlives himself, though unlike the surviving chums I have examined, he has no story of maturation. Bon lives, too, in a way—in the descendant Jim Bond, who Shreve predicts will go on living and conquer the globe in a few thousand years. And they each live on, of course, through Quentin and Shreve's telling, in the shivering body of Quentin himself. Consider, then, how far from the narrative of postbellum marriage—Herbert's to Leonora after Claiborne's death, Tom's to Nettie after Ned's death, John's to his dead friend's sister, even the Stoneman-Cameron pairs after their brothers' deaths—we have come. If those maturation narratives conform to a developmental view of sexuality's transition, where youthful homoeroticism gives way to heterosexual maturity, Faulkner offers a static, post-Freudian view of arrested development. He retains, however, a sense of Civil War history mapped onto a male body, Quentin, "not a being" and not "an entity" but "a commonwealth," "a barracks filled with stubborn back-looking ghosts."[56] Not just the Pelhams, but also the Cookes, the Claibornes and Herberts, the Toms and Neds, the Macs and Lales, the Babes in the Woods, and the Tods and Wades, are among the back-looking ghosts.

ACKNOWLEDGMENTS

NLIKE ABRAHAM LINCOLN, who was friendless, unassisted, unaided, and alone (see chapter 1), I have benefited significantly from the advice and assistance of many individuals and institutions. It is a pleasure to acknowledge and thank them here. One begins such acknowledgments with one's teachers. Amanda Claybaugh's gift was the high bar she set and the belief that I could meet it. I am a better thinker, reader, and writer as a result of her influence. Robin Bernstein, Louis Menand, and Robert Reid-Pharr each helped transform this book beyond what I thought it could be. I have benefited, as well, from many teachers, among whom Deidre Lynch, Joe Nugent, and John Stauffer deserve special recognition for shaping my thinking and this work. Kevin Ohi, who taught me how to read and gave generous feedback on parts of this work, gets his own sentence, though one neither as long nor exquisite as he doubtless deserves.

Cristie Ellis, Travis Foster, and Jaime Harker read the entirety of this work at a crucial stage; their feedback on the manuscript transformed it for the better. Caroline Wigginton made that review happen, as she does so much else, and I'm exceedingly grateful for her encouragement and advice. Katie McKee never let me forget the joy and possibility of being a nineteenth-century Americanist, and I only wish I could acknowledge her as well as she does others. Great improvement came, as well, from the expertise of Brook Thomas, Jim Downs, Karen Kilcup, and reviewers at *Civil War History* and *ESQ*. The comments and advice of the following, along the way, were so beneficial that they may not even recognize this work's genesis in something they read: Michael Allen, Will Baldwin, Deborah Barker, Marina Bilbija, Phoebe Braithwaite, Isabel Duarte-Gray, Dan Farbman, Eliza Holmes, Geoffrey Kirsch, Tess McNulty, Ernie Mitchell, Martin Quinn, Nick Rinehart, Hannah Rosefield, Chris Schlegel, Emily Silk, Dave Weimer, and Michael Weinstein— Phoebe and Nick, especially, corrected my mistaken ideas. Steph Dick, Ralph Eubanks, Brian Highsmith, Devin Kennedy, Gili Vidan, and Jay Watson each provided exceedingly helpful comments. The reviewers for UNC Press helped pull out the fundamental themes that made this book cohere. The entire UNC Press team deserves my gratitude, starting with Mark Simpson-Vos, as well as the Gender and American Culture Series editors, Mary Kelley and Martha S.

Jones. For a final close reading, I am especially grateful to Riley Moran. Projects beyond this one also sustained this work, and I thank LaToysha Brown, Kate Gluckman, Ki Harris, Sam Klug, Vaish Shastry, Niha Singh, Jeremiah Smith, and many others for working with me. Emily Gowen deserves recognition in at least two categories, if not more.

The Loring Fellowship on the Civil War, Its Origins, and Its Consequences and an Andrew W. Mellon Foundation Fellowship enabled invaluable research at the Boston Athenaeum, Massachusetts Historical Society, the Library Company of Philadelphia, and the Historical Society of Pennsylvania. Staff and archivists at these institutions assisted me thoroughly at every turn. I wrote portions of this book while supported by the Mellon Foundation and the American Council of Learned Societies as a Public Fellow at the National Book Foundation. Time spent there thinking about how books connect with real readers in the world, especially witnessing the inspiring work of libraries around the country to build and serve interest in cultural history, shaped this book into the one you hold or have downloaded. I am grateful to Lisa Lucas, Ruth Dickey, and Jordan Smith for making that workplace one where the work we did was not alienated from the work of thinking, reading, and writing. I'm grateful to colleagues, especially Natalie Green, Anna Dobben, Anja Kuipers, and Chris Wisniewski, for conversations that kept this project alive. So, too, did a few brief conversations with Ian Maloney at St. Francis College, for which I remain grateful.

The Center for the Study of Southern Culture proved a perfect home to develop this book; I benefited from the knowledge and enthusiasm of the center's faculty, staff, and graduate students. Andy Harper went out of his way to assist me with the images. Unbelievably generous colleagues in the University of Mississippi's English Department—to those already named add, at least, Sheila Sundar, Justin Raden, Dee Kreisel, Scott Mackenzie, and Leigh Anne Duck—shaped my thinking and sustained my work. My University of Memphis colleagues (Darry Domingo, Katie Fredlund, Donal Harris, Terrence Tucker, among others) gave this project a welcome hearing and crucial encouragement in its final stages to see it through to completion.

There remain some of the most important people to thank, beginning with my parents, from whom I received a curiosity about history, books, and words and a whole lot more. For being in the life of its author, this book has significant debts to Seth and Lucie, Steve, Pat, Raquel, Sam, Wesley, Riley, Alison, Emerson, and Rowan. Lastly, the ideas here were always shared with Marc, both in the sense that he read them and that he often had them first. But that's life with this guy, a life that, by some embarrassment of fortune, I get to share.

NOTES

ABBREVIATIONS

HW   *Harper's Weekly*

JCL   Henry James, *Complete Letters of Henry James*

INTRODUCTION

1. The conductor, Peter Doyle, described meeting Whitman in an interview to Richard Maurice Bucke, who published Whitman's letters to Doyle in 1897. Bucke, *Calamus*, 23; Murray, "'Pete the Great,'" 13–14; DeFerrari, *Capital Streetcars*, 45–46. Doyle was not Whitman's first intimate locomotive encounter; in 1863, Whitman wrote in his notebook of a fellow passenger, "[I] felt I loved that boy, from the first, and saw he returned it." Quoted in Shively, *Calamus Lovers*, 99.

2. Whitman's friend John Burroughs called Doyle Whitman's "intimate friend." Bucke, *Calamus*, 13. Whitman's biographers concur: he "fell in love at least once, with the young Southerner Peter Doyle," who "came closer than anyone else to being the love of his life," was "the heart's companion he had been looking for all the while," "the longest affectional relationship of his life," and "Walt's dearest friend" who "may or may not have been Whitman's lover" and about whom he penned an "anguished confession of his love." Callow, *From Noon*, 258; David S. Reynolds, *Walt Whitman's America*, 487; Justin Kaplan, *Walt Whitman*, 287; Folsom and Price, *Re-scripting Walt Whitman*, 83; Loving, *Walt Whitman*, 297; Zweig, *Walt Whitman*, 196.

3. "Walt Whitman Letters and 'Leaves,'" *Critic*, January 1, 1898, 4. See Murray, "'Pete the Great,'" 42–43.

4. Bucke, *Calamus*, 55.

5. Asselineau, *Evolution of Walt Whitman*, 144–53; David S. Reynolds, *Walt Whitman's America*, 410–47; Loving, *Walt Whitman*, 266–95; Morris, *Better Angel*.

6. Murray, "'Pete the Great,'" 8; "Walt Whitman Letters and 'Leaves.'"

7. In 1875 war remembrances, Whitman wrote that "three or four hundred more escapees from the Confederate Army" arriving in Washington proved "the unscrupulous tyranny exercised by the Secession government in conscripting the common people by absolute force everywhere." Whitman, *Memoranda during the War*, 41. A chronicler of Whitman's hospital service cites this moment as characteristic of the poet's "special affinity for Southerners." Morris, *Better Angel*, 207.

8. See Crain, *American Sympathy*; and Godbeer, *Overflowing of Friendship*.

9. Whitman, *Leaves of Grass*, 349–51.

10. Whitman, *Drum-Taps*, 49.

11. See Asselineau, *Evolution of Walt Whitman*, 121–27; David S. Reynolds, *Walt Whitman's America*, 391–403; Erkkila, *Whitman the Political Poet*, 155–89; and Erkkila, *Whitman Revolution*, 79–100.

12. Take Whitman's electoral choices: In 1848 and 1852, the Jacksonian Democrat voted for the breakaway, minority Free Soil Party, resistant to slavery's expansion. In 1856, he gave reluctant support to the losing upstart Republican Party. He supported Democrat Stephen Douglas in the late 1850s and likely in 1860 as well, in the four-way race that Lincoln won. Only from 1864 to 1884 did his presidential preferences match electoral outcomes. After voting for Lincoln's reelection, he was warm to successor Andrew Johnson. Although he skipped a few elections, he supported winning Republican candidates Ulysses S. Grant, Rutherford B. Hayes, and James A. Garfield, until defecting, with the mugwump Republicans, for Grover Cleveland. Slightly older than the typical mugwump, Whitman had a longer history of advocating a nationally unifying political project. In 1890, Whitman praised a speech by one of his literary executors as "good (independent-mugwump)." Whitman, *Correspondence*, 105. For Whitman's Reconstruction years, see Mancuso, *Strange Sad War Revolving*; and Buinicki, *Walt Whitman's Reconstruction*.

13. Foner, *Reconstruction*, 499.

14. For Liberal Republican and mugwump sympathies, developed in reaction to the era's democratic expansions, see Sproat, *Best Men*, esp. 26–44; Nancy Cohen, *Reconstruction of American Liberalism*, 61–85; and Richard White, *Republic*, 61, 191–93. For the classic account of mugwumps as elites reacting to a status revolution, see Hofstadter, *Age of Reform*, 137–41. For positive accounts of mugwumps as good government reformers, see McFarland, *Mugwumps, Morals, and Politics*; and Tucker, *Mugwumps*.

15. See Du Bois, *Black Reconstruction in America*, 605–34; C. Vann Woodward, *Reunion and Reaction*, 24–37; Richardson, *Death of Reconstruction*, 83–121; Downs and Masur, "Echoes of War," 6–14; and Kidada E. Williams, *I Saw Death Coming*, 188–90.

16. A historian of antebellum Black masculinity writes, "Unfortunately, source material on romantic friendship among enslaved men in the antebellum South is notably absent," although "intense same-sex friendships . . . most likely existed, and indeed flourished in slave communities." Lussana, *My Brother Slaves*, 103. For recent fiction, see Jones, *Prophets*.

17. John Brown's father, Owen Brown, cited his youthful relationship with an enslaved boy as the source of his abolitionism: "He used to carry me on his back, and I fell in love with him." Sanborn, *Life and Letters*, 10; Du Bois, *John Brown*, 80.

18. Hints of this potential are found in Dearing, *Veterans in Politics*, 81; McConnell, *Glorious Contentment*, 177–85; and Brian Matthew Jordan, *Marching Home*, 24–25, 81–84.

19. As one notable example, a historical archaeologist finds traces of a homosexual subculture among Black soldiers in the early 1870s at Fort Davis, Texas. Among the questions of what the likeness of Antinous, the male lover of the Roman emperor Hadrian, was doing discarded in the barracks, we might ask what political feelings were cultivated within a homosexual subculture among Black soldiers stationed there. Wilkie, *Unburied Lives*, 177–83.

20. By the 1930s, Wilde's lines about a condemned prisoner, whose "wretched" status "few men can claim," were among the most famous in proletarian literature. By ending his

chapter with these lines, Du Bois aimed to unite the Black proletariat with the European as an especially marked outcast. Wilde's identification with this class—"Two outcast men we were: / The world had thrust us from its heart"—through his imprisonment for homosexual acts makes Du Bois's quotation an early linking of Black, proletariat, and queer solidarity. Wilde, *Ballad of Reading Gaol*, 13, 28; Du Bois, *Black Reconstruction in America*, 709. For Du Bois's complicated experience with homosexual men, including his daughter's divorce from the poet Countee Cullen (after Cullen disclosed to her his same-sex attraction), his firing of protégé Augustus Granville Dill, arrested for homosexual acts, and his later regret at that firing with the statement that he had "no conception of homosexuality. I had never understood the tragedy of an Oscar Wilde," see Du Bois, *Autobiography*, 179; and Ross, *Manning the Race*, 254–55.

21. Since *Black Reconstruction in America*, generations of scholars have attended to the seemingly always-prior power of whiteness and the demonstrable evidence of its formation. See, e.g., Du Bois, *Black Reconstruction in America*, 699–704; Roediger, *Wages of Whiteness*, 13–15; Blum, *Reforging the White Republic*, 7–8; and Painter, *History of White People*, x–xii. In his exploration of postbellum culture, Travis Foster argues for anti-Blackness operating within ordinary life, suggesting that anti-Blackness both preceded and was the product of postbellum white supremacist discourse, actions, and laws. Travis M. Foster, *Genre and White Supremacy*, 4–6.

22. Silber, *Romance of Reunion*, 6–7. See Blight, *Race and Reunion*, 216–17; Amy Murrell Taylor, *Divided Family*, 183–89; Thomas, *Literature of Reconstruction*, 56–64; and Kathryn B. McKee, *Reading Reconstruction*, 178–99.

23. Griffith, *Birth of a Nation*. For the film's racism and depiction of Black sexuality, see Franklin, "'Birth of a Nation'"; Baldwin, *Devil Finds Work*, 43–56; Rogin, "'Sword,'" 170–84; Wood, *Lynching and Spectacle*, 147–78; and Barker, *Reconstructing Violence*, 53–64.

24. See Stokes, *Color of Sex*, 159–77.

25. According to Griffith's synopsis submitted to the Library of Congress in 1915, "On the battlefield, the chums—the younger Cameron and [S]toneman sons—meet once again and die in each other's arms." Usai, *Griffith Project*, 53. Which of the two Cameron brothers, Wade or Duke, dies in this scene has generated some confusion. A 1966 article, relying on interviews with the actor George (André) Beranger, confirms that he played the "Young Cameron" who "falls to the ground beside his chum and they die in each other's arms." Presuming the much-printed cast list correct, I therefore use "Wade" for the Confederate chum. The third Cameron brother, played by Maxfield Stanley, also dies in some versions of the film, with the intertitle "Death of the second Cameron son." Versions that omit this death include, after the chums' death, a scene informing the family of "news of the death of the youngest Cameron." Either the cast list has mixed up Beranger's and Stanley's roles or that news is of a third Cameron not depicted. In the latter case, the "second son's" death in alternative versions of the film would be the error. Barbara Duarte, "Lagunan Beranger Helped It Happen," *South Coast News*, March 25, 1966, 9. Also see Cosgrove, "Missing in Action."

26. See Rotundo, *American Manhood*, 85–86; and Rohy, *Anachronism and Its Others*, 4–6.

27. Film scholar Mimi White reads "homosexuality in their relationship" through "the extent of the physical expression of their affection for one another, culminating at the

moment of their deaths." She further argues that their deaths represent the need for such queer impulses to be eliminated in order for the heteronormative family to survive and build the nation. That view overlooks the deeply nostalgic and tragic tone that accompanies the soldiers' kiss and deaths. Mimi White, "Birth of a Nation," 222.

28. Bryony Cosgrove, "Stuff of Silent Legend," *Sydney Morning Herald*, March 3, 2012.

29. Schickel, *D. W. Griffith*, 439.

30. For the "cultural work" of sympathy, see Jane Tompkins, *Sensational Designs*; and Fisher, *Hard Facts*. For its biological effects, impressed from one body to another, see Burgett, *Sentimental Bodies*; and Schuller, *Biopolitics of Feeling*, 9–10. For sympathy as political tool in US history, see Burstein, "Political Character of Sympathy." Burstein's 2001 essay accompanied a wave of scholarship on sympathy and sentiment (e.g., Stern, *Plight of Feeling*; Burstein, *Sentimental Democracy*; Noble, *Masochistic Pleasures*; Boudreau, *Sympathy in American Literature*; and Hendler, *Public Sentiments*).

31. Harriet Beecher Stowe, *Uncle Tom's Cabin*, 404. For histories of sympathy and antislavery, see Elizabeth B. Clark, "'Sacred Rights'"; Levecq, *Slavery and Sentiment*; Pratt, *Strangers Book*; and Sinha, *Slave's Cause*, 436–50. Antislavery's appeal to sympathy came under criticism, contemporaneously by Martin Delany (see Rollin, *Life and Public Services*, 73–76) and by later critics such as Douglas, *Feminization of American Culture*; and Berlant, *Female Complaint*.

32. For antislavery mobilization around sexual abuse, see Walters, "Erotic South"; Yee, *Black Women Abolitionists*, 122–25; Sánchez-Eppler, *Touching Liberty*, 14–49; Fuentes, *Dispossessed Lives*, 124–43; and Sinha, *Slave's Cause*, 456–60.

33. Barnes, *States of Sympathy*. For the seduction plot, see Davidson, *Revolution and the Word*; and Armstrong, "Why Daughters Die."

34. Sumner, *Crime against Kansas*, 94. To justify the violent attack on Sumner that followed his speech, the proslavery press made Sumner the source of licentiousness: "Cataline was purity itself compared with the Massachusetts Senator." *Richmond Examiner*, quoted in "Refuge of Oppression," *Liberator*, June 9, 1856. Sexualized attacks on Sumner were not new; when Sumner accused slaveholders of sexually abusing enslaved women he was repeating a charge (of interracial sexual desire) made frequently against abolitionists. See Sinha, "Caning of Charles Sumner," 242–43.

35. Fahs, *Imagined Civil War*, 94. For the sympathies of wartime literature, see Amy Murrell Taylor, *Divided Family*; Bernath, *Confederate Minds*; and Hutchison, *Apples and Ashes*. For soldiers' feelings, see Broomall, *Private Confederacies*. For the era's history of emotions, see Michael E. Woods, *Emotional and Sectional Conflict*; and Dwyer, *Mastering Emotions*.

36. For "crisis in gender," see Clinton and Silber, *Divided Houses*; Whites, *Civil War*; Clinton and Silber, *Battle Scars*; and Frank and Whites, *Household War*. For a crisis in masculinity, see Reid Mitchell, *Vacant Chair*; Berry, *All That Makes*; Gallman, *Defining Duty*; and Broomall, *Private Confederacies*. For crises in Democratic masculinity preceding the war, see Haumesser, *Democratic Collapse*.

37. For Civil War–era ideologies of sexuality, see Gaines M. Foster, *Moral Reconstruction*; Giesberg, *Sex*; and Berry and Harris, *Sexuality and Slavery*. For Confederate nationalism and the Confederate soldier as symbol, see Faust, *Creation of Confederate Nationalism*; Faust, "Race, Gender"; Rubin, *Shattered Nation*; and Gallagher, *Becoming Confederates*.

38. For the suffering of Black soldiers as reason for expanded rights, see Thomas Waterman Wood's 1866 painting *A Bit of War History*; the regimental flag of the Twenty-Fourth Regiment US Colored Troops, with the motto "Let Soldiers in War, Be Citizens in Peace"; or Frances E. W. Harper, "National Salvation: A Lecture Delivered Last Evening at National Hall," *Telegraph*, February 1, 1867. For Reconstruction-era contests of racialized sympathies, see Laura F. Edwards, *Gendered Strife*; Feimster, *Southern Horrors*, 37–61; Rosen, *Terror*; Egerton, *Wars of Reconstruction*, 168–210; Summers, *Ordeal of the Reunion*, 37–45; Prince, "Burnt District"; Kidada E. Williams, "Wounds That Cried Out"; Lang, *Contest of Civilizations*, 261–81, 355–58; William A. Blair, *Record*; and Sinha, *Rise and Fall*, 119–32.

39. See Slap, *Doom of Reconstruction*, 86.

40. For Liberal Republicans' view of activist administration, see Nancy Cohen, *Reconstruction of American Liberalism*, 121–22; and Richard White, "What Counts as Corruption?," 1044–46. For a classic account of sorting into deserving and undeserving government beneficiaries, see Skocpol, *Protecting Soldiers and Mothers*, 148–51. For this sorting as a feature of liberal governance, see Michael B. Katz, *In the Shadow*, 33–36.

41. Prince, *Stories of the South*, 2.

42. *Harper's Weekly* editor George William Curtis, *Scribner's* (later *Century*) editor Richard Watson Gilder, and *Nation* editor E. L. Godkin were among the most prominent mugwumps. Through 1876, the editors of the *North American Review* (though less literary) were the liberals James Russell Lowell, Charles Eliot Norton, and Henry Adams; after 1876, its Republican owner, C. Allen Thorndike Rice, changed much but preserved the magazine's reputation for political independence. The *Galaxy*, founded by brothers William C. and Francis P. Church, included a broad set of views but skewed toward the moderate reconciliationism of its founders until the magazine was folded into the *Atlantic Monthly* in 1878. The *Atlantic's* editor after 1881, Thomas Bailey Aldrich, was a mugwump. Before 1881, the editor had been William Dean Howells, a more complicated liberal who espoused reform ideas in the 1870s but stuck with the Republican Party in 1884. See Thomas, "The *Galaxy*, National Literature, and Reconstruction." For Howells's political views, see William Alexander, *William Dean Howells*, 32–33; Goodman and Dawson, *William Dean Howells*, 252; Richard White, *Republic*, 209–11, 471–76.

43. Tourgée, "South as a Field," 405. For assessments of Tourgée's claim, see Buck, *Road to Reunion*, 294–97; Blight, *Race and Reunion*, 216–21; and Prince, *Stories of the South*, 136–38. Despite Tourgée's claim, the period's literature was not monolithic, as his own fiction shows. See Thomas, *Literature of Reconstruction*, 33–56.

44. The New Hampshire–born Woolson spent her 1870s summers in Florida. Her "Rodman the Keeper" was published in the *Atlantic Monthly* in 1877. Cable's New Orleans stories were published in *Scribner's* in the 1870s. Harris first placed Uncle Remus in Henry Grady's *Atlanta Constitution* in 1879 before replanting him in the *Century* in the 1880s. Page's "Marse Chan: A Tale of Old Virginia" was published in the *Century* in 1884. At the time of Tourgée's essay, the historical novels set during Reconstruction that, for many scholars, best confirm his claim—i.e., Page's *Red Rock* (1898) and Thomas Dixon's Ku Klux Klan trilogy (1902, 1905, 1907)—had not yet been written. For a survey of 1880s realist novels with Southern settings and Confederate sympathies (often written in direct response to Tourgée's fiction), see Donnelly, "Voting." For a history of the *Century*, see

Noonan, *Reading the Century*. For overviews of Southern regionalists, see Hardwig, *Upon Provincialism*; Prince, *Stories of the South*, 138–65; and Kennedy-Nolle, *Writing Reconstruction*, 10–19.

45. Tourgée, "South as a Field," 406. For more on Tourgée's claim, the realists, and race, see Warren, *Black and White Strangers*, 1–17.

46. Henry James, *Small Boy and Others*, 131.

47. Henry James, *Notes*, 290.

48. Henry James, *American Scene*, 377.

49. Sedgwick, *Epistemology of the Closet*, 9–12. Similarly Joan Wallach Scott writes, "The project of making experience visible . . . excludes, or at least understates, the historically variable interrelationship between the meanings 'homosexual' and 'heterosexual,' the constitutive force each has for the other, and the contested and changing nature of the terrain that they simultaneously occupy." Joan Wallach Scott, "Evidence of Experience," 778.

50. Foucault, *History of Sexuality*, 1:43.

51. For the emergence of homo/heterosexuality in the United States, see David F. Greenberg, *Construction of Homosexuality*, 397–433; Jonathan Ned Katz, *Invention of Heterosexuality*, 1–33; Terry, *American Obsession*, 74–119; Hatheway, *Gilded Age Construction*; and Engel, *Fragmented Citizens*, 61–108.

52. Coviello, *Tomorrow's Parties*, 3.

53. For same-sex sexuality before homosexual identity, see Rupp, *Desired Past*; Jonathan Ned Katz, *Love Stories*; and Thomas A. Foster, *Long before Stonewall*.

54. In the second and third volumes, Foucault revised what "sexuality" meant: not a historically singular experience originating at the end of the eighteenth century but a consistent domain of inquiry into how humans problematize sex and desire across history, within which volume 1's "birth of sexuality" was one highly visible, episteme-shaping moment. Foucault, *History of Sexuality*, 2:3–13. See also Michel Foucault and Richard Sennett, "Sexuality and Solitude," *London Review of Books*, May 21, 1981.

55. Foucault, *History of Sexuality*, 1:100–102, 115–31. For revisions to Foucault's chronology, see David M. Halperin, *One Hundred Years*, 15–18; Chauncey, *Gay New York*, 26–28; Sedgwick, *Epistemology of the Closet*, 44–48; D'Emilio and Freedman, *Intimate Matters*, 222–29; Stoler, *Race*, 5–9; and LaFleur, *Natural History of Sexuality*, 9–16.

56. Supreme Court justice Anthony Kennedy's landmark gay-rights decisions succeeded in changing history only by, well, changing history. In overruling *Bowers v. Hardwick* (1986), Kennedy's *Lawrence v. Texas* (2003) decision replaced one historical tradition in Western civilization (state condemnation of homosexuality) with another (state nonintervention in the private affairs of consenting adults). His *Obergefell v. Hodges* (2015) supersession of provisions in the Defense of Marriage Act (1996) rested upon a right so "fundamental" and "ancient" that it became apparent only to "new generations" as "new dimensions of freedom." Obergefell v. Hodges, 576 U.S. 644 (2015). The contradictions between two notions of time—the universal time of permanent rights and the historical time that fails to realize those rights—follow the classic form of the American jeremiad. In Herman Melville's terms, "by their very contradictions," the universal time of the *chronometer* and the historical time of the *horologe* have been "made to correspond." Melville, *Pierre*, 212; Bercovitch, *American Jeremiad*, 28–30.

57. That historical situatedness, and self-conscious relation to its own historicity, makes homosexual representation a ripe site to contest normative temporality, as scholars theorizing queer temporalities have argued. See, e.g., Elizabeth Freeman, *Time Binds*.

58. Indeed, Jameson treats homosexuality as one of those "diachronic constructs" that reveals its own "synchronic" situatedness—its appearance across time betrayed by its historical boundedness. In his analysis of an 1826 German novella, it is homosexuality's referentiality to other texts and times (namely the easily resolved homosexual overtones of Renaissance drama) that reveals the novella's displacement of a more explosive class transgression into familiar, less dangerous taboos. For Jameson, then, homosexuality's appearance, like magic or form, is never the discovery but a construct to be read through to the political horizon. Jameson, *Political Unconscious*, 137–39.

59. Valerie Traub, *Thinking Sex*, 81. In a 2005 review, Susan McCabe defined "queer historicism" as efforts "to analyze and situate historical texts as cultural material, fusing the work of excavation with the recognition that sexualities are socially constructed and can take multiple forms." Susan McCabe, "To Be," 121. A decade later, when many queer theorists found historicist inquiry limiting in describing queer lives and identities, Traub defended the methodology in a *PMLA* essay, "The New Unhistoricism in Queer Studies."

60. Lott, *Love and Theft*, 54–56.

61. Abdur-Rahman, *Against the Closet*; Woodard, *Delectable Negro*; Kyla Wazana Tompkins, *Racial Indigestion*, 5, 185–86; Thomas A. Foster, *Rethinking Rufus*, 94–112. For narratives of nonheteronormative racial reproduction, see Fielder, *Relative Races*. For homoerotic race-making after 1900, see Pérez, *Taste for Brown Bodies*. For an overview of this scholarship, see Donnelly, "Whiteness and Queer Studies."

62. Somerville, *Queering the Color Line*; Carter, *Heart of Whiteness*; Melissa N. Stein, *Measuring Manhood*. For an earlier intersection of gender difference and racial science, within the practices of enslavement, see Snorton, *Black on Both Sides*, 17–53.

63. Fiedler, "Come Back"; Fiedler, *Love and Death*, 348–60.

64. Looby, "'Innocent Homosexuality,'" 538–39.

65. After debate within queer theory questioning its fundamental antinormativity (see Wiegman and Wilson, "Antinormativity's Queer Conventions"), the "bad gays" are, according to a 2023 article, "having their moment in the spotlight." Doubtless there is something symptomatic about the return of gay male villains in a culture where being gay can no longer get one out of the military, marriage, a job, or blood donation. This book's inquiry may be a product of this moment, but the history itself is not: not a counterhistory but a prehistory to homoeroticism's antinormativity. Mark Harris, "Yes, These Gays Are Trying to Murder You," *New York Times*, August 17, 2023. See Lemmey and Miller, *Bad Gays*, 1–18.

66. Eng, *Feeling of Kinship*, 2–8.

67. Puar, *Terrorist Assemblages*, 10.

68. For primitivist fascism as a libidinal politics of recovery, see Chaudhary, "Paranoid Publics." For a case study of twentieth-century gay fascism, see Buchanan, "Gay Neo-Nazis." For the twenty-first century, see Blake Smith, "Bronze Age Pervert's Dissertation on Leo Strauss," *Tablet*, February 13, 2023.

69. Two recent studies of postbellum literature testify to insights of reading, and generalizing, across broad sets of novels in order to perform interpretive close readings at the

scale of historiographic interventions. Thomas, *Literature of Reconstruction*, 15; Travis M. Foster, *Genre and White Supremacy*, 16–17.

CHAPTER 1

1. Washington, *Farewell Address*, 5, 10.

2. Quoted in Jonathan Ned Katz, *Gay American History*, 453. See Flexner, *Young Hamilton*, 255–63; and Jonathan Ned Katz, "Alexander Hamilton's Nose," *Advocate*, October 10, 1988, 29.

3. Godbeer, *Overflowing of Friendship*, 13. For Revolutionary-era friendship, see Crain, *American Sympathy*; Schweitzer, *Perfecting Friendship*; and Good, *Founding Friendships*.

4. For Democratic discontinuities, see Schlesinger, *Age of Jackson*; Wilentz, *Chants Democratic*; and Earle, *Jacksonian Antislavery*. For continuities, see Saxton, *Rise and Fall*; and Lynn, *Preserving*.

5. Lynn, *Preserving*, 6.

6. Nelson, *National Manhood*, 18–22.

7. Coviello, *Intimacy in America*, 10–12.

8. See, e.g., Yacovone, "Abolitionists."

9. Van Buren to Ritchie, January 13, 1827, Van Buren Papers, Library of Congress. This chapter embraces Justine Murison's description of this partisan literary period as "the Age of Van Buren," while complicating the final part of her suggestion that such periodization would be a throwback to "masculinist, white, straight" literary history. Murison, "Age of Van Buren," 171.

10. Nelson describes this symbolic consolidation, "the concrete correlative of national manhood," within the male body of the president himself as *presidentialism*. Nelson, *National Manhood*, 218.

11. On Jacksonian manhood, see David G. Pugh, *Sons of Liberty*; Kimmel, *Manhood in America*, 25–27; Burstein, *Passions of Andrew Jackson*; Zagarri, *Revolutionary Backlash*, 148–80; and Cheathem, *Andrew Jackson, Southerner*.

12. Amy S. Greenberg, *Manifest Manhood*, 11–13. For ideologies of masculinity within US expansionism, see Morrissey, "Engendering the West"; Streeby, *American Sensations*, 81–101; and Hahn, *Nation without Borders*, 125. For Young America as political movement, see Eyal, *Young America Movement*.

13. For the section-by-section Whig campaign, see Holt, *Rise and Fall*, 33–59; and Daniel Walker Howe, *What Hath God Wrought*, 485–88.

14. For the crisis of Van Buren's manhood, see Kimmel, *Manhood in America*, 27–29; Holt, *Rise and Fall*, 105–11; and Greven, *Men beyond Desire*, 111–16.

15. Holt, *Rise and Fall*, 163–64; Earle, *Jacksonian Antislavery*, 62–63.

16. H. Bucholzer and James S. Baillie, "Polk in His Extremity," 1844, American Cartoon Print Filing Series, Library of Congress.

17. H. Bucholzer and James S. Baillie, "Loco-Foco Triumphal Honors," 1844, American Cartoon Print Filing Series, Library of Congress.

18. For Polk-Dallas's victory, see Holt, *Rise and Fall*, 172–76; and Daniel Walker Howe, *What Hath God Wrought*, 682–90.

19. For overviews of nineteenth-century male romantic friendship, see D'Emilio and Freedman, *Intimate Matters*, 121–30; Yacovone, "Surpassing"; Rotundo, *American Manhood*, 75–91; and Jonathan Ned Katz, *Love Stories*, 8–12. For a contrasting view that attempts to distinguish minoritarian homosexual experience from nonsexual romantic friendships, see Benemann, *Male-Male Intimacy*. For female romantic friendships, see Smith-Rosenberg, "Female World"; and Faderman, *Surpassing*.

20. That testing boundaries teaches and reinforces those boundaries has long been an insight of theories of queerness, discipline, and pedagogy. See, e.g., D. A. Miller, *Novel and the Police*, 196–207; Foucault, *Discipline and Punish*, 276–82; and Ambrose, *Jacob and the Happy Life*, 133.

21. Quoted in Burg, *American Seafarer*, 80.

22. Burg, *American Seafarer*, 88. For Van Buskirk's antimasturbatory reading, see Burg, 21–31. To believe his diaries, many of Van Buskirk's fellow sailors had less guilt-bound attitudes about male-male sex, a difference Burg attributes to Van Buskirk's middle-class status, but this might also have been a difference between present experience and reflection in his diary. See also Knip, "Homosocial Desire."

23. When Howe's Laurence, as a stand-in for Juliet in their college play, enraptures the actor playing Romeo, the roommate defends Laurence's manhood by challenging Romeo to a duel. Injured from the duel, the roommate then reveals his love for, and then attempts to rape, Laurence, saying, "You shall be a man to all the world, if you will, but a woman, a sweet, warm, living woman to me." Twenty-first-century readers schooled in homo- and heterosexual difference might presume that knowing that the same-sex college roommate you desire is potentially a member of the opposite sex would resolve the problem of same-sex desire. Not so in Howe's novel, where the protagonist's bi/agendered nature disrupts the collegiate male-male intimacy. Julia Ward Howe, *Hermaphrodite*, 86.

24. Twentieth-century critics noted *Pierre*'s thorough presentation of sexual transgression: incest, homosexuality, and bigamy. Freudian readings suggested that Pierre's, or Glen's, "latent homosexuality" manifested itself in the novel's violence. Melville, however, stressed just how normal, stabilizing, and appropriate Pierre and Glen's intimacy was, an exemplar of "the friendship of fine-hearted generous boys" that "revels for a while in the empyrean of a love which only comes short, by one degree, of the sweetest sentiment entertained between the sexes." Sexual anarchy, incest, and bigamy descend upon the plot only when that male intimacy disappears. Melville, *Pierre*, 216; Matthiessen, *American Renaissance*, 480.

25. Winthrop, *Cecil Dreeme*. For romantic friendship in the novel, see Nissen, *Manly Love*, 57–88. For Winthrop's biography and literary efforts, see Timothy J. Williams, "'Gold of the Pen.'"

26. See, e.g., the letters of Virgil Maxcy to his "chum" William Blanding in 1800, quoted in Godbeer, *Overflowing of Friendship*, 57–58; and the letters of Daniel Webster to James Hervey Bingham, quoted in Rotundo, *American Manhood*, 77–80. For the potential sexual meaning of "chum," see Martin, *Hero, Captain, and Stranger*, 62; and Jonathan Ned Katz, *Love Stories*, 47.

27. Quoted in Duberman, "'Writhing Bedfellows,'" 155–56. For more on Hammond and Withers, see Steven M. Stowe, *Intimacy and Power*, 82–84.

28. In his diary, Hammond responded to this check on his freedom with self-pity and self-victimization: "Is there a man, with manhood in him and a heart susceptible of any emotions of tenderness, who could tear himself from such a cluster of lovely, loving, such amorous and devoted beings? Nay are there many who would have the self-control to stop where I did? Am I not after all entitled to some, the smallest portion of, credit for not going further?" His biographer Drew Gilpin Faust somehow excuses him as well, writing of the abuse of the teenagers: "Within a society that prescribed rigid standards of purity for ladies of their social position, the girls' behavior was perhaps even more unorthodox than that of their uncle"! James Henry Hammond, *Secret and Sacred*, 173; Faust, *James Henry Hammond*, 242.

29. James Henry Hammond, "Hammond's Letters on Slavery"; Cong. Globe, 35th Cong., 1st Sess. 962 (1858). Hammond's notion of freedom would even curtail the later encroachment of the Confederate government on citizens' property in its military effort to preserve their enslaved property. Faust, *James Henry Hammond*, 368–69.

30. Nelson, *National Manhood*, 148–51. See Coviello, *Intimacy in America*, 10–11.

31. Quoted in Burg, *American Seafarer*, xi.

32. According to Burg, after deserting the Confederate army, Van Buskirk for the rest of his life had sex almost exclusively with women, many of whom were nonwhite and whom he encountered during naval service in the Pacific Islands. Burg, *Rebel at Large*, 135–41.

33. Burg, *American Seafarer*, 130–31.

34. Whitman, a follower of leading Locofoco journalist William Leggett, was called during an 1840 political debate "a well known loco foco of the town." Hawthorne, in "The Custom House" preface to *The Scarlet Letter*, called himself "a Locofoco Surveyor." Melville's lawyer brothers Gansevoort and Allan, with whom he stayed in New York City in the mid-1840s, were Democratic speechmakers in the wake of Locofocoism. Melville entered the city's literary-political world through his brothers' connections. David S. Reynolds, *Walt Whitman's America*, 67; Hawthorne, *Scarlet Letter*, 7; Delbanco, *Melville*, 66–67.

35. Wilentz, *Chants Democratic*, 256–58; Stansell, *City of Women*, 89–100; Horowitz, *Rereading Sex*, 125–43; David S. Reynolds, *Waking Giant*, 305–6; Dennis, *Licentious Gotham*, 22–25.

36. For the masculinity of Locofoco leaders, see Joshua R. Greenberg, *Advocating the Man*, 190–206.

37. Cornelius Mathews, *Pen-and-Ink Panorama*, 124–25.

38. Cornelius Mathews, *Big Abel*, 78.

39. Perry Miller alludes to the pairing of a "white boy" and a "dying Negro companion" as within the Fiedler formula. Perry Miller, *Raven and the Whale*, 245.

40. Cornelius Mathews, *Big Abel*, dedication page.

41. Stott, *Jolly Fellows*, 99–103.

42. Stott, *Jolly Fellows*, 50.

43. Quoted in Cohen, Gilfoye, and Horowitz, *Flash Press*, 192–98. See also Cohen, Gilfoye, and Horowitz, 73–75; Jonathan Ned Katz, *Love Stories*, 45–59; and Horowitz, *Rereading Sex*, 169–76.

44. Cornelius Mathews, *Pen-and-Ink Panorama*, 124. Perry Miller faults Mathews, and his contemporaries, for an obliviousness on matters of sex, meaning that Mathews was

more interested in documenting the variety of men than the Bowery's female sex workers. Perry Miller, *Raven and the Whale*, 235.

45. Poe, "Cornelius Mathews," 271; Perry Miller, *Raven and the Whale*, 333; Widmer, *Young America*, 110, 117; Allen F. Stein, *Cornelius Mathews*, 15.

46. One vehicle for Mathews's satirical political commentary was a magazine possibly titled with a nationalist, phallic pun: *Yankee Doodle*. On that pun, see Abelove, "Yankee Doodle Dandy."

47. Wilentz, *Chants Democratic*, 256.

48. Melville, *Moby-Dick*, 416. For Melville's democratic homoeroticism, see Erkkila, *Whitman Revolution*, 174–77; and Greiman, *Melville's Democracy*, 261–64.

49. Whitman quoted in Traubel, *With Walt Whitman*, 342–43. For Whitman's democratic homoeroticism, see David S. Reynolds, *Walt Whitman's America*, 66–67, 100–106; Lawson, *Walt Whitman*, 14–15; and Erkkila, *Whitman Revolution*, 82–89.

50. For Melville and the 1848 European revolutions, see Rogin, *Subversive Genealogy*, 19–23; and Delbanco, *Melville*, 103–8. For Whitman, see Zweig, *Walt Whitman*, 74–75; David S. Reynolds, *Walt Whitman's America*, 131–33; Erkkila, *Whitman Revolution*, 123–43; and Graber, *Twice-Divided Nation*, 76–97. For both (though a notably more reactionary Melville), see Larry J. Reynolds, *European Revolutions*, 97–152.

51. Despite Auld, Evert Duyckinck, Jones, and John L. O'Sullivan marrying in the 1840s or later, the *bachelor* status of these meetings has long been emphasized in Melville studies. The frequent criticism that the Young America set was a mutual congratulation society occasionally had homoerotic undertones. For example, the *New York Tribune* called Duyckinck and Mathews the "Damon and Pythias of the drama of real life"; another critic called Young America a "you-tickle-me-I'll-tickle-you-school." Quoted in Widmer, *Young America*, 110, 245n63.

52. By the mid-1850s, Melville repudiated Young America, mocking its project of nationalist literature in *Pierre*. As I argue in the next chapter, his *Benito Cereno* reverses Mathews's political image of cross-racial male intimacy. But in 1848, Melville remained a party man, sending up the Whig nominee Zachary Taylor for Mathews's *Yankee Doodle*.

53. John L. O'Sullivan, "Great Nation of Futurity," *Democratic Review*, November 1839, 426–30.

54. For Walker and slavery, see May, *Manifest Destiny's Underworld*, 267–72; Amy S. Greenberg, *Manifest Manhood*, 40–42; Johnson, *River of Dark Dreams*, 390–94; and Gobat, *Empire by Invitation*, 243–51.

55. In June 1857, it was at the Bowery Theatre that Walker, on tour in the United States, received cheering crowds. May, *Manifest Destiny's Underworld*, 71; Gobat, *Empire by Invitation*, 105.

56. Amy S. Greenberg, *Manifest Manhood*, 149–51; Beer, "Martial Men," 115–19.

57. Gobat, *Empire by Invitation*, 218–20; Amy S. Greenberg, *Manifest Manhood*, 124–26.

58. Amy S. Greenberg, *Manifest Manhood*, 148. See also Dufour, *Gentle Tiger*, 82–83; and May, *Manifest Destiny's Underworld*, 110–11.

59. Walker, *War in Nicaragua*, 53.

60. May, *Manifest Destiny's Underworld*, 95–96; Amy S. Greenberg, *Manifest Manhood*, 147–48.

61. Greene, *Filibuster*, 21; Rosengarten, *Freebooters Must Die!*, 3; Teilhet, *Lion's Skin*, 145.

62. David S. Reynolds, *Walt Whitman's America*, 401–3.

63. For Walsh, see Wilentz, *Chants Democratic*, 326–35; David S. Reynolds, *Walt Whitman's America*, 102–3; and Stott, *Jolly Fellows*, 116–21.

64. "How to Show a Friendship for Mike Walsh and His Principles," *Subterranean*, November 14, 1846.

65. "Calhoun Ball," *Subterranean*, January 10, 1846.

66. [Melville], "Hawthorne and His Mosses," 250. For Cornelius Mathews's suggested influence, see Bousquet, "Mathews's Mosses?" For the essay's picture of New England's sexual conquest of the South, see Greeson, *Our South*, 195–96.

67. Widmer, *Young America*, 22. For their relationship, see Argersinger and Person, *Hawthorne and Melville*.

68. Whigs, too, adopted cross-sectional tickets, though their nationally famous generals made these pairings (Louisiana's Zachary Taylor and New York's Millard Fillmore in 1848; New Jersey's Winfield Scott and North Carolina's William Graham in 1852) less the senatorial compacts of the Democrats.

69. Landis, *Northern Men*, 3–5.

70. Patricia Clark, "A. O. P. Nicholson," 60–63. See Holt, *Rise and Fall*, 357; and Landis, *Northern Men*, 103–4.

71. Lewis Cass, "Letter from Gen. Cass," *Signal of Liberty*, January 22, 1848.

72. "Another Short and Sour Letter from Gen. Cass," *Charlotte Journal*, October 13, 1848.

73. Shelden, *Washington Brotherhood*, 63–119.

74. Balcerski, *Bosom Friends*, 84.

75. For Barnburners in the 1848 election, see Holt, *Rise and Fall*, 338–45; Earle, *Jacksonian Antislavery*, 68–77; and Daniel Walker Howe, *What Hath God Wrought*, 831–32.

76. Cong. Globe, 31st Cong., 1st Sess. 182 (1850).

77. For the role of campaign biographies, see William Burlie Brown, *People's Choice*, 3–14, 104–21; Troy, *See How They Ran*, 44–45; and Daniel Walker Howe, *What Hath God Wrought*, 276. For their literary status, see Blouin, *Literary Interventions*.

78. Hawthorne, *Life of Franklin Pierce*, 14–15. See Balcerski, "'Work of Friendship.'"

79. Hawthorne, *Life of Franklin Pierce*, 13.

80. James Buchanan, "Letter," *Daily Dispatch*, June 23, 1852.

81. For speculation on the Buchanan-King relationship, see Baker, *James Buchanan*, 25–26; Strauss, *Worst. President. Ever.*, 85–94; Loewen, *Lies across America*, 367–70; and Ezekiel Emanuel, "America Has Already Had a Gay President," *Washington Post*, March 26, 2019. For King as (erroneously) "a kind of First Gentleman to bachelor president James Buchanan," see Daniel Brook, "The Forgotten Confederate Jew," *Tablet*, July 17, 2012.

82. Balcerski, *Bosom Friends*, 14.

83. For the political status of bachelorhood, see McCurdy, *Citizen Bachelors*, 4–6; Balcerski, *Bosom Friends*, 66–69; and Lynn, *Preserving*, 121–22.

84. "W. R. King and James Buchanan," *True Democrat*, October 14, 1856.

85. Horton, *Life and Public Services*, 424. See Landis, *Northern Men*, 56–57.

86. For popular sovereignty as principle of white-male fraternity, see Nelson, *National Manhood*, 60. For Buchanan's body as its symbol, see Lynn, *Preserving*, 119–45.

87. "Democratic Rallying Song for 1852," *Daily Indiana State Sentinel*, June 8, 1852.

88. J. L. Magee, "The Great Presidential Race of 1856," Stern Collection of Lincolniana, Library of Congress, 1856.

89. Gienapp, "Nativism"; Gienapp, *Origins*, 92–102. See Foner, *Free Soil*, 226–60; and Walters, "Erotic South," 193–94.

90. For "Sisterhood of Reforms," see Higginson, *Cheerful Yesterdays*, 119; Foner, *Free Soil*, 109–11; and Walters, *American Reformers*, xii. For "Sodom," see James A. Thome, "The Licentiousness of Slavery," *Anti-slavery Record*, December 1, 1836. For the role of sexual reform within the Republican Party's formation, see Perry, *Radical Abolitionism*, 215–16; Walters, "Erotic South"; and Gaines M. Foster, *Moral Reconstruction*, 9–26.

91. William Lloyd Garrison, "Masturbation," *Liberator*, January 16, 1846.

92. Graham mentioned his desire to write a history of US slavery. Graham to Garrison, March 13, 1849, Anti-Slavery Collection, Boston Public Library. For Graham's and contemporaries' antimasturbation campaigns, see Walters, *American Reformers*, 149–52; Nissenbaum, *Sex, Diet, and Debility*, 25–38; D'Emilio and Freedman, *Intimate Matters*, 68–69; Horowitz, *Rereading Sex*, 92–122; Laqueur, *Solitary Sex*, 46–48; and David S. Reynolds, *Waking Giant*, 206–9. For Graham's masturbatory and diet restrictions, in their mutual reference to invented nonwhite practices, as constructive of whiteness, see Kyla Wazana Tompkins, *Racial Indigestion*, 53–88.

93. For Graham and Weld's friendship, see Abzug, *Passionate Liberator*, 157–59. For antislavery and sexual restraint, see Foner, *Politics and Ideology*, 24–25; Castronovo, "Sexual Purity"; and French, *Against Sex*, 69–71, 90–93.

94. Foucault, *History of Sexuality*, 1:17–35. For antislavery's sensational, even pornographic, discourse, see Halttunen, "Humanitarianism"; Lasser, "Voyeuristic Abolitionism"; and the classic discussion of "pornotroping" in Spillers, "Mama's Baby, Papa's Maybe," 67.

95. Despite Foucault's scope encompassing the West, we should not dismiss that the transformation in epistemologies of sexuality took place in the United States alongside and within political divisions. In the broadest view of US history, the Republican Party's political ascendance coincides with forces ushering in epistemological changes in sexuality, bourgeois liberalism, and capital.

96. Trent, *Manliest Man*, 89. See also Showalter, *Civil Wars*, 39.

97. See Samuel Gridley Howe, *Report*, 84–88. Howe states the causal argument forcefully in the section "Self-Abuse," but to be fair, other parts of his report leave open whether masturbation is a cause or result of idiocy.

98. Samuel Gridley Howe, *Report*, 86.

99. Samuel Gridley Howe, *Report*, 88.

100. For Van Buskirk's terms, including "mutual self-pollution" and "going chaw for chaw," see Burg, *American Seafarer*, 76–77. On overlap between masturbation and homosexuality, see Horowitz, *Rereading Sex*, 104–5; and Laqueur, *Solitary Sex*, 254–63.

101. Howe was not ignorant of sex between men. In his journals from the Greek Revolution, he described Turkish soldiers sexually abusing Greek men they had captured

before killing them, "unless someone is very young and beautiful, then he is kept for the embraces of some high officer." Quoted in Showalter, *Civil Wars*, 28.

102. Howe's intimacy with Sumner appears to have caused considerable difficulty for his wife, the poet Julia Ward Howe. In a letter to Sumner about the Howes' honeymoon, he wrote, "When my heart is full of joy or sorrow, it turns to you & yearns for your sympathy; in fact, as Julia often says, Sumner ought to have been a woman & you to have married her." The statement may be more easily dismissed given Howe's playful tone in sharing the anecdote with Sumner had it not found resonance in Ward Howe's writing, both in her diaries and in her unpublished 1847 manuscript, published later as *The Hermaphrodite*. The first readers of Ward Howe's unearthed manuscript saw its bi/agendered hero as a means of understanding her husband's "indifference to her (and responsiveness to Charles Sumner) as somehow corporeal, a principle of his very constitution." Showalter, *Civil Wars*, 69; Bergland and Williams, introduction to *Philosophies of Sex*, 8.

103. Sumner, *Crime against Kansas*, 9.

104. Mann, *Life and Works*, 486. For indignation meetings, see Michael E. Woods, "'Indignation of Freedom-Loving People.'"

105. See Gienapp, "Crime against Sumner"; Joanne B. Freeman, *Field of Blood*, 223–34; and Karp, "People's Revolution of 1856," 533–34.

106. Smucker, *Life*, 52. This use of "truculent" likely derives from the verb "to truck," as in "to exchange"; *Oxford English Dictionary*, under "truculent" (adj.), sense 2, July 2023, www.oed.com.

107. Smucker, *Life*, 50.

108. Smucker, *Life*, 52.

109. Haumesser, *Democratic Collapse*, 14–22.

110. Shelden, *Washington Brotherhood*, 149–52, 172–73.

111. Quoted in Donald, *We Are Lincoln Men*, 55.

112. Quoted in Donald, *We Are Lincoln Men*, 67.

113. Barrett, *Life of Abraham Lincoln*, 130.

114. See Haumesser, *Democratic Collapse*, 105–9.

115. See John David Smith, "Gentlemen."

116. Quoted in Nicolay and Hay, *Abraham Lincoln*, 3:343–44.

CHAPTER 2

1. Fiedler, "Come Back," 671. See also Wiegman, "Fiedler and Sons."

2. Thomas Gossett, in 1985, listed twenty-seven responses to *Uncle Tom's Cabin* before the Civil War; Stephen Railton, Joy Jordan-Lake, David S. Reynolds, and Sarah Roth each added a few more. To narrow in on novelistic responses to Stowe's novel, of those mentioned by these scholars, David Brown's *The Planter* (1853) was a proslavery autobiographical essay, not narrative fiction; Wiley's *Life in the South* (1852) was a reprint of Wiley's 1849 novel *Roanoke*; Grayson's *The Hireling and the Slave* (1856), like *The Patent Key to Uncle Tom's Cabin* (1853), was a verse essay; and Thorpe's *The Master's House* (1854), while certainly a racist novel, should be read as a limited antislavery, not proslavery, argument. Simms's *The Sword and the Distaff* (Charleston, SC, 1852; then Philadelphia, 1853) is decidedly a proslavery novel in Stowe's wake but, for reasons discussed

in this chapter, is treated separately. If we count the borderline cases of *White Acre vs. Black Acre*, an allegorical novel responding to Stowe, and *Abolitionism Unveiled*, a book-length proslavery essay with a narrative frame, thirty novels respond to Stowe defending slavery: Criswell, *"Uncle Tom's Cabin" Contrasted with Buckingham Hall, the Planter's Home* (New York, 1852); Eastman, *Aunt Phillis's Cabin* (Philadelphia, 1852); Baynard Rush Hall, *Frank Freeman's Barber Shop* (New York, 1852); McIntosh, *Lofty and the Lowly* (New York, 1852); Charles Jacobs Peterson, *Cabin and Parlor* (Philadelphia, 1852); Rush, *North and South* (Philadelphia, 1852); William L. G. Smith, *Life at the South* (Buffalo, 1852); Butt, *Antifanaticism* (Philadelphia, 1853); Hale, *Liberia* (New York, 1853); Herndon, *Louise Elton* (Philadelphia, 1853); John White Page, *Uncle Robin, in His Cabin in Virginia, and Tom without One in Boston* (Richmond, 1853); Vidi, *Mr. Frank* (Philadelphia, 1853); Chase, *English Serfdom and American Slavery* (New York, 1854); Hentz, *Planter's Northern Bride* (Philadelphia, 1854); Holmes, *Tempest and Sunshine* (New York, 1854); Estes, *Tit for Tat* (London, 1855); Neville, *Edith Allen* (Richmond, 1855); Burwell, *White Acre vs. Black Acre* (Richmond, 1856); Henry Field James, *Abolitionism Unveiled* (Cincinnati, 1856); *Olive-Branch*, written by an anonymous author (Philadelphia, 1857); Smythe, *Ethel Somers* (Augusta, 1857); Hungerford, *Old Plantation* (New York, 1859); Texan, *Yankee Slave-Dealer* (Nashville, 1860); Cowdin, *Ellen* (Mobile, 1860); Flanders, *Ebony Idol* (New York, 1860); Joseph Holt Ingraham, *Sunny South* (Philadelphia, 1860); Schoolcraft, *Black Gauntlet* (Philadelphia, 1860); Starnes, *Slaveholder Abroad* (Philadelphia, 1860); Nehemiah Adams, *Sable Cloud* (Boston, 1861); and Theodore Dehone Mathews, *Old Toney and His Master* (Nashville, 1861). Biographical details for these authors are noted below. See Gossett, *Uncle Tom's Cabin*, 429n1; Uncle Tom's Cabin and American Culture, accessed June 28, 2024, http://utc.iath.virginia.edu; Karen Manners Smith, "Southern Women Writers' Responses"; Jordan-Lake, *Whitewashing Uncle Tom's Cabin*, xviii–xix; David S. Reynolds, *Mightier Than the Sword*, 153–54; and Roth, *Gender and Race*, 143–45.

3. The only titles mentioned in the extant Lippincott business ledgers from this period are Simms's *Sword and the Distaff* and Schoolcraft's *Black Gauntlet*. In what may have been the pattern for these novels, the latter was published at the author's expense. At least 350 copies were printed, but at least 274 remained unsold by 1864. Account books, series 1, J. B. Lippincott Company Records, Historical Society of Pennsylvania. (Thanks to Michael Winship, who interpreted the ledger.)

4. For gendered sexual violence in *Incidents*, see Sánchez-Eppler, *Touching Liberty*, 83–104; Berlant, *Queen of America*, 225–35; Hartman, *Scenes of Subjection*, 102–12; and Sielke, *Reading Rape*, 23–26.

5. Jacobs, *Incidents*, 246–47. For this scene as example of homosexual abuse, see Abdur-Rahman, *Against the Closet*, 25–50; Greven, *Gender Protest*, 45–46; and Thomas A. Foster, "Sexual Abuse," 129–31.

6. For the sexual abuse of enslaved women, see Jennings, "Us Colored Women"; Camp, *Closer to Freedom*, 64–68; and Jones-Rogers, "Rethinking Sexual Violence." For male-male sexual violence in Brazilian slavery, see Sigal, "(Homo)Sexual Desire"; and Aidoo, *Slavery Unseen*, 29–65.

7. Hartman, *Scenes of Subjection*, 85. For readings of cultural texts that evidence sexual violation as constitutive of enslavement, see Saillant, "Black Body Erotic"; and Woodard, *Delectable Negro*, 95–125.

8. Thomas A. Foster, *Rethinking Rufus*, 94–102.

9. Some of the earliest and most notable US narratives mentioning the sexual abuse of enslaved women point to offspring or aggrieved wives as evidence: Roper, *Narrative*, 1–3; Martineau, *Society in America*, 328–29; Kemble, *Journal of a Residence*, 14–16; and Chesnut, *Private Mary Chesnut*, 42–43.

10. See Yee, *Black Women Abolitionists*, 40–59; and Sinha, *Slave's Cause*, 269–71.

11. Jane Tompkins, *Sensational Designs*, 122–46; Tennenhouse, "Libertine America," 17–20.

12. For a classic account of this logic, see Cleaver, *Soul on Ice*, 97–117. For slavery's homosexual violence contemplated in more complexity than a narrative of sexual subordination, see the recent novel Jones, *Prophets*, 202–8.

13. Edelman, *Homographesis*, 42–78; Reid-Pharr, "Tearing the Goat's Flesh"; Woodard, *Delectable Negro*, 22–24.

14. For the South as always already queer, see Donna Jo Smith, "Queering the South"; and Brasell, "'Degeneration of Nationalism.'"

15. Little evidence exists of these novels' reception or significant readership. Historian Timothy Williams's survey of Civil War–era Southern white reading habits suggests that political novels were not among popularly read works. Readers interested in politics often read nonfiction and histories, whereas novel readers preferred fiction that avoided sectional politics. Timothy J. Williams, "Readers' South."

16. See Meer, *Uncle Tom Mania*, 73–101; Burleigh, *Intimacy and Family*, 125–42; Capitani, *Truthful Pictures*; and Roth, *Gender and Race*, 141–65.

17. Harriet Beecher Stowe, *Key*, 133. For these novels' contrast between abolitionism's abstract arguments and slavery's concrete intimate familial relationships, see Burleigh, *Intimacy and Family*, 127–30.

18. John White Page, *Uncle Robin*, 66. Page was the clerk of the court in Frederick County, Virginia. Gold, *History of Clarke County*, 92–93.

19. For North-South differences in defining family, see Arthur Wallace Calhoun, *Social History*, 171–357; Cashin, "Structure"; Levine, *Half Slave*, 23–27, 71–75; Glover, *All Our Relations*; and Pierson, *Free Hearts*.

20. As a proslavery newspaper put it in a review of William L. G. Smith's *Life at the South*, "Such a book almost out of necessity must be, rather dull; justice is apt to be dull, and to drawl out its words monotonously." New Books, *Charleston Mercury*, August 21, 1852.

21. For the abolitionist as wolf in sheep's clothing, see Hentz, *Planter's Northern Bride*, 2:159; Cowdin, *Ellen*, 34, 57; and Theodore Dehone Mathews, *Old Toney*, 266.

22. Tennenhouse, "Libertine America," 16.

23. Fear, both of slave revolt and of abolitionist success, is remarkably absent in these novels. And yet the stridency with which they deny such threats may be the strongest evidence for fear as this propaganda's underlying motivation. The Irish journalist William Howard Russell, in 1861, would see "something suspicious in the constant never-ending statement that 'We are not afraid of our slaves'" as proved by "the curfew and the night patrol in the streets, the prisons and watch-houses, and the police regulations." Russell, *Civil War in America*, 61.

24. *Frank Freeman's Barber Shop* opens after a thwarted insurrection, with the insurrectionists put to death. The real victim is the protagonist, Frank, who has lost the trust of

the whites because of others' disloyalty. Sarah Josepha Buell Hale's *Liberia* also opens with a family hunkering down against a rumored slave revolt that never arrives. Caroline Lee Hentz's *The Planter's Northern Bride* treats insurrection as a Northern fear for the titular bride to overcome. Her primary development across the novel is learning to not be afraid of the enslaved.

25. On slavery's expansion as necessary for its survival, see (politically) Oakes, *Ruling Race*; (economically) Baptist, *Half Has Never*; and (globally) Grandin, *Empire of Necessity*.

26. McIntosh was probably the most successful female writer before the 1850s who responded to Stowe's novel. For more on the Georgia-born author, who spent time in New York, see Weaks-Baxter, "Gender Issues," 39–40; Karen Manners Smith, "Novel," 55–57; Gardner, *Blood and Irony*, 32–34; and Burnett, "Proslavery Social Problem."

27. These names reflect the tradition in which Southerners saw the US sectional dispute, as descended from the English civil war, with New England abolitionists as Cromwellian Puritans, racially Anglo-Saxon or English, and Southerners as Royalist Cavaliers, racially Norman or Scotch Irish. See Fischer, *Albion's Seed*, 831–63; William Robert Taylor, *Cavalier and Yankee*; Fox-Genovese and Genovese, *Mind*, 665–67; and Ritchie D. Watson Jr., *Normans and Saxons*.

28. *The Ebony Idol* was written by a Mrs. G. M. Flanders, who was advertised as "a lady of New England" who had "lived South." Apparently, the identity of the author raised some speculation, as a *Liberator* article stated: "The story has been started in England that Miss [Harriet Elizabeth] Prescott [Spofford], author of 'Sir Rohan's Ghost' wrote 'The Ebony Idol.' This is a slander on a gifted woman." Pink, "Correspondence of the Courier," *Charleston Tri-weekly Courier*, August 21, 1860; "A Story," *Liberator*, September 14, 1860.

29. McIntosh, *Lofty and the Lowly*, 2:146–51.

30. The anonymous author of *Mr. Frank* used the pseudonym "Vidi." One newspaper believed his or hers to be "a voice from south of Mason and Dixon." New Publications, *Daily Atlas*, October 28, 1853.

31. Vidi, *Mr. Frank*, 220.

32. Mary H. Eastman, the author of *Aunt Phillis's Cabin*, was born to a slaveholding family in Virginia and lived with her husband in Minnesota Territory in the 1840s and in Washington, DC, in the 1850s. Eastman's novel was one of the best-selling responses to Stowe's. See Beverly Peterson, "'Aunt Phillis's Cabin.'"

33. *Frank Freeman's Barber Shop* author Bayard Rush Hall was a classicist from Pennsylvania, teaching at the state university in Indiana when he wrote the novel. *Antifanaticism* author Mary Haines Butt was twenty when her novel was published. Possibly a pupil of *Planter's Northern Bride* author Hentz, Butt had a successful career in the 1860s as a writer of moral tales and children's short stories. Karen Manners Smith, "Southern Women Writers' Responses," 100.

34. *Aunt Phillis's Cabin* describes one young enslaved woman as being "seduced off by the Abolitionists"; she "threw herself, trembling and dismayed, into the arms and tender mercies of the Abolitionists." Eastman, *Aunt Phillis's Cabin*, 57–58.

35. Hentz, *Planter's Northern Bride*, 2:112–13. Caroline Lee Hentz was a Kentucky schoolteacher and author of more than a dozen antebellum works. See Shillingsburg, "Caroline Lee Hentz."

36. Charles Jacobs Peterson, *Cabin and Parlor*, 51, 27; Cowdin, *Ellen*, 16. Charles Peterson was a magazine editor in Philadelphia for *Graham's Magazine* and the *Saturday*

Evening Post. For analysis of the novel, see Stokes, *Color of Sex*, 35–50. According to a music historian, Virginia Cowdin lived in Liberty, Mississippi, and was the author of the music "Gen. Beauregard's Grand March." Bailey, *Music*, 156–57.

37. For Adolph's gendered foppishness, see Borgstrom, "Passing Over"; and Greven, *Men beyond Desire*, 161–62. For Adolph and St. Clare as homoerotically attached, see Foreman, "'This Promiscuous Housekeeping'"; and Benemann, *Male-Male Intimacy*, 146–49. For Adolph as Black dandy, see Monica L. Miller, *Slaves to Fashion*, 94–114. For enslaved valets as vulnerable to same-sex violence, see Thomas A. Foster, *Rethinking Rufus*, 102–12.

38. Harriet Beecher Stowe, *Uncle Tom's Cabin*, 303.

39. Smith was a resident of Buffalo and the city's treasurer from 1856 to 1857. A lifelong Democrat, Smith also wrote a biography of 1848 Democratic presidential candidate Lewis Cass.

40. William L. G. Smith, *Life at the South*, 47; Fowler, *Illustrated Self-Instructor*, 57.

41. William L. G. Smith, *Life at the South*, 511.

42. Lynch, "'Here Is Adhesiveness,'" 84; David S. Reynolds, "'Affection'"; Zweig, *Walt Whitman*, 194–95. Also see David F. Greenberg, *Construction of Homosexuality*, 404–6.

43. Fowler, *Phrenology Proved*, 31–32. Schoolcraft, *Black Gauntlet*, also used adhesiveness to describe an enslaved woman's attachment to the young white heroine: "No mother on earth could have been more loving than this sympathizing, adhesive slave" (346).

44. Hale, *Liberia*, 20, 24, 25. Hale was a New Englander who served as the editor of *Godey's Lady Book* from 1837 to 1877. For Hale and her novel, see Baym, *American Women Writers*, 26–28, 63; and Ryan, "Errand into Africa."

45. Amy Kaplan, *Anarchy of Empire*, 37–42. Etsuko Taketani argues that Hale's novel adds complexity to the narrative of a childlike Liberia by describing an independent Liberia in which "unequal relations of colonial rule are reinscribed into a subtler form." Taketani, "Postcolonial Liberia," 481.

46. See discussion of Mathews in chapter 1. For Harris, see Bier, "'Bless You, Chile'"; and Bernstein, *Racial Innocence*, 93.

47. Theodore Dehone Mathews, *Old Toney*, 47, 94, 47.

48. Schoolcraft, *Black Gauntlet*, 202. Mary Howard Schoolcraft's novel is autobiographical fiction, describing its heroine's upbringing on a Virginia slave plantation and her marriage to a widower, like her real-life husband Henry Schoolcraft, who studied Native American culture and had been married to an Ojibwe woman.

49. Theodore Dehone Mathews, *Old Toney*, 48.

50. Theodore Dehone Mathews, *Old Toney*, 195.

51. Theodore Dehone Mathews, *Old Toney*, 19–20.

52. US Census Bureau, 1860 Federal Slave Schedules, St. Peter's Parish, Beaufort County, South Carolina, 74, accessed January 30, 2022, Ancestry.com. Mathews died in 1860, before his book's publication.

53. Lott, *Love and Theft*, 170.

54. See, e.g., the anti-antislavery pamphlet "God Bless Abraham Lincoln! A Solemn Discourse," ca. 1864, 14–16, Stern Collection of Lincolniana, Library of Congress, Washington, DC.

55. The nearest one of these novels comes to deriding homoeroticism is when, within the novel's humorous tone, a loquacious Irish character in *Mr. Frank* compliments an enslaved man on being "the handsomest individual of the human species" to get information about a nearby plantation. Vidi, *Mr. Frank*, 151.

56. Baynard Rush Hall, *Frank Freeman's Barber Shop*, 60.

57. Baynard Rush Hall, *Frank Freeman's Barber Shop*, 62. For vows within the novel, see Burleigh, *Intimacy and Family*, 138–39.

58. The famous British Society for the Abolition of the Slave Trade medallion, designed by Josiah Wedgwood in 1787, depicted a kneeling enslaved man entreating justice. For analysis of these images in *Frank Freeman's Barber Shop* and *The Planter's Northern Bride*, see Roth, *Gender and Race*, 151–53.

59. Hentz, *Planter's Northern Bride*, vol. 2 frontispiece.

60. Dew, *Review of the Debate*, 109–10.

61. See Genovese, *World the Slaveholders Made*, 127–36; and Faust, "Proslavery Argument in History," 8–10.

62. Dew, *Review of the Debate*, 109.

63. Legaré, *Writings*, 428–29; Thomas Read Rootes Cobb, *Inquiry*, 13–14; Sawyer, *Southern Institutes*, 37. Another proslavery writer, George Fitzhugh, would explain that God "instituted slavery from the first, as he instituted marriage and parental authority." Fitzhugh, *Sociology for the South*, 167. For this analogy in proslavery thought, see Fox-Genovese and Genovese, *Mind*, 201, 274–75; and Brophy, *University, Court, and Slave*, 231–32.

64. Sawyer, *Southern Institutes*, 236–48. One narrator says about Stowe: "Although she is here speaking of slavery *politically*, can you not apply it to matrimony in this miserable country of ours? . . . Take advantage of it, wives and negroes!" Eastman, *Aunt Phillis's Cabin*, 111.

65. Thomas Read Rootes Cobb, *Inquiry*, 13–14.

66. Thomas Read Rootes Cobb, *Inquiry*, xxxv.

67. Dew, *Review of the Debate*, 110.

68. Schoolcraft, *Black Gauntlet*, 83–84.

69. Nyong'o, *Amalgamation Waltz*, 82–85.

70. Simms, *Letters*, 222–23.

71. Ridgely, "Woodcraft"; Charles S. Watson, "Simms's Answer"; Roth, *Gender and Race*, 149–51, 155–56.

72. For Simms's proslavery essays, see Foley, "Social and Political Prose."

73. For an overview of Simms's romances and context, see Moltke-Hansen, "Revolutionary Romances." For *The Sword and the Distaff*, see Kibler, "Woodcraft."

74. Moran, "Contributions," lv.

75. Sarah Meer's comment that the novel "does not labor to defend slavery or the South" is misleading, but it points to the complete absence from the novel of an abolitionist threat to Southern society. Meer, *Uncle Tom Mania*, 82.

76. Kolodny, "Unchanging Landscape," 61–67. For masculinity in Simms, see Mayfield, "'Soul of a Man!'"

77. Simms, *Sword and the Distaff*, 591.

78. Simms, *Sword and the Distaff*, 124.

79. Dale, "William Gilmore Simms's Porgy," 70.

80. Jones-Rogers, *They Were Her Property*, xiv–xvii.

81. Before Yancey's departure as the Confederacy's minister to the United Kingdom in 1861, he lectured throughout the United States (including at Richmond) about the nobility of slavery, but I have been unable to identify specific language to which this envelope refers. A biographer does mention "a faithful slave of many years" named Joe but only to demonstrate Yancey's cold indifference to the lives of the enslaved. Walther, *William Lowndes Yancey*, 153–54.

82. Bernstein, *Racial Innocence*, 94–105.

83. Melville, *Benito Cereno*, 49.

84. Melville, *Benito Cereno*, 61, 87–89, 116, 63.

85. Melville, *Benito Cereno*, 63.

CHAPTER 3

1. For gender crisis scholarship, see n36 in this book's introduction.

2. For writing the history of homosexuality beyond "simply a story of aberration," see Downs, "With Only a Trace," 28–29.

3. Beyond the three misconduct charges Thomas Lowry documented in the wartime US Navy for "indecent intercourse" and "unnatural crime" between two men, there is little evidence of same-sex sex as a new or intensified social problem during the Civil War. Many accounts of soldiers' lives treat as routine male co-sleeping arrangements and homosocial nudity. Jonathan Ned Katz summarizes such wartime intimacies, including in the Andersonville memoirs discussed in the next chapter, and Randy Shilts points to Confederate captain Irving Buck's description of sleeping with Gen. Patrick Cleburne. Union army surgeon general William A. Hammond, who directed medical attention to the problems of "pederasty" and "sexual inversion" in the 1880s, published two volumes one might expect to mention homosexual behavior. While his 1863 *Treatise on Hygiene* posed "masturbation" as a core problem of army camp life due to soldiers' boredom, neither that volume nor his 1864 *Lectures on Venereal Diseases*, a collection of his 1861 talks, mentions sexual contact between people of the same sex. Lowry, *Story*, 109–13; Jonathan Ned Katz, *Love Stories*, 134–46; Shilts, *Conduct Unbecoming*, 14–15; Higginson, *Army Life*, 74–76, 226–27; Billings, *Hardtack and Coffee*, 52; McCarthy, *Detailed Minutiæ*, 89; William A. Hammond, *Treatise on Hygiene*, 139–43; William A. Hammond, *Lectures on Venereal Diseases*.

4. A partial list of this trope includes Bradshaw, *Pauline of the Potomac* (1862); Bradshaw, *Maud of the Mississippi* (1863); Barclay, *Lady Lieutenant* (1862); Buntline, *Rattlesnake* (1862); *Dora, the Heroine of the Cumberland* (1864); Edgeville, *Castine* (1865); Abby Buchanan Longstreet, *Remy St. Remy* (1865); Hazel, *Virginia Graham* (1867); Cooke, *Hilt to Hilt* (1869); and Dowling, *Southern Prisons* (1870). For at least 250 real-life analogues to these fictional soldiers, see Blanton and Cook, *They Fought Like Demons*. Such real-life figures, most prominently Union soldier Sarah Emma Edmonds (author of the semifictional 1864 memoir *Nurse and Spy*) and Confederate soldier Loreta Janeta Velázquez (author of the semifictional 1876 memoir *The Woman in Battle*), have received significant recent

treatment as protofeminist figures in popular histories such as Leonard, *All the Daring*; and Karen Abbott, *Liar, Temptress, Soldier, Spy*. For histories of cross-dressing adventure stories beyond the Civil War, see Dugaw, *Warrior Women*; Daniel A. Cohen, *Female Marine*; Gustafson, "Genders of Nationalism"; and LaFleur, *Natural History of Sexuality*, 137–63.

5. Literary scholar Marjorie Garber suggested that a cross-gendered character in a text often "indicates a *category crisis elsewhere*, an irresolvable conflict or epistemological crux." For the Civil War years, the crisis seems obvious, and these stories usually enfold the period of gender transgression between Sumter and Appomattox. Marjorie B. Garber, *Vested Interests*, 17.

6. Elizabeth Young, *Disarming the Nation*, 169–75; Fahs, *Imagined Civil War*, 240–41.

7. Barclay, *Lady Lieutenant*, 17; Buntline, *Rattlesnake*, 47, 64. Erastus Elmer Barclay had established a publishing career in Philadelphia in the 1840s with sensational reportages of violent crimes in the city. McDade, "Lurid Literature." Under the pen name Ned Buntline, Edward Judson wrote many dime novels before and after the Civil War. After being dishonorably discharged from the Union army for drunkenness, he wrote sensational novels popularizing Buffalo Bill and became the namesake of a pistol. Harry Hazel's *Virginia Graham, the Spy of the Grand Army* (1867) also uses gender disguise to suggest homoeroticism. Under that pen name, Justin Jones wrote over forty sensational novellas often featuring military adventures. The gun advertisements at the back of *Virginia Graham* indicate the book's place within a genre of adventure books for boys. Hazel, *Virginia Graham*, 135. In such writing, these authors are hardly exploring the range of female sexuality as they are presenting scenes between women as the objects of sexual fantasy.

8. Abby Buchanan Longstreet, *Remy St. Remy*, 239. Aside from being the only of these novels that demonstrates any consternation over male-male sexual desire, *Remy St. Remy* appears to be the only one by a woman author. Under the pen name Mrs. C. H. Gildersleeve, Abbie Peters Buchanan Longstreet, a New Yorker, wrote several articles for magazines such as the *Home Monthly* as well as for books such as *Social Etiquette of New York*. "Mrs. C. H. Gildersleeve," Beadle and Adams Dime Novel Digitization Project, 2023, https://ulib.niu.edu/badndp/gildersleeve_c.html.

9. When a Catholic review dismissed *Remy St. Remy*, it did not mention the captain's pining over his comrade, only that "the heroine is no model for any virtuous modest girl; for no woman of correct training or good morals could dress herself in the habiliments of the opposite sex." New Publications, *Catholic World*, November 1865, 287.

10. Cooke, *Hilt to Hilt*, 73.

11. Cooke, *Hilt to Hilt*, 44, 82, 85, 89, 92, 97.

12. Mountaineer, "Ned Arlington, or Harper's Ferry Scenes," *Southern Illustrated News*, September 27, 1862, 2. For the sexual threat in the story, see Fahs, *Imagined Civil War*, 251–52.

13. See Rable, *Civil Wars*; Faust, *Mothers of Invention*; Censer, *Reconstruction*; Roberts, *Confederate Belle*; and Whites, *Gender Matters*.

14. See, e.g., Osterweis, *Myth*; Connelly, *Marble Man*; Charles Reagan Wilson, *Baptized in Blood*; Gallagher, *Causes Won*; and Cox, *Dixie's Daughters*. For overviews of the Lost Cause, see Gaines M. Foster, *Ghosts of the Confederacy*; Gallagher and Nolan, *Myth*; and Janney, *Remembering the Civil War*, 133–59.

15. Silber, *Romance of Reunion*, 34. See also Kenneth S. Greenberg, *Honor and Slavery*, 25–33.

16. For Lincoln and Stanton, see "This Is Old Mother Lincoln Explaining to Old Mother Stanton," *New York Illustrated News*, January 1, 1863; and Rothberg, "Father Abraham." For Hendricks, see Thomas Nast, "HEN(dricks)-PECKED," *HW*, August 5, 1876, 630.

17. Robert R. Rowison, "History of the War," *Southern Literary Messenger*, September 1863, 516. Twenty-four years after that account a Confederate officer wrote, "There was no truth in the statement that Col. Zarvona was 'dressed in female apparel.'" Scharf, *History*, 121.

18. Frank Battle, "Entering the Union Lines in a Petticoat," *Confederate Veteran*, February 1899, 79.

19. Fiske, *Mississippi Valley*, 16–17. Having derided this story as "too absurd for belief," John Fiske wrote that he was told the story by Gen. Francis P. Blair's widow and son as well as by a colonel on Lyons's staff.

20. Grimes, *Confederate Mail Runner*, 44.

21. John N. Edwards, *Noted Guerillas*, 172–73. These stories were compiled in a blog post: G. E. Rule, "Manly Missouri Crossdressers of the Civil War," *Civil War St. Louis* (blog), March 7, 2001, www.civilwarstlouis.com/articles/manly-missouri-crossdressers-of-the-civil-war.

22. The story of Stringfellow's disguise appeared in a 1936 *Dictionary of American Biography*, written by William E. Dodd, the eventual US ambassador to Nazi Germany, who claimed that he heard Stringfellow's lectures himself. The story of the Union ball comes from a 1960 work, for which the episode gets an entire chapter and a single footnote that begins, "For this episode, the author could find no actual documentation." Dodd, "Stringfellow, Franklin"; R. Shepard Brown, *Stringfellow of the Fourth*, 298n98.

23. Quoted in Looby, "'As Thoroughly Black,'" 79.

24. Reid Mitchell, *Vacant Chair*, 71–72.

25. Quoted in Maxwell, *Perfect Lion*, 317.

26. "The Gallant Pelham," *Richmond Sentinel*, March 21, 1863.

27. "The War," *Richmond Whig*, March 21, 1863. For Confederate funerals—focusing on Stonewall Jackson's in 1863 and Robert E. Lee's in 1870—see Purcell, *Spectacle of Grief*.

28. Quoted in Maxwell, *Perfect Lion*, 293–94.

29. Cooke, *Surry of Eagle's-Nest*, 377–78, 379. In *Wearing of the Gray*, Cooke remembers Pelham in "the bed where he so often slept with me, prolonging his gay talk deep into the night" (129).

30. Edmund Wilson, *Patriotic Gore*, 442–49; Aaron, *Unwritten War*, 245–46; Blight, *Race and Reunion*, 156–57. See also Beaty, *John Esten Cooke, Virginian*.

31. See Steve Davis, "John Esten Cooke"; Ritchie D. Watson Jr., "John Esten Cooke"; Bernath, *Confederate Minds*, 186; Hettle, *Inventing Stonewall Jackson*, 53–68; and Templeton, *Politics*, 148–61.

32. Cooke, *Surry of Eagle's-Nest*, 377–79.

33. Cooke, *Wearing of the Gray*, 132.

34. Cooke, *Life of Gen. Robert E. Lee*, 206. Pelham is also featured in Cooke's *Life of Stonewall Jackson* (1863), *Mohun* (1869), *Hammer and Rapier* (1870), and the poem "Band in the Pines" (1866).

35. Von Borcke, *Memoirs*, 2:14n.

36. Blackford, *War Years*, 200, 90. The phrase "child-like and bland" is lifted from Bret Harte's description of the Chinese cardplayer's smile in the 1870 poem "Plain Language from Truthful James," later known as "The Heathen Chinee." As the cardplayer's apparent innocent simplicity masks his cunning, so does Pelham's innocence mask his flirtatiousness.

37. Brooks, *Visible Confederacy*, 100–114, 150–61.

38. Many of the surviving Pelham prints were printed by E. & H. T. Anthony at 501 Broadway in New York City or at the Gilbert Studios in Philadelphia. Another full-length photo of Pelham in a suit from 1860 was not as reprinted as Brady's was. *John Pelham as a Student*, 1860, Photographs Collection, Alabama Department of Archives and History.

39. Faust, *This Republic of Suffering*, 85. See also Faust, "Race, Gender"; and Janney, *Burying the Dead*, 34–35.

40. James R. Randall, "John Pelham." Reprinted countless times after the war, the poem was first published by the *Southern Literary Messenger* in May 1863.

41. For a succinct account of "how thoroughly Pelham's memory became a part of the Lost Cause narrative," see John Byers Nesbit III, "The Gallant Pelham," *Disunion* (blog), *New York Times*, April 1, 2013, https://archive.nytimes.com/opinionator.blogs.nytimes .com/2013/04/01/the-gallant-pelham.

42. Gallagher, *Confederate War*.

43. Rubin, *Shattered Nation*, 4.

44. Rubin, *Shattered Nation*, 172–200; Broomall, *Private Confederacies*, 120–30.

45. Pater, *Renaissance*, 221.

46. See, e.g., André-Naquian Wheeler, "Why Can't Black Men Be Twinks?," *i-D*, May 22, 2018.

47. Quoted in Archie K. Davis, *Boy Colonel*, 82.

48. Bennett H. Young, "Col. John R. Lane and His Regiment," *Confederate Veteran*, March 1909, 110.

49. Archie K. Davis, *Boy Colonel*, 4.

50. Quoted in Archie K. Davis, *Boy Colonel*, 339.

51. Charles Ingraham's biography of Ellsworth includes a newspaper's description of him: "A boyish figure, not exceeding five feet six inches in height, with well-formed, shapely limbs . . . a well-balanced head crowned with a wealth of dark brown hair that fell in careless, clinging curls about his neck, eyes of dark hazel that sparkled and flashed with excitement or melted with tenderness . . . a face as smooth and as fair as a maiden's." To which biographer Ruth Painter Randall, quoting Ingraham, adds: "What boy could resist him?" When Ellsworth died, his body lay in state in the White House's East Room with a glass oval allowing viewers to see his face. Accounts of Ellsworth's death emphasized Lincoln's reaction, the language of which led to C. A. Tripp using Ellsworth as an example of Lincoln's homosexual interest. Lincoln, however, appears no more enamored of the dead soldier than was the rest of the country. Charles A. Ingraham, *Elmer E. Ellsworth*, 8–9; Ruth Painter Randall, *Lincoln's Sons*, 61; "Obsequies of Col. Ellsworth," *New York Herald*, May 27, 1861; Tripp, *Intimate World*, 109–24.

52. See Timothy J. Williams, "'Gold of the Pen.'"

53. See Guy-Bray, "Elegy"; Boehrer, "'Lycidas'"; and Craft, "'Descend.'"

54. Quoted in Archie K. Davis, *Boy Colonel*, 338.

55. Archie K. Davis, *Boy Colonel*, 21.

56. Archie K. Davis, *Boy Colonel*, 248.

57. Cooke, *Wearing of the Gray*, 132; Blackford, *War Years*, 163; Hassler, *Colonel John Pelham*, 101; Maxwell, *Perfect Lion*, 184.

58. Quoted in Maxwell, *Perfect Lion*, 26.

59. Edward Porter Alexander, *Fighting for the Confederacy*, 174. Alexander mentions another Confederate officer, Gen. Thomas Muldrup Logan, who "was slight, slender, blue eyed, youthful looking & with such delicate features that his college nickname, like 'the gallant Pelham's,' had been a girl's. Pelham's was Sally Pelham. Logan's was Molly Logan" (315).

60. Von Borcke, *Memoirs*, 2:184, 187.

61. Blackford, *War Years*, 201.

62. Von Borcke states, "My thoughts constantly reverting to my dear friend Pelham, with an obstinate foreboding that some dreadful fate must have befallen him." Von Borcke, *Memoirs*, 2:186.

63. Blackford, *War Years*, 201.

64. Hassler, *Colonel John Pelham*, 160.

65. Quoted in Maxwell, *Perfect Lion*, 312.

66. Bernstein, *Racial Innocence*, 4–8.

67. See Kincaid, *Erotic Innocence*, 17–19.

68. Shelton, *Dreamworlds of Alabama*, 27. Pelham's coat, in the back, connects to a tree-trunk strut for support, which may give to the viewer's imagination the outline of curvature underneath, slight by the standards of male statuary. But such is Pelham's power of provocation upon the perceptions of older men.

69. Shelton, *Dreamworlds of Alabama*, xx, xi, 27, xii.

70. Horwitz, *Confederates in the Attic*, 276–77; Coates, *We Were Eight Years*, 81; Burns, "Universe of Battle." See Marrs, *Not Even Past*, 121–22.

71. Faulkner, *Intruder in the Dust*, 190.

72. Horwitz, *Confederates in the Attic*, 277.

73. For modernism's mixing of identification and desire, I am referring to how canonical modernist novels, where they incorporate male homoerotic desire, often do so through their transformation of the Jamesian observer-actor fictional formula, such as in F. Scott Fitzgerald's *The Great Gatsby* (1925) or Ernest Hemingway's *The Sun Also Rises* (1926). For the insights of queer theory on identification and desire, see Sedgwick, *Epistemology of the Closet*, 161–64.

74. Fiedler includes *Intruder* within the cross-racial male pattern following "the erotic tie at the heart of *Huckleberry Finn*." Fiedler, *Love and Death*, 352. Chick also has a Black boy companion, Aleck Sander, in a youthful friendship staged as more typical of normative Southern white male development in *Intruder* and *The Town* (1957). A younger Mallison narrates that second novel of the Snopes trilogy from the perspective of male sexual innocence, precociously on the verge of sexual knowledge. He returns for the third Snopes novel, *The Mansion* (1959), as an adult and veteran, although his final appearance, after asking his uncle's permission to "try to lay" Linda Snopes Kohl and being told that he can't, concludes with her closing the door on him while he meditates on an ensnared

"spider lover" whose "gal" empties "him of his blood too while all he thinks he is risking is his semen." Which is to say that, in Faulkner, Charles Mallison, whether it is sex or Gettysburg, is perpetually paused on the verge of action but innocent of it, the one who wonders, as he does in *The Town*, "how any boys live long enough to grow up." Faulkner, *Mansion*, 388, 395; Faulkner, *Town*, 56.

75. Evans, *Macaria*, 170–72. For ideologies of purity in *Macaria*, see Faust, "Altars of Sacrifice"; Gardner, *Blood and Irony*, 25–30; and Greven, *Men beyond Desire*, 186–91.

76. James R. Randall, "John Pelham"; W. Gordon McCabe, "John Pegram"; John R. Thompson, "Captain Latane."

77. La Coste, "Somebody's Darling"; Kentucky Girl, "Rebel Soldier"; Timrod, "Unknown Dead," 251–52.

78. Cooke, "Broken Mug," 273, 269, 272.

79. Bernath, *Confederate Minds*, 211–18; Hutchison, *Apples and Ashes*, 4–14; Binnington, *Confederate Visions*, 97–101.

80. Hayne, "Memoir of Henry Timrod"; Hayne, "Our Martyrs," 279. For Timrod's elegiac debts to Tennyson, see Henderson, "Nation."

81. Timrod, "Ode."

82. Rubin, *Shattered Nation*, 233–39; Janney, *Burying the Dead*, 39–68.

83. Tim Lockette, "Anniston Council Again Votes to Remove Monument," *Anniston Star*, September 15, 2020; Tim Lockette, "Community Leaders React to Removal of Anniston's Confederate Monument," *Anniston Star*, September 27, 2020.

84. Hardy Jackson, "Commemorating John Pelham," *Observer*, April 25, 2018. Distinguishing between slaveholders and Pelham makes little sense: he was also a slaveholder. He had two enslaved attendants during the war, whom Von Borcke romanticized as being as attached to the young man as everyone else. At Pelham's death, Von Borcke writes, the attendants "begged to be allowed at once to go and take charge of their master's body—a permission which I was, however, constrained to refuse." Von Borcke, *Memoirs*, 2:188.

85. "A Reminiscence," *Richmond Whig*, April 14, 1863.

86. Maxwell, *Perfect Lion*, ix; Schaff, *Spirit*, 133.

87. Schaff, *Spirit*, 131–33.

88. Travis M. Foster, *Genre and White Supremacy*, 20.

89. For Whitman's hospital experience caring for soldiers, see Asselineau, *Evolution of Walt Whitman*, 144–53; Shively, *Calamus Lovers*, 56–72; David S. Reynolds, *Walt Whitman's America*, 424–32; Loving, *Walt Whitman*, 262–78; Jonathan Ned Katz, *Love Stories*, 148–63; Morris, *Better Angel*; Coviello, *Tomorrow's Parties*, 48–63; and Robert Leigh Davis, *Whitman*, 33–42.

90. Walt Whitman, "Our Wounded and Sick Soldiers," *New York Times*, December 11, 1864; Whitman, *Complete Prose Works*, 37.

91. Quoted in Jonathan Ned Katz, *Gay American History*, 500; Timrod, "Two Portraits," 94.

92. Halleck, *Young America*, 26, 31. See Hallock, *American Byron*. Halleck's relationship with Joseph Rodman Drake is the model for the male romantic friendship in Bayard Taylor, *Joseph and His Friend*.

93. Halleck, *Young America*, 11–12, 35, 28–30.

94. Whitman, *Sequel to Drum-Taps*, 23. For the reconciliationist project of white nationalism in Whitman's elegies, see Travis M. Foster, *Genre and White Supremacy*, 72–74.

95. Whitman, *Memoranda during the War*, 13.

96. Whitman, *Notebooks*, 67.

97. Folsom, "'Yet More Terrible." For Whitman and Black Americans, see the essays in Ivy Wilson, *Whitman Noir*, esp. Folsom, "Erasing Race"; and Freeburg, "Walt Whitman"; and see Goldberg, "Unspeakable Whiteness."

CHAPTER 4

1. "Rebel Cruelty," *HW*, June 18, 1864, 385. For a history of these images, see Collins, "Living Skeletons"; and Cross, "'Pictures.'"

2. See, e.g., Halttunen, "Humanitarianism"; and Lasser, "Voyeuristic Abolitionism."

3. Giesberg, *Sex*, 42.

4. "A Typical Negro," *HW*, July 4, 1863, 429–30. For history of this image, see Silkenat, "'Typical Negro.'"

5. Historian Benjamin Cloyd suggests in his book on Civil War prisons in American memory that "it would not be unfair to change the subtitle of the book to 'Andersonville in American Memory,'" so much does it stand in for the prison experience generally. Cloyd, *Haunted by Atrocity*, 2.

6. For a classic account of these debates, see McPherson, *Battle Cry of Freedom*, 798–803. Witnesses at Wirz's trial, as well as John McElroy, record the general in command of Confederate prisoners as saying something like "I am killing off more Yankees than twenty regiments in Lee's Army." McElroy, *Andersonville*, 651.

7. For a detailed account of soldiers' sensory experiences at Andersonville and other Civil War prisons, see Kutzler, *Living by Inches*. For histories of Confederate prisons, see Sanders, *While in the Hands*; and Pickenpaugh, *Captives in Blue*.

8. "Rebel Cruelties," *HW*, June 17, 1865, 379–80. When this image was reproduced in the corner of a large lithograph depicting the horrors at Andersonville, the description named the pair as "Smith and Churchill," who were "known to the rest of the prisoners by the nickname 'Siamese Twins.'" Felix La Baume, "Andersonville Prison Stockade and Hospital," John W. January, printer (Chicago), 1865, Graphic Arts Department, Library Company of Philadelphia.

9. Confederates Champ Ferguson and Henry Clay Magruder were each tried and hanged in October 1865, a month before Wirz.

10. For an overview of prisoners' memoirs, see Fabian, *Unvarnished Truth*, 120–25.

11. Thomas Nast, "Let Us Clasp Hands over the Bloody Chasm," *HW*, September 21, 1872, 729.

12. Jonathan Ned Katz, *Love Stories*, 138–41.

13. Blight, *Race and Reunion*, 242–43.

14. As many have argued, the Federal government had additional incentives in a halted exchange, namely that the Union's greater resources and larger population made a larger prison population on both sides advantageous. For Confederate apologists, these facts make the Federal government more responsible for the conditions at Andersonville than

Confederate leaders themselves. For example, the monument to prison commandant Henry Wirz erected by the Daughters of the Confederacy in 1905 names the Federal government as "solely responsible for the condition of affairs at Andersonville." "Georgia U. D. C. to Honor Henry Wirz," *Confederate Veteran*, April 1906, 181.

15. Quoted in McElroy, *Andersonville*, 310. McElroy defended his government for refusing to "yield up the negro soldiers and their officers to the unrestrained brutality of the Rebel authorities" (652).

16. See Fabian, *Unvarnished Truth*, 129–57; and Blight, *Race and Reunion*, 243.

17. Northup, *Twelve Years a Slave*, 182–86. Another man, Wiley, returns to the plantation with bite marks from the dogs that had pursued him. In his second attempted escape, he flees to the swamps to evade them. Northup himself recognizes that in order to realize his own escape, he would have to train the slaveholder's dogs to obey him.

18. The slave trader does not use the dogs in his chase because the enslaved men, secretly assisting Eliza, make the trader think the plantation's dogs are useless for this purpose. Harriet Beecher Stowe, *Uncle Tom's Cabin*, 52.

19. Long, *Twelve Months in Andersonville*, 175.

20. For slave-hunting dogs chasing escaped prisoners, see A. O. Abbott, *Prison Life*, 100; Ferguson, *Life-Struggles in Rebel Prisons*, 69–71; Glazier, *Capture*, 231–32; Goss, *Soldier's Story*, 129–32; Hamlin, *Martyria*, 66–67; Kellogg, *Life and Death*, 62–65; McElroy, *Andersonville*, 183–86; Ransom, *John Ransom's Diary*, 69; and Sabre, *Nineteen Months*, 140. In Morgan Dowling's mostly fictional Andersonville narrative, the prisoners get their revenge by capturing and eating the Confederate commanding officer's dog. Dowling, *Southern Prisons*, 67–68. See Fabian, *Unvarnished Truth*, 139–40.

21. Goss, *Soldier's Story*, 133–34.

22. Dowling, *Southern Prisons*, 295. Dowling's narrative also includes the trope discussed in the previous chapter, of cross-dressing narratives that allow for imagined homoeroticism. The narrator writes that during his time in the Atlanta prison, "my attention was attracted by the pleasing countenance of a young fellow, also a prisoner, who gave me his name as Frank Holmes, and said he belonged to an Indiana regiment. Only two days, however, had passed when it was discovered by the rebel surgeon in charge of the prison that my new acquaintance was a pretty girl disguised in a Union uniform. . . . Frank and I had become very good friends during the brief term of our acquaintance, and our parting was more like that of two lovers than a gentleman and a lady but lately strangers." Frank Holmes is not, however, the narrator's love interest, Josie, but her friend. Dowling, *Southern Prisons*, 35.

23. James W. Turner, "Spot" and "Hero," 1869, Warren L. Goss publisher, Graphic Arts Department, Library Company of Philadelphia.

24. *Trial of Henry Wirz*, 72–73; see also 60–61, 74–75, 78, 79, 88, 92, 97, 109.

25. *Trial of Henry Wirz*, 813–14. Compare to Harriet Beecher Stowe, *Uncle Tom's Cabin*, 339–40; and Jacobs, *Incidents*, 246–47.

26. By charging Wirz with "combining, confederating, and conspiring," prosecutors attempted to establish the Confederacy itself a treasonous conspiracy, laying a framework by which the officials of its government and army could be brought to trial. Wirz refused to implicate Davis, who was released from prison in 1867 on bail posted by Horace Greeley and never tried for treason. *Trial of Henry Wirz*, 3.

27. McElroy, *Andersonville*, 66. Another memoirist wrote about a large Southern crowd viewing the prisoners: "Many of them have supposed, until very recently, that the Yankees actually wore horns." Glazier, *Capture*, 250.

28. See, e.g., William Parker, "Freedman's Story," *Atlantic Monthly*, February 1, 1866.

29. Isham, Davidson, and Furness, *Prisoners of War*.

30. Skocpol, *Protecting Soldiers and Mothers*, 107–15.

31. Costa and Kahn, "Surviving Andersonville," 1475.

32. For intimacy as survival strategy, see Kutzler, *Living by Inches*, 5.

33. First, Goss's memoir describes the adjutant of Florence prison, Rufus Sidney Cheatham, as "very kind to his Yankee boys, as he termed us." Cheatham kept "one or two fine-looking fellows around the office, whom he made great pets of." Cheatham apparently told women in Florence, South Carolina, that the boys he had living with him were girls. When the women arrived with curious inquiries at Cheatham's office, he had the boys style their hair in a feminine manner and coached them to answer yes to the question of whether they were "Yankee girls." When the women asked them, "Where do you stop o'nights?" they responded, "'O, right in here with the Adjutant.' Whereupon each Secesh dame took her snuff stick, which she had sat chewing, from her mouth, and sat in blank amazement, and when the Adjutant was out, said among themselves, 'This Cheatum is a drefful man.'" Second, Bernhard Domschcke's German-language memoir portrays the sycophant behavior of a Union prisoner, Col. James M. Sanderson. Generalizing about men like Sanderson, Domschcke describes prisoners receiving favorable treatment from Confederate officers in exchange for "schmutzige Dienste," or dirty services. A 1987 translator, Frederic Trautmann, interpreted this statement with possible sexual implications: "And then, [worst of all,] suspicion had it that, to gain favor and win a place on the list of those recommended [for exchange], some [of us] did obscene favors for Rebels." Goss, *Soldier's Story*, 254–55; Domschcke, *Zwanzig Monate in Kriegs-Gefangenschaft*, 53–54; Domschcke, *Twenty Months in Captivity*, 51.

34. McElroy, *Andersonville*, 104, 560.

35. Ransom, *John Ransom's Diary*, 10; McElroy, *Andersonville*, 167.

36. McElroy, *Andersonville*, 339.

37. McElroy, *Andersonville*, 50.

38. Burg, *American Seafarer*, 79. See also Jonathan Ned Katz, *Love Stories*, 78–80.

39. McElroy, *Andersonville*, 361–63.

40. McElroy, *Andersonville*, 203–4, 339, 560.

41. Long, *Twelve Months in Andersonville*, 61, 71.

42. Ransom tried to pass the diary off as having been written while at Andersonville. See Marvel, "Johnny Ransom's Imagination."

43. Ransom, *John Ransom's Diary*, 9, 10, 62, 47, 32, 76, 102, 182.

44. Ransom, *John Ransom's Diary*, 62, 83–84, 93, 145, 179, 202. Battese was likely John Battice, or Batties, a private in Company K of the First Minnesota Sharpshooters.

45. McElroy, *Andersonville*, 503, 406, 543.

46. McElroy, *Andersonville*, 593, 543.

47. McElroy, *Andersonville*, 625, 598, 581.

48. John McElroy married twice and lived in Toledo, Ohio, then Washington, DC, until his death in 1929. His chum Bezaleel Andrews married as well and lived in Nebraska until his death in 1915. Lessel Long married, too, and lived in Andrews, Indiana, until his

death also in 1915. Both John Ransom and George Hendryx each married twice. Ransom eventually lived in Pasadena, California, where he died in 1919. His chum Hendryx died in 1888 in Belding, Michigan. The cousins David and Eli Buck lived near each other in Michigan, both married after the war, and died in 1878 and 1889.

49. A. O. Abbott, *Prison Life*, 51; Ferguson, *Life-Struggles in Rebel Prisons*, 160; Sabre, *Nineteen Months*, 42; Glazier, *Capture*, 93; Goss, *Soldier's Story*, 182–83, 207.

50. Billings, *Hardtack and Coffee*, 52; McCarthy, *Detailed Minutiæ*, 89.

51. Goss, *Soldier's Story*, 216–17.

52. Blight, *Race and Reunion*, 183.

53. McElroy, *Andersonville*, 654.

54. Talk About Books, *Chautauquan*, November 1889, 252.

55. Books and Authors, *Christian Union*, January 1889, 151.

56. Collingwood, with a degree from the Michigan Agricultural College, was better known as a writer on farm issues while living in upstate New York in the 1880s.

57. Collingwood, *Andersonville Violets*, 9, 11, 18. An introduction by David Rachels and Robert Baird from 2000 describes the two men's relationship as "increasingly homo-erotic" (xii). For more on Collingwood's novel, see Cloyd, *Haunted by Atrocity*, 80–81; and Cook, *Civil War Memories*, 114–15.

58. Woolson, *Rodman the Keeper*, 23. Albion Tourgée also has a story, from 1889, about a post-prisoner-of-war reunion, different from Woolson's in significant ways. "A Conflict between Church and State" is triply removed from the cross-sectional intimacy of the prisoner of war: Two decades after a wounded Confederate veteran nursed a dying Union escapee from a Confederate prison, the Confederate veteran's brother seeks legal help from the dead soldier's father. In gratitude to the Southerner for caring for his son, the Northern lawyer welcomes the case—but also because the lawyer sees the Southerner's arrest for interracial marriage as unjust. Brook Thomas, who contrasts Tourgée's story with Woolson's, writes, "As much as Tourgée is moved by individual acts . . . [he] felt that the best way to honor the Union dead was to perpetuate the ideal for which they fought." Tourgée, *With Gauge and Swallow*, 163–78; Thomas, *Literature of Reconstruction*, 74.

59. Dunlap, "Calvin Bates Fraud." Among the chronological errors Lloyd Dunlap found: Billy enlisted in a company four months before it was organized; he was captured prior to his leaving Ohio; he left Millen prison and arrived at Andersonville both a year before each prison opened; and he interacted with Wirz though he had left the prison before the date Wirz arrived. Most damning, Dunlap finds no "Ralph Orr Bates" in the records of the Ninth Ohio. In the narrative, Bates claims that after his release from Andersonville, he was appointed lieutenant in the 129th Indiana Volunteers. There was a Ralph Bates in that regiment, albeit a private not a lieutenant. And Ralph's description of his regimental service, in a single paragraph on the penultimate page of his narrative, concurs with that history. The Indiana Volunteer Ralph Bates obtained a pension card in 1870; his widow filed a few months after his death in 1910. Needless to say, about the claim that "Dick and I were subsequently subpoenaed to give evidence on the trial of Captain Wirz," neither one by name or nickname appears in the trial's transcript. Bates, *Billy and Dick*, 97.

60. Bates, *Billy and Dick*, 21, 45, 69, 89–90.

61. Benét, *John Brown's Body*; Kantor, *Andersonville*; Levitt, *Andersonville Trial*; George C. Scott, *Andersonville Trial*; Frankenheimer, *Andersonville*.

62. Benét, *John Brown's Body*, 324, 268, 131, 206.

63. Kantor, *Andersonville*, 351, 417, 414.

64. During World War II, Kantor was a journalist who covered the American liberation of the Buchenwald concentration camp. He followed the Nuremberg trials closely and wrote Wirz as a prison bureaucrat whose desire for orderly competence results in the mass death of prisoners.

65. Kantor, *Andersonville*, 309.

66. Kantor, *Andersonville*, 717.

67. For this moment of intense, popular Civil War interest, see Faust, "'We Should.'"

68. Frankenheimer, *Andersonville*.

69. Horwitz, *Confederates in the Attic*, 212.

70. Tilla-2, "One of the best Civil War films Ever," Andersonville User Reviews, IMDb, November 25, 2002, www.imdb.com/title/tt0115097/reviews.

71. Horwitz, *Confederates in the Attic*, 12.

72. Horwitz, *Confederates in the Attic*, 210.

CHAPTER 5

1. Beale, *Critical Year*, 129–38; Wagstaff, "Arm-in-Arm Convention"; Summers, *Ordeal of the Reunion*, 94–95.

2. "South Carolina and Massachusetts Arm and Arm," *HW*, September 1, 1866, 551.

3. Thomas Nast, "The Tearful Convention," *HW*, September 29, 1866, 617.

4. Hosmer, *Thinking Bayonet*, 257, 20, 95, 97. Hosmer was a Massachusetts Unitarian minister before the war, a professor at Antioch College, then University of Missouri, then Washington University after the war, and then director of the Minnesota Public Library. He married twice, once in 1863 and again, after his first wife's death, in 1878.

5. For distinctions between reunion and reconciliation, see Janney, *Remembering the Dead*, 5–7.

6. Historians trained by Dunning at Columbia are more ideologically diverse than those meant by the term "Dunning School," a subset of Dunning's students who wrote state-by-state histories of Reconstruction in the South. That group remains defined by W. E. B. Du Bois's collective characterization of their "endless sympathy with the South," "ridicule, contempt, or silence for the Negro," and "judicial attitude towards the North." Du Bois, *Black Reconstruction in America*, 719.

7. Hart to Hosmer, February 9, 1907, Hosmer Papers, Minnesota Historical Society. The fact that Hart, who commissioned Hosmer and Dunning to write Civil War and Reconstruction history, was also W. E. B. Du Bois's dissertation adviser—and invited Du Bois to give a talk on the benefits of Reconstruction before historians, including Dunning, at the American Historical Association—demonstrates that the Dunning School was less the historical hegemon than often presented.

8. There is considerable scholarship on the figure of the "Black male rapist," including accounts of the figure as a psychic invention (Cash, *Mind of the South*, 115–19; Fanon, *Black Skin, White Masks*, 120–84; Winthrop D. Jordan, *White over Black*, 154–63; Hernton, *Sex and Racism*; Fredrickson, *Black Image*, 256–82); as constructed in opposition to the invented purity of white womanhood (Trudier Harris, *Exorcising Blackness*; Jacquelyn Dowd Hall, "'Mind That Burns'") or in opposition to white manhood (Bederman, *Manliness and Civilization*, 45–76); as a method of emasculation, feminization, and control of

Black men (Wiegman, "Anatomy of Lynching"; Harper, *Are We Not Men?*, 8–10); and as a tool of white supremacist power (Whites, *Gender Matters*, 177–92), patriarchal power (Painter, "'Social Equality'"), or imperialist power (Hoganson, *Fighting for American Manhood*, 134–35). For historical accounts of the figure's emergence within Reconstruction and post-Reconstruction politics, see Hodes, *White Women, Black Men*; and Sommerville, *Rape and Race*.

9. Nelson, *National Manhood*.

10. Nissen, *Manly Love*, 49.

11. See Rotundo, *American Manhood*, 90. For scholarship on antebellum intimacies and romantic friendship, see chapter 1 of this book.

12. Nissen's anthology of nineteenth-century male romantic friendship includes one Civil War soldier, Theodore Winthrop, and three novels about soldiers, by Henry James, William Dean Howells, and Frederick Loring. Nissen, *Romantic Friendship Reader*.

13. For the classic account of the war-wrought transformation from romanticism to realism, see Edmund Wilson, *Patriotic Gore*, 684–87.

14. Howells, *Mrs. Farrell*, 99. Howells's 1874 novel was republished as *Mrs. Farrell* in 1924. See Nissen, *Manly Love*, 16–17.

15. See Nissen, *Manly Love*, 151.

16. Haw, *Rivals*, 16, 3.

17. Evans, *St. Elmo*, 60, 310.

18. Sidney Lanier, *Tiger-Lilies*, 26, 248. For Lanier's novel, see Aaron, *Unwritten War*, 263–71; and MacKethan, *Dream of Arcady*, 20–26.

19. The novel's most extensive treatment, that of literary scholar Cruce Stark in 1975, describes the novel as "a remarkably inept piece of literature." In 1964, historian Joyce Appleby included Hosmer's novel among several that "depict relations between Confederate and Union soldiers as friendly and respectful." In 2010, religion scholar Douglas Walworth discussed the role of a minister character, while literary scholar Elizabeth Duquette discussed the picture of an impulsive, irrational South within the novel. A 2017 book mentions only its provocative title. Stark, "Man of Letters," 56; Appleby, "Reconciliation," 126; Walrath, *Displacing the Divine*, 234–35; Duquette, *Loyal Subjects*, 30; Vincent, *Health of the State*, 17.

20. Hosmer, *Thinking Bayonet*, 95.

21. Hosmer, *Thinking Bayonet*, 79, 82.

22. Homer White, *Norwich Cadets*, 8, 20–21, 54. A Methodist minister, White was chaplain for and a trustee of Norwich University and lived in Randolph, Vermont. He married twice, once in 1864 and again, after his first wife's death, in 1880. His daughter was named after the state for which his character Wolfe fights.

23. Shand-Tucci, *Crimson Letter*, 29–36; Loring, *Two College Friends*, 93.

24. Loring, *Two College Friends*, 47, 84. The sense of Ned's impossible adulthood is mirrored by the Massachusetts author's death at twenty-two in the same year as the novel's publication.

25. Loring, *Two College Friends*, 89, 138, 159. Travis Foster contextualizes this novel within the postbellum campus-novel genre to argue that the novel's homoeroticism, for present-day readers, distracts from its generically consistent celebration of white supremacist fraternity. Travis M. Foster, *Genre and White Supremacy*, 39–41.

26. Giesberg, *Sex*, 77–81.

27. Henry Clay Trumbull, *Friendship the Master-Passion*. About the relationship between Trumbull and Comstock, Comstock's chosen biographer, Trumbull's son Charles, wrote that it "grew into intimacy and friendship as the years passed; the two men loved and admired each other throughout the lifetime of the elder." Charles Gallaudet Trumbull, *Anthony Comstock, Fighter*, 32.

28. Carpenter, *Ioläus*. Carpenter's biographer writes that *Ioläus* "adopted a reassuring form, the sentimental friendship miscellany, as a means of breaking the ban on any discussion in a popular idiom of homosexuality or lesbianism." Carpenter himself said that "sex-things are not mentioned, tho they may here and there be read between the lines." Rowbotham, *Edward Carpenter*, 268.

29. Henry Clay Trumbull, *Knightly Soldier*, vi, 97, 100. For Trumbull and Camp's relationship, see Amico, "Union of Two Henrys."

30. Blustein, *Preserve Your Love*, 69–75; Devine, *Learning from the Wounded*, 13–52; Jim Downs, *Sick from Freedom*, 33–34.

31. Injuries to the groin, such as those suffered by Herbert in *The Thinking Bayonet* or by Gettysburg hero and future Maine governor Joshua Chamberlain, were especially prevalent among Civil War veterans, due to military directives to aim for an enemy's center or to the relative survivability of such injuries. Herr, "'Privates Were Shot.'"

32. William A. Hammond, *Sexual Impotence*, 55.

33. William A. Hammond, *Sexual Impotence*, 35, 64, 14. Moreover, Hammond differentiated between active and passive participants in pederasty, treating the latter as more pathological; the active participant he tended to treat as following behavior not inconsistent with heterosexual marital outcomes.

34. For the birth of sexuality as "the self-affirmation of one class [the bourgeoisie] rather than the enslavement of another," see Foucault, *History of Sexuality*, 1:123.

35. Knoper, *Literary Neurophysiology*, 15.

36. William A. Hammond, *Sexual Impotence*, 55. Hammond's treatment included a thrice-daily "bromide of sodium," "continuous association with virtuous women," "severe study of subjects that would require abstract thought," such as "mathematics," and the application of a cauterizing iron to the nape of the neck (63, 67–68).

37. Kiernan, "Responsibility in Sexual Perversion," 198; Lydston, "Sexual Perversion," 244–45.

38. Melissa S. Stein, *Measuring Manhood*, 17–18; Somerville, *Queering the Color Line*, 15–38.

39. McGuire and Lydston, *Sexual Crimes*, 1.

40. See, e.g., Bruce, *Plantation Negro as Freeman*, 32–39. For the development of racialized crime statistics, see Muhammad, *Condemnation of Blackness*, 49–54.

41. Lydston, *Diseases of Society*, 384.

42. Melissa S. Stein, *Measuring Manhood*, 171–72.

43. Lydston, *Diseases of Society*, 121, 267; McGuire and Lydston, *Sexual Crimes*, 17.

44. McGuire and Lydston, *Sexual Crimes*, 10.

45. Pike, *Prostrate State*. If Lydston and Kiernan got their history from colleagues in the University of Chicago History Department, those influences would have been the German-born chair Hermann von Holst, who wrote the antislavery biographies *John Brown* (1888) and *John C. Calhoun* (1882), or the lecturer Edwin E. Sparks, who would go

on to write a two-part US history with an anti-Reconstruction chapter, *United States of America*, pt. 2 (1900).

46. "Kiernan, James George," 158; "Lydston Would Have Whites."

47. Lydston, *Diseases of Society*, 13–30.

48. Lydston, *Over the Hookah*, 59–64.

49. Lydston, *Diseases of Society*, 309.

50. Monroe, "Sodomy-Pederasty," 432.

51. Lydston, *Diseases of Society*, 338.

52. Howard, "Sexual Perversion in America," 9.

53. Jelliffe, "Homosexuality and the Law," 96.

54. Ellis, *Sexual Inversion*, n20.

55. D'Emilio, *Sexual Politics, Sexual Communities*, 11. See Engel, *Fragmented Citizens*, 71–75.

56. Beard, *American Nervousness*, 187.

57. Beard, *Sexual Neurasthenia*, 103.

58. Stiles, "Go Rest, Young Man."

59. Silas Weir Mitchell, *Roland Blake*; Stiles, "'Intimate Language.'"

60. Quoted in Jonathan Ned Katz, *Gay American History*, 43.

61. Ellis, *Sexual Inversion*, nn19–20.

62. Mayne, *Intersexes*, 639.

63. For the incoherence of the analogic linking of Blackness and queerness, see Rohy, *Anachronism and Its Others*, 1–20. Add to the racial incoherence other discontinuities among what appears, in hindsight, to be a unified field: Hammond and Beard were famously rivals who despised each other; Ellis's work was animated by disagreement with the German sexologists, but he praised Kiernan's and Lydston's taxonomies, which they saw bolstered, in turn, by his affirmation. For discontinuities in late nineteenth-century sexological literature, see Knoper, *Literary Neurophysiology*, 144–55.

64. Ellis, *Sexual Inversion*, n120.

65. Dixon, *Leopard's Spots*, 325, 328, 329.

66. Rhodes, *History*, 1:336–37; Martineau, *Society in America*, 325–29.

67. Rhodes, *History*, 5:212.

68. Blight, *Race and Reunion*, 357–60. See also Janney, *Remembering the Dead*, 269–70.

69. Charles Francis Adams, *Some Phases of the Civil War*.

70. Charles Francis Adams, *Some Phases of Sexual Morality*.

71. Both Dunning and his mentor John Burgess had academic training in Berlin. For Burgess as part of the same intellectual origins as sexual science, see Engel, *Fragmented Citizens*, 69–70.

72. W. E. B. Du Bois offered another interpretation of sexuality's Civil War history. In brief, Du Bois followed Rhodes in seeing the Civil War and emancipation as a corrective to slavery's "sexual chaos," a corrective that could have been fixed by the propriety of an empowered Black middle class. Instead, the counterrevolution of property that ended Reconstruction gave the worst elements of white society total license for self-governance, which made no check on the return of sexual chaos and immorality. Du Bois, *Black Reconstruction in America*, 35, 699–702.

73. William Watson Davis, *Civil War and Reconstruction*, 3.

74. Fleming, *Civil War and Reconstruction*, 231, 763.

75. Garner, *Reconstruction in Mississippi*, 116.

76. Garner was from Summit, Mississippi; Fleming from Brundidge, Alabama; Davis from Pensacola, Florida, and Oak Grove, Alabama; Charles Ramsdell from Salado, Texas; Joseph G. de Roulhac Hamilton, from Hillsborough, North Carolina; Ulrich Phillips from LaGrange, Georgia; Thomas Staples, who wrote *Reconstruction in Arkansas* (1924), from Roopville, Georgia; and Paul Haworth from Indiana, an outlier in content and ideology, who wrote a less Democratically partisan history of the 1876 election. For accounts of Dunning School historians, see Smith and Lowery, *Dunning School*.

77. Addresses compiled from student directories, in Columbia University, *Catalogue of the Officers*. For history of Harlem's Black neighborhoods, see Osofsky, *Harlem*, 84.

78. Eric Garber, "Spectacle in Color"; Chauncey, *Gay New York*, 244–67.

79. Garner, "Plan of the Journal," 6; Lydston, "Malingering among Criminals."

80. Lindsey, "International Congress," 581.

81. Garner, "Asexualization of Hereditary Criminals," 125.

82. Hosmer to Adams, February 20, 1914, Correspondence, Adams Papers, Massachusetts Historical Society. See also Adams to Hosmer, April 23, 1896, July 20, November 1, 1907, January 22, 1912, Hosmer Papers, Minnesota Historical Society; and Hosmer to Adams, May 7, 1896, September 12 1905, June 28, 1906, Correspondence, Adams Papers, Massachusetts Historical Society.

83. Hosmer, *Appeal to Arms*, 14; Hosmer, *Outcome*, 229.

84. Hosmer, *Outcome*, 285, 288, 305, 306.

85. Dunning, *Reconstruction, Political and Economic*, xv. See Thomas, "Unfinished Task," 24–27.

86. Schaff was an Ohioan who moved to Massachusetts after the war, becoming the superintendent of his wife's father's company, Berkshire Glass Works. In advertising for Schaff's *Sunset of the Confederacy*, the *Atlantic Monthly* stated, "Nothing which the Atlantic has published has touched the quick sympathies of Southern as well as of Northern readers like the two previous Atlantic series, 'The Spirit of Old West Point' and 'The Battle of the Wilderness.'" At least one Union veteran, George Haven Putnam, complained of Schaff's "whitewashing" of the Confederacy: "Schaff writes, if not with acceptance of, at least with sympathy for, the Southern contention that the Union was not a nation, but a confederation of independent States which had reserved to themselves full liberty of action." "Sunset of the Confederacy," *Atlantic Monthly*, December 1911, 78; Putnam, *Some Memories*, 80.

87. Mayne, *Intersexes*, 210.

88. Mayne (Edward I. Prime-Stevenson) wrote to a friend in 1907 that while he read "little except Italian or French" he had "*held-on* to the 'Atlantic Monthly' for many years," in which he would have encountered Schaff's *Spirit*. Quoted in Mayne, *Imre*, 184.

89. Schaff, *Spirit*, 110–11.

90. Schaff, *Spirit*, 192. Due to Mayne's celebration of the text, the passage is featured in Gifford, *Glances Backward*, 348–50.

91. The pairs were Thomas Rosser (Confederate) and John Pelham (Confederate), Campbell Emory (Union) and Adelbert Ames (Union), Nathaniel Chambliss (Confederate) and Llewellyn Hoxton (Confederate), Jacob Kent (Union) and Eugene Beaumont

(Union), Peter Haines (Union) and Alonzo Cushing (Union), James Dearing (Confederate) and George Gillespie (Union), and Henry Du Pont (Union) and Francis Farquhar (Union). Comly was Lt. Clifton Comly, who returned to West Point after the war as a professor in the Ordnance and Gunnery Department. See Kirshner, *Class of 1861*; and McEnany, *For Brotherhood and Duty*.

92. Mayne, *Intersexes*, 210.

93. Nash, *Life and Times*, 77.

94. Herbert, *History*, 77.

95. For a history of Ezekiel's *New South*, see Cox, "Confederate Monument at Arlington"; and Cox, *Dixie's Daughters*, 67–69.

96. Loewen and Sebesta, *Confederate and Neo-Confederate Reader*, 373; Levin, *Searching for Black Confederates*, 98–99.

97. Ezekiel, *Memoirs*, 440.

CHAPTER 6

1. Henry James, *Bostonians*, 8, 15.

2. Jagose, *Inconsequence*, 65; Henry James, *Bostonians*, 15.

3. Henry James, *Bostonians*, 2, 331.

4. Sedgwick, *Tendencies*, 172.

5. For example, Major Carroll in Constance Fenimore Woolson's *For the Major* (1883) or Colonel Woodburne in William Dean Howells's *Hazard of New Fortunes* (1889).

6. Silber, *Romance of Reunion*, 185–96.

7. See Amy Murrell Taylor, *Divided Family*, 183–89; Thomas, *Literature of Reconstruction*, 56–64; and Kathryn B. McKee, *Reading Reconstruction*, 178–99.

8. [Henry Adams], *Democracy*, 22; Twain and Warner, *Gilded Age*, 173: Tourgée, *Bricks without Straw*, 350, 419, 241. James's Ransom is "nearly thirty years of age"; John W. De Forest's Colonel Carter is "anywhere from thirty-three to thirty-seven." Henry James, *Bostonians*, 10; De Forest, *Miss Ravenel's Conversion*, 27.

9. C. Vann Woodward, *Origins*, 6–7.

10. Wister, *Virginian*, 4.

11. For Twain and Warner, in *The Gilded Age*, Colonel Selby's attractiveness was his mode of (the novel's favorite activity) deceit: Laura Hawkins falls for his handsome Southern gentility only to be abandoned by him. That presentation follows the attractive Virginian cavalier, though a Union not a Confederate soldier, in John W. De Forest's *Miss Ravenel's Conversion from Secession to Loyalty* (1867). De Forest's lesson was to distrust the appeal of dishonest Southern men in favor of plainer, though more honest, New England men. For Adams and, we will see, James, the lesson about attraction and honesty was the opposite: Adams's Carrington, in contrast to his rival, the New Englander Ratcliffe, is good-looking insofar as he is honest, not corrupt. Finally, Tourgée's *Bricks without Straw* offered the former slaveholder Le Moyne, who, through his love for the New England schoolteacher, becomes committed to the defense of Black citizens. While their romance can only be realized after his ideological conversion, the schoolteacher finds "this quiet maimed veteran of a lost cause" attractive immediately, "not to her as other men." Le Moyne's appeal, then, represented the potential of moderate Southern aristocrats,

whether old Whigs or Douglas Democrats (as Tourgée alternatively labels Le Moyne's father), to join the cause of equal rights. Tourgée, *Bricks without Straw*, 243.

12. Sedgwick, *Touching Feeling*, 40. See also Stevens, *Henry James and Sexuality*, 164–73; Person, *Henry James*, 10–15; Gunter and Jobe, *Dearly Beloved Friends*, 1–12; and Rawlings, *Henry James*, 34–39.

13. C. Vann Woodward, *Burden of Southern History*, 126–40.

14. "Political Views of a Humorist," *New York Herald*, August 28, 1876. On Twain's mugwump views, see Thomas, *Civic Myths*, 125–76; and Thomas, "Twain and Tourgée."

15. Richard White, *Republic*, 460–61. As a historian of religion in this period puts it, "Coming out for 'character' in the 1870s was the rough equivalent of coming out for 'family' in the 1970s." Fox, *Trials of Intimacy*, 35. An electoral historian concurs about character's predominance in the period but cites Civil War celebrity and expanded access to candidates by changing media as its cause. Troy, *See How They Ran*, 82–83.

16. Individual campaign biographies for specific elections are noted below. For lists of campaign biographies, see Miles, *Image Makers*. For the history of postbellum elections, see Summers, *Party Games*; and Charles W. Calhoun, *From Bloody Shirt*.

17. Richard White, "What Counts as Corruption?," 1035–37. For liberals and corruption, see Sproat, *Best Men*, 244–71; and Nancy Cohen, *Reconstruction of American Liberalism*, 53–55.

18. See, e.g., Dailey, *Before Jim Crow*, 89–96; Sommerville, *Rape and Race*, 196–97; and Muhammad, *Condemnation of Blackness*, 15–17. That epistemologies of sexuality contribute to corruption's social construction, and its character types, may be exemplified by those racialized villains of the 1980s and 1990s liberal imagination described in Cammett, "Deadbeat Dads."

19. Warren argues that Black characters in James's writing, no matter how backgrounded they may be in plots, encroach on the private realm from appearances in public spaces as the symbolic social consequences of political change. Warren, *Black and White Strangers*, 120–30. For anti-Black racism in James's writing, see Morrison, *Playing in the Dark*, 13–14; Michaels, "Jim Crow Henry James?"; Sara Blair, *Henry James*, 190–210; and Patricia McKee, *Producing American Races*, 31–98.

20. Henry James, *Notes*, 290.

21. Quoted in Edel, *Henry James: The Untried Years*, 169. For more on James Sr.'s speech, the younger James boys' service, and the older James boys' application to join the freedmen's relief efforts, see Edel, 168–73. For James's and his family's abolitionism, see Fredrickson, *Inner Civil War*, 156–61; and Warren, *Black and White Strangers*, 19–20.

22. Henry James, "Democracy and Theodore Roosevelt," 215.

23. Henry James, *American Scene*, 374–75.

24. Henry James, "Miss Ravenel's Conversion," *Nation*, June 20, 1867, 491.

25. Sometimes taken to mean James's inventiveness, from "ingenious," in finding sympathies with Southerners, the phrase derives from Alexander Maclaren's commentary on a biblical passage James would know well: the call in 2 Corinthians for *ambassadors for Christ*. Explaining "ingenuity of tenderness," Maclaren compares God's orientation toward human sin to a mother's "foolish fondness" and "injudicious kindness" that leads her to ignore her child's wrongdoing. This quality of belief connects directly to the sympathy James cannot help but feel toward Southerners. Maclaren, *St. Paul's Epistles*, 385.

26. Henry James, *American Scene*, 387–88, 371–74.

27. Henry James, *American Scene*, 387–89. For contrasting readings of this parenthetical, see Haviland, *Henry James' Last Romance*, 127–29; and Buelens, *Henry James*, 41–43.

28. Henry James, *American Scene*, 375.

29. Henry James, *American Scene*, 377.

30. Henry James, *Ambassadors*, 78–79.

31. Henry James, *Ambassadors*, 319; Henry James, *American*, 5; Sedgwick, *Touching Feeling*, 42–43.

32. Quoted in Gunter and Jobe, *Dearly Beloved Friends*, 147.

33. Ohi, *Henry James*, 166–70.

34. Henry James, *Hawthorne*, 112–14. See Greven, "Homoerotics of James' Hawthorne." For Hawthorne's Pierce biography (and friendship), see chapter 1 of this book.

35. Henry James, "Democracy and Theodore Roosevelt," 215.

36. Henry James, *Roderick Hudson*, 41, xvii.

37. See Gregory Woods, "Art of Friendship"; Collister, *Writing the Self*, 77.

38. Martin, "'High Felicity' of Comradeship," 103.

39. Henry James, *Roderick Hudson*, 189.

40. For the myth that James suffered castration, and that his asexuality caused an inverse outpouring of prose, see Edmund Wilson, *Patriotic Gore*, 654–63; and Aaron, *Unwritten War*, 106–17. For an account of the "obscure" injury described in *Notes*, see Edel, *Henry James: The Untried Years*, 176–83; and Hoffman and Hoffman, "Henry James." For the myth that James manually stimulated a convalescent Oliver Wendell Holmes Jr.—which, in an inversion of the celibate, asexual James, produced a forthright homosexual James—see Novick, *Henry James*, 110, 472n48. For the veracity of that anecdote, see the exchange among Leon Edel, Sheldon Novick, and Fred Kaplan in *Slate* beginning with Edel "Oh Henry!," *Slate*, December 12, 1996, https://slate.com/news-and-politics/1996/12/oh-henry.html, through Edel, Novick, and Kaplan, "Henry James's Love Life," *Slate*, January 30, 1997, https://slate.com/tag/henry-james-love-life. For James's wartime experience as crucial to his sexual and writerly self-development, see John Halperin, "Henry James's Civil War"; and Collister, *Writing the Self*, 81–97.

41. Rawlings, *Henry James*, 24–32.

42. Henry James, *American Scene*, 338.

43. Ratcliffe professes a desire to "use vice" if "virtue won't answer our purpose" and is guilty in the novel of two corrupt acts. First, as governor of Illinois during the war, he manipulated the vote count to ensure the Republican president won reelection. Although she later regrets it, Mrs. Lee excused this as an emergency measure to save the country. Second, as revealed in a letter from Carrington, Ratcliffe received a bribe from the Inter-Oceanic Mail Steamship Company in exchange for a federal subsidy to expand its global services. [Henry Adams], *Democracy*, 141.

44. [Henry Adams], *Democracy*, 76, 374.

45. [Henry Adams], *Democracy*, 22, 140–41. If, as Amanda Claybaugh suggests, Washington, DC, functioned in postbellum fiction as a synecdoche of governmental corruption, Mount Vernon beyond and above the city served as its symbolic opposite. Claybaugh, "Washington Novels."

46. See O'Brien, *Henry Adams*, 109–12; and Kreyling, *Figures of the Hero*, 59–61. For accounts of Adams's history of the Jefferson and Madison administrations, see Stevenson, *Henry Adams*, 220–45; and Samuels, *Henry Adams*, 180–93.

47. [Henry Adams], *Democracy*, 22, 214. For the Lee myth, see Connelly, *Marble Man*, 116–21.

48. Coit, *American Snobs*, 4–9. Coit situates James's reaction within an international liberalism, linked to John Stuart Mill and Matthew Arnold, rather than one confined to US politics. For that international liberalism, and its relation to mugwumpery, see Butler, *Critical Americans*.

49. Even when describing James's aversion to political labels, literary history has long taken the novelist's mugwump sensibilities as the starting point for analysis. For example, while disagreeing about whether a private realm wrenches itself free from a public space or constructs itself through contractual exchanges between individuals, Philip Fisher and Brook Thomas asserted the mugwumpian triumph of privacy over publicity in *The Bostonians*. Fisher, "Appearing and Disappearing"; Thomas, *American Literary Realism*, 53–87.

50. Hofstadter, *Age of Reform*, 135–39. Building from Richard Hofstadter, Alan Trachtenberg argued that as much as these reformers responded to the rising power of newly wealthy businessmen, their model for government efficiency was business administration. Trachtenberg, *Incorporation of America*, 153–73. For William James's embrace of the mugwump label, and Henry James's resistance to political labels, see Posnock, *Trial of Curiosity*, 6–7.

51. Edel, *Henry James: The Conquest of London*, 1–34, 75–80.

52. For Liberal Republicans' criticism of the Grant administration, see Sproat, *Best Men*, 74–88. For Godkin and Adams, see Slap, *Doom of Reconstruction*. For Godkin and Norton, see Tucker, *Mugwumps*, 1–14. For Godkin, Norton, and Lowell, see Butler, *Critical Americans*, 175–220. For Lowell, see Scudder, *James Russell Lowell*, 190–202. The exception was James's friend Howells, who had Liberal sympathies but would stick with the Republicans through the mugwump defection.

53. JCL *1872–1876*, 1:15.

54. JCL *1872–1876*, 3:87.

55. JCL *1855–1872*, 450. For the disappointment of Liberal Republican organizers at Greeley's nomination, see Slap, *Doom of Reconstruction*, 164–69.

56. Republican National Convention, *Proceedings*, 23.

57. Democratic National Convention, *Official Proceedings*, 123.

58. People and Politics, *Daily Rocky Mountain News*, July 13, 1876; Political Points, *Inter Ocean*, August 22, 1876.

59. Ingersoll, *Great Speeches*, 264.

60. One historian of the 1876 election comments on Ingersoll's insults, "The implication was clear to the audience: Tilden was a homosexual," adding, as evidence, cartoons drawn by Thomas Nast of Tilden in a dress. But none of the "bachelor" attacks on Tilden made him out to be a woman, and Nast frequently depicted other politicians in female dress, including Tilden's married running mate, Thomas Hendricks. Another historian, without elaboration, cites "Tilden's alleged homosexuality" as a campaign issue. A third claims, "Tilden was a lifelong bachelor whom some historians have described as utterly asexual." Morris, *Fraud of the Century*, 142; Beatty, *Age of Betrayal*, 208; Holt, *By One Vote*, 100. Most contemporaneous attacks on Tilden's bachelor status did not mention his aversion to women but rather—in a lesson to voters—women's aversion to him. See, e.g., Campaign Reports, *Inter Ocean*, July 26, 1876; and "Glorious!," *Milwaukee Daily Sentinel*, November 7, 1876.

61. Ingersoll, *Great Speeches*, 193, 258.

62. JCL *1872–1876*, 3:165.

63. JCL *1880–1883*, 1:94; JCL *1883–1884*, 228. James's concern with the personnel consequences of presidential elections continued through the decade. In 1888, he suggested that for supporting Grover Cleveland's reelection, his friend Francis Boott ought to be named minister to England. The previous year, he discussed proposing that Cleveland appoint another friend, Samuel Dana Horton, as a special commissioner in Europe on monetary policy, an appointment made instead by Cleveland's successor, President Benjamin Harrison, in 1890. JCL *1887–1888*, 2:324, 1:227.

64. JCL *1876–1878*, 5.

65. JCL *1876–1878*, 79.

66. JCL *1876–1878*, 95.

67. JCL *1880–1883*, 1:153.

68. Garfield's biographer details how he managed to maintain an image, even as he leaned away from 1860s radicalism toward laissez-faire liberalism, as a Reconstruction Republican. Peskin, *Garfield*, 420–48. Garfield's platform, and inaugural speech, would include commitments to protect Black voters and bolster public education for Black Southerners. The extent to which he would have recommitted national policy toward Reconstruction efforts had he not been shot five months into his presidency is an open question. Remarkably, Garfield is the only candidate from 1872 to 1892 to have both Albion Tourgée's and Henry Adams's support.

69. Quoted in Hinsdale, *Republican Text-Book*, 169; Coffin, *Life*, 341; quoted in Bundy, *Life*, 40. For Hancock's corset, see Quad, *Comic Biography*.

70. JCL *1880–1883*, 2:88.

71. [Henry Adams], *Letters of Henry Adams*, 444.

72. JCL *1880–1883*, 2:84–92.

73. Henry James, "Pandora," 131, 158.

74. JCL *1887–1888*, 2:358.

75. See Summers, *Rum, Romanism, and Rebellion*, 179–96; Charles W. Calhoun, *From Bloody Shirt*, 90–92; and Richard White, *Republic*, 470–75.

76. Charles W. Calhoun, *Conceiving a New Republic*, 79–81; Summers, *Rum, Romanism, and Rebellion*, 64–65; Richard White, *Republic*, 361–62.

77. If the resolution to the disputed 1876 election was, as historian Gregory Downs has written, "just one episode in a longer process of peeling back the federal government's authority," then Cleveland's 1884 election, a political revolution in the executive branch, must be seen as another monumental episode. Gregory P. Downs, *After Appomattox*, 239.

78. "Mr. Roosevelt's Creed," *New York Times*, October 19, 1884.

79. See, e.g., Novick, *Henry James*, 309; Horne, *Henry James*, 163; Andrew Taylor, *Henry James*, 2; Mendelssohn, *Henry James*, 47; and Bailey and Joslin, *Theodore Roosevelt*, 105–6.

80. Murphy, *Political Manhood*, 11–37. Murphy also describes how Roosevelt was subject to similarly gendered and sexualized attacks on his good-government politics four years earlier in 1882. For sexualized caricature of the mugwumps, see also Makemson, "'Dude and Pharisee."

81. "Mr. Roosevelt's Creed."

82. Roosevelt appears to have been correct in imputing James's support for Cleveland. In 1888, William James wrote to his brother that their mutual friend Oliver Wendell

Holmes Jr. was "going to vote for [Benjamin] Harrison, God knows why, except to show the shady side of himself—he couldn't give an articulate reason for it the other night." An October scandal that election year involved the British ambassador to the United States Lionel Sackville-West endorsing Cleveland as more favorable to British interests than Harrison. Republicans had secretly solicited and then published the ambassador's letter to rouse suspicions of British intervention on behalf of Cleveland, possibly propelling Harrison to his electoral count victory. James, characteristically, called the ambassador's endorsement "silly Lord Sackville's bit of innocence." When the US secretary of state for the outgoing Cleveland administration dismissed Sackville-West, James criticized this action as "coming round to a pretended horror—to please the clumsy, blundering many-headed monster." What's worse, the incoming Republican president would replace that secretary of state with "the hideous Blaine!" James and James, *Selected Letters*, 205; JCL *1887–1888*, 2:339, 358. See also Charles W. Calhoun, *Minority Victory*, 160–61.

83. The reviews demonstrate an interest for James and literary culture on the Civil War past, and the possibly arbitrary pairings, e.g., the autobiography of General Grant alongside the published volume *Calamus*, of Walt Whitman's letters to Peter Doyle, are provocative for questions of the Civil War and sexuality—though James does not comment on this element.

84. Henry James, "Democracy and Theodore Roosevelt," 214.

85. JCL *1884–1886*, 11.

86. Gabler, "Narrator's Script"; Boudreau, "Narrative Sympathy"; Kearns, "Narrative Discourse"; Jagose, *Inconsequence*, 57–58.

87. Henry James, *Bostonians*, 18.

88. Henry James, *Bostonians*, 206–7.

89. See Free, *Suffrage Reconstructed*.

90. Henry James, *Bostonians*, 180.

91. Henry James, *Bostonians*, 387.

92. Sherman quoted in Guernsey and Alden, *Harper's Pictorial History*, 673.

93. Henry James, *Bostonians*, 392–93.

94. Henry James, *Bostonians*, 318.

95. For links among perverse sexuality, hermaphroditism, and racial upheaval in *The Bostonians*, see Shaheen, *Androgynous Democracy*, 20–33.

96. Fetterley, *Resisting Reader*, 101–53; Stevens, *Henry James and Sexuality*, 90–103; Coviello, *Tomorrow's Parties*, 169–86.

97. Henry James, *American Scene*, 373.

98. Anderson, "James's Portrait"; Kreyling, *Figures of the Hero*, 64–75; Silber, *Romance of Reunion*, 118–20; Shaheen, "Henry James's Southern Mode."

99. Henry James, *Bostonians*, 2, 19.

100. Wilt, "Desperately Seeking Verena," 308–9.

101. Henry James, *Bostonians*, 10, 381.

102. Henry James, *Bostonians*, 414, 53.

103. Hochman, "Reading Historically/Reading Selectively"; Noonan, *Reading the Century*. Coit argues *The Bostonians* expresses a deep skepticism about the Reconstruction promise to achieve democracy through programs of universal education for Black Southerners. Coit, *American Snobs*, 54–68. For attacks on Gilder's mugwumpian masculinity, see Murphy, *Political Manhood*, 12–17.

104. Henry James, *Bostonians*, 233.

105. Henry James, *Notes*, 240. For this scene, see also Brigham, "Touring Memorial Hall."

106. Henry James, *Bostonians*, 232.

107. Ryan, *"Bostonians,"* 269.

108. Henry James, *Notes*, 199.

109. Henry James, *Bostonians*, 2.

110. Henry James, *Notes*, 94–95.

111. Henry James, *Notes*, 75–77.

112. King, *Life and Public Services*, 220.

113. JCL *1884–1886*, 196; Habegger, *Henry James*, 193–94.

114. Lamar, "On Sumner," 187.

CONCLUSION

1. Beard and Beard, *Rise of American Civilization*, 2:768, 441.

2. Hofstadter, *Progressive Historians*, 394.

3. For James's anticonsumerism as a theory of capitalism, see Posnock, "Henry James."

4. Hofstadter, *Progressive Historians*, 394–95.

5. I am tempted to say their experience of gender, but if men historians were anxious about being men of inaction who write about men of action, twentieth-century women historians often shared anxieties relative to masculinity compounded by entering an up-to-then male-dominated field.

6. Sedgwick, *Epistemology of the Closet*, 9–12.

7. Hayden White, "Historical Text," 92.

8. Hayden White, *Metahistory*.

9. See, e.g., Sedgwick, *Between Men*, 91–93; D. A. Miller, *Novel and the Police*, 152–91; and Sedgwick, *Epistemology of the Closet*, 160–61.

10. Lanser, *Sexuality of History*, 3.

11. Historians of slavery and capitalism as an integrated system, skeptical of the Beards' "clash of civilizations" thesis, have worked to debunk the myth of the antebellum South's premodernity. See Du Bois, *Black Reconstruction in America*; Eric Williams, *Capitalism and Slavery*; Johnson, "Pedestal and the Veil"; and Beckert and Rockman, *Slavery's Capitalism*.

12. Greene, *Filibuster*, 21; Teilhet, *Lion's Skin*, 214. In a footnote to a history of filibuster representations, Andreas Beer remarks that several authors "speculated about Walker's homosexuality." In addition to the works by biographer Laurence Greene (1937) and the novelist Darwin L. Teilhet (1955), Albert Carr's 1963 pro-Walker biography begins with Walker leaving "his first hopeless encounter with a laughing Parisian prostitute . . . indignant, disturbed, unwilling to admit his frustration even to himself, determined more than ever to maintain his knightly ideals." Frederic Rosengarten's equally celebratory 1976 account describes the young Walker as "sometimes considered a mama's boy and a sissy." The narrator of Robert Houston's 1984 novel asks a failed female lover of Walker, "Does he like men then?" She answers that he is "afraid to touch anybody, like a priest." When Houston wrote the preface to a new edition of Walker's memoir the following year, he stated that in his research on Walker he had never encountered material that "mentioned the word

'homosexual' in relation to Walker, though there is sufficient evidence at least strongly to suggest the possibility." These themes, of the invasion of Nicaragua as a way to deal with sexual insecurities, get exhaustive treatment in Alejandro Bolaños Geyer's five-volume 1988 biography, with Freudian chapters such as "Mama's Boy" and "Oedipus." Geyer concludes the episode in which the Parisian prostitute mocked Walker's "impotence" with the "appropriate French insult, somewhat stronger than the *girl-boy!* of his childhood days," with: "Grandiose fantasies of power rush in to compensate for sexual inadequacy." Beer, *Transnational Analysis of Representations*, 195; Carr, *World and William Walker*, 5–6; Rosengarten, *Freebooters Must Die!*, 1; Houston, *Nation Thief*, 181; Walker, *War in Nicaragua*, 3; Geyer, *William Walker*, 130. See also May, *Manifest Destiny's Underworld*, 103.

13. Harrison, *Agent of Empire*, 148.

14. Instead, Gobat confines discussion of Walker's sexuality to rumors of an affair with Irene O'Horan Espinosa, the keeper of the boardinghouse where Walker first lived. Gobat, *Empire by Invitation*, 219.

15. Presumptions of their incompatibility underlie James Shapiro's analysis of an 1845 incident in which the young soldier Ulysses S. Grant was replaced by a professional female actor for the role of Desdemona in an army performance of *Othello*. Because "martial manhood" was a dominating masculine ideal during the US-Mexico War, Shapiro argues, a male soldier in the female role and her staged kiss with Lt. Theodoric Porter's Othello "would force them to confront the discomfort they themselves felt about manliness." Certainly, the US-Mexico War involved anxieties about manhood, but kisses between military men did not necessarily undermine one's masculine power. Instead, homoeroticism could be a tool for the expansion of male power—as Iago uses it. Shapiro, *Shakespeare*, 24–31. See James Longstreet, *From Manassas to Appomattox*, 20.

16. Charles Henry Brown, *Agents of Manifest Destiny*, 3.

17. Isenberg, *Fallen Founder*, 248–56, 410–12. For legacies of Burr's homoerotic attractiveness, see Eudora Welty's 1943 "First Love," about a deaf boy who falls in love with the filibuster Burr. Charles Henry Brown, *Agents of Manifest Destiny*, 174.

18. Johnson, *River of Dark Dreams*, 9–10, 381–84.

19. Johnson, *River of Dark Dreams*, 382.

20. Walker, *War in Nicaragua*, 49; Johnson, *River of Dark Dreams*, 386–87.

21. Joan Wallach Scott, "Psychoanalysis," 38. For psychoanalysis in history writing, and the work of the discipline to exclude it, see Connolly, "Psychoanalysis."

22. Another way to put this is that Johnson's Freud is not Scott's "'post-Freudian' Freud, the one read through the lenses of poststructuralism," but the Freud of structuralist myth-making, the one abused by Gilles Deleuze and Felix Guattari for reducing the multiplicities of the unconscious always to the Oedipal structure. Joan Wallach Scott, "Psychoanalysis," 38; Deleuze and Guattari, *Anti-Oedipus*, esp. 44–45, 56–58.

23. Walter Johnson, "Guns in the Family," *Boston Review*, March 23, 2018.

24. Faust, *James Henry Hammond*, 18–19n18. See the discussion of Withers's letters to Hammond in chapter 1 of this book.

25. See William C. Davis, foreword to *Judah P. Benjamin*, xiv; Daniel Brook, "The Forgotten Confederate Jew," *Tablet*, July 17, 2012; and James Traub, *Judah Benjamin*, 94–98.

26. Jonathan Ned Katz, *Love Stories*, 3–25.

27. Nicolay and Hay, *Abraham Lincoln*, 1:194.

28. R. T. Stevenson, "Abraham Lincoln and Joshua Speed," *Christian Advocate*, February 9, 1905, 217.

29. Sandburg, *Abraham Lincoln*, 431, 264.

30. Quoted in Donald, *We Are Lincoln Men*, 38. Strozier was responding to claims that Lincoln was a homosexual made in Tripp, *Intimate World*.

31. Donald, *We Are Lincoln Men*, 36.

32. Donald, *Charles Sumner*, 271, 315–16.

33. Crowe, *Age of Civil War*, 199.

34. Fawn M. Brodie, "Abolitionists and American Historians," *Dissent*, Summer 1965, 356–57. Brodie herself was a practitioner of what she called "psychobiography" and wrote biographies that incorporated the sexual lives of figures like Joseph Smith, Thaddeus Stevens, and Thomas Jefferson, the latter one of the first biographies to treat the president's relationship with Sally Hemings.

35. Barzun and Graff, *Modern Researcher*, 212. Cf. p. 212 of other 1957 editions as well as every subsequent edition.

36. Charles C. Calhoun, *Longfellow*, 136. Longfellow and Sumner's friendship is explored in Blue, "Poet and the Reformer." Sumner appears on LGBTQ tours of Mount Auburn Cemetery due to his romantic friendship with Samuel Gridley Howe, though the evidence there is Howe's letters to Sumner. Tinker Ready, "Gay History Comes Alive on Mount Auburn Cemetery Tour," *Boston Globe*, July 7, 2016.

37. Chernow, *Grant*, 681. Grant's performance of gender deserves its own treatment. His twenty-first-century celebrants make the butch and bearded president the avatar of muscular Federal intervention. They mostly dismiss the origin story emphasized by earlier biographers, who were more critical of a failed, impotent, scandalized presidency: "A broad streak of the feminine in his personality," one writes. "He was almost half-woman" and nicknamed "Little Beauty" by officers during the US-Mexico War. William E. Woodward, *Meet General Grant*, 25.

38. Donald, *Lincoln Reconsidered*, 36.

39. See Twelve Southerners, *I'll Take My Stand*; Cash, *Mind of the South*, 137–41; O'Brien, *Idea*, 14–27; Tindall, "Mythology," 8–12; and James C. Cobb, *Away Down South*, 112–22.

40. See Beard and Beard, *Rise of American Civilization*, 2:3–51; Luraghi, "Civil War"; and Foner, *Politics and Ideology*, 19–21.

41. Bibler, *Cotton's Queer Relations*; Tison Pugh, *Queer Chivalry*.

42. Bibler, "Queer/Quare," 202. For the South as premodern problem, see Greeson, *Our South*; and Ring, *Problem South*.

43. Wise, *William Alexander Percy*, 164.

44. Percy, *Sappho in Levkas*, 5, 44; Percy, *In April Once*, 109.

45. Faulkner, "Books and Things," 71–72.

46. Percy, *Lanterns on the Levee*, 16–24. See Gulledge, "William Alexander Percy."

47. See Lyle H. Lanier, "Critique," 146–50. For the Agrarians' antipathy to homosexuality, see Richards, *Lovers and Beloveds*, 13–17.

48. Stark Young, "Not in Memoriam," 340.

49. Lawrance Thompson, *Robert Frost*, 105–21; Parini, *Robert Frost*, 185–91. When Amherst College president Alexander Meiklejohn refused to fire Young, Frost resigned from Amherst. For Young's homosexuality, see Gordon, *Gay Faulkner*, 12–15.

50. Jonathan Ned Katz, *Gay American History*, 74–76.

51. See Ohi, *Dead Letters Sent*, 177–210.

52. Bibler, *Cotton's Queer Relations*, 73, 81, 95.

53. Bibler, *Cotton's Queer Relations*, 81.

54. Faulkner, *Absalom, Absalom!*, 76–77, 93.

55. Faulkner, *Absalom, Absalom!*, 269, 275.

56. Faulkner, *Absalom, Absalom!*, 7.

BIBLIOGRAPHY

ARCHIVES

Alabama
    Department of Archives and History, Montgomery
        Photographs Collection
Massachussetts
    Boston Athenæum
        Confederate Collection
    Boston Public Library
        Anti-Slavery Collection
    Harvard Houghton Library
        MOLLUS Civil War Collection: Patriotic Covers
    Massachusetts Historical Society, Boston
        Charles Francis Adams (1835–1915) Papers
        Civil War Correspondence, Diaries, and Journals
Minnesota
    Minnesota Historical Society, St. Paul
        James K. Hosmer Papers
Mississippi
    University of Mississippi Libraries, Oxford
        Special Collections
New Jersey
    Princeton University Library
        Special Collections
Pennsylvania
    Historical Society of Pennsylvania, Philadelphia
        J. B. Lippincott Company Records
    Library Company of Philadelphia
        Graphic Arts Department: Cartes de visit, 1860–70
        McAllister Collection of Civil War Envelopes
Washington, DC
    Library of Congress
        American Cartoon Print Filing Series
        Feinberg-Whitman Collection
        Alfred Whital Stern Collection of Lincolniana
        Martin Van Buren Papers
    Smithsonian Institution
        National Portrait Gallery, Antebellum Portraits of West Pointers

PERIODICALS

Advocate (Los Angeles)
Anniston (AL) Star
Anti-slavery Record (New York)
Atlantic Monthly
Boston Globe
Boston Review
Catholic World (New York)
Charleston (SC) Mercury
Charleston (SC) Tri-weekly Courier
Charlotte (NC) Journal
Chautauquan (Meadville, Pennsylvania)
Christian Advocate (New York)
Christian Union (New York)
Confederate Veteran
Critic (New York)
Daily Atlas (Boston)
Daily Dispatch (Richmond, Virginia)
Daily Indiana State Sentinel (Indianapolis)
Daily Rocky Mountain News (Denver, Colorado)
Democratic Review
Dissent
Harper's Weekly
i-D
Inter Ocean (Chicago)
Liberator (Boston)
London Review of Books
Milwaukee (WI) Daily Sentinel
Nation
New York Herald
New York Illustrated News
New York Times
Observer (Opelika, Alabama)
Puck
Richmond (VA) Sentinel
Richmond (VA) Whig
Signal of Liberty (Ann Arbor, Michigan)
South Coast News (Laguna Beach, California)
Southern Illustrated News (Richmond, Virginia)
Southern Literary Messenger (Richmond, Virginia)
Subterranean (New York)
Sydney (Australia) Morning Herald
Tablet
Telegraph (Philadelphia)
True Democrat (Little Rock, Arkansas)
Washington Post

FILM

Burns, Ken, dir. "The Universe of Battle." Season 1, episode 5, of *The Civil War*. Aired September 25, 1990, on PBS.

Frankenheimer, John, dir. *Andersonville*. 2 episodes. Aired March 3–4, 1996, on Turner Network Television.

Griffith, D. W., dir. *The Birth of a Nation*. Griffith Corp., 1915.

Scott, George C., dir. *The Andersonville Trial*. National Education Television, May 17, 1970.

BOOKS AND ARTICLES

Aaron, Daniel. *The Unwritten War: American Writers and the Civil War*. 1973. Madison: University of Wisconsin Press, 1987.

Abbott, A. O. *Prison Life in the South*. New York: Harper and Brothers, 1865.

Abbott, Karen. *Liar, Temptress, Soldier, Spy: Four Women Undercover in the Civil War*. New York: HarperCollins, 2014.

Abdur-Rahman, Aliyyah I. *Against the Closet: Black Political Longing and the Erotics of Race*. Durham, NC: Duke University Press, 2012.

Abelove, Henry. "Yankee Doodle Dandy." *Massachusetts Review* 49, no. 1/2 (2008): 13–21.

Abzug, Robert H. *Passionate Liberator: Theodore Dwight Weld and the Dilemma of Reform*. New York: Oxford University Press, 1980.

Adams, Charles Francis. *Some Phases of Sexual Morality and Church Discipline in Colonial New England*. Cambridge, MA: John Wilson and Son, 1891.

——. *Some Phases of the Civil War: An Appreciation and Criticism of Mr. James Ford Rhodes's Fifth Volume*. Cambridge, MA: John Wilson and Son, 1905.

[Adams, Henry]. *Democracy: An American Novel*. New York: H. Holt, 1880.

——. *The Letters of Henry Adams*. Vol. 2, *1868–1885*. Edited by J. C. Levenson, Ernest Samuels, Charles Vandersee, and Viola Hopkins Winner. Cambridge, MA: Harvard University Press, 1982.

Adams, Nehemiah. *The Sable Cloud: A Southern Tale, with Northern Comments*. Boston: Ticknor and Fields, 1861.

Aidoo, Lamonte. *Slavery Unseen: Sex, Power, and Violence in Brazilian History*. Durham, NC: Duke University Press, 2018.

Alexander, Edward Porter. *Fighting for the Confederacy: The Personal Recollections of General Edward Porter Alexander*. Chapel Hill: University of North Carolina Press, 1989.

Alexander, William. *William Dean Howells: The Realist as Humanist*. New York: Franklin, 1981.

Ambrose, *Jacob and the Happy Life*. In *Saint Ambrose: Seven Exegetical Works*. Translated by Michael P. McHugh. The Fathers of the Church 65. Washington, DC: Catholic University of America Press, 1972.

Amico, Michael Joseph. "The Union of Two Henrys." PhD diss., Yale University, 2017.

Anderson, Charles R. "James's Portrait of the Southerner." *American Literature* 27, no. 3 (1955): 309–31.

Appleby, Joyce. "Reconciliation and the Northern Novelist, 1865–1880." *Civil War History* 10, no. 2 (1964): 117–29.

Argersinger, Jana L., and Leland S. Person, eds. *Hawthorne and Melville: Writing a Relationship*. Athens: University of Georgia Press, 2008.

Armstrong, Nancy. "Why Daughters Die: The Racial Logic of American Sentimentalism." *Yale Journal of Criticism* 7, no. 2 (1994): 1–24.

Asselineau, Roger. *The Evolution of Walt Whitman*. Iowa City: University of Iowa Press, 1999.

Bailey, Candace. *Music and the Southern Belle: From Accomplished Lady to Confederate Composer*. Carbondale: Southern Illinois University Press, 2010.

Bailey, Thomas, and Katherine Joslin. *Theodore Roosevelt: A Literary Life*. Lebanon, NH: University Press of New England, 2018.

Baker, Jean H. *James Buchanan: The 15th President, 1857–1861*. American Presidents Series. New York: Macmillan, 2004.

Balcerski, Thomas J. *Bosom Friends: The Intimate World of James Buchanan and William Rufus King*. New York: Oxford University Press, 2019.

———. "'A Work of Friendship': Nathaniel Hawthorne, Franklin Pierce, and the Politics of Enmity in the Civil War Era." *Journal of Social History* 50, no. 4 (2017): 655–79.

Baldwin, James. *The Devil Finds Work*. New York: Knopf Doubleday, 2013.

Baptist, Edward E. *The Half Has Never Been Told: Slavery and the Making of American Capitalism*. New York: Basic Books, 2016.

Barclay, Erastus Elmer. *The Lady Lieutenant: A Wonderful, Startling and Thrilling Narrative of the Adventures of Miss Madeline Moore*. Philadelphia: Barclay, 1862.

Barker, Deborah E. *Reconstructing Violence: The Southern Rape Complex in Film and Literature*. Baton Rouge: Louisiana State University Press, 2015.

Barnes, Elizabeth. *States of Sympathy: Seduction and Democracy in the American Novel*. New York: Columbia University Press, 1997.

Barrett, Joseph Hartwell. *Life of Abraham Lincoln*. Indianapolis, IN: Asher, 1860.

Barzun, Jacques, and Henry F. Graff. *The Modern Researcher*. New York: Harcourt, Brace, 1957.

Bates, Ralph Orr. *Billy and Dick from Andersonville Prison to the White House*. Santa Cruz, CA: Press Sentinel, 1910.

Baym, Nina. *American Women Writers and the Work of History, 1790–1860*. New Brunswick, NJ: Rutgers University Press, 1995.

Beale, Howard K. *The Critical Year: A Study of Andrew Johnson and Reconstruction*. 1930. New York: F. Ungar, 1958.

Beard, George Miller. *American Nervousness, Its Causes and Consequences: A Supplement to Nervous Exhaustion (Neurasthenia)*. New York: Putnam, 1881.

———. *Sexual Neurasthenia*. New York: E. B. Treat, 1886.

Beard, Mary Ritter, and Charles A. Beard. *The Rise of American Civilization*. 2 vols. New York: Macmillan, 1930.

Beatty, Jack. *Age of Betrayal: The Triumph of Money in America, 1865–1900*. New York: Knopf Doubleday, 2008.

Beaty, John Owen. *John Esten Cooke, Virginian*. New York: Columbia University Press, 1922.

Beckert, Sven, and Seth Rockman. *Slavery's Capitalism: A New History of American Economic Development*. Philadelphia: University of Pennsylvania Press, 2016.

Bederman, Gail. *Manliness and Civilization: A Cultural History of Gender and Race in the United States, 1880–1917*. Chicago: University of Chicago Press, 2008.

Beer, Andreas. "Martial Men in Virgin Lands? Nineteenth-Century Filibustering, Nation-Building, and Competing Notions of Masculinity in the United States and Nicaragua." In *Masculinities and the Nation in the Modern World: Between Hegemony and Marginalization*, edited by Pablo Dominguez Andersen and Simon Wendt, 113–28. New York: Palgrave Macmillan, 2015.

———. *A Transnational Analysis of Representations of the US Filibusters in Nicaragua, 1855–1857*. New York: Palgrave Macmillan, 2016.

Benemann, William. *Male-Male Intimacy in Early America: Beyond Romantic Friendships*. New York: Haworth, 2006.

Benét, Stephen Vincent. *John Brown's Body*. Garden City, NY: Doubleday, Doran, 1928.

Bercovitch, Sacvan. *The American Jeremiad*. Madison: University of Wisconsin Press, 1978.

Bergland, Renée L., and Gary Williams. Introduction to *Philosophies of Sex: Critical Essays on the Hermaphrodite*, edited by Renée L. Bergland and Gary Williams, 1–14. Columbus: Ohio State University Press, 2012.

Berlant, Lauren. *The Female Complaint: The Unfinished Business of Sentimentality in American Culture*. Durham, NC: Duke University Press, 2008.

———. *The Queen of America Goes to Washington City: Essays on Sex and Citizenship*. Durham, NC: Duke University Press, 1997.

Bernath, Michael T. *Confederate Minds: The Struggle for Intellectual Independence in the Civil War South*. Chapel Hill: University of North Carolina Press, 2010.

Bernstein, Robin. *Racial Innocence: Performing American Childhood from Slavery to Civil Rights*. New York: New York University Press, 2011.

Berry, Daina Ramey, and Leslie M. Harris, eds. *Sexuality and Slavery: Reclaiming Intimate Histories in the Americas*. Athens: University of Georgia Press, 2018.

Berry, Stephen W. *All That Makes a Man: Love and Ambition in the Civil War South*. New York: Oxford University Press, 2002.

Bibler, Michael P. *Cotton's Queer Relations: Same-Sex Intimacy and the Literature of the Southern Plantation, 1936–1968*. Charlottesville: University of Virginia Press, 2009.

———. "Queer/Quare." In *Keywords for Southern Studies*, edited by Scott Romine and Jennifer Rae Greeson, 200–212. Athens: University of Georgia Press, 2016.

Bier, Jesse. "'Bless You, Chile': Fiedler and 'Huck Honey' a Generation Later." *Mississippi Quarterly* 34, no. 4 (1981): 456–62.

Billings, John Davis. *Hardtack and Coffee*. Boston: G. M. Smith, 1887.

Binnington, Ian. *Confederate Visions: Nationalism, Symbolism, and the Imagined South in the Civil War*. Charlottesville: University of Virginia Press, 2013.

Blackford, W. W. *War Years with Jeb Stuart*. New York: Scribner, 1945.

Blair, Sara. *Henry James and the Writing of Race and Nation*. New York: Cambridge University Press, 1996.

Blair, William A. *The Record of Murders and Outrages: Racial Violence and the Fight over Truth at the Dawn of Reconstruction*. Chapel Hill: University of North Carolina Press, 2021.

Blanton, DeAnne, and Lauren M. Cook. *They Fought Like Demons: Women Soldiers in the American Civil War*. Baton Rouge: Louisiana State University Press, 2002.

Blight, David W. *Race and Reunion*. Cambridge, MA: Harvard University Press, 2009.

Blouin, Michael J. *Literary Interventions in the Campaign Biography*. New York: Routledge, 2021.

Blue, Frederick J. "The Poet and the Reformer: Longfellow, Sumner, and the Bonds of Male Friendship, 1837–1874." *Journal of the Early Republic* 15, no. 2 (1995): 273–97.

Blum, Edward J. *Reforging the White Republic: Race, Religion, and American Nationalism, 1865–1898*. Baton Rouge: Louisiana State University Press, 2007.

Blustein, Bonnie Ellen. *Preserve Your Love for Science: Life of William A. Hammond, American Neurologist*. New York: Cambridge University Press, 1991.

Boehrer, Bruce. "'Lycidas': The Pastoral Elegy as Same-Sex Epithalamium." *PMLA* 117, no. 2 (2002): 222–36.

Borgstrom, Michael. "Passing Over: Setting the Record Straight in 'Uncle Tom's Cabin.'" *PMLA* 118, no. 5 (2003): 1290–304.

Boudreau, Kristin. "Narrative Sympathy in *The Bostonians*." *Henry James Review* 14, no. 1 (1993): 17–33.

———. *Sympathy in American Literature: American Sentiments from Jefferson to the Jameses*. Gainesville: University Press of Florida, 2002.

Bousquet, P. Marc. "Mathews's Mosses? Fair Papers and Foul: A Note on the Northwestern-Newberry Edition of Melville's 'Hawthorne and His Mosses.'" *New England Quarterly* 67, no. 4 (1994): 622–49.

Bradshaw, Wesley [Charles Wesley Alexander]. *Maud of the Mississippi*. Philadelphia: C. W. Alexander, 1864.

———. *Pauline of the Potomac*. Philadelphia: Barclay, 1862.

Brasell, R. Bruce. "'The Degeneration of Nationalism': Colonialism, Perversion, and the American South." *Mississippi Quarterly* 56, no. 1 (2002): 33–54.

Brigham, Ann. "Touring Memorial Hall: The State of the Union in *The Bostonians*." *Arizona Quarterly* 62, no. 3 (2006): 5–29.

Brooks, Ross A. *The Visible Confederacy: Images and Objects in the Civil War South*. Baton Rouge: Louisiana State University Press, 2019.

Broomall, James J. *Private Confederacies: The Emotional Worlds of Southern Men as Citizens and Soldiers*. Chapel Hill: University of North Carolina Press, 2019.

Brophy, Alfred L. *University, Court, and Slave: Pro-slavery Thought in Southern Colleges and Courts and the Coming of Civil War*. New York: Oxford University Press, 2016.

Brown, Charles Henry. *Agents of Manifest Destiny: The Lives and Times of the Filibusters*. Chapel Hill: University of North Carolina Press, 1980.

Brown, David. *The Planter, or Thirteen Years in the South, by a Northern Man*. Philadelphia: H. Hooker, 1853.

Brown, R. Shepard. *Stringfellow of the Fourth*. New York: Crown, 1960.

Brown, William Burlie. *The People's Choice: The Presidential Image in the Campaign Biography*. Baton Rouge: Louisiana State University Press, 1960.

Bruce, Philip A. *The Plantation Negro as Freeman: Observations on His Character, Condition, and Prospects in Virginia*. New York: Putnam's, 1889.

Buchanan, Blu. "Gay Neo-Nazis in the United States: Victimhood, Masculinity, and the Public/Private Spheres." *GLQ: A Journal of Lesbian and Gay Studies* 28, no. 4 (October 2022): 489–513.

Buck, Paul Herman. *The Road to Reunion: 1865–1900*. Boston: Little, Brown, 1937.

Bucke, Richard Maurice. *Calamus: A Series of Letters Written during the Years 1868–1880 by Walt Whitman to a Young Friend (Peter Doyle)*. Boston: Laurens Maynard, 1897.

Buelens, Gert. *Henry James and the "Aliens": In Possession of the American Scene*. New York: Rodopi, 2002.

Buinicki, Martin T. *Walt Whitman's Reconstruction: Poetry and Publishing between Memory and History*. Iowa City: University of Iowa Press, 2011.

Bundy, Jonas Mills. *The Life of Gen. James A. Garfield*. New York: A. S. Barnes, 1880.

Buntline, Ned [Edward Judson]. *The Rattlesnake, or The Rebel Privateer, a Tale of the Present Time*. New York: Frederic A. Brady, 1862.

Burg, B. R. *An American Seafarer in the Age of Sail: The Erotic Diaries of Philip C. Van Buskirk 1851–1870*. New Haven, CT: Yale University Press, 1994.

———. *Rebel at Large: The Diary of Confederate Deserter Philip Van Buskirk*. Jefferson, NC: McFarland, 2009.

Burgett, Bruce. *Sentimental Bodies: Sex, Gender, and Citizenship in the Early Republic*. Princeton, NJ: Princeton University Press, 1998.

Burleigh, Erica. *Intimacy and Family in Early American Writing*. New York: Palgrave Macmillan, 2014.

Burnett, Katharine A. "The Proslavery Social Problem Novel: Maria J. Mcintosh's Narrative of Reform in the Plantation South." *College Literature* 42, no. 4 (2015): 619–47.

Burstein, Andrew. *The Passions of Andrew Jackson*. New York: Knopf, 2003.

———. "The Political Character of Sympathy." *Journal of the Early Republic* 21, no. 4 (2001): 601–32.

———. *Sentimental Democracy: The Evolution of America's Romantic Self-Image*. New York: Macmillan, 2000.

Burwell, William MacCreary. *White Acre vs. Black Acre: A Case at Law*. Richmond, VA: J. W. Randolph, 1856.

Butler, Leslie. *Critical Americans: Victorian Intellectuals and Transatlantic Liberal Reform*. Chapel Hill: University of North Carolina Press, 2009.

Butt, Martha Haines. *Antifanaticism: A Tale of the South*. Philadelphia: Lippincott, Grambo, 1853.

Calhoun, Arthur Wallace. *A Social History of the American Family from Colonial Times to the Present*. Vol. 2, *From Independence through the Civil War*. Cleveland, OH: Arthur H. Clark, 1918.

Calhoun, Charles C. *Longfellow: A Rediscovered Life*. Boston: Beacon, 2004.

Calhoun, Charles W. *Conceiving a New Republic: The Republican Party and the Southern Question, 1869–1900*. Lawrence: University Press of Kansas, 2006.

———. *From Bloody Shirt to Full Dinner Pail: The Transformation of Politics and Governance in the Gilded Age*. New York: Farrar, Straus and Giroux, 2010.

———. *Minority Victory: Gilded Age Politics and the Front Porch Campaign of 1888*. Lawrence: University Press of Kansas, 2008.

Callow, Philip. *From Noon to Starry Night: A Life of Walt Whitman*. Chicago: Ivan R. Dee, 1996.

Cammett, Ann. "Deadbeat Dads and Welfare Queens: How Metaphor Shapes Poverty Law." *Boston College Journal of Law and Social Justice* 34, no. 2 (Spring 2014): 233–65.

Camp, Stephanie M. H. *Closer to Freedom: Enslaved Women and Everyday Resistance in the Plantation South*. Chapel Hill: University of North Carolina Press, 2004.

Capitani, Diane N. *Truthful Pictures: Slavery Ordained by God in the Domestic Sentimental Novel of the Nineteenth-Century South*. New York: Lexington Books, 2009.

Carpenter, Edward. *Ioläus: An Anthology of Friendship*. Boston: Charles E. Goodspeed, 1902.

Carr, Albert H. Zolotkoff. *The World and William Walker*. New York: Harper and Row, 1963.

Carter, Julian B. *The Heart of Whiteness: Normal Sexuality and Race in America, 1880–1940*. Durham, NC: Duke University Press, 2007.

Cash, W. J. *The Mind of the South*. New York: Knopf, 1941.

Cashin, Joan E. "The Structure of Antebellum Planter Families: 'The Ties That Bound Us Was Strong.'" *Journal of Southern History* 56, no. 1 (1990): 55–70.

Castronovo, Russ. "Sexual Purity, White Men, and Slavery: Emerson and the Self-Reliant Body." *Prospects*, no. 25 (October 2000): 193–227.

Censer, Jane Turner. *The Reconstruction of White Southern Womanhood, 1865–1895*. Baton Rouge: Louisiana State University Press, 2003.

Chase, Lucien Bonaparte. *English Serfdom and American Slavery, or Ourselves—As Others See Us*. New York: H. Long and Brother, 1854.

Chaudhary, Zahid R. "Paranoid Publics." *History of the Present: A Journal of Critical History* 12, no. 1 (April 2022): 103–26.

Chauncey, George. *Gay New York: Gender, Urban Culture, and the Making of the Gay Male World, 1890–1940*. 1994. New York: Basic Books, 2008.

Cheathem, Mark Renfred. *Andrew Jackson, Southerner*. Baton Rouge: Louisiana State University Press, 2013.

Chernow, Ron. *Grant*. New York: Penguin, 2017.

Chesnut, Mary Boykin. *The Private Mary Chesnut: The Unpublished Civil War Diaries*. Edited by C. Vann Woodward and Elisabeth Muhlenfeld. New York: Oxford University Press, 1984.

Clark, Elizabeth B. "'The Sacred Rights of the Weak': Pain, Sympathy, and the Culture of Individual Rights in Antebellum America." *Journal of American History* 82, no. 2 (1995): 463–93.

Clark, Patricia. "A. O. P. Nicholson of Tennessee: Editor, Statesman, and Jurist." Master's thesis, University of Tennessee, 1965.

Claybaugh, Amanda. "Washington Novels and the Machinery of Government." In *The World the Civil War Made*, edited by Gregory P. Downs and Kate Masur, 206–225. Chapel Hill: University of North Carolina Press, 2015.

Cleaver, Eldridge. *Soul on Ice*. New York: McGraw-Hill, 1967.

Clinton, Catherine, and Nina Silber, eds. *Battle Scars: Gender and Sexuality in the American Civil War*. New York: Oxford University Press, 2006.

———, eds. *Divided Houses: Gender and the Civil War*. New York: Oxford University Press, 1992.

Cloyd, Benjamin G. *Haunted by Atrocity: Civil War Prisons in American Memory*. Baton Rouge: Louisiana State University Press, 2010.

Coates, Ta-Nehisi. *We Were Eight Years in Power: An American Tragedy*. New York: One World, 2017.

Cobb, James C. *Away Down South: A History of Southern Identity*. New York: Oxford University Press, 2005.

Cobb, Thomas Read Rootes. *An Inquiry into the Law of Negro Slavery in the United States of America: To Which Is Prefixed, an Historical Sketch of Slavery*. Philadelphia: T. and J. W. Johnson, 1858.

Coffin, Charles Carleton. *The Life of James A. Garfield*. Boston: J. H. Earle, 1880.

Cohen, Daniel A. *The Female Marine and Related Works: Narratives of Cross-dressing and Urban Vice in America's Early Republic*. Amherst: University of Massachusetts Press, 1997.

Cohen, Nancy. *The Reconstruction of American Liberalism, 1865–1914*. Chapel Hill: University of North Carolina Press, 2003.

Cohen, Patricia Cline, Timothy J. Gilfoyle, and Helen Lefkowitz Horowitz. *The Flash Press: Sporting Male Weeklies in 1840s New York*. Chicago: University of Chicago Press, 2008.

Coit, Emily. *American Snobs: Transatlantic Novelists, Liberal Culture and the Genteel Tradition*. Edinburgh, UK: Edinburgh University Press, 2022.

Collingwood, Herbert Winslow. *Andersonville Violets: A Story of Northern and Southern Life*. With an introduction by David Rachels and Robert Baird. 1889. Tuscaloosa: University of Alabama Press, 2000.

Collins, Kathleen. "Living Skeletons: Carte-de-Visite Propaganda in the American Civil War." *History of Photography* 12, no. 2 (April 1988): 103–20.

Collister, Peter. *Writing the Self: Henry James and America*. New York: Routledge, 2015.

Columbia University. *Catalogue of the Officers and Students of Columbia College*. New York: Columbia University, 1900–1906.

Connelly, Thomas Lawrence. *The Marble Man: Robert E. Lee and His Image in American Society*. Baton Rouge: Louisiana State University Press, 1978.

Connolly, Brian. "Psychoanalysis." In *The Routledge Companion to Historical Theory*, edited by Chel van den Akker, 179–96. New York: Routledge, 2022.

Cook, Robert J. *Civil War Memories: Contesting the Past in the United States since 1865*. Baltimore: Johns Hopkins University Press, 2017.

Cooke, John Esten. "The Band in the Pines (Heard after Pelham Died)." In *War Poetry of the South*, edited by William Gilmore Simms, 209–10. New York: Richardson, 1866.

———. "The Broken Mug." In *War Poetry of the South*, edited by William Gilmore Simms, 269–74. New York: Richardson, 1866.

———. *Hammer and Rapier*. New York: Carleton, 1870.

———. *Hilt to Hilt, or Days and Nights on the Banks of the Shenandoah in the Autumn of 1864*. New York: Carleton, 1869.

———. *A Life of Gen. Robert E. Lee*. New York: Appleton, 1871.

———. *The Life of Stonewall Jackson: From Official Papers, Contemporary Narratives, and Personal Acquaintance*. New York: C. B. Richardson, 1863.

———. *Mohun, or The Last Days of Lee and His Paladins*. New York: F. J. Huntington, 1869.

———. *Surry of Eagle's-Nest, or The Memoirs of a Staff-Officer Serving in Virginia*. New York: F. J. Huntington, 1866.

———. *Wearing of the Gray: Being Personal Portraits, Scenes and Adventures of the War*. New York: E. B. Treat, 1867.

Cosgrove, Bryony. "Missing in Action, Caught on Film: Silent Film Actor 'André de Beranger' Goes to War." *Screening the Past*, no. 32 (December 2011). https://www.screeningthepast.com/issue-32-first-release/missing-in-action-caught-on-film-silent-film-actor-andre-de-beranger-goes-to-war/.

Costa, Dora L., and Matthew E. Kahn. "Surviving Andersonville: The Benefits of Social Networks in POW Camps." *American Economic Review* 97, no. 4 (2007): 1467–87.

Coviello, Peter. *Intimacy in America: Dreams of Affiliation in Antebellum Literature*. Minneapolis: University of Minnesota Press, 2005.

———. *Tomorrow's Parties: Sex and the Untimely in Nineteenth-Century America*. New York: New York University Press, 2013.

Cowdin, V. G. *Ellen, or The Fanatic's Daughter*. Mobile, AL: S. H. Goetzel, 1860.

Cox, Karen L. "The Confederate Monument at Arlington: A Token of Reconciliation." In *Monuments to the Lost Cause: Women, Art, and the Landscapes of Southern Memory*, edited by Cynthia J. Mills and Pamela Hemenway Simpson, 149–62. Knoxville: University of Tennessee Press, 2003.

———. *Dixie's Daughters: The United Daughters of the Confederacy and the Preservation of Confederate Culture*. Gainesville: University Press of Florida, 2019.

Craft, Christopher. "'Descend, and Touch, and Enter': Tennyson's Strange Manner of Address." *Genders*, no. 1 (March 1988): 83–101.

Crain, Caleb. *American Sympathy: Men, Friendship, and Literature in the New Nation*. New Haven, CT: Yale University Press, 2001.

Criswell, Robert. *"Uncle Tom's Cabin" Contrasted with Buckingham Hall, the Planter's Home, or A Fair View of Both Sides of the Slavery Question*. New York: D. Fanshaw, 1852.

Cross, Anne Strachan. "'The Pictures Which We Publish To-day Are Fearful to Look Upon': The Circulation of Images of Atrocity during the American Civil War." *History of Photography* 45, no. 1 (January 2021): 20–33.

Crowe, Charles Robert. *The Age of Civil War and Reconstruction, 1830–1900*. Homewood, IL: Dorsey, 1966.

Dailey, Jane. *Before Jim Crow: The Politics of Race in Postemancipation Virginia*. Chapel Hill: University of North Carolina Press, 2009.

Dale, Corinne. "William Gilmore Simms's Porgy as Domestic Hero." *Southern Literary Journal* 13, no. 1 (1980): 55–71.

Davidson, Cathy N. *Revolution and the Word: The Rise of the Novel in America*. New York: Oxford University Press, 2004.

Davis, Archie K. *Boy Colonel of the Confederacy: The Life and Times of Henry King Burgwyn, Jr.* Chapel Hill: University of North Carolina Press, 1985.

Davis, Robert Leigh. *Whitman and the Romance of Medicine*. Berkeley: University of California Press, 2023.

Davis, Steve. "John Esten Cooke and Confederate Defeat." *Civil War History* 24, no. 1 (1978): 66–83.

Davis, William C. Foreword to *Judah P. Benjamin: Confederate Statesman*, by Robert
    Douthat Meade, xi–xiv. Baton Rouge: Louisiana State University Press, 2001.
Davis, William Watson. *The Civil War and Reconstruction in Florida*. New York: Colum-
    bia University, 1913.
Dearing, Mary Rulkotter. *Veterans in Politics: The Story of the G.A.R.* Westport, CT:
    Greenwood, 1974.
DeFerrari, John. *Capital Streetcars: Early Mass Transit in Washington*. Dover, NH:
    Arcadia, 2015.
De Forest, John W. *Miss Ravenel's Conversion from Secession to Loyalty*. New York:
    Harper and Brothers, 1867.
Delbanco, Andrew. *Melville: His World and Work*. New York: Knopf, 2005.
Deleuze, Gilles, and Felix Guattari, *Anti-Oedipus: Capitalism and Schizophrenia*. Trans-
    lated by Robert Hurley, Mark Seem, and Helen R. Lane. Minneapolis: University of
    Minnesota Press, 1983.
D'Emilio, John. *Sexual Politics, Sexual Communities: The Making of a Homosexual
    Minority in the United States, 1940–1970*. Chicago: University of Chicago Press, 1998.
D'Emilio, John, and Estelle B. Freedman. *Intimate Matters: A History of Sexuality in
    America*. Chicago: University of Chicago Press, 2012.
Democratic National Convention. *Official Proceedings of the National Democratic Con-
    vention*. St. Louis, MO: Woodward, Tiernan, and Hale, 1876.
Dennis, Donna. *Licentious Gotham: Erotic Publishing and Its Prosecution in Nineteenth-
    Century New York*. Cambridge, MA: Harvard University Press, 2009.
Devine, Shauna. *Learning from the Wounded: The Civil War and the Rise of American
    Medical Science*. Chapel Hill: University of North Carolina Press, 2014.
Dew, Thomas Roderick. *Review of the Debate in the Virginia Legislature of 1831 and
    1832*. Richmond, VA: T. W. White, 1832.
Dixon, Thomas. *The Leopard's Spots: A Romance of the White Man's Burden, 1865–1900*.
    New York: Grosset and Dunlap, 1902.
Dodd, William E. "Stringfellow, Franklin." In *The Dictionary of American Biography*,
    edited by Dumas Malone, 18:138–39. New York: Charles Scribner's Sons, 1936.
Domschcke, Bernhard. *Twenty Months in Captivity: Memoirs of a Union Officer in Con-
    federate Prisons*. Edited and translated by Frederic Trautmann. Rutherford, NJ: Fair-
    leigh Dickinson University Press, 1987.
———. *Zwanzig Monate in Kriegs-Gefangenschaft*. Milwaukee, WI: W. W. Coleman, 1865.
Donald, David Herbert. *Charles Sumner and the Rights of Man*. New York: Knopf, 1970.
———. *Lincoln Reconsidered: Essays on the Civil War Era*. New York: Vintage Books,
    2000.
———. *We Are Lincoln Men: Abraham Lincoln and His Friends*. New York: Simon and
    Schuster, 2007.
Donnelly, Andrew. "Voting in the Reconstruction Novel: Black Suffrage, Election-Day
    Violence, and the Regulation of the Vote." *American Literary History* 35, no. 1 (Febru-
    ary 2023): 38–52.
———. "Whiteness and Queer Studies." In *Whiteness and American Literature*, edited by
    Jolene Hubbs. New York: Cambridge University Press, forthcoming.
Dora, the Heroine of the Cumberland: The Western Amazon. Philadelphia: Barclay, 1864.

Douglas, Ann. *The Feminization of American Culture*. New York: Farrar, Straus and Giroux, 1998.

Dowling, Morgan E. *Southern Prisons, or Josie the Heroine of Florence*. Detroit, MI: William Graham, 1870.

Downs, Gregory P. *After Appomattox: Military Occupation and the Ends of War*. Cambridge, MA: Harvard University Press, 2019.

Downs, Gregory P., and Kate Masur. "Echoes of War: Rethinking Post–Civil War Governance and Politics." In *The World the Civil War Made*, edited by Gregory P. Downs and Kate Masur, 1–21. Chapel Hill: University of North Carolina Press, 2015.

Downs, Jim. *Sick from Freedom: African-American Illness and Suffering during the Civil War and Reconstruction*. New York: Oxford University Press, 2012.

———. "With Only a Trace: Same-Sex Sexual Desire and Violence on Slave Plantations, 1607–1865." In *Connexions: Histories of Race and Sex in North America*, edited by Jennifer Brier, Jim Downs, and Jennifer L. Morgan, 15–37. Urbana: University of Illinois Press, 2016.

Duberman, Martin Bauml. "'Writhing Bedfellows' in Antebellum South Carolina: Historical Interpretation and the Politics of Evidence." In *Hidden from History: Reclaiming the Gay and Lesbian Past*, edited by Martin Bauml Duberman, Martha Vicinus, and George Chauncey, 153–68. New York: Meridian, 1989.

Du Bois, W. E. B. *The Autobiography of W. E. B. Du Bois: A Soliloquy on Viewing My Life from the Last Decade of Its First Century*. 1968. New York: Oxford University Press, 2007.

———. *Black Reconstruction in America, 1860–1880*. 1935. New York: Simon and Schuster, 1998.

———. *John Brown*. Philadelphia: George W. Jacobs, 1909.

Dufour, Charles L. *Gentle Tiger: The Gallant Life of Roberdeau Wheat*. Baton Rouge: Louisiana State University Press, 1999.

Dugaw, Dianne. *Warrior Women and Popular Balladry, 1650–1850*. Chicago: University of Chicago Press, 1996.

Dunlap, Lloyd A. "The Calvin Bates Fraud." *Abraham Lincoln Quarterly* 6, no. 8 (December 1951): 438–42.

Dunning, William Archibald. *Reconstruction, Political and Economic, 1865–1877*. Vol. 22 of *The American Nation: A History*, edited by Albert Bushnell Hart. New York: Harper and Brothers, 1877.

Duquette, Elizabeth. *Loyal Subjects: Bonds of Nation, Race, and Allegiance in Nineteenth-Century America*. New Brunswick, NJ: Rutgers University Press, 2010.

Dwyer, Erin Austin. *Mastering Emotions: Feelings, Power, and Slavery in the United States*. Philadelphia: University of Pennsylvania Press, 2021.

Earle, Jonathan Halperin. *Jacksonian Antislavery and the Politics of Free Soil, 1824–1854*. Chapel Hill: University of North Carolina Press, 2004.

Eastman, Mary Henderson. *Aunt Phillis's Cabin, or Southern Life as It Is*. Philadelphia: Lippincott, Grambo, 1852.

Edel, Leon. *Henry James: The Conquest of London, 1870–1881*. 1962. New York: Avon Books, 1978.

———. *Henry James: The Untried Years, 1843–1870*. 1953. New York: Avon Books, 1978.

Edelman, Lee. *Homographesis: Essays in Gay Literary and Cultural Theory*. 1994. New York: Routledge, 2013.

Edgeville, Edward. *Castine*. Raleigh, NC: Wm. B. Smith, 1865.

Edmonds, Sarah Emma. *Nurse and Spy of the Union Army*. Hartford, CT: W. S. Williams, 1865.

Edwards, John N. *Noted Guerillas, or The Warfare of the Border*. St. Louis, MO: Bryan, Brand, 1877.

Edwards, Laura F. *Gendered Strife and Confusion: The Political Culture of Reconstruction*. Urbana: University of Illinois Press, 1997.

Egerton, Douglas. *The Wars of Reconstruction: The Brief, Violent History of America's Most Progressive Era*. New York: Bloomsbury, 2014.

Ellis, Havelock. *Sexual Inversion*. Vol. 2 of *Studies in the Psychology of Sex*. Philadelphia: F. A. Davis, 1915.

Eng, David L. *The Feeling of Kinship: Queer Liberalism and the Racialization of Intimacy*. Durham, NC: Duke University Press, 2010.

Engel, Stephen M. *Fragmented Citizens: The Changing Landscape of Gay and Lesbian Lives*. New York: New York University Press, 2016.

Erkkila, Betsy. *The Whitman Revolution: Sex, Poetry, and Politics*. Iowa City: University of Iowa Press, 2020.

———. *Whitman the Political Poet*. New York: Oxford, 1989.

Estes, Mathew [Julia]. *Tit for Tat, or American Fixings of English Humanity*. London: Clarke and Beeton, 1855.

Evans, Augusta Jane. *Macaria, or Altars of Sacrifice*. Richmond, VA: West and Johnston, 1864.

———. *St. Elmo*. New York: G. W. Dillingham, 1866.

Eyal, Yonatan. *The Young America Movement and the Transformation of the Democratic Party, 1828–61*. New York: Cambridge University Press, 2007.

Ezekiel, Moses. *Memoirs from the Baths of Diocletian*. Detroit, MI: Wayne State University Press, 1975.

Fabian, Ann. *The Unvarnished Truth: Personal Narratives in Nineteenth-Century America*. Berkeley: University of California Press, 2000.

Faderman, Lillian. *Surpassing the Love of Men: Romantic Friendship and Love between Women from the Renaissance to the Present*. New York: HarperCollins, 1998.

Fahs, Alice. *The Imagined Civil War: Popular Literature of the North and South, 1861–1865*. Chapel Hill: University of North Carolina Press, 2001.

Fanon, Frantz. *Black Skin, White Masks*. 1952. New York: Grove, 2008.

Faulkner, William. *Absalom, Absalom!* 1936. New York: Random House, 1986.

———. "Books and Things." In *William Faulkner: Early Prose and Poetry*, edited by Carvel Collins, 71–73. London: Jonathan Cape, 1962.

———. *Intruder in the Dust*. 1948. New York: Random House, 1948.

———. *The Mansion*. 1959. New York: Random House, 2011.

———. *The Town*. 1957. New York: Random House, 2011.

Faust, Drew Gilpin. "Altars of Sacrifice: Confederate Women and the Narratives of War." *Journal of American History* 76, no. 4 (1990): 1200–1228.

——. *The Creation of Confederate Nationalism: Ideology and Identity in the Civil War South*. Baton Rouge: Louisiana State University Press, 1989.

——. *James Henry Hammond and the Old South: A Design for Mastery*. Baton Rouge: Louisiana State University Press, 1985.

——. *Mothers of Invention: Women of the Slaveholding South in the American Civil War*. Chapel Hill: University of North Carolina Press, 2004.

——. "The Proslavery Argument in History." Introduction to *The Ideology of Slavery: Proslavery Thought in the Antebellum South; 1830–1860*, edited by Drew Gilpin Faust, 1–20. Baton Rouge: Louisiana State University Press, 1981.

——. "Race, Gender, and Confederate Nationalism: William D. Washington's 'Burial of Latané.'" *Southern Review* 25, no. 2 (April 1989): 297.

——. *This Republic of Suffering: Death and the American Civil War*. New York: Knopf, 2008.

——. "'We Should Grow Too Fond of It': Why We Love the Civil War." *Civil War History* 50, no. 4 (2004): 368–83.

Feimster, Crystal N. *Southern Horrors: Women and the Politics of Rape and Lynching*. Cambridge, MA: Harvard University Press, 2009.

Ferguson, Joseph. *Life-Struggles in Rebel Prisons: A Record of the Sufferings, Escapes, Adventures and Starvation of the Union Prisoners*. Philadelphia: James M. Ferguson, 1865.

Fetterley, Judith. *The Resisting Reader: A Feminist Approach to American Fiction*. Bloomington: Indiana University Press, 1978.

Fiedler, Leslie. "Come Back to the Raft Ag'in, Huck Honey!" *Partisan Review* 15, no. 6 (June 1948): 664–71.

——. *Love and Death in the American Novel*. 1960. Funks Grove, IL: Dalkey Archive, 1997.

Fielder, Brigitte. *Relative Races: Genealogies of Interracial Kinship in Nineteenth-Century America*. Durham, NC: Duke University Press, 2020.

Fischer, David Hackett. *Albion's Seed: Four British Folkways in America*. New York: Oxford University Press, 1989.

Fisher, Philip. "Appearing and Disappearing in Public: Social Space in Late-Nineteenth-Century Literature and Culture." In *Reconstructing American Literary History*, edited by Sacvan Bercovitch, 155–88. Cambridge, MA: Harvard University Press, 1986.

——. *Hard Facts: Setting and Form in the American Novel*. New York: Oxford, 1987.

Fiske, John. *The Mississippi Valley in the Civil War*. Boston: Houghton, Mifflin, 1900.

Fitzhugh, George. *Sociology for the South, or The Failure of Free Society*. Richmond, VA: Morris, 1854.

Flanders, G. M. *The Ebony Idol*. New York: Appleton, 1860.

Fleming, Walter Lynwood. *Civil War and Reconstruction in Alabama*. New York: Columbia University Press, 1905.

Flexner, James Thomas. *The Young Hamilton: A Biography*. Boston: Little, Brown, 1978.

Foley, Ehren. "Social and Political Prose: Slavery in America and Father Abbott." In *Reading William Gilmore Simms: Essays of Introduction to the Author's Canon*, edited by Todd Hagstette, 374–85. Columbia: University of South Carolina Press, 2017.

Folsom, Ed. "Erasing Race: The Lost Black Presence in Whitman's Manuscripts." In Ivy Wilson, *Whitman Noir*, 3–31.

———. "'A Yet More Terrible and More Deeply Complicated Problem': Walt Whitman, Race, Reconstruction, and American Democracy." *American Literary History* 30, no. 3 (September 2018): 531–58.

Folsom, Ed, and Kenneth M. Price. *Re-scripting Walt Whitman: An Introduction to His Life and Work*. Malden, MA: Blackwell, 2008.

Foner, Eric. *Free Soil, Free Labor, Free Men: The Ideology of the Republican Party before the Civil War*. 1970. New York: Oxford University Press, 1995.

———. *Politics and Ideology in the Age of the Civil War*. New York: Oxford University Press, 1980.

———. *Reconstruction: America's Unfinished Revolution, 1863–1877*. 1988. New York: HarperCollins, 2014.

Foreman, P. Gabrielle. "'This Promiscuous Housekeeping': Death, Transgression, and Homoeroticism in Uncle Tom's Cabin." *Representations*, no. 43 (1993): 51–72.

Foster, Gaines M. *Ghosts of the Confederacy: Defeat, the Lost Cause, and the Emergence of the New South, 1865–1913*. New York: Oxford University Press, 1987.

———. *Moral Reconstruction: Christian Lobbyists and the Federal Legislation of Morality, 1865–1920*. Chapel Hill: University of North Carolina Press, 2003.

Foster, Thomas A., ed. *Long before Stonewall: Histories of Same-Sex Sexuality in Early America*. New York: New York University Press, 2007.

———. *Rethinking Rufus: Sexual Violations of Enslaved Men*. Athens: University of Georgia Press, 2019.

———. "The Sexual Abuse of Black Men under American Slavery." In Berry and Harris, *Sexuality and Slavery*, 124–44.

Foster, Travis M. *Genre and White Supremacy in the Postemancipation United States*. New York: Oxford University Press, 2019.

Foucault, Michel. *Discipline and Punish: The Birth of the Prison*. 1975. New York: Knopf Doubleday, 2012.

———. *The History of Sexuality*. Vol. 1, *An Introduction*. 1976. Translated by Robert Hurley. New York: Knopf Doubleday, 2012.

———. *The History of Sexuality*. Vol. 2, *The Use of Pleasure*. 1984. Translated by Robert Hurley. New York: Knopf Doubleday, 1990.

Fowler, Orson Squire, and Lorenzo Niles Fowler. *The Illustrated Self-Instructor in Phrenology and Physiology*. New York: Fowlers and Wells, 1853.

———. *Phrenology Proved, Illustrated, and Applied*. New York: Fowler and Brevcourt, 1838.

Fox, Richard Wightman. *Trials of Intimacy: Love and Loss in the Beecher-Tilton Scandal*. Chicago: University of Chicago Press, 1999.

Fox-Genovese, Elizabeth, and Eugene D. Genovese. *The Mind of the Master Class: History and Faith in the Southern Slaveholders' Worldview*. New York: Cambridge University Press, 2005.

Frank, Lisa Tendrich, and LeeAnn Whites, eds. *Household War: How Americans Lived and Fought the Civil War*. Athens: University of Georgia Press, 2020.

Franklin, John Hope. "'Birth of a Nation': Propaganda as History." *Massachusetts Review* 20, no. 3 (1979): 417–34.

Fredrickson, George M. *The Black Image in the White Mind: The Debate on Afro-American Character and Destiny, 1817–1914.* Middletown, CT: Wesleyan University Press, 1987.

———. *The Inner Civil War: Northern Intellectuals and the Crisis of the Union.* Urbana: University of Illinois Press, 1965.

Free, Laura E. *Suffrage Reconstructed: Gender, Race, and Voting Rights in the Civil War Era.* Ithaca, NY: Cornell University Press, 2015.

Freeburg, Christopher. "Walt Whitman, James Weldon Johnson, and the Violent Paradox of US Progress." In Ivy Wilson, *Whitman Noir,* 82–103.

Freeman, Elizabeth. *Time Binds: Queer Temporalities, Queer Histories.* Durham, NC: Duke University Press, 2010.

Freeman, Joanne B. *The Field of Blood: Violence in Congress and the Road to Civil War.* New York: Farrar, Straus and Giroux, 2018.

French, Kara M. *Against Sex: Identities of Sexual Restraint in Early America.* Chapel Hill: University of North Carolina Press, 2021.

Fuentes, Marisa J. *Dispossessed Lives: Enslaved Women, Violence, and the Archive.* Philadelphia: University of Pennsylvania Press, 2016.

Gabler, Janet A. "The Narrator's Script: James's Complex Narration in 'The Bostonians.'" *Journal of Narrative Technique* 14, no. 2 (1984): 94–109.

Gallagher, Gary W. *Becoming Confederates: Paths to a New National Loyalty.* Athens: University of Georgia Press, 2013.

———. *Causes Won, Lost, and Forgotten: How Hollywood and Popular Art Shape What We Know about the Civil War.* Chapel Hill: University of North Carolina Press, 2008.

———. *The Confederate War.* Cambridge, MA: Harvard University Press, 1999.

Gallagher, Gary W., and Alan T. Nolan, eds. *The Myth of the Lost Cause and Civil War History.* Bloomington: Indiana University Press, 2000.

Gallman, J. Matthew. *Defining Duty in the Civil War: Personal Choice, Popular Culture, and the Union Home Front.* Chapel Hill: University of North Carolina Press, 2015.

Garber, Eric. "A Spectacle in Color: The Lesbian and Gay Subculture of Jazz Age Harlem." In *Hidden from History: Reclaiming the Gay and Lesbian Past,* edited by Martin Bauml Duberman, Martha Vicinus, and George Chauncey, 318–31. New York: Meridian, 1989.

Garber, Marjorie B. *Vested Interests: Cross-dressing and Cultural Anxiety.* New York: Routledge, 1992.

Gardner, Sarah E. *Blood and Irony: Southern White Women's Narratives of the Civil War, 1861–1937.* Chapel Hill: University of North Carolina Press, 2004.

Garner, James W. "Asexualization of Hereditary Criminals." *Journal of the American Institute of Criminal Law and Criminology* 1, no. 2 (1910): 124–25.

———. "Plan of the Journal." *Journal of the American Institute of Criminal Law and Criminology* 1, no. 1 (1910): 5–7.

———. *Reconstruction in Mississippi.* New York: Macmillan, 1901.

Genovese, Eugene D. *The World the Slaveholders Made: Two Essays in Interpretation.* New York: Pantheon Books, 1969.

Geyer, Alejandro Bolaños. *William Walker: The Gray-Eyed Man of Destiny*. Vol. 1, *The Crescent City*. Lake Saint Louis, MO: Alejandro Bolaños Geyer, 1988.

Gienapp, William E. "The Crime against Sumner: The Caning of Charles Sumner and the Rise of the Republican Party." *Civil War History* 25, no. 3 (1979): 218–45.

———. "Nativism and the Creation of a Republican Majority in the North before the Civil War." *Journal of American History* 72, no. 3 (1985): 529–59.

———. *The Origins of the Republican Party, 1852–1856*. New York: Oxford University Press, 1987.

Giesberg, Judith. *Sex and the Civil War: Soldiers, Pornography, and the Making of American Morality*. Chapel Hill: University of North Carolina Press, 2017.

Gifford, James J., ed. *Glances Backward: An Anthology of American Homosexual Writing, 1830–1920*. Peterborough, ON: Broadview, 2006.

Glazier, Willard W. *The Capture, the Prison Pen and the Escape, Giving an Account of Prison Life in the South*. Albany, NY: R. H. Ferguson, 1865.

Glover, Lorri. *All Our Relations: Blood Ties and Emotional Bonds among the Early South Carolina Gentry*. Baltimore: Johns Hopkins University Press, 2000.

Gobat, Michel. *Empire by Invitation: William Walker and Manifest Destiny in Central America*. Cambridge, MA: Harvard University Press, 2018.

Godbeer, Richard. *The Overflowing of Friendship: Love between Men and the Creation of the American Republic*. Baltimore: Johns Hopkins University Press, 2009.

Gold, Thomas Daniel. *History of Clarke County, Virginia and Its Connection with the War between the States*. Berryville, VA: Gold, 1914.

Goldberg, Jesse A. "The Unspeakable Whiteness in Whitman's Democracy: Empire and the Limits of American Literature." *College Literature* 49, no. 4 (2022): 652–81.

Good, Cassandra A. *Founding Friendships: Friendships between Men and Women in the Early American Republic*. New York: Oxford University Press, 2015.

Goodman, Susan, and Carl Dawson. *William Dean Howells: A Writer's Life*. Berkeley: University of California Press, 2005.

Gordon, Phillip. *Gay Faulkner: Uncovering a Homosexual Presence in Yoknapatawpha and Beyond*. Jackson: University Press of Mississippi, 2020.

Goss, Warren Lee. *The Soldier's Story of His Captivity at Andersonville, Belle Isle, and Other Rebel Prisons*. Boston: Lee and Shepard, 1866.

Gossett, Thomas F. *Uncle Tom's Cabin and American Culture*. University Park, TX: Southern Methodist University Press, 1985.

Graber, Samuel. *Twice-Divided Nation: National Memory, Transatlantic News, and American Literature in the Civil War Era*. Charlottesville: University of Virginia Press, 2019.

Grandin, Greg. *The Empire of Necessity: Slavery, Freedom, and Deception in the New World*. New York: Henry Holt, 2014.

Grayson, William John. *The Hireling and the Slave, Chicora, and Other Poems*. Charleston, SC: McCarter, 1856.

Greenberg, Amy S. *Manifest Manhood and the Antebellum American Empire*. New York: Cambridge University Press, 2005.

Greenberg, David F. *The Construction of Homosexuality*. Chicago: University of Chicago Press, 1990.

Greenberg, Joshua R. *Advocating the Man: Masculinity, Organized Labor, and the House-hold in New York, 1800–1840*. New York: Columbia University Press, 2009.

Greenberg, Kenneth S. *Honor and Slavery: Lies, Duels, Noses, Masks, Dressing as a Woman, Gifts, Strangers, Humanitarianism, Death, Slave Rebellions, the Proslavery Argument, Baseball, Hunting, and Gambling in the Old South*. Princeton, NJ: Princeton University Press, 1998.

Greene, Laurence. *The Filibuster: The Career of William Walker*. Indianapolis, IN: Bobbs-Merrill, 1937.

Greeson, Jennifer Rae. *Our South: Geographic Fantasy and the Rise of National Literature*. Cambridge, MA: Harvard University Press, 2010.

Greiman, Jennifer. *Melville's Democracy: Radical Figuration and Political Form*. Stanford, CA: Stanford University Press, 2023.

Greven, David. *Gender Protest and Same-Sex Desire in Antebellum American Literature: Margaret Fuller, Edgar Allan Poe, Nathaniel Hawthorne, and Herman Melville*. Burlington, VT: Ashgate, 2014.

———. "The Homoerotics of James' *Hawthorne*: Race, Aesthetics, and American Masculinity." *American Literary Realism* 46, no. 2 (January 2014): 137–57.

———. *Men beyond Desire: Manhood, Sex, and Violation in American Literature*. New York: Palgrave Macmillan, 2005.

Grimes, Absalom. *Confederate Mail Runner*. New Haven, CT: Yale University Press, 1926.

Guernsey, Alfred Hudson, and Henry Mills Alden. *Harper's Pictorial History of the Civil War*. New York: Harper and Brothers, 1866.

Gulledge, Jo, ed. "William Alexander Percy and the Fugitives: A Literary Correspondence, 1921–1923." With an introduction by Walker Percy. *Southern Review* 21, no. 2 (April 1985): 415–27.

Gunter, Susan E., and Steven H. Jobe. *Dearly Beloved Friends: Henry James's Letters to Younger Men*. Ann Arbor: University of Michigan Press, 2004.

Gustafson, Sandra M. "The Genders of Nationalism." In *Possible Pasts*, edited by Robert Blair St. George, 380–400. Ithaca, NY: Cornell University Press, 2000.

Guy-Bray, Stephen. "Elegy." In *The Gay and Lesbian Literary Heritage: A Reader's Companion to the Writers and Their Works, from Antiquity to the Present*, edited by Claude J. Summers, 205–7. New York: Routledge, 2002.

Habegger, Alfred. *Henry James and the "Woman Business."* New York: Cambridge University Press, 2004.

Hahn, Steven. *A Nation without Borders: The United States and Its World in an Age of Civil Wars, 1830–1910*. New York: Penguin, 2016.

Hale, Sarah Josepha Buell. *Liberia, or Mr. Peyton's Experiments*. New York: Harper and Brothers, 1853.

Hall, Baynard Rush. *Frank Freeman's Barber Shop: A Tale*. New York: Scribner, 1852.

Hall, Jacquelyn Dowd. "'The Mind That Burns in Each Body': Women, Rape, and Racial Violence." In *Powers of Desire: The Politics of Sexuality*, edited by Ann Snitow, Christine Stansell, and Sharon Thompson, 328–49. New York: New York University Press, 1983.

Halleck, Fitz-Greene. *Young America: A Poem*. New York: Appleton, 1865.

Hallock, John W. M. *The American Byron: Homosexuality and the Fall of Fitz-Greene Halleck*. Madison: University of Wisconsin Press, 2000.

Halperin, David M. *One Hundred Years of Homosexuality: And Other Essays on Greek Love*. New York: Routledge, 2012.

Halperin, John. "Henry James's Civil War." *Henry James Review* 17, no. 1 (1996): 22–29.

Halttunen, Karen. "Humanitarianism and the Pornography of Pain in Anglo-American Culture." *American Historical Review* 100, no. 2 (1995): 303–34.

Hamlin, Augustus Choate. *Martyria, or Andersonville Prison*. Boston: Lee and Shepard, 1866.

Hammond, James Henry. "Hammond's Letters on Slavery." In *The Pro-slavery Argument: As Maintained by the Most Distinguished Writers of the Southern States*. Philadelphia: Lippincott, Grambo, 1853.

———. *Secret and Sacred: The Diaries of James Henry Hammond, a Southern Slaveholder*. Edited by Carol K. Rothrock Bleser. New York: Oxford University Press, 1988.

Hammond, William A. *Lectures on Venereal Diseases*. Philadelphia: Lippincott, 1864.

———. *Sexual Impotence in the Male*. New York: Bermingham, 1883.

———. *A Treatise on Hygiene: With Special Reference to the Military Service*. Philadelphia: Lippincott, 1863.

Hardwig, Bill. *Upon Provincialism: Southern Literature and National Periodical Culture, 1870–1900*. Charlottesville: University of Virginia Press, 2013.

Harper, Phillip Brian. *Are We Not Men? Masculine Anxiety and the Problem of African-American Identity*. New York: Oxford University Press, 1996.

Harris, Trudier. *Exorcising Blackness: Historical and Literary Lynching and Burning Rituals*. Bloomington: Indiana University Press, 1984.

Harrison, Brady. *Agent of Empire: William Walker and the Imperial Self in American Literature*. Athens: University of Georgia Press, 2004.

Harte, Bret. "Plain Language from Truthful James." *Overland Monthly* 5, no. 3 (September 1870): 287–88.

Hartman, Saidiya. *Scenes of Subjection: Terror, Slavery, and Self-Making in Nineteenth-Century America*. New York: Oxford, 1997.

Hassler, William W. *Colonel John Pelham: Lee's Boy Artillerist*. Chapel Hill: University of North Carolina Press, 1995.

Hatheway, Jay. *The Gilded Age Construction of Modern American Homophobia*. New York: Palgrave Macmillan, 2003.

Haumesser, Lauren N. *The Democratic Collapse: How Gender Politics Broke a Party and a Nation, 1856–1861*. Chapel Hill: University of North Carolina Press, 2022.

Haviland, Beverly. *Henry James' Last Romance: Making Sense of the Past and the American Scene*. New York: Cambridge University Press, 1997.

Haw, Mary Jane. *The Rivals: A Chickahominy Story*. Richmond, VA: Ayres and Wade, 1864.

Hawthorne, Nathaniel. *Life of Franklin Pierce*. Boston: Ticknor, Reed, and Fields, 1852.

———. *The Scarlet Letter*. Boston: Ticknor, Reed, and Fields, 1850.

Hayne, Paul H. "Memoir of Henry Timrod." In *The Poems of Henry Timrod*, edited by Paul H. Hayne, 7–69. New York: E. J. Hale and Son, 1873.

———. "Our Martyrs." In *War Poetry of the South*, edited by William Gilmore Simms, 277–79. New York: Richardson, 1866.

Hazel, Harry. *Virginia Graham, the Spy of the Grand Army*. New York: Loring, 1867.

Henderson, Christina. "A Nation of the Continual Present: Timrod, Tennyson, and the Memorialization of the Confederacy." *Southern Literary Journal* 45, no. 2 (2013): 19–38.

Hendler, Glenn. *Public Sentiments: Structures of Feeling in Nineteenth-Century American Literature*. Chapel Hill: University of North Carolina Press, 2003.

Hentz, Caroline Lee. *The Planter's Northern Bride*. 2 vols. Philadelphia: Hart, 1854.

Herbert, Hilary A. *History of the Arlington Confederate Monument*. Washington, DC: United Daughters of the Confederacy, 1914.

Herndon, Mary Eliza. *Louise Elton, or Things Seen and Heard*. Philadelphia: Lippincott, Grambo, 1853.

Hernton, Calvin C. *Sex and Racism in America*. 1965. New York: Anchor Books, 1992.

Herr, Harry. "'The Privates Were Shot': Urological Wounds and Treatment in the Civil War." In *Years of Change and Suffering: Modern Perspectives on Civil War Medicine*, edited by James M. Schmidt and Guy R. Hasegawa, 89–105. Roseville, MN: Edinborough Press, 2009.

Hettle, Wallace. *Inventing Stonewall Jackson: A Civil War Hero in History and Memory*. Baton Rouge: Louisiana State University Press, 2011.

Higginson, Thomas Wentworth. *Army Life in a Black Regiment*. 1870. Cambridge, MA: Riverside, 1900.

———. *Cheerful Yesterdays*. Boston: Houghton, Mifflin, 1898.

Hinsdale, Burke Aaron. *The Republican Text-Book for the Campaign of 1880: A Full History of General James A. Garfield's Public Life*. New York: Appleton, 1880.

Hochman, Barbara. "Reading Historically/Reading Selectively: *The Bostonians* in the *Century*, 1885–1886." *Henry James Review* 34, no. 3 (2013): 270–78.

Hodes, Martha. *White Women, Black Men*. New Haven, CT: Yale University Press, 2014.

Hoffmann, Tess, and Charles Hoffmann. "Henry James and the Civil War." *New England Quarterly* 62, no. 4 (1989): 529–52.

Hofstadter, Richard. *The Age of Reform*. New York: Knopf Doubleday, 2011.

———. *The Progressive Historians: Turner, Beard, Parrington*. New York: Knopf, 1968.

Hoganson, Kristin L. *Fighting for American Manhood: How Gender Politics Provoked the Spanish-American and Philippine-American Wars*. New Haven, CT: Yale University Press, 1998.

Holmes, Mary Jane. *Tempest and Sunshine, or Life in Kentucky*. New York: Appleton, 1855.

Holt, Michael F. *By One Vote: The Disputed Presidential Election of 1876*. Lawrence: University Press of Kansas, 2008.

———. *The Rise and Fall of the American Whig Party: Jacksonian Politics and the Onset of the Civil War*. New York: Oxford University Press, 1999.

Horne, Philip. *Henry James: A Life in Letters*. New York: Penguin, 1999.

Horowitz, Helen Lefkowitz. *Rereading Sex: Battles over Sexual Knowledge and Suppression in Nineteenth-Century America*. New York: Knopf, 2003.

Horton, Rushmore G. *The Life and Public Services of James Buchanan*. New York: Derby and Jackson, 1856.

Horwitz, Tony. *Confederates in the Attic: Dispatches from the Unfinished Civil War*. New York: Pantheon, 1998.

Hosmer, James Kendall. *The Appeal to Arms, 1861–1863*. Vol. 20 of *The American Nation: A History*, edited by Albert Bushnell Hart. New York: Harper and Brothers, 1907.

———. *Outcome of the Civil War, 1863–1865*. Vol. 21 of *The American Nation: A History*, edited by Albert Bushnell Hart. New York: Harper and Brothers, 1907.

———. *The Thinking Bayonet*. Boston: Walker, Fuller, 1865.

Houston, Robert. *The Nation Thief*. New York: Ballantine Books, 1985.

Howard, William Lee. "Sexual Perversion in America." *American Journal of Dermatology and Genito-urinary Diseases* 8, no. 1 (January 1904): 9–14.

Howe, Daniel Walker. *What Hath God Wrought: The Transformation of America, 1815–1848*. New York: Oxford University Press, 2007.

Howe, Julia Ward. *The Hermaphrodite*. Edited by Gary Williams. Lincoln: University of Nebraska Press, 2004.

Howe, Samuel Gridley. *Report Made to the Legislature of Massachusetts, upon Idiocy*. Boston: Coolidge and Wiley, 1848.

Howells, William Dean. *A Hazard of New Fortunes*. New York: Harper and Brothers, 1889.

———. *Mrs. Farrell [Private Theatricals]*. New York: Harper and Brothers, 1921.

Hungerford, James. *The Old Plantation: And What I Gathered There in an Autumn Month*. New York: Harper and Brothers, 1859.

Hutchison, Coleman. *Apples and Ashes: Literature, Nationalism, and the Confederate States of America*. Athens: University of Georgia Press, 2012.

Ingersoll, Robert Green. *Great Speeches of Col. R. G. Ingersoll, Complete*. Chicago: Rhodes and McClure, 1900.

Ingraham, Charles A. *Elmer E. Ellsworth and the Zouaves of '61*. Vol. 11. Chicago Historical Society's Collection. Chicago: University of Chicago Press, 1925.

Ingraham, Joseph Holt. *The Sunny South, or The Southerner at Home*. Philadelphia: G. G. Evans, 1860.

Isenberg, Nancy. *Fallen Founder: The Life of Aaron Burr*. New York: Penguin, 2007.

Isham, Asa Brainerd, Henry M. Davidson, and H. B. Furness. *Prisoners of War and Military Prisons: Personal Narratives of Experience in the Prisons at Richmond, Danville, Macon, Andersonville, Savannah, Millen, Charleston, and Columbia*. Cincinnati, OH: Lyman and Cushing, 1890.

Jacobs, Harriet A. *Incidents in the Life of a Slave Girl: Written by Herself*. Edited by Jean Fagan Yellin. 1861. Cambridge, MA: Harvard University Press, 2009.

Jagose, Annamarie. *Inconsequence: Lesbian Representation and the Logic of Sexual Sequence*. Ithaca, NY: Cornell University Press, 2018.

James, Henry. *The Ambassadors*. 1903. New York: Cambridge University Press, 2015.

———. *The American: An Authoritative Text, Backgrounds and Sources, Criticism*. 1877. New York: Norton, 1978.

———. *The American Scene*. 1907. Edited by Leon Edel. Bloomington: Indiana University Press, 1968.

———. *The Bostonians*. 1886. World's Classics. New York: Oxford University Press, 1984.

———. *The Complete Letters of Henry James, 1855–1872*. Vol. 2. Edited by Pierre A. Walker and Greg W. Zacharias. Lincoln: University of Nebraska Press, 2006.

———. *The Complete Letters of Henry James, 1872–1876*. Vols. 1 and 3. Edited by Pierre A. Walker and Greg W. Zacharias. Lincoln: University of Nebraska Press, 2008.

———. *The Complete Letters of Henry James, 1876–1878*. Vol. 1. Edited by Pierre A. Walker and Greg W. Zacharias. Lincoln: University of Nebraska Press, 2012.

———. *The Complete Letters of Henry James, 1880–1883*. Vols. 1–2. Edited by Michael Anesko and Greg W. Zacharias. Lincoln: University of Nebraska Press, 2016, 2017.

———. *The Complete Letters of Henry James, 1883–1884*. Vol. 2. Edited by Michael Anesko and Greg W. Zacharias. Lincoln: University of Nebraska Press, 2019.

———. *The Complete Letters of Henry James, 1884–1886*. Vol. 1. Edited by Michael Anesko and Greg W. Zacharias. Lincoln: University of Nebraska Press, 2020.

———. *The Complete Letters of Henry James, 1887–1888*. Vols. 1–2. Edited by Michael Anesko and Greg W. Zacharias. Lincoln: University of Nebraska Press, 2022, 2023.

———. "Democracy and Theodore Roosevelt." In *The American Essays*, 212–16. Princeton, NJ: Princeton University Press, 1989.

———. *Hawthorne*. 1879. Ithaca, NY: Cornell University Press, 1997.

———. *Notes of a Son and Brother, and The Middle Years*. 1914, 1917. Charlottesville: University of Virginia Press, 2011.

———. "Pandora." In *Daisy Miller, Pandora, The Patagonia, and Other Stories*. Vol. 18 of *The Novels and Tales of Henry James*, 95–168. 1884. New York: Charles Scribner's Sons, 1909.

———. *Roderick Hudson*. Vol. 1 of *The Novels and Tales of Henry James*. 1875. New York: Charles Scribner's Sons, 1907.

———. *A Small Boy and Others*. 1913. Charlottesville: University of Virginia Press, 2011.

James, Henry Field. *Abolitionism Unveiled, or Its Origin, Progress, and Pernicious Tendency Fully Developed*. Cincinnati, OH: E. Morgan and Sons, 1856.

James, William, and Henry James. *Selected Letters*. Edited by Ignas K. Skrupskelis and Elizabeth M. Berkeley. Charlottesville: University Press of Virginia, 1997.

Jameson, Fredric. *The Political Unconscious: Narrative as a Socially Symbolic Act*. Ithaca, NY: Cornell University Press, 1981.

Janney, Caroline E. *Burying the Dead but Not the Past: Ladies' Memorial Associations and the Lost Cause*. Chapel Hill: University of North Carolina Press, 2008.

———. *Remembering the Civil War: Reunion and the Limits of Reconciliation*. Chapel Hill: University of North Carolina Press, 2013.

Jelliffe, Smith Ely. "Homosexuality and the Law." *Journal of the American Institute of Criminal Law and Criminology* 3, no. 1 (1912): 95–96.

Jennings, Thelma. "'Us Colored Women Had to Go through a Plenty': Sexual Exploitation of African-American Slave Women." *Journal of Women's History* 1, no. 3 (1990): 45–74.

Johnson, Walter. "The Pedestal and the Veil: Rethinking the Capitalism/Slavery Question." *Journal of the Early Republic* 24, no. 2 (2004): 299–308.

———. *River of Dark Dreams*. Cambridge, MA: Harvard University Press, 2013.

Jones, Robert, Jr. *The Prophets*. New York: Penguin, 2021.

Jones-Rogers, Stephanie. "Rethinking Sexual Violence and the Marketplace of Slavery: White Women, the Slave Market, and Enslaved People's Sexualized Bodies in the Nineteenth-Century South." In Berry and Harris, *Sexuality and Slavery*, 109–23.

———. *They Were Her Property: White Women as Slave Owners in the American South*. New Haven, CT: Yale University Press, 2019.

Jordan, Brian Matthew. *Marching Home: Union Veterans and Their Unending Civil War*. New York: Norton, 2014.

Jordan, Winthrop D. *White over Black: American Attitudes toward the Negro, 1550–1812*. Chapel Hill: University of North Carolina Press, 2013.

Jordan-Lake, Joy. *Whitewashing Uncle Tom's Cabin: Nineteenth-Century Women Novelists Respond to Stowe*. Nashville, TN: Vanderbilt University Press, 2005.

Kantor, MacKinlay. *Andersonville*. New York: Plume, 1993.

Kaplan, Amy. *The Anarchy of Empire in the Making of U.S. Culture*. Cambridge, MA: Harvard University Press, 2002.

Kaplan, Justin. *Walt Whitman: A Life*. New York: HarperCollins, 1980.

Karp, Matthew. "The People's Revolution of 1856: Antislavery Populism, National Politics, and the Emergence of the Republican Party." *Journal of the Civil War Era* 9, no. 4 (2019): 524–45.

Katz, Jonathan Ned. *Gay American History: Lesbians and Gay Men in the U.S.A.: A Documentary History*. New York: Meridian, 1992.

———. *The Invention of Heterosexuality*. Chicago: University of Chicago Press, 2007.

———. *Love Stories: Sex between Men before Homosexuality*. Chicago: University of Chicago Press, 2001.

Katz, Michael B. *In the Shadow of the Poorhouse: A Social History of Welfare in America*. New York: Basic Books, 1996.

Kearns, Michael S. "Narrative Discourse and the Imperative of Sympathy in *The Bostonians*." *Henry James Review* 17, no. 2 (1996): 162–81.

Kellogg, Robert H. *Life and Death in Rebel Prisons*. Hartford, CT: L. Stebbins, 1865.

Kemble, Fanny. *Journal of a Residence on a Georgian Plantation in 1838–1839*. New York: Harper and Brothers, 1864.

Kennedy-Nolle, Sharon D. *Writing Reconstruction: Race, Gender, and Citizenship in the Postwar South*. Chapel Hill: University of North Carolina Press, 2015.

Kentucky Girl, A. "A Rebel Soldier Killed in the Trenches before Petersburg, VA, April 15, 1865." In *War Poetry of the South*, edited by William Gilmore Simms, 389–91. New York: Richardson, 1866.

Kibler, James Everett. "Woodcraft; or, Hawks about the Dovecote." In *Reading William Gilmore Simms: Essays of Introduction to the Author's Canon*, edited by Todd Hagstette, 455–66. Columbia: University of South Carolina Press, 2017.

Kiernan, James G. "Responsibility in Sexual Perversion." *Chicago Medical Recorder*, no. 3 (May 1892): 185–210.

"Kiernan, James George, 1852–." In *New York University: Its History, Influence, Equipment and Characteristics, with Biographical Sketches and Portraits of Founders, Benefactors, Officers and Alumni*, edited by Joshua Lawrence Chamberlain, 157–58. Boston: R. Herndon, 1903.

Kimmel, Michael S. *Manhood in America: A Cultural History*. New York: Oxford University Press, 2012.

Kincaid, James R. *Erotic Innocence: The Culture of Child Molesting*. Durham, NC: Duke University Press, 1998.

King, Pendleton. *Life and Public Services of Grover Cleveland*. New York: G. P. Putnam's Sons, 1884.

Kirshner, Ralph. *The Class of 1861: Custer, Ames, and Their Classmates after West Point*. Carbondale: Southern Illinois University Press, 2008.

Knip, Matthew. "Homosocial Desire and Erotic Communitas in Melville's Imaginary: The Evidence of Van Buskirk." *ESQ: A Journal of Nineteenth-Century American Literature and Culture* 62, no. 2 (2016): 355–414.

Knoper, Randall K. *Literary Neurophysiology: Memory, Race, Sex, and Representation in U.S. Writing, 1860–1914*. New York: Oxford University Press, 2021.

Kolodny, Annette. "The Unchanging Landscape: The Pastoral Impulse in Simms's Revolutionary War Romances." *Southern Literary Journal* 5, no. 1 (1972): 46–67.

Kreyling, Michael. *Figures of the Hero in Southern Narrative*. Baton Rouge: Louisiana State University Press, 1987.

Kutzler, Evan A. *Living by Inches: The Smells, Sounds, Tastes, and Feeling of Captivity in Civil War Prisons*. Chapel Hill: University of North Carolina Press, 2019.

La Coste, Marie. "Somebody's Darling." In *War Poetry of the South*, edited by William Gilmore Simms, 369–71. New York: Richardson, 1866.

Lady in New-York. *The Patent Key to Uncle Tom's Cabin*. New York: Pudney and Russell, 1853.

LaFleur, Greta. *The Natural History of Sexuality in Early America*. Baltimore: Johns Hopkins University Press, 2020.

Lamar, Lucius Q. C. "On Sumner and the South." In *Lucius Q. C. Lamar: His Life, Times, and Speeches; 1825–1893*, edited by Edward Mayes, 184–87. Nashville, TN: Publishing House of the Methodist Episcopal Church, South, 1895.

Landis, Michael Todd. *Northern Men with Southern Loyalties: The Democratic Party and the Sectional Crisis*. Ithaca, NY: Cornell University Press, 2014.

Lang, Andrew F. *A Contest of Civilizations: Exposing the Crisis of American Exceptionalism in the Civil War Era*. Chapel Hill: University of North Carolina Press, 2021.

Lanier, Lyle H. "A Critique of the Philosophy of Progress." In Twelve Southerners, *I'll Take My Stand*, 122–54.

Lanier, Sidney. *Tiger-Lilies*. New York: Hurd and Houghton, 1867.

Lanser, Susan Sniader. *The Sexuality of History: Modernity and the Sapphic, 1565–1830*. Chicago: University of Chicago Press, 2014.

Laqueur, Thomas Walter. *Solitary Sex: A Cultural History of Masturbation*. New York: Zone Books, 2003.

Lasser, Carol. "Voyeuristic Abolitionism: Sex, Gender, and the Transformation of Antislavery Rhetoric." *Journal of the Early Republic* 28, no. 1 (2008): 83–114.

Lawson, Andrew. *Walt Whitman and the Class Struggle*. Iowa City: University of Iowa Press, 2009.

Legaré, Hugh Swinton. *Writings*. Charleston, SC: Burges, 1846.

Lemmey, Huw, and Ben Miller. *Bad Gays: A Homosexual History*. New York: Verso, 2022.

Leonard, Elizabeth D. *All the Daring of the Soldier: Women of the Civil War Armies*. New York: Norton, 1999.

Levecq, Christine. *Slavery and Sentiment: The Politics of Feeling in Black Atlantic Antislavery Writing, 1770–1850*. Lebanon, NH: University Press of New England, 2012.

Levin, Kevin M. *Searching for Black Confederates: The Civil War's Most Persistent Myth*. Chapel Hill: University of North Carolina Press, 2019.

Levine, Bruce. *Half Slave and Half Free: The Roots of Civil War*. New York: Farrar, Straus and Giroux, 2005.

Levitt, Saul. *The Andersonville Trial*. New York: Dramatists Play Service, 1961.

Lindsey, Edward. "The International Congress of Criminal Anthropology: A Review." *Journal of the American Institute of Criminal Law and Criminology* 1, no. 4 (1910): 578–83.

Loewen, James W. *Lies across America: What Our Historic Sites Get Wrong*. New York: New Press, 2019.

Loewen, James W., and Edward H. Sebesta. *The Confederate and Neo-Confederate Reader: The Great Truth about the Lost Cause*. Jackson: University Press of Mississippi, 2011.

Long, Lessel. *Twelve Months in Andersonville*. Huntington, IN: Butler, 1886.

Longstreet, Abby Buchanan [C. H. Gildersleeve]. *Remy St. Remy, or The Boy in Blue*. New York: James O'Kane, 1865.

Longstreet, James. *From Manassas to Appomattox: Memoirs of the Civil War in America*. Philadelphia: Lippincott, 1896.

Looby, Christopher. "'As Thoroughly Black as the Most Faithful Philanthropist Could Desire': Erotics of Race in Higginson's Army Life in a Black Regiment." In *Race and the Subject of Masculinities*, edited by Harilaos Stecopoulos and Michael Uebel, 71–115. Durham, NC: Duke University Press, 1997.

———. "'Innocent Homosexuality': The Fiedler Thesis in Retrospect." In *Adventures of Huckleberry Finn: A Case Study in Critical Controversy*, edited by Gerald Graff and James Phelan, 535–50. New York: St. Martin's, 1995.

Loring, Frederic Wadsworth. *Two College Friends*. Boston: Loring, 1871.

Lott, Eric. *Love and Theft: Blackface Minstrelsy and the American Working Class*. New York: Oxford University Press, 2013.

Loving, Jerome. *Walt Whitman: The Song of Himself*. Berkeley: University of California Press, 2000.

Lowry, Thomas P. *The Story the Soldiers Wouldn't Tell: Sex in the Civil War*. Mechanicsburg, PA: Stackpole Books, 2012.

Luraghi, Raimondo. "The Civil War and the Modernization of American Society: Social Structure and Industrial Revolution in the Old South before and during the War." *Civil War History* 18, no. 3 (1972): 230–50.

Lussana, Sergio. *My Brother Slaves: Friendship, Masculinity, and Resistance in the Antebellum South*. Lexington: University Press of Kentucky, 2016.

Lydston, G. Frank. *The Diseases of Society: The Vice and Crime Problem*. Philadelphia: Lippincott, 1904.

———. "Malingering among Criminals." *Journal of the American Institute of Criminal Law and Criminology* 2, no. 3 (1911): 386–88.

———. *Over the Hookah: The Tales of a Talkative Doctor*. Chicago: F. Klein, 1896.

————. "Sexual Perversion." In *Addresses and Essays*, 243–64. Louisville, KY: Renz and Henry, 1892.

"Lydston Would Have Whites and Negroes Marry." *Texas State Journal of Medicine* 5, no. 7 (November 1909): 284–85.

Lynch, Michael. "'Here Is Adhesiveness': From Friendship to Homosexuality." *Victorian Studies* 29, no. 1 (1985): 67–96.

Lynn, Joshua A. *Preserving the White Man's Republic: Jacksonian Democracy, Race, and the Transformation of American Conservatism*. Charlottesville: University of Virginia Press, 2019.

MacKethan, Lucinda Hardwick. *The Dream of Arcady: Place and Time in Southern Literature*. Baton Rouge: Louisiana State University Press, 1999.

Maclaren, Alexander. *St. Paul's Epistles to the Corinthians: To II Corinthians, Chapter V*. Expositions of Holy Scripture. New York: A. C. Armstrong and Son, 1910.

Makemson, Harlen. "A 'Dude and Pharisee.'" *Journalism History* 29, no. 4 (January 2004): 179–89.

Mancuso, Luke. *The Strange Sad War Revolving: Walt Whitman, Reconstruction, and the Emergence of Black Citizenship, 1865–1876*. Columbia, SC: Camden House, 1997.

Mann, Horace. *Life and Works of Horace Mann*. Boston: Lee and Shepard, 1891.

Marrs, Cody. *Not Even Past: The Stories We Keep Telling about the Civil War*. Baltimore: Johns Hopkins University Press, 2020.

Martin, Robert K. *Hero, Captain, and Stranger: Male Friendship, Social Critique, and Literary Form in the Sea Novels of Herman Melville*. Chapel Hill: University of North Carolina Press, 1986.

————. "The 'High Felicity' of Comradeship: A New Reading of *Roderick Hudson*." *American Literary Realism, 1870–1910* 11, no. 1 (1978): 100–108.

Martineau, Harriet. *Society in America*. Vol. 2. London: Saunders and Otley, 1837.

Marvel, William. "Johnny Ransom's Imagination." *Civil War History* 41, no. 3 (1995): 181–89.

Mathews, Cornelius. *Big Abel, and the Little Manhattan*. New York: Wiley and Putnam, 1845.

————. *A Pen-and-Ink Panorama of New-York City*. New York: J. S. Taylor, 1853.

Mathews, Theodore Dehone [Desmos]. *Old Toney and His Master, or The Abolitionist and the Land-Pirate*. Nashville, TN: Southwestern, 1861.

Matthiessen, F. O. *American Renaissance: Art and Expression in the Age of Emerson and Whitman*. New York: Oxford University Press, 1968.

Maxwell, Jerry H. *The Perfect Lion: The Life and Death of Confederate Artillerist John Pelham*. Tuscaloosa: University of Alabama Press, 2011.

May, Robert E. *Manifest Destiny's Underworld: Filibustering in Antebellum America*. Chapel Hill: University of North Carolina Press, 2003.

Mayfield, John. "'The Soul of a Man!': William Gilmore Simms and the Myths of Southern Manhood." *Journal of the Early Republic* 15, no. 3 (1995): 477–500.

Mayne, Xavier [Edward I. Prime-Stevenson]. *Imre: A Memorandum*. Edited by James J. Gifford. Peterborough, ON: Broadview, 2003.

————. *The Intersexes: A History of Similisexualism as a Problem in Social Life*. New York: Arno, 1975.

McCabe, Susan. "To Be and to Have: The Rise of Queer Historicism." *GLQ: A Journal of Lesbian and Gay Studies* 11, no. 1 (2005): 119–34.

McCabe, W. Gordon. "John Pegram." In *War Poetry of the South*, edited by William Gilmore Simms, 371–72. New York: Richardson, 1866.

McCarthy, Carlton. *Detailed Minutiæ of Soldier Life in the Army of Northern Virginia, 1861–1865*. Richmond, VA: B. F. Johnson, 1882.

McConnell, Stuart. *Glorious Contentment: The Grand Army of the Republic, 1865–1900*. Chapel Hill: University of North Carolina Press, 1992.

McCurdy, John Gilbert. *Citizen Bachelors: Manhood and the Creation of the United States*. Ithaca, NY: Cornell University Press, 2011.

McDade, Thomas M. "Lurid Literature of the Last Century: The Publications of E. E. Barclay." *Pennsylvania Magazine of History and Biography* 80, no. 4 (1956): 452–64.

McElroy, John. *Andersonville: A Story of Rebel Military Prisons*. Toledo, OH: D. R. Locke, 1879.

McEnany, Brian R. *For Brotherhood and Duty: The Civil War History of the West Point Class of 1862*. Lexington: University Press of Kentucky, 2015.

McFarland, Gerald W. *Mugwumps, Morals, and Politics, 1884–1920*. Amherst: University of Massachusetts Press, 1975.

McGuire, Hunter, and G. Frank Lydston. *Sexual Crimes among the Southern Negroes*. Louisville, KY: Rentz and Henry, 1893.

McIntosh, Maria Jane. *The Lofty and the Lowly, or Good in All and None All-Good*. 2 vols. New York: Appleton, 1852.

McKee, Kathryn B. *Reading Reconstruction: Sherwood Bonner and the Literature of the Post–Civil War South*. Baton Rouge: Louisiana State University Press, 2019.

McKee, Patricia. *Producing American Races: Henry James, William Faulkner, Toni Morrison*. Durham, NC: Duke University Press, 1999.

McPherson, James M. *Battle Cry of Freedom: The Civil War Era*. New York: Oxford University Press, 2003.

Meer, Sarah. *Uncle Tom Mania: Slavery, Minstrelsy, and Transatlantic Culture in the 1850s*. Athens: University of Georgia Press, 2005.

Melville, Herman. *Benito Cereno*. In *The Piazza Tales, and Other Prose Pieces, 1839–1860*, 46–117. 1855. Evanston, IL: Northwestern University Press, 1987.

———. "Hawthorne and His Mosses." In *The Piazza Tales, and Other Prose Pieces, 1839–1860*, 239–53. 1850. Evanston, IL: Northwestern University Press, 1987.

———. *Moby-Dick; or, The Whale*. 1851. Evanston, IL: Northwestern University Press, 1988.

———. *Pierre; or, The Ambiguities*. 1852. Evanston, IL: Northwestern University Press, 1971.

Mendelssohn, Michèle. *Henry James, Oscar Wilde and Aesthetic Culture*. Edinburgh, UK: Edinburgh University Press, 2014.

Michaels, Walter Benn. "Jim Crow Henry James?" *Henry James Review* 16, no. 3 (1995): 286–91.

Miles, William. *The Image Makers: A Bibliography of American Presidential Campaign Biographies*. Metuchen, NJ: Scarecrow, 1979.

Miller, D. A. *The Novel and the Police*. Berkeley: University of California Press, 1988.

Miller, Monica L. *Slaves to Fashion: Black Dandyism and the Styling of Black Diasporic Identity*. Durham, NC: Duke University Press, 2009.

Miller, Perry. *The Raven and the Whale: Poe, Melville, and the New York Literary Scene*. Baltimore: Johns Hopkins University Press, 1997.

Mitchell, Reid. *The Vacant Chair: The Northern Soldier Leaves Home*. New York: Oxford University Press, 1995.

Mitchell, Silas Weir. *Roland Blake*. New York: Century, 1886.

Moltke-Hansen, David. "The Revolutionary Romances: The Partisan; Mellichampe; The Scout; Katherine Walton; Woodcraft; The Forayers; Eutaw; and Joscelyn." In *Reading William Gilmore Simms: Essays of Introduction to the Author's Canon*, edited by Todd Hagstette, 295–316. Columbia: University of South Carolina Press, 2017.

Monroe, George J. "Sodomy-Pederasty." *St. Louis Medical Era* 9, no. 12 (August 1900): 431–34.

Moran, Benjamin. "Contributions towards a History of American Literature." In *Bibliographical Guide to American Literature*, by Nicolas Trübner, xxxvii–civ. London: Trübner, 1859.

Morris, Roy, Jr. *The Better Angel: Walt Whitman in the Civil War*. New York: Oxford University Press, 2000.

———. *Fraud of the Century: Rutherford B. Hayes, Samuel Tilden, and the Stolen Election of 1876*. New York: Simon and Schuster, 2007.

Morrison, Toni. *Playing in the Dark: Whiteness and the Literary Imagination*. Cambridge, MA: Harvard University Press, 1992.

Morrissey, Katherine G. "Engendering the West." In *Under an Open Sky: Rethinking America's Western Past*, edited by William Cronon, George Miles, and Jay Gitlin, 132–44. New York: Norton, 1992.

Muhammad, Khalil Gibran. *The Condemnation of Blackness: Race, Crime, and the Making of Modern Urban America*. Cambridge, MA: Harvard University Press, 2010.

Murison, Justine S. "The Age of Van Buren." In *Timelines of American Literature*, edited by Cody Marrs and Christopher Hager, 170–88. Baltimore: Johns Hopkins University Press, 2019.

Murphy, Kevin P. *Political Manhood: Red Bloods, Mollycoddles, and the Politics of Progressive Era Reform*. New York: Columbia University Press, 2010.

Murray, Martin G. "'Pete the Great': A Biography of Peter Doyle." *Walt Whitman Quarterly Review* 12, no. 1 (July 1994): 1–51.

Nash, Peter Adam. *The Life and Times of Moses Jacob Ezekiel American Sculptor, Arcadian Knight*. Madison, NJ: Fairleigh Dickinson University Press, 2014.

Nelson, Dana D. *National Manhood: Capitalist Citizenship and the Imagined Fraternity of White Men*. Durham, NC: Duke University Press, 1998.

Neville, Laurence. *Edith Allen, or Sketches of Life in Virginia*. Richmond, VA: J. W. Randolph, 1855.

Nicolay, John George, and John Hay. *Abraham Lincoln: A History*. Vols. 1 and 3. New York: Century, 1890.

Nissen, Axel. *Manly Love: Romantic Friendship in American Fiction*. Chicago: University of Chicago Press, 2009.

———. *The Romantic Friendship Reader: Love Stories between Men in Victorian America*. Boston: Northeastern University Press, 2003.

Nissenbaum, Stephen. *Sex, Diet, and Debility in Jacksonian America: Sylvester Graham and Health Reform*. Westport, CT: Praeger, 1980.

Noble, Marianne. *The Masochistic Pleasures of Sentimental Literature*. Princeton, NJ: Princeton University Press, 2000.

Noonan, Mark J. *Reading the Century Illustrated Monthly Magazine: American Literature and Culture, 1870–1893*. Kent, OH: Kent State University Press, 2010.

Northup, Solomon. *Twelve Years a Slave*. Baton Rouge: Louisiana State University Press, 1968.

Novick, Sheldon M. *Henry James: The Young Master*. New York: Random House, 1996.

Nyong'o, Tavia. *The Amalgamation Waltz: Race, Performance, and the Ruses of Memory*. Minneapolis: University of Minnesota Press, 2009.

Oakes, James. *The Ruling Race*. New York: Knopf Doubleday, 2013.

O'Brien, Michael. *Henry Adams and the Southern Question*. Athens: University of Georgia Press, 2007.

———. *The Idea of the American South, 1920–1941*. Baltimore: Johns Hopkins University Press, 1979.

Ohi, Kevin. *Dead Letters Sent: Queer Literary Transmission*. Minneapolis: University of Minnesota Press, 2015.

———. *Henry James and the Queerness of Style*. Minneapolis: University of Minnesota Press, 2011.

The Olive-Branch, or White Oak Farm. Philadelphia: Lippincott, 1857.

Osofsky, Gilbert. *Harlem, the Making of a Ghetto: Negro New York, 1890–1930*. Chicago: Ivan R. Dee, 1996.

Osterweis, Rollin G. *The Myth of the Lost Cause, 1865–1900*. Hamden, CT: Archon Books, 1973.

Page, John White. *Uncle Robin, in His Cabin in Virginia, and Tom without One in Boston*. Richmond, VA: J. W. Randolph, 1853.

Page, Thomas Nelson. "Marse Chan: A Tale of Old Virginia." *Century* 27, no. 6 (April 1884): 932–42.

———. *Red Rock: A Chronicle of Reconstruction*. New York: Charles Scribner's Sons, 1898.

Painter, Nell Irvin. *The History of White People*. New York: Norton, 2010.

———. "'Social Equality,' Miscegenation, Labor, and Power." In *The Evolution of Southern Culture*, edited by Numan V. Bartley, 47–67. Athens: University of Georgia Press, 1988.

Parini, Jay. *Robert Frost: A Life*. London: Heinemann, 1998.

Pater, Walter. *The Renaissance: Studies in Art and Poetry*. New York: Macmillan, 1903.

Percy, William Alexander. *In April Once*. New Haven, CT: Yale University Press, 1920.

———. *Lanterns on the Levee: Recollections of a Planter's Son*. New York: Knopf, 1941.

———. *Sappho in Levkas and Other Poems*. New Haven, CT: Yale University Press, 1915.

Pérez, Hiram. *A Taste for Brown Bodies: Gay Modernity and Cosmopolitan Desire*. New York: New York University Press, 2015.

Perry, Lewis. *Radical Abolitionism: Anarchy and the Government of God in Antislavery Thought*. Knoxville: University of Tennessee Press, 1995.

Person, Leland S. *Henry James and the Suspense of Masculinity*. Philadelphia: University of Pennsylvania Press, 2003.

Peskin, Allan. *Garfield*. Kent, OH: Kent State University Press, 1999.

Peterson, Beverly. "'Aunt Phillis's Cabin': One Reply to Uncle Tom." *Southern Quarterly* 33, no. 1 (1994): 97.

Peterson, Charles Jacobs. *The Cabin and Parlor, or Slaves and Masters*. Philadelphia: T. B. Peterson, 1852.

Pickenpaugh, Roger. *Captives in Blue: The Civil War Prisons of the Confederacy*. Tuscaloosa: University of Alabama Press, 2013.

Pierson, Michael D. *Free Hearts and Free Homes: Gender and American Antislavery Politics*. Chapel Hill: University of North Carolina Press, 2003.

Pike, James Shepherd. *The Prostrate State: South Carolina under Negro Government*. New York: Appleton, 1874.

Poe, Edgar Allan. "Cornelius Mathews." In *The Works of the Late Edgar Allan Poe: The Literati*, edited by Rufus Wilmot Griswold, Nathaniel Parker Willis, and James Russell Lowell, 262–71. New York: Redfield, 1850.

Posnock, Ross. "Henry James, Veblen and Adorno: The Crisis of the Modern Self." *Journal of American Studies* 21, no. 1 (1987): 31–54.

———. *The Trial of Curiosity: Henry James, William James, and the Challenge of Modernity*. New York: Oxford University Press, 1991.

Pratt, Lloyd. *The Strangers Book: The Human of African American Literature*. Philadelphia: University of Pennsylvania Press, 2015.

Prince, K. Stephen. "The Burnt District: Making Sense of the Ruins in the Postwar South." In *The World the Civil War Made*, edited by Gregory P. Downs and Kate Masur, 106–31. Chapel Hill: University of North Carolina Press, 2015.

———. *Stories of the South: Race and the Reconstruction of Southern Identity, 1865–1915*. Chapel Hill: University of North Carolina Press, 2014.

Puar, Jasbir K. *Terrorist Assemblages: Homonationalism in Queer Times*. Durham, NC: Duke University Press, 2007.

Pugh, David G. *Sons of Liberty: The Masculine Mind in Nineteenth-Century America*. Westport, CT: Greenwood, 1984.

Pugh, Tison. *Queer Chivalry: Medievalism and the Myth of White Masculinity in Southern Literature*. Baton Rouge: Louisiana State University Press, 2013.

Purcell, Sarah J. *Spectacle of Grief: Public Funerals and Memory in the Civil War Era*. Chapel Hill: University of North Carolina Press, 2022.

Putnam, George Haven. *Some Memories of the Civil War*. New York: G. P. Putnam's Sons, 1924.

Quad, M. *The Comic Biography of Winfield S. Hancock: Prepared from Carefully Selected Stock and Warranted Perfectly Fresh*. New York: Chic, 1880.

Rable, George C. *Civil Wars: Women and the Crisis of Southern Nationalism*. Urbana: University of Illinois Press, 2022.

Randall, James R. "John Pelham." In *War Poetry of the South*, edited by William Gilmore Simms, 235–37. New York: Richardson, 1866.

Randall, Ruth Painter. *Lincoln's Sons*. Boston: Little, Brown, 1955.

Ransom, John L. *John Ransom's Diary*. New York: P. S. Eriksson, 1963.

Rawlings, Peter. *Henry James and the Abuse of the Past*. New York: Palgrave Macmillan, 2005.

Reid-Pharr, Robert F. "Tearing the Goat's Flesh." In *Black Gay Man: Essays*, 99–134. New York: New York University Press, 2001.

Republican National Convention. *Proceedings of the Republican National Convention Held at Cincinnati, Ohio*. Edited by M. A. Clancy. Concord, NH: Republican Press Association, 1876.

Reynolds, David S. "'Affection Shall Solve Every One of the Problems of Freedom': Calamus Love and the Antebellum Political Crisis." *Huntington Library Quarterly* 73, no. 4 (2010): 629–42.

———. *Mightier Than the Sword: Uncle Tom's Cabin and the Battle for America*. New York: Norton, 2011.

———. *Waking Giant: America in the Age of Jackson*. New York: HarperCollins, 2009.

———. *Walt Whitman's America: A Cultural Biography*. New York: Knopf Doubleday, 2011.

Reynolds, Larry J. *European Revolutions and the American Literary Renaissance*. New Haven, CT: Yale University Press, 1988.

Rhodes, James Ford. *History of the United States from the Compromise of 1850*. Vols. 1 and 5. New York: Macmillan, 1892, 1904.

Richards, Gary. *Lovers and Beloveds: Sexual Otherness in Southern Fiction, 1936–1961*. Baton Rouge: Louisiana State University Press, 2007.

Richardson, Heather Cox. *The Death of Reconstruction: Race, Labor, and Politics in the Post–Civil War North, 1865–1901*. Cambridge, MA: Harvard University Press, 2009.

Ridgely, Joseph V. "Woodcraft: Simms's First Answer to Uncle Tom's Cabin." *American Literature* 31, no. 4 (1960): 421–33.

Ring, Natalie J. *The Problem South: Region, Empire, and the New Liberal State, 1880–1930*. Athens: University of Georgia Press, 2012.

Roberts, Giselle. *The Confederate Belle*. Columbia: University of Missouri Press, 2003.

Roediger, David R. *The Wages of Whiteness: Race and the Making of the American Working Class*. New York: Verso, 2007.

Rogin, Michael. *Subversive Genealogy: The Politics and Art of Herman Melville*. Berkeley: University of California Press, 1985.

———. "'The Sword Became a Flashing Vision': D. W. Griffith's *The Birth of a Nation*." *Representations*, no. 9 (1985): 150–95.

Rohy, Valerie. *Anachronism and Its Others: Sexuality, Race, Temporality*. Albany: State University of New York Press, 2009.

Rollin, Frank A. *Life and Public Services of Martin R. Delany, Sub-assistant Commissioner Bureau Relief of Refugees, Freedmen, and of Abandoned Lands, and Late Major 104th U.S. Colored Troops*. Boston: Lee and Shepard, 1868.

Roper, Moses. *A Narrative of the Adventures and Escape of Moses Roper from American Slavery*. London: Darton, Harvey, and Darton, 1837.

Rosen, Hannah. *Terror in the Heart of Freedom: Citizenship, Sexual Violence, and the Meaning of Race in the Postemancipation South*. Chapel Hill: University of North Carolina Press, 2009.

Rosengarten, Frederic, Jr. *Freebooters Must Die! The Life and Death of William Walker, the Most Notorious Filibuster of the Nineteenth Century*. Wayne, PA: Haverford House, 1976.

Ross, Marlon Bryan. *Manning the Race: Reforming Black Men in the Jim Crow Era*. New York: New York University Press, 2004.

Roth, Sarah N. *Gender and Race in Antebellum Popular Culture*. New York: Cambridge University Press, 2014.

Rothberg, Emma. "Father Abraham and Mother Lincoln: Cartoons of Abraham Lincoln and Manhood." Paper presented at the annual Popular Culture Association meeting, Washington, DC, April 18, 2019.

Rotundo, E. Anthony. *American Manhood: Transformations in Masculinity from the Revolution to the Modern Era*. New York: Basic Books, 1993.

Rowbotham, Sheila. *Edward Carpenter: A Life of Liberty and Love*. New York: Verso, 2009.

Rubin, Anne Sarah. *A Shattered Nation: The Rise and Fall of the Confederacy, 1861–1868*. Chapel Hill: University of North Carolina Press, 2009.

Rupp, Leila J. *A Desired Past: A Short History of Same-Sex Love in America*. Chicago: University of Chicago Press, 1999.

Rush, Caroline E. *The North and South, or Slavery and Its Contrasts: A Tale of Real Life*. Philadelphia: Crissy and Markley, 1852.

Russell, William Howard. *The Civil War in America*. Boston: G. A. Fuller, 1861.

Ryan, Susan M. "*The Bostonians* and the Civil War." *Henry James Review* 26, no. 3 (2005): 265–72.

———. "Errand into Africa: Colonization and Nation Building in Sarah J. Hale's *Liberia*." *New England Quarterly* 68, no. 4 (1995): 558–83.

Sabre, Gilbert E. *Nineteen Months a Prisoner of War*. New York: American News Company, 1865.

Saillant, John. "The Black Body Erotic and the Republican Body Politic, 1790–1820." *Journal of the History of Sexuality* 5, no. 3 (1995): 403–28.

Samuels, Ernest. *Henry Adams*. Cambridge, MA: Harvard University Press, 1989.

Sanborn, Franklin B. *Life and Letters of John Brown: Liberator of Kansas, and Martyr of Virginia*. Boston: Roberts Brothers, 1891.

Sánchez-Eppler, Karen. *Touching Liberty: Abolition, Feminism, and the Politics of the Body*. Berkeley: University of California Press, 1993.

Sandburg, Carl. *Abraham Lincoln: The Prairie Years*. Vol. 2. New York: Harcourt, Brace, 1926.

Sanders, Charles W., Jr. *While in the Hands of the Enemy: Military Prisons of the Civil War*. Baton Rouge: Louisiana State University Press, 2005.

Sawyer, George S. *Southern Institutes, or An Inquiry into the Origin and Early Prevalence of Slavery and the Slave-Trade*. Philadelphia: Lippincott, 1858.

Saxton, Alexander. *The Rise and Fall of the White Republic: Class Politics and Mass Culture in Nineteenth-Century America*. New York: Verso, 1990.

Schaff, Morris. *The Spirit of Old West Point, 1858–1862*. Boston: Houghton Mifflin, 1907.

Scharf, John Thomas. *History of the Confederate States Navy from Its Organization to the Surrender of Its Last*. New York: Rogers and Sherwood, 1887.

Schickel, Richard. *D. W. Griffith: An American Life*. New York: Hal Leonard, 1996.

Schlesinger, Arthur M. *The Age of Jackson*. Boston: Little, Brown, 1945.

Schoolcraft, Mary Howard. *The Black Gauntlet: A Tale of Plantation Life in South Carolina*. Philadelphia: Lippincott, 1860.

Schuller, Kyla. *The Biopolitics of Feeling: Race, Sex, and Science in the Nineteenth Century*. Durham, NC: Duke University Press, 2018.

Schweitzer, Ivy. *Perfecting Friendship: Politics and Affiliation in Early American Literature*. Chapel Hill: University of North Carolina Press, 2006.

Scott, Joan Wallach. "The Evidence of Experience." *Critical Inquiry* 17, no. 4 (Summer 1991): 773–97.

———. "Psychoanalysis and the Indeterminacy of History." In *Situation Critical: Critique, Theory, and Early American Studies*, edited by Max Cavitch and Brian Connolly, 33–51. Durham, NC: Duke University Press, 2024.

Scudder, Horace Elisha. *James Russell Lowell: A Biography*. Boston: Houghton, Mifflin, 1901.

Sedgwick, Eve Kosofsky. *Between Men: English Literature and Male Homosocial Desire*. New York: Columbia University Press, 2016.

———. *Epistemology of the Closet*. Berkeley: University of California Press, 2008.

———. *Tendencies*. Durham, NC: Duke University Press, 1993.

———. *Touching Feeling: Affect, Pedagogy, Performativity*. Durham, NC: Duke University Press, 2003.

Shaheen, Aaron. *Androgynous Democracy: Modern American Literature and the Dual-Sexed Body Politic*. Knoxville: University of Tennessee Press, 2010.

———. "Henry James's Southern Mode of Imagination: Men, Women, and the Image of the South in *The Bostonians*." *Henry James Review* 24, no. 2 (2003): 180–92.

Shand-Tucci, Douglass. *The Crimson Letter: Harvard, Homosexuality, and the Shaping of American Culture*. New York: St. Martin's, 2003.

Shapiro, James. *Shakespeare in a Divided America: What His Plays Tell Us about Our Past and Future*. New York: Penguin, 2020.

Shelden, Rachel A. *Washington Brotherhood: Politics, Social Life, and the Coming of the Civil War*. Chapel Hill: University of North Carolina Press, 2013.

Shelton, Allen. *Dreamworlds of Alabama*. Minneapolis: University of Minnesota Press, 2007.

Shillingsburg, Miriam J. "Caroline Lee Hentz." In *The History of Southern Women's Literature*, edited by Carolyn Perry and Mary Weaks-Baxter, 82–86. Baton Rouge: Louisiana State University Press, 2002.

Shilts, Randy. *Conduct Unbecoming: Gays and Lesbians in the U.S. Military*. New York: Macmillan, 2005.

Shively, Charley. *Calamus Lovers: Walt Whitman's Working-Class Camerados*. San Francisco: Gay Sunshine, 1987.

Showalter, Elaine. *The Civil Wars of Julia Ward Howe: A Biography*. New York: Simon and Schuster, 2016.

Sielke, Sabine. *Reading Rape: The Rhetoric of Sexual Violence in American Literature and Culture, 1790–1990*. Princeton, NJ: Princeton University Press, 2009.

Sigal, Pete. "(Homo)Sexual Desire and Masculine Power in Colonial Latin America: Notes toward an Integrated Analysis." In *Infamous Desire: Male Homosexuality in Colonial Latin America*, edited by Pete Sigal, 1–24. Chicago: University of Chicago Press, 2003.

Silber, Nina. *The Romance of Reunion: Northerners and the South, 1865–1900*. Chapel Hill: University of North Carolina Press, 2000.

Silkenat, David. "'A Typical Negro': Gordon, Peter, Vincent Colyer, and the Story behind Slavery's Most Famous Photograph." *American Nineteenth Century History* 15, no. 2 (May 2014): 169–86.

Simms, William Gilmore. *The Letters of William Gilmore Simms*. Vol. 3. Columbia: University of South Carolina Press, 1954.

———. *The Sword and the Distaff, or "Fair, Fat and Forty": A Story of the South, at the Close of the Revolution*. Charleston, SC: Walker, Richards, 1852.

Sinha, Manisha. "The Caning of Charles Sumner: Slavery, Race, and Ideology in the Age of the Civil War." *Journal of the Early Republic* 23, no. 2 (2003): 233–62.

———. *The Rise and Fall of the Second American Republic: Reconstruction, 1860–1920*. New York: Liveright, 2024.

———. *The Slave's Cause: A History of Abolition*. New Haven, CT: Yale University Press, 2016.

Skocpol, Theda. *Protecting Soldiers and Mothers: The Political Origins of Social Policy in the United States*. Cambridge, MA: Harvard University Press, 2009.

Slap, Andrew L. *The Doom of Reconstruction: The Liberal Republicans in the Civil War Era*. New York: Fordham University Press, 2010.

Smith, Donna Jo. "Queering the South: Constructions of Southern/Queer Identity." In *Carryin' on in the Lesbian and Gay South*, edited by John Howard, 370–85. New York: New York University Press, 1997.

Smith, John David. "'Gentlemen, I Too, Am a Kentuckian': Abraham Lincoln, the Lincoln Bicentennial, and Lincoln's Kentucky in Recent Scholarship." *Register of the Kentucky Historical Society* 106, no. 3/4 (2008): 433–70.

Smith, John David, and J. Vincent Lowery, eds. *The Dunning School: Historians, Race, and the Meaning of Reconstruction*. Lexington: University Press of Kentucky, 2013.

Smith, Karen Manners. "The Novel." In *The History of Southern Women's Literature*, edited by Carolyn Perry and Mary Weaks-Baxter, 48–58. Baton Rouge: Louisiana State University Press, 2002.

———. "Southern Women Writers' Responses to Uncle Tom's Cabin." In *The History of Southern Women's Literature*, edited by Carolyn Perry and Mary Weaks-Baxter, 97–102. Baton Rouge: Louisiana State University Press, 2002.

Smith, William L. G. *Life at the South, or "Uncle Tom's Cabin" as It Is*. Buffalo, NY: George H. Derby, 1852.

Smith-Rosenberg, Carroll. "The Female World of Love and Ritual: Relations between Women in Nineteenth-Century America." *Signs* 1, no. 1 (Autumn 1975): 1–29.

Smucker, Samuel Mosheim. *The Life of Col. John Charles Fremont*. New York: Miller, Orton and Mulligan, 1856.

Smythe, James M. *Ethel Somers, or The Fate of the Union*. Augusta, GA: H. D. Norrell, 1857.

Snorton, C. Riley. *Black on Both Sides: A Racial History of Trans Identity*. Minneapolis: University of Minnesota Press, 2017.

Somerville, Siobhan B. *Queering the Color Line: Race and the Invention of Homosexuality in American Culture*. Durham, NC: Duke University Press, 2000.

Sommerville, Diane Miller. *Rape and Race in the Nineteenth-Century South*. Chapel Hill: University of North Carolina Press, 2005.

Spillers, Hortense J. "Mama's Baby, Papa's Maybe: An American Grammar Book." *Diacritics* 17, no. 2 (1987): 65–81.

Sproat, John G. *The Best Men: Liberal Reformers in the Gilded Age*. New York: Oxford University Press, 1968.

Stansell, Christine. *City of Women: Sex and Class in New York, 1789–1860*. Urbana: University of Illinois Press, 1987.

Stark, Cruce. "The Man of Letters as a Man of War: James K. Hosmer's *The Thinking Bayonet*." *New England Quarterly* 48, no. 1 (1975): 47–64.

Starnes, Ebenezer. *The Slaveholder Abroad, or Billy Buck's Visit, with His Master, to England*. Philadelphia: Lippincott, 1860.

Stein, Allen F. *Cornelius Mathews*. New York: Twayne, 1974.

Stein, Melissa N. *Measuring Manhood: Race and the Science of Masculinity, 1830–1934*. Minneapolis: University of Minnesota Press, 2015.

Stern, Julia A. *The Plight of Feeling: Sympathy and Dissent in the Early American Novel*. Chicago: University of Chicago Press, 1997.

Stevens, Hugh. *Henry James and Sexuality*. New York: Cambridge University Press, 1998.

Stevenson, Elizabeth. *Henry Adams: A Biography*. New York: Transaction, 1997.

Stiles, Anne M. "Go Rest, Young Man." *Monitor on Psychology* 43, no. 1 (2012): 32.

———. "'The Intimate Language of Friendship with Men': Same-Sex Attraction in the Civil War Fiction of S. Weir Mitchell." *Literature and Medicine* 32, no. 1 (2014): 193–217.

Stokes, Mason. *The Color of Sex: Whiteness, Heterosexuality, and the Fictions of White Supremacy*. Durham, NC: Duke University Press, 2001.

Stoler, Ann Laura. *Race and the Education of Desire: Foucault's History of Sexuality and the Colonial Order of Things*. Durham, NC: Duke University Press, 1995.

Stott, Richard. *Jolly Fellows: Male Milieus in Nineteenth-Century America*. Baltimore: Johns Hopkins University Press, 2009.

Stowe, Harriet Beecher. *A Key to Uncle Tom's Cabin: Presenting the Original Facts and Documents upon Which the Story Is Founded*. Boston: J. P. Jewett, 1853.

———. *Uncle Tom's Cabin, or Life among the Lowly*. 1852. New York: Norton, 2010.

Stowe, Steven M. *Intimacy and Power in the Old South: Ritual in the Lives of the Planters*. Baltimore: Johns Hopkins University Press, 1987.

Strauss, Robert. *Worst. President. Ever.: James Buchanan, the POTUS Rating Game, and the Legacy of the Least of the Lesser Presidents*. Guilford, CT: Rowman and Littlefield, 2016.

Streeby, Shelley. *American Sensations: Class, Empire, and the Production of Popular Culture*. Berkeley: University of California Press, 2002.

Summers, Mark Wahlgren. *The Ordeal of the Reunion: A New History of Reconstruction*. Chapel Hill: University of North Carolina Press, 2014.

———. *Party Games: Getting, Keeping, and Using Power in Gilded Age Politics*. Chapel Hill: University of North Carolina Press, 2005.

———. *Rum, Romanism, and Rebellion*. Chapel Hill: University of North Carolina Press, 2000.

Sumner, Charles. *The Crime against Kansas: The Apologies for the Crime; The True Remedy*. Boston: J. P. Jewett, 1856.

Taketani, Etsuko. "Postcolonial Liberia: Sarah Josepha Hale's Africa." *American Literary History* 14, no. 3 (2002): 479–504.

Taylor, Amy Murrell. *The Divided Family in Civil War America*. Chapel Hill: University of North Carolina Press, 2009.

Taylor, Andrew. *Henry James and the Father Question*. New York: Cambridge University Press, 2002.

Taylor, Bayard. *Joseph and His Friend: A Story of Pennsylvania*. New York: G. P. Putnam and Sons, 1870.

Taylor, William Robert. *Cavalier and Yankee: The Old South and American National Character*. New York: Oxford University Press, 1993.

Teilhet, Darwin L. *The Lion's Skin*. New York: William Sloane, 1955.

Templeton, Peter. *The Politics of Southern Pastoral Literature, 1785–1885: Jeffersonian Afterlives*. New York: Palgrave Macmillan, 2019.

Tennenhouse, Leonard. "Libertine America." *Differences: A Journal of Feminist Cultural Studies* 11, no. 3 (1999): 1–28.

Terry, Jennifer. *An American Obsession: Science, Medicine, and Homosexuality in Modern Society*. Chicago: University of Chicago Press, 2010.

Texan. *The Yankee Slave-Dealer, or An Abolitionist Down South: A Tale for the Times*. Nashville, TN: Printed by the author, 1860.

Thomas, Brook. *American Literary Realism and the Failed Promise of Contract*. Berkeley: University of California Press, 1997.

———. *Civic Myths: A Law-and-Literature Approach to Citizenship*. Chapel Hill: University of North Carolina Press, 2007.

———. "*The Galaxy*, National Literature, and Reconstruction." *Nineteenth-Century Literature* 75, no. 1 (2020): 50–81.

———. *The Literature of Reconstruction: Not in Plain Black and White*. Baltimore: Johns Hopkins University Press, 2017.

———. "Twain and Tourgée on Gilded Age Presidential Elections and Voting Rights." *J19* 11, no. 2 (2023): 301–32.

———. "The Unfinished Task of Grounding Reconstruction's Promise." *Journal of the Civil War Era* 7, no. 1 (2017): 16–38.

Thompson, John R. "Captain Latane." In *War Poetry of the South*, edited by William Gilmore Simms, 385–87. New York: Richardson, 1866.

Thompson, Lawrance. *Robert Frost: The Years of Triumph, 1915–1938*. New York: Holt, Rinehart and Winston, 1970.

Thorpe, Thomas Bangs. *The Master's House: A Tale of Southern Life*. New York: T. L. McElrath, 1854.

Timrod, Henry. "Ode Sung on the Occasion of Decorating the Graves of the Confederate Dead, at Magnolia Cemetery, Charleston, S.C., 1867." In *The Poems of Henry Timrod*, edited by Paul H. Hayne, 209–10. New York: E. J. Hale and Son, 1873.

———. "Two Portraits." In *The Poems of Henry Timrod*, edited by Paul H. Hayne, 87–97. New York: E. J. Hale and Son, 1873.

———. "The Unknown Dead." In *War Poetry of the South*, edited by William Gilmore Simms, 251–52. New York: Richardson, 1866.

Tindall, George B. "Mythology: A New Frontier in Southern History." In *Myth and Southern History: The New South*, edited by Patrick Gerster and Nicholas Cords, 1–15. Urbana: University of Illinois Press, 1989.

Tompkins, Jane. *Sensational Designs: The Cultural Work of American Fiction, 1790–1860*. New York: Oxford University Press, 1986.

Tompkins, Kyla Wazana. *Racial Indigestion: Eating Bodies in the 19th Century*. New York: New York University Press, 2012.

Tourgée, Albion. *Bricks without Straw*. Edited by Carolyn Karcher. 1880. Durham, NC: Duke University Press, 2009.

———. "The South as a Field for Fiction." *Forum*, no. 6 (December 1888): 404–13.

———. *With Gauge and Swallow, Attorneys*. Philadelphia: Lippincott, 1889.

Trachtenberg, Alan. *The Incorporation of America: Culture and Society in the Gilded Age*. New York: Macmillan, 1982.

Traub, James. *Judah Benjamin: Counselor to the Confederacy*. New Haven, CT: Yale University Press, 2021.

Traub, Valerie. "The New Unhistoricism in Queer Studies." *PMLA* 128, no. 1 (2013): 21–39.

———. *Thinking Sex with the Early Moderns*. Philadelphia: University of Pennsylvania Press, 2016.

Traubel, Horace. *With Walt Whitman in Camden*. Vol. 6. Carbondale: Southern Illinois University Press, 1982.

Trent, James W. *The Manliest Man: Samuel G. Howe and the Contours of Nineteenth-Century American Reform*. Amherst: University of Massachusetts Press, 2012.

Trial of Henry Wirz: Letter from the Secretary of War Ad Interim, in Answer to a Resolution of the House of April 16, 1866. Washington, DC: Government Printing Office, 1868.

Tripp, C. A. *The Intimate World of Abraham Lincoln*. New York: Simon and Schuster, 2005.

Troy, Gil. *See How They Ran: The Changing Role of the Presidential Candidate*. Cambridge, MA: Harvard University Press, 1996.

Trumbull, Charles Gallaudet. *Anthony Comstock, Fighter: Some Impressions of a Lifetime Adventure in Conflict with the Powers of Evil*. New York: Fleming H. Revell, 1913.

Trumbull, Henry Clay. *Friendship the Master-Passion*. Philadelphia: J. D. Wattles, 1891.

———. *The Knightly Soldier: A Biography of Major Henry Ward Camp, Tenth Conn. Vols.* Boston: Nichols and Noyes, 1865.

Tucker, David M. *Mugwumps: Public Moralists of the Gilded Age*. Columbia: University of Missouri Press, 1998.

Twain, Mark, and Charles Dudley Warner. *The Gilded Age: A Tale of To-day*. Hartford, CT: American Publishing, 1874.

Twelve Southerners. *I'll Take My Stand: The South and the Agrarian Tradition*. New York: Harper and Row, 1962.

Usai, Paolo Cherchi, ed. *The Griffith Project*. Vol. 8, *Films Produced in 1914–15*. London: Bloomsbury, 2019.

Velasquez, Loreta Janeta. *The Woman in Battle*. Richmond, VA: Dustin, Gilman, 1876.

Vidi. *Mr. Frank: The Underground Mail-Agent*. Philadelphia: Lippincott, Grambo, 1853.

Vincent, Jonathan E. *The Health of the State: Modern US War Narrative and the American Political Imagination, 1890–1964*. New York: Oxford University Press, 2017.

Von Borcke, Heros. *Memoirs of the Confederate War for Independence*. 2 vols. Edinburgh, UK: W. Blackwood and Sons, 1866.

Wagstaff, Thomas. "The Arm-in-Arm Convention." *Civil War History* 14, no. 2 (1968): 101–19.

Walker, William. *The War in Nicaragua*. 1860. Tucson: University of Arizona Press, 1985.

Walrath, Douglas Alan. *Displacing the Divine: The Minister in the Mirror of American Fiction*. New York: Columbia University Press, 2010.

Walters, Ronald G. *American Reformers, 1815–1860*. New York: Macmillan, 1978.

———. "The Erotic South: Civilization and Sexuality in American Abolitionism." *American Quarterly* 25, no. 2 (1973): 177–201.

Walther, Eric H. *William Lowndes Yancey and the Coming of the Civil War*. Chapel Hill: University of North Carolina Press, 2006.

Warren, Kenneth W. *Black and White Strangers: Race and American Literary Realism*. Chicago: University of Chicago Press, 1993.

Washington, George. *Farewell Address: Delivered September 17th, 1796*. New York: Appleton, 1861.

Watson, Charles S. "'Simms's Answer to 'Uncle Tom's Cabin': Criticism of the South in 'Woodcraft.'" *Southern Literary Journal* 9, no. 1 (1976): 78–90.

Watson, Ritchie D., Jr. "John Esten Cooke." In *Fifty Southern Writers before 1900: A Bio-bibliographical Sourcebook*, edited by Robert Bain and Joseph M. Flora, 15–16. New York: Bloomsbury Academic, 1987.

———. *Normans and Saxons: Southern Race Mythology and the Intellectual History of the American Civil War*. Baton Rouge: Louisiana State University Press, 2008.

Weaks-Baxter, Mary. "Gender Issues in the Old South." In *The History of Southern Women's Literature*, edited by Carolyn Perry and Mary Weaks-Baxter, 32–42. Baton Rouge: Louisiana State University Press, 2002.

Welty, Eudora. "First Love." In *The Collected Stories of Eudora Welty*, 153–168. 1943. New York: Harcourt, 1980.

White, Hayden. "The Historical Text as Literary Artifact." In *Tropics of Discourse: Essays in Cultural Criticism*, 81–100. Baltimore: Johns Hopkins University Press, 1978.

———. *Metahistory: The Historical Imagination in Nineteenth-Century Europe*. 1973. Baltimore: Johns Hopkins University Press, 2014.

White, Homer. *The Norwich Cadets: A Tale of the Rebellion*. St. Albans, VT: Albert Clarke, 1873.

White, Mimi. "The Birth of A Nation: History as Pretext." In *The Birth of a Nation*, edited by Robert Lang, 5:214–24. New Brunswick, NJ: Rutgers University Press, 1994.

White, Richard. *The Republic for Which It Stands: The United States during Reconstruction and the Gilded Age, 1865–1896*. New York: Oxford University Press, 2017.

———. "What Counts as Corruption?" *Social Research: An International Quarterly* 80, no. 4 (2013): 1033–56.

Whites, LeeAnn. *Civil War as a Crisis in Gender: Augusta, Georgia, 1860–1890*. Athens: University of Georgia Press, 2000.

———. *Gender Matters: Race, Class and Sexuality in the Nineteenth-Century South*. New York: Palgrave Macmillan, 2016.

Whitman, Walt. *Complete Prose Works*. Philadelphia: McKay, 1892.

———. *The Correspondence, 1890–1892*. Edited by Edwin Haviland Miller. New York: New York University Press, 2007.

———. *Drum-Taps*. New York: Whitman, 1865.

———. *Leaves of Grass*. Boston: Thayer and Eldridge, 1860.

———. *Memoranda during the War*. Camden, NJ: Walt Whitman, 1876.

———. *Notebooks and Unpublished Prose Manuscripts: Family Notes and Autobiography, Brooklyn and New York*. Edited by Edward F. Grier. New York: New York University Press, 1984.

———. *Sequel to Drum-Taps*. New York: Walt Whitman, 1866.

Widmer, Edward L. *Young America: The Flowering of Democracy in New York City*. New York: Oxford University Press, 1999.

Wiegman, Robyn. "The Anatomy of Lynching." *Journal of the History of Sexuality* 3, no. 3 (1993): 445–67.

———. "Fiedler and Sons." In *Race and the Subject of Masculinities*, edited by Harilaos Stecopoulos and Michael Uebel, 45–68. Durham, NC: Duke University Press, 1997.

Wiegman, Robyn, and Elizabeth Wilson. "Antinormativity's Queer Conventions." *Differences*, no. 26 (June 2015): 1–25.

Wilde, Oscar. *The Ballad of Reading Gaol*. 1898. Little Blue Book 2. Girard, KS: Haldeman-Julius, 1923.

Wilentz, Sean. *Chants Democratic: New York City and the Rise of the American Working Class, 1788–1850*. 1984. New York: Oxford University Press, 2004.

Wiley, Calvin Henderson. *Life in the South: A Companion to Uncle Tom's Cabin*. Philadelphia: T. B. Peterson, 1852.

Wilkie, Laurie A. *Unburied Lives: The Historical Archaeology of Buffalo Soldiers at Fort Davis, Texas, 1869–1875*. Albuquerque: University of New Mexico Press, 2021.

Williams, Eric. *Capitalism and Slavery*. 1944. Chapel Hill: University of North Carolina Press, 2014.

Williams, Kidada E. *I Saw Death Coming: A History of Terror and Survival in the War against Reconstruction*. New York: Bloomsbury, 2023.

———. "The Wounds That Cried Out: Reckoning with African Americans' Testimonies of Trauma and Suffering from Night Riding." In *The World the Civil War Made*, edited by Gregory P. Downs and Kate Masur, 159–82. Chapel Hill: University of North Carolina Press, 2015.

Williams, Timothy J. "'The Gold of the Pen and the Steel of the Sword': The Unlikely and Fleeting Celebrity of Theodore Winthrop." *Civil War History* 68, no. 2 (2022): 164–77.

———. "The Readers' South: Literature, Region, and Identity in the Civil War Era." *Journal of the Civil War Era* 8, no. 4 (2018): 564–90.

Wilson, Charles Reagan. *Baptized in Blood: The Religion of the Lost Cause, 1865–1920*. Athens: University of Georgia Press, 2011.

Wilson, Edmund. *Patriotic Gore: Studies in the Literature of the American Civil War*. New York: Oxford University Press, 1962.

Wilson, Ivy, ed. *Whitman Noir: Black America and the Good Gray Poet*. Iowa City: University of Iowa Press, 2014.

Wilt, Judith. "Desperately Seeking Verena: A Resistant Reading of 'The Bostonians.'" *Feminist Studies* 13, no. 2 (1987): 293–316.

Winthrop, Theodore. *Cecil Dreeme*. Edited by Peter Coviello. New York: New York University Press, 2016.

Wise, Benjamin E. *William Alexander Percy: The Curious Life of a Mississippi Planter and Sexual Freethinker*. Chapel Hill: University of North Carolina Press, 2012.

Wister, Owen. *The Virginian: A Horseman of the Plains*. New York: Macmillan, 1902.

Wood, Amy Louise. *Lynching and Spectacle: Witnessing Racial Violence in America, 1890–1940*. Chapel Hill: University of North Carolina Press, 2011.

Woodard, Vincent. *The Delectable Negro: Human Consumption and Homoeroticism within US Slave Culture*. Edited by Justin A. Joyce and Dwight A. McBride. New York: New York University Press, 2014.

Woods, Gregory. "The Art of Friendship in Roderick Hudson." In *Henry James and Homo-erotic Desire*, edited by John Bradley, 69–77. New York: Macmillan, 1999.

Woods, Michael E. *Emotional and Sectional Conflict in the Antebellum United States*. New York: Cambridge University Press, 2014.

———. "'The Indignation of Freedom-Loving People': The Caning of Charles Sumner and Emotion in Antebellum Politics." *Journal of Social History* 44, no. 3 (2011): 689–705.

Woodward, C. Vann. *The Burden of Southern History*. Baton Rouge: Louisiana State University Press, 1960.

———. *Origins of the New South, 1877–1913*. Baton Rouge: Louisiana State University Press, 1971.

———. *Reunion and Reaction: The Compromise of 1877 and the End of Reconstruction*. Boston: Little, Brown, 1951.

Woodward, William E. *Meet General Grant*. New York: Horace Liveright, 1928.

Woolson, Constance Fenimore. *For the Major, a Novelette*. New York: Harper and Brothers, 1883.

———. *Rodman the Keeper: Southern Sketches*. New York: Appleton, 1880.

Yacovone, Donald. "Abolitionists and the 'Language of Fraternal Love.'" In *Meanings for Manhood: Constructions of Masculinity in Victorian America*, edited by Mark C. Carnes and Clyde Griffen. Chicago: University of Chicago Press, 1990.

———. "'Surpassing the Love of Women': Victorian Manhood and the Language of Fraternal Love." In *A Shared Experience: Men, Women, and the History of Gender*, edited by Laura McCall and Donald Yacovone, 195–221. New York: New York University Press, 1998.

Yee, Shirley J. *Black Women Abolitionists: A Study in Activism, 1828–1860*. Knoxville: University of Tennessee Press, 1992.

Young, Elizabeth. *Disarming the Nation: Women's Writing and the American Civil War*. Chicago: University of Chicago Press, 1999.

Young, Stark. "Not in Memoriam, but in Defense." In Twelve Southerners, *I'll Take My Stand*, 328–59.

Zagarri, Rosemarie. *Revolutionary Backlash: Women and Politics in the Early American Republic*. Philadelphia: University of Pennsylvania Press, 2007.

Zweig, Paul. *Walt Whitman: The Making of the Poet*. New York: Basic Books, 1984.

INDEX